THE UNIVERSITY OF WINCHESTER

New Deal / New South

AN ANTHONY J. BADGER READER

The University of Arkansas Press
FAYETTEVILLE
2007

Library of Congress Cataloging-in-Publication Data

Badger, Anthony J.
   New Deal/New South : an Anthony J. Badger reader.
      p. cm.
   Includes bibliographical references and index.
   ISBN-13: 978-1-55728-843-1 (cloth : alk. paper)
   ISBN-13: 978-1-55728-844-8 (paper : alk. paper)
   1. Southern States—History—20th century. 2. Southern States—History—
1951- 3. New Deal, 1933–1939—Southern States. 4. Southern States—Politics
and government—20th century. 5. African Americans—Civil rights—Southern
States—History—20th century. 6. Civil rights movements—Southern States—
History—20th century. 7. Whites—Southern States—History—20th century.
8. Southern States—Race relations—History—20th century. I. Title.
   F215.B24 2007
      975'.043--dc22   2007009472

For Nick and Chris

Acknowledgments

"Huey Long and the New Deal" was first published in *Nothing Else to Fear: New Perspectives on America in the Thirties,* 1985, edited by S. Baskerville and R. Willetts, reproduced with permission from Manchester University Press.

"How Did the New Deal Change the South?" was first published in *Looking Inward, Looking Outward: From the 1930s through the 1940s,* 1990, edited by S. Ickringill, published by VU University Press.

"The Modernization of the South: The Lament for Rural Worlds Lost" was first published in *Rewriting the South: History and Fiction,* 1993, edited by Lothar Honnighausen and Valeria Gennaro Lerda, reproduced with permission from Stauffenberg Verlag.

"Southerners Who Did Not Sign the Southern Manifesto" was first published in the *Historical Journal* 42:2 in 1999, reproduced with permission from Cambridge University Press.

"Whatever Happened to Roosevelt's New Generation of Southerners?" was first published in *The Roosevelt Years: New Essays on the United States, 1933–1945,* 1999, edited by Robert A. Garson and Stuart Kidd, reproduced with permission from Edinburgh University Press.

"The White Reaction to *Brown*: Arkansas, the Southern Manifesto and Massive Resistance" was first published in *Understanding the Little Rock Crisis: An Exercise in Remembrance and Reconciliation,* 1999, edited by Elizabeth Jacoway and C. Fred Williams, reproduced with permission from the University of Arkansas Press.

"'Closet Moderates': Why White Liberals Failed, 1940–1970" was first published in *The Role of Ideas in the Civil Rights South,* 2002, edited by Ted Ownby, reproduced with permission from the University Press of Mississippi.

"Southern History from the Outside" was first published in *Shapers of Southern History: Autobiographical Reflections,* 2004, edited by John Boles, reproduced with permission from the University of Georgia Press.

"From Defiance to Moderation: South Carolina Governors and Racial Change" was first published in *Making a New South: Race, Leadership, and Community after the Civil War,* edited by Paul A. Cimbala and Barton C. Shaw, reproduced with permission from the University Press of Florida.

Contents

Foreword

Tony Badger has explained that, even as a youth, he was drawn to southern politics because the shenanigans of a Huey Long or a Jim Folsom "seemed very, very different from the gray world of British politics" in the 1950s. I have to admit it stills startles me sometimes to hear a colorful anecdote about a Long or a Folsom or a Talmadge coming from someone who looks and sounds like the distinguished Cambridge don that he is. I should know better, for from the moment I met him nearly two decades ago, I realized that Tony was anything but the stereotypical stiff-lipped British academic. (I doubt seriously that many of them actually prefer Budweiser to Guinness or care in the slightest whether the Atlanta Braves win the National League East.) Getting to know Tony as a person has been a very rewarding experience for me, and, as readers are about to discover, getting to know him as a historian is no less satisfying.

This book promises to inform and enlighten in a multitude of ways, not the least of them being the insights it offers into the progression of an exceptionally talented historian's interests and awareness as Tony shares his professional and personal odyssey from New Deal historian to southern historian. Indeed, taken together, the essays offered here amount to an extremely thoughtful consideration of the short- and long-term impact of the New Deal on the South.

For starters, Tony takes us into the vast, little-explored area between the interpretive polar extremes of the New Deal as a rip-roaring, revolutionary success and a disappointing, dismal failure to address the South's real needs, examining possible policy alternatives with the hard-nosed realism that pervades all his work. This realism is much in evidence in Tony's subsequent writing on civil rights and southern politics. He considers the New Deal and post–New Deal generation of southern Democrats such as Folsom, Sid McMath, and Earl Long, assessing what they accomplished as well as what they were up against and delving into the broader question of how political leaders either shape or are shaped by majority opinion—and sometimes minority opinion as well.

Badger astutely diagnoses the failure of the South's more progressive post–New Deal leadership to play a more active and forthright role in promoting racial changes. He concludes that the region's racial "moderates" were generally too moderate, too timid, too reluctant to urge southern whites to let go of Jim Crow for fear of unloosing what they believed would be a tidal wave of white-hot rage culminating in widespread violence and bloodshed. However, Tony points out that the staunchest defenders of segregation were convinced that the white masses did not fully perceive the gravity of the threat to the "southern way of life," and the sound and fury of their exhortations to resist integration at all costs only made the moderates more reticent and ineffective. Ultimately, he demonstrates it was not the hesitant moralizing of the moderates but the congressional and executive pressures generated by black activism, as well as the growing sense that die-hard segregationism was economic suicide, that finally brought the barricades of massive resistance tumbling down.

Tony offers as cogent an explanation of the difficulties of winning and sustaining biracial political support in the South since the Voting Rights Act of 1965 as I have seen, and his account of Tennessee senator Albert Gore Sr.'s defeat in 1970 clearly shows just how ugly the GOP's "southern strategy" could actually get. Badger brings his treatment full circle by examining the clash between Gore and his fellow southern New Dealer Lyndon Johnson over Vietnam.

My favorite piece in this collection, I must admit, is Tony's appraisal of Ernest F. Hollings and John C. West as southern governors in an age of racial change. I had the pleasure of sitting in the audience, watching Hollings and West on the stage with him in Charleston as he delivered his analysis of their gubernatorial roles in advancing or impeding the cause of civil rights in South Carolina. He was exceedingly respectful and polite, but he pulled no punches, giving credit when it was due but withholding it when it was not. Both Hollings and West flinched perceptibly a time or two, but Tony's talk was so balanced and informed that they could find no real fault with what he had to say. In the end, I came away from the evening feeling very proud, not simply because Tony is my friend, but because he had shown how powerful and important historical analysis can be when it is done right. Needless to say, I believe readers of this volume will go away from it feeling the same way I did that night in Charleston.

James C. Cobb

Introduction

SOUTHERN HISTORY FROM THE OUTSIDE

Jim Holt, a fine New Zealand historian of U.S. Progressivism, claimed there was always one book that so captured your interest in a subject that you would always be able to remember where and when you first read it. What made Jim an American historian was reading Richard Hofstadter's *The Age of Reform* (1955). Twenty years later he could still remember the exact location in his university library where he had found the book and first read it. In my case the book was William E. Leuchtenburg's *Franklin D. Roosevelt and the New Deal* (1963). It was 1966 after my first year exams at Cambridge; the book had just come out in paperback, and I was going to be taking my first-ever course in American history the following year. I devoured the book in the pub behind Sidney Sussex College while England won the world cup at soccer and Tom Graveney, my schoolboy hero, made a triumphant return at the age of thirty-eight to the national cricket team. Leuchtenburg's dramatic narrative, the sheer scale of the Great Depression, the personality of Roosevelt and other colorful politicians, the bewildering range of bold government programs—all seemed so different from what, at that time, I took to be the gray conservatism of the national government in Britain in the 1930s. My response to Leuchtenburg's historical reconstruction, I later discovered, was the same as that of young British intellectuals like Isaiah Berlin and Denis Brogan to the New Deal at the time. Herbert Nicholas, the first Rhodes Professor of American History at Oxford, recalled the hopes invested by the younger generation of academics in the 1930s, who contrasted the "positive affirmations of the New Deal" with "the appeasing record of the Chamberlain government":

> Yet partly because the Democrats had succeeded in presenting themselves as a party of hope (there was *no* British party of hope in the 1930), partly because of F.D.R's personal dynamism (there was *no* dynamic British party leader in the 1930s except Sir Oswald Mosley), one could and did nourish the conviction that one now realizes to be partly illusion that the America of Franklin Roosevelt would, somehow or other, either avert the war or, when it came, rescue the democracies of Europe from their common foe.[1]

Leuchtenburg's book made me want to be an American historian. I did not suspect that a quarter of a century later I would be organizing a conference in Cambridge—a stone's throw from the pub where I had first read it—to mark the thirtieth anniversary of the book's publication. Bill responded at that conference to British and American historians who reflected on writing about the New Deal "In the Shadow of Leuchtenburg." Even less did I suspect that I would later crisscross the South working in the archival collections of southern congressmen in the vain hope of beating Leuchtenburg to one of those collections.[2]

Leuchtenburg's book also reintroduced me to Huey Long. When I was twelve, I read about the Kingfish in a book on my father's shelves, *America Came My Way*, by a young English baronet who toured the United States in 1935. Sir Anthony Jenkinson had crossed the United States from the America's Cup races off Rhode Island to Hollywood. Armed with influential introductions, he met and wrote about celebrities from Walter Winchell to Shirley Temple. Long afterward I discovered that the book had been dismissively reviewed by the doyen of British commentators on the United States, Alistair Cooke. Cooke, his biographer noted, "swiftly spotting an interloper on his territory, accuse[d] [Jenkinson] of making sweeping statements based on a highly superficial experience of the country."[3]

Jenkinson's chapter on Huey Long stuck in my mind, not only because of its title, "Huey Long Takes His Shirt Off," but because of the footnote that pointed out that he had subsequently been assassinated. To a twelve-year-old in 1959, assassinations of politicians in democracies seemed exotic rather than all too frequent, as they would in the years to come. When I discovered in Leuchtenburg's narrative of the New Deal that Huey Long was an important political figure, my curiosity was piqued. I read Allan P. Sindler and Harnett Thomas Kane and gave a paper on Long to the college undergraduate history society, largely relying on anecdotes about Huey that, to the England of Harold Wilson and Ted Heath, made politics in Louisiana seem from another planet. T. Harry Williams was actually in Oxford that year as Harmsworth Professor, and I acquired a copy of his inaugural lecture, which previewed his massive biography of Huey. In the modest way of 1960s liberals I championed Long's record for poor whites and accepted that his corruption and power grabs were necessitated by the ruthlessness and conservatism of his enemies. Subsequently, I was suspicious of Williams's wide-eyed acceptance of the most specious defenses of Long's behavior. Almost twenty years after that first undergraduate paper, I finally had the chance to publish an essay that was a modest contribution to the revisionist interpretation of Long more vigorously and convincingly undertaken by Alan Brinkley, William Ivy Hair, and Glen Jeansonne. Thirty-five years later I had the chance to be a visiting professor at Tulane University during the trial of Governor Edwin Edwards and to chronicle the havoc wrought with governance in Louisiana by conservative segregationists and Republicans on the one hand, and corrupt Long-style welfare liberals on the other. In my Mellon Lecture there in 2000 I summarized my new understanding about the state: "The future for the have-nots in Louisiana and for the state's economy look bleak. The legacy of corrupt welfare liberalism and racial moderation has produced a system of public governance that has proved incapable of delivering a modernized economy. The legacy of good government and racial and economic conservatism has equally failed to produce a vision that can see beyond the next tax cut or the next toxic waste dump. Politics as TV wrestling is a great spectator sport and it has been for me a subject of endless fascination over the past forty years, but I have to confess, as I head to the airport, that the quality of governance it provides is more easily coped with at a distance of three thousand miles."[4]

Leuchtenburg's reawakening of this dormant interest in Huey Long did not make me a southern historian. It did make me want to look at the New Deal in the South. The British, used to national, ideologically distinct, and coherent political parties, found the association of New Deal liberals and southern conservatives in the same party strange. How that relationship functioned in the 1930s, when that tension became so apparent, was what I wanted to understand. Armed with one survey course in American history and this sketchy ambition, I set out to do a Ph.D. in American history at the University of Hull, which had given me a three-year studentship.

In Cambridge, American history had been championed by Frank Thistlethwaite, but he was in the economics faculty and had left to be the first vice chancellor of the University of East Anglia; by Denis Brogan, an idiosyncratic professor of political science who retired in 1967; and by Pitt professors, distinguished but transient, on annual appointments from the United States. The history faculty had sent William R. Brock, a noted historian of Lord Liverpool, to the United States to re-tool as an American historian, but he left in my final year to go to Glasgow. J. R. Pole, initially appointed on outside funding, was only rather grudgingly taken on the university's payroll when that funding ended. For all the very considerable scholarly distinction of these Americanists, it was difficult to avoid the feeling that, for Cambridge, American history was not a proper subject. "American history is not a fit subject for a gentleman," intoned one college director of studies in turning down the request of an undergraduate, Harry Porter, to take the optional course on American history.

In Hull, by contrast, American history was taken seriously. Hull had an American Studies department, established in the 1960s on the model of the pioneering interdisciplinary programs at the Universities of Manchester and Keele. The excellence of the Hull library's American holdings was due in part to funding from the United States Information Agency (USIA), in part to the energy and bibliographic interests of members of the department, and in part to the benign support and encouragement of the university's librarian, the poet Philip Larkin, who shared the historian John White's passion for jazz.

There was no critical mass of graduate students: I was the only one. There was no coursework, no training in historiography, and no training in research methods. My supervisor was a specialist in immigration history. Of vast swathes of American history I was wholly ignorant. Yet it was a wonderful time. I read widely in New Deal historiography and in contemporary American politics. The members of staff seemed to treat me as a colleague rather than as a student. Philip A. M. Taylor was a model supervisor. Like William Brock, Taylor marched to his own intellectual drumbeat. Both had an inner self-confidence as historians that their interpretation of the sources, whatever the subject, would be of value. Their independent conclusions at critical points intersected with simultaneous developments in American historiography. Brock's careful reading of congressional debates during Reconstruction in which he took the rhetoric of radical Republicans seriously led to the landmark *An American Crisis: Congress and Reconstruction, 1865–1867* (1963), which appeared just as the revisionist historiography of Reconstruction came to fruition. His later work on state government agencies in the late nineteenth and early twentieth centuries coincided with the explosion of work on "state development" in the United States. Taylor's whole approach to immigration, summed up in *The Distant Magnet: European Migration to the U.S.A.* (1971), paralleled the work of Rudolf Vecoli and others that stressed the persistent importance of European experiences and values in the immigrant experience. Taylor had few qualms about supervising a Ph.D. on the New Deal. He read whatever I wrote quickly and carefully. He consistently prodded me to greater clarity and to be certain about what questions I was trying to answer. He was immensely encouraging, gave me the chance to lecture to undergraduates on the New Deal, and displayed a reassuring, if, in retrospect, foolhardy, confidence that I would obtain an academic job at the end of the three years. He also arranged for me to fund a year's archival research by asking an old friend to give me a teaching assistantship at North Carolina State University at Raleigh. In September 1969 I set off for the first time to America and to the South.

In 1997 I was invited back to North Carolina State to give the Harrelson Lecture. I flew in direct from London to Raleigh-Durham airport, an airport now almost identical to any other major international airport. I sat next to a Swedish telecommunications specialist from Ericcson who was visiting his company's office in the Research Triangle. I was entertained in excellent restaurants and held up in endless traffic jams—all the trappings of a modern city. It had been very different in 1969. Then I had flown in from New York, walked from the bottom of the aircraft steps to a small, single-story building, and gone outside to pick up my baggage from a carousel open to the elements. The first night I spent in the Carolina Hotel, now demolished, which, unknown to me, had been the campaign headquarters for the liberal faction in the state's politics, the headquarters of Kerr Scott and Frank Graham. (Candidates of the Shelby Dynasty used the Sir Walter). Searching that night for a meal, I could only find an indifferent Chinese restaurant. Asking that Sunday evening for a drink, I was given my first, and last, root beer. Looking at the wallpaper paste on my plate next morning at breakfast, I tasted my first, and last, grits.

But if the Triangle in 1969 was not a gourmet or beer drinker's delight, it was an archival treasure trove, at the State Archives in Raleigh and over at the Southern Historical Collection at Chapel Hill. In a year I knew more about the New Deal tobacco program, I suspect, than anybody has ever wanted to know with the exception of Pete Daniel. Teaching the history of Western civilization to textile majors equipped me for anything I was ever likely to face in a classroom in the future.

I left North Carolina as a New Deal historian who happened to be studying the South. My interest in the tobacco program was in the policy options available to New Dealers, in the implementation of those policies at the local level, and in what that said about the radical opportunities or the constraints that confronted Roosevelt and his advisers. I just happened to be studying that question in North Carolina, rather than Montana. My consciousness of race was intermittent and marginal. In my dissertation, African Americans were acted upon; they had no agency, if they appeared at all. My concern was with sharecropping as an object of policy, not with the life of the sharecroppers themselves. I did manage to capture, from a 1946 dissertation and its interviews, the sense of a greater breathing space that alternative sources of credit and votes in crop control elections gave African Americans, but the experience of sharecroppers, black or white, did not loom large as it would later for Pete Daniel and Jack Kirby. I was working at a tokenly integrated university. Only one African American started on the basketball and football teams. The Atlantic Coast Conference was only on the edge of the desegregation that Charles Martin has so expertly described. Concern and awareness about race relations in general, not about race relations in my own community, was my dominant emotion. As a schoolboy in Bristol in 1963, I had waxed suitably indignant about apartheid in South Africa. Only thirty years after the event did I discover that there had been a bus boycott in my own city by West Indians that same year. In Raleigh in 1969–70 I could not avoid being aware of Jesse Helms, of Nixon's southern strategy, of the strike of cafeteria workers at the University of North Carolina, or of substantial school desegregation for the first time in early 1970 when the greatest white flight from the public schools occurred in the areas inhabited by Duke faculty. But I met few black students, and I did not understand the daily humiliations of segregation in the way that white southern students radicalized by the civil rights movement did. While I was in Raleigh, eleven-year-old Tim Tyson was told that his friend's father had killed a "nigger." My recollection is that I was entirely unaware of the rioting that followed in Oxford. Oxford, North Carolina, was known to me only as the home of New Deal congressman and 1938 senatorial candidate Frank Hancock.[5]

I returned from my year in North Carolina (I would go back there every summer in the 1970s), started writing up my dissertation, and applied for a university lectureship at Newcastle University advertised in British history with a preference for someone who could also teach American history. I turned up in the administrative offices of the university at the appropriate time, was interviewed for thirty minutes, told to come back in two hours' time, and then sat in a small room with the other candidates while the committee made up its mind. It transpired that the department really wanted an Americanist but all the other applicants were British historians. So an administrator came out and announced that the committee wished to offer the job to me—and I set off to the train station with one of the defeated candidates. At the age of twenty-four, with an unfinished dissertation and still ignorant of vast chunks of American history, I was a tenured university academic and determined to make my reputation as a historian of the New Deal—and that is what I published on for the next twenty years.

But teaching undergraduates made me a southern historian.

In Newcastle I taught a survey course on American history from 1965 and a final year special subject on the New Deal. That specialist course was the basis of my later general overview of the New Deal. But in the early 1970s any American historian was conscious that the most exciting work was being done in the field of slavery. As one after another major studies by John Blassingame, George Rawick, Robert W. Fogel and Stanley L. Engerman, Eugene D. Genovese, Peter H. Wood, Edmund S. Morgan, Herbert Gutman, Lawrence N. Levine, and others appeared, there was a powerful imperative to engage with this literature. To me, it seemed the best way to make sure that I read these books was to promise to teach a seminar course on them myself; subsequently I introduced a course on "The South and Race: From Slavery to Civil Rights." In the first couple of years the students and I taught one another. There was no copy, for example, of Gutman's book on the black family in Newcastle, and the students had to rely on my laboriously typed-up notes. In time, the course became a large lecture course and the staple of my teaching at Newcastle in the 1980s.

There were a number of consequences from this indirect way into southern history. First, unlike so many southern historians, I did not come to southern history through C. Vann Woodward's *The Origins of the New South* (1951). I had read it as an undergraduate, but I did not grasp why the book was so important. Not having been exposed to traditional southern historiography, I failed to understand how it challenged the conventional pieties and why it was such an eye-opening book to that generation of southern historians immediately preceding me. The book that shaped my teaching of the course on the South was *The Strange Career of Jim Crow* (1955) and the debate about the forgotten alternatives to segregation which was ideally suited to small-group class discussion. By contrast, Michael O'Brien, like me an undergraduate in Cambridge, had gone to Vanderbilt University for a master's degree, and he addressed from the start of his career questions of southern identity and southerners' sense of self. Unknown to each other, we followed each other round southern archives on very different quests. For O'Brien, Vann Woodward loomed large, and in 1974 he published an article in the *American Historical Review* quizzically exploring Woodward's liberalism.[6]

Second, my introduction to the historiography of slavery (and later women) changed the way I wrote about the history of the New Deal. It was my first serious engagement with the new social history, with the history of "the inarticulate many rather than the articulate few." I began to appreciate the limitations of my political and administrative approach to the history of the New Deal, no matter that I was stressing the local and state impact of the New Deal and the implementation of its programs. I therefore tried to incorporate the new work on rank-and-file labor militancy, on the unemployed, on native Americans, and on blacks into my New Deal account. I have to confess that my study of women came later. In 1974 Carl Degler came to Newcastle and gave a version of his Harmsworth inaugural lecture at Oxford, "Is There a History of Women?" In Newcastle the answer in 1974 was definitely no. Only slowly did I fully understand the implications of this omission. History in Britain was a notably "stag" affair in the 1970s. We lacked that cohort of older American women historians who reentered graduate school and the profession in the 1970s in the aftermath of the women's movement. We also lagged in equal opportunity employment policy. Again, teaching women's history was my entry point into belatedly incorporating women into my New Deal narrative.

Third, my engagement with the modern South was slow. The historiography of slavery, Reconstruction, and the New South was so rich that a course based on seminar discussions of major historiographical issues inevitably focused on the earlier period. The historiography of the civil rights movement, for example, was largely stillborn at that point. When the course became a lecture course, I had to address the civil rights movement more substantively;

and it became clear that that was what the students wanted to hear about. I therefore replaced the final year New Deal special subject with a course on "Martin Luther King, Jr., and the Civil Rights Movement." The subject matter made it the most popular special subject in Newcastle before I was appointed—to my surprise—to the chair at Cambridge in 1991. The appointment process at Cambridge was even more austere than it had been at Newcastle. In 1991, two years to the day after the closing date for applications, I received out of the blue a letter from the vice chancellor indicating that the electors wished to offer me the chair. In the intervening twenty-four months there had been no communication from Cambridge, no interview, and no meeting with the electors.

Once there, however, my priority in Cambridge was to try and make American history more central to the faculty's provisions for students so that some of the best Cambridge undergraduates might choose to stay on for research in American rather than early modern British history, for example. Teaching a popular course on civil rights that now had a rich and rapidly developing historiography seemed one way of achieving that goal. The faculty board was skeptical but tolerant. Teaching King and the civil rights movement was, said one member, "dreadfully modern." Another wondered if any student would choose the course, given that the students could choose to study, for example, charters in medieval Florence. As a result I was assigned the smallest room in the building. When seventy-five students crowded into a room with sixteen chairs, my hopes were justified, and over the next four years the course broke records for the number taking a Cambridge special subject paper.

It was one thing to teach the civil rights movement, another to change tack and carry out research in the modern South. Having written a local case study of the New Deal, my thoughts first turned to a local case study of the civil rights movement in Mississippi, modeled on William Chafe's study of Greensboro. James T. Patterson swiftly disabused me of that notion: John Dittmer was already at work on just such a study. I also doubted that any British scholar could spend enough time in the United States to carry out the necessary archival and oral history work. Subsequently, Adam Fairclough and Stephen G. N. Tuck with their studies of Louisiana and Georgia respectively triumphantly proved me wrong. My next thought also sprang from my New Deal specialization. When Norman Thomas chided Roosevelt for being so fearful of upsetting southern conservatives in tackling the plight of sharecroppers in the Arkansas Delta, Roosevelt explained that they had to be patient: there was, he said, a new generation of southerners on the horizon. I wanted to know how that new generation of southern liberals handled the race issue when civil rights came to center stage after 1945. I set out to look at the liberal governors in the postwar South who appealed on economic issues to a biracial coalition of lower-income whites and the small, but slowly increasing black electorate. Were politicians like Jim Folsom, Sid McMath, Kerr Scott, and Earl Long simply overwhelmed in the aftermath of *Brown* by the overwhelming forces of popular mass racism? I tried to understand this relationship between constituency pressure and political stances on race by looking also at the Southern Manifesto of 1956. What happened to those southerners who refused to sign the Manifesto, particularly the three North Carolina congressmen whose early careers I had been familiar with during the New Deal? And who faced primary elections immediately after they refused to sign?[7]

But could I be an effective historian of the South? Could I understand the South, if, unlike Quentin Compson, I had not been born there? Like other British Americanists of my generation, I had consciously tried to make my work indistinguishable from that of U.S.-based historians. Unlike many of our predecessors who saw their role as interpreting the U.S. to a British audience or pursuing distinctive Anglo-American themes, we had tried to produce works as well researched as those of our American counterparts, on domestic American topics at the heart of American-centered debates, published by American university presses and reviewed in the leading American journals. But, when I started to write about the South, could I overcome the handicap of not having been born there?[8]

A number of critics, whose work I greatly respected, believed not. In 1993 I spoke at the Southern Historical Association as a member of an all-British panel on civil rights. The commentator warned the audience not to be seduced by our "charming British accents" because the study of southern race relations hid many traps for unsuspecting outsiders. (I apparently had fallen into these traps more heedlessly than the other panelists, Brian Ward and Adam Fairclough.) Four years later at an excellent conference on the fortieth anniversary of the Little Rock crisis, another commentator on another all-British panel thought that our outsider status prevented John Kirk and me from displaying enough empathy with the dilemmas faced by white southerners trapped by a paralyzing racial culture. (The belief that one could not adequately write American history without being born there had also been held by the electors of the Paul Mellon chair at Cambridge in 1991. As the vice chancellor wrote to me, they had been seeking an American-based historian for the chair "as a matter of principle, not *simply* [emphasis mine] because of doubts about the quality of the British Americanists."[9] A distinguished Ivy League historian made a subtly different point to me when a great friend of mine and noted southern historian refused to move to his university. The best southern historians, the Ivy Leaguer argued, were those who were born in the South but moved North and achieved a certain detachment. He cited David Potter, David Donald, and C. Vann Woodward.)

Such criticisms of our outsider-ness, gently and charmingly made, gave me pause. Far from being unsympathetic to the plight of white southerners, I had imagined myself a sort of honorary good ole' boy described recently by James C. Cobb as "a disarmingly down-home, diehard Braves fan who prefers Budweiser to Guinness." I believed that I was as likely to spring to the defense of white southerners criticized by supercilious Yankees as any native. I could understand how C. Vann Woodward reacted at the Selma-Montgomery march. He and other historians on the march rather self-consciously gathered round to give three cheers for Martin Luther King. As he told Willie Morris, he looked over to see the raw hatred of the white Alabamans watching from behind the ranks of the National Guard. And part of him sympathized with their view. In 1984 Alger Hiss took me to see some of his white liberal friends on Long Island. He told them that I had wonderful things to report from the South. (I had been telling Alger about what John Shelton Reed described as the transformation of day-to-day race relations in the South.) I was listened to with the careful attention and astonishment that a missionary returning from a foreign country would receive. One couple worried about the physical safety of their son, who was going to Montgomery to clerk for an African American federal judge. Should he discard his New York car tags? Would we provide a safe house for him in Atlanta when he broke his journey south? I suppressed the desire to reply that he was less likely to be attacked by rednecks in Alabama than by his fellow New Yorkers on the streets of Manhattan.[10]

My work argued that both conservatives and moderates in the South believed that public opinion was arrayed against them. Conservatives believed that ordinary white southerners were entirely too indifferent to the threat posed to white supremacy. Moderates believed, on the contrary, that ordinary whites were entirely too stirred up over the race issue, and that defiance of that popular sentiment would be fatal politically. The difference was that the conservatives were prepared to mount a righteous crusade to stir up white opposition to desegregation, to persuade ordinary whites that the Supreme Court could be defied, but the moderates and liberals for the most part were silent, fearing that too much agitation would harm the prospects of gradual racial change. In a contest between conservative dynamism and liberal fatalism, there could be only one victor. As critics rightly noted, there was an undoubted implication in my argument not only that liberal failings mattered and enabled the triumph of Massive Resistance, but that they did not need to be so supine. I had to acknowledge that it was all-too-easy for historians to second-guess politicians and to ascribe a freedom of maneuver that

may have been illusory. It was undoubtedly true that to second-guess courageous politicians like Frank Smith, Carl Elliott, or Hale Boggs from a distance of three thousand miles was even easier.

Nevertheless, I retained some hope that an outsider's perspective might
not be crippling. Part of that optimism lay in the achievements of a remarkable trio of graduate students who started in Cambridge as my first Ph.D.
students there in 1992. Tim Minchin, Stephen Tuck, and Clive Webb left me
in no doubt as to the value of British scholars working on southern history.
The British Ph.D. undoubtedly has its faults. The absence of coursework and
an empirical emphasis may contribute to the tin ear that many British
Americanists, as Richard King notes, have for theory. Our work can seem traditional and even old-fashioned. But there are compelling virtues in the
British system as well. On a prosaic level, the concentration on the dissertation enables students to complete their dissertations quickly and to enable a
scholar like Tim Minchin to have written four substantial research mono-
graphs within ten years of starting as a graduate student at the age of twenty-
two. That speed does not come at the expense of archival research. Most of
them have spent well over a year in southern archives during their Ph.D.
studies—archival research that was unhindered by teaching responsibilities.
The oral history interviews that Tuck conducted, the voluminous National
Labor Relations Board hearings that Minchin explored, and the geographi-
cal range of the collections that Webb consulted, all testify to the thorough-
ness of their research. Even more important, the freedom granted to highly
intelligent students to pursue their own topic is valuable. Would an American
Ph.D. student have been given the license to study an entire state for a case
study of the civil rights movement as Tuck was, would such a student have
been allowed to follow Webb's determined path to cover black-Jewish relations in the South all the way from slavery to the present? Distance perhaps
also allowed them to challenge the conventional pieties and to undermine
rather celebratory accounts of resistance and protest in the South. Tuck was
as interested in Georgia communities where there was no civil rights protest
as in those that were hotbeds of activism. Webb made it impossible to sustain easy generalizations about mutual black and Jewish interests in civil
rights in the South. Minchin found the failure of textile unionism in the
South not in a distinctive culture of southern workers but in the structure of
the industry and the circumstances of wartime and postwar prosperity.[11]

The obvious obstacles facing an outside observer and some possibly
compensating benefits from a measure of detachment were brought home to
me at the 2003 conference organized by Vernon Burton and Winfred B. "Bo"
Moore Jr. at The Citadel, the first major conference to examine the civil
rights movement in South Carolina. I could not help but feel an interloper

as I listened to the moving testimony from African American participants in the movement, particularly survivors of the Orangeburg massacre, about the violence and intimidation they faced. I could also not match the eloquent appraisal of white South Carolinians who, as students in the early 1960s in Columbia, had courageously been part of the small interracial movement in the state: Selden Smith, Charles Joyner, Dan T. Carter, and Hayes Mizell. Could I bring anything to this family reunion?[12]

To be asked to talk about the reaction of South Carolina governors to racial change and to do so on the same platform as former governors Fritz Hollings and John C. West was certainly likely to expose any comfortable academic second-guessing of southern moderates. I noted that it took "no little courage and no little political skill to reorient the state toward economic development and peaceful racial change." I did, however, raise questions about what I described as the "self-exculpatory model" of massive resistance in South Carolina—that the responsibility for massive resistance lay with everybody *except* the white political leaders of the state. I also queried the more panglossian versions of "the self-congratulatory model" of the state's peaceful adaptation to racial change in the 1960s. How much congratulation was due to a white leadership for eventually and belatedly complying with the law? How much credit was due the white leadership for averting the threat of violence, a threat that that leadership had unleashed in the first place? Critics have argued that I, as a nonsoutherner, have failed to understand politicians like Hollings and West on their own terms. What I argued in Charleston was that we do need to understand, not patronize or demonize, the white southern leaders of the 1950s and 1960s. But to understand them is not to absolve them of responsibility.[13]

Jack E. Davis recently exclaimed in effect that "the British are coming" as he noted the large number of British scholars publishing on the civil rights movement.[14] In fact, southern history as a whole, not just the post-1945 South, disproportionately engages the interest of American historians in Britain. From Betty Wood on colonial Georgia to Mike Tadman on the slave trade to Adam Fairclough on modern black protest, many of the leading British Americanists work on the South. They do so at a time when interest in southern history appears to be on the decline in the United States. Fewer posts in southern history and literature seem to be filled in American universities outside the South than they were a generation ago. In southern universities like Emory and Georgia, leading southern historians acutely feel the scorn of their Ivy League–trained colleagues in American and European history who regard southern history as mere "local" history.

Why does the South exert such a pull over British academics? It may be the universality of the southern experience of war, poverty, defeat, and guilt that C. Vann Woodward identified. Michael O'Brien noted that Columbia, South Carolina, burned to the ground by Sherman, was instantly recognizable to someone who grew up in a Plymouth flattened by the Luftwaffe. Stephen Tuck claimed an affinity between the British West Midlands and the South as marginal regions. A former imperial power coming to terms with its own history of racial oppression might be seen to have a special interest in a region coping with slavery, its own form of apartheid, and the dramatic collapse of white supremacy. The trials and tribulations of a fledgling nation-state have powerful contemporary European resonance. The Civil War has had a never-ending fascination for British observers interested in the constitutional workings of federalism and the scale of the military conflict. The southern roots of so much American popular culture attracted scholars like Brian Ward.

Contingency also plays a part, however. The presence of expatriate scholars who happened to work on the South, Bill Dusinberre and Richard King, has been enormously important. Teaching demands turned Peter Parish into a southern historian as they had me. His head of department in Glasgow, Esmond Wright, who was tired of teaching a special subject, told Peter to introduce one instead. When Peter suggested his own speciality, Wright told him to teach instead the American Civil War, which would be more popular with the students. The results, some years down the road, were Peter's magisterial studies of the Civil War and of slavery and its historians. The paucity of graduate awards in Britain in the 1970s and 1980s led historians like Mark Newman, Richard Follett, and Keith Mason to pursue their Ph.D.s at southern universities. The accidents of appointments and funding opportunities allied to student demand have shaped the importance of southern history in British universities as much as the universality of the southern historical experience. Indeed, for many scholars and students what has always been attractive about the South has been the appeal of its difference, rather than its similarity: its exotic politics, its brutal race relations, its compelling nonviolent social protest.

Jack Davis compared the "invasion" of British historians to the arrival of the Beatles in America.[15] He rightly doubts that we will have the same impact, though he is generous about our work. The outsiders' perspective has perhaps some value for the pursuit of southern history at this particular time. The interest in the South in Britain and Europe should bolster the confidence of southern historians that theirs is not a parochial subject. But the outsider can also challenge the sense of proprietorial ownership of their own history by southerners, especially white southerners. The outsider status neither guarantees authenticity nor precludes it. What I hope the essays in this volume show is a sympathetic, but not uncritical, understanding of the South by an outsider.

The essays are representative of a quarter of a century's work on southern history. They follow from a generous comment by James T. Patterson at the 2003 OAH meeting that many of my articles and chapters were not easily available in the United States. Of the twelve essays in this volume only three were originally published in the United States: four have never been published. I have tried to excise the most egregious repetitions but I have not tried to improve the essays in the light of subsequent scholarship or my own changing views. Hasty, premature, or simply misguided judgments remain for all to see: they represent my best effort at the time they were written.

The first four chapters deal with the impact of the New Deal in the South. "Huey Long and the New Deal" examines the structural reasons why Long unlike other reformers or other demagogues was able to overcome the conservative hegemony in southern politics in the first half of the twentieth century. While acknowledging his real achievements and his personal popularity, it raises questions about his supposed racial moderation and suggests that the New Deal did more for the poorest Louisianans than Long did. It doubts that Long posed either a radical or a powerful challenge to the New Deal.

"How Did the New Deal Change the South" extends the discussion of the local impact of the New Deal to the region as a whole. It shows how the New Deal left the South in many ways as it found it: a one-party, poor rural region, over-dependent on one-crop agriculture in which African Americans were rigidly segregated and politically powerless. It shows how persistent local conservative political power stymied the New Dealers' bottom-up economic modernization strategies. The New Deal may have raised the expectations of the federal government held by African American leaders and white southern liberals but its impact on the eventual modernization of the South and the collapse of segregation was tangential and often unintended.

The "Lament for Rural Worlds Lost" examines that eventual modernization: the transformation from a poor, rural, and small-town South to a booming industrial and urban region. I argue that the decisive flight from the land and the stimulus to agricultural mechanization came with World War II, not the New Deal. I question whether there were alternative policies in the 1930s that would have led to a modernization that would have sustained a model of self-sufficient, small farms. Nostalgia for "rural worlds lost" was in any case more common among white than among African Americans. Distinctive southern values survived modernization but I attempt to draw up a balance sheet of what was excoriated as distinctively southern in the 1950s and 1960s but celebrated in the New South of the 1970s and 1980s: southern race relations.

Finally, "Roosevelt's New Generation of Southerners" looks at the legacy of FDR for younger, issue-oriented, liberal southern politicians elected to

Congress and state houses in the late 1930s and 1940s. These politicians saw the federal government exemplified by the New Deal, as the solution, not the cause, of the region's problems. Just as the TVA had regenerated an entire river valley, so the federal government could transform the infrastructure of the whole region. They appealed to a biracial alliance of lower-income voters, labor, women, and veterans by providing long-overdue government welfare and public services for those voters. But, at the same time, they confronted a racial and economic backlash that in the end would be more powerful.

In the next four essays I examine the way white southern liberal politicians handled the race issue after 1945. They had hoped that economic development would in itself resolve racial problems in the South and permit gradual racial change. But the federal courts and African American protest forced southern politicians to confront the issue head-on. Were those politicians overwhelmed by the sheer mass of popular white racism?

"Southerners Who Refused to Sign the Southern Manifesto" shows what happened to a small group in Congress who refused to sign the blast of defiance at the Supreme Court in 1956, which, its drafters hoped, would demonstrate a united regional stance against desegregation. The essay shows that a variety of personal, sometimes idiosyncratic impulses prompted the nonsigners: national political ambition, economic liberalism, factional in-fighting in Texas, service in World War II, concern for cold war foreign policy, urban constituents, and religion. In Texas, Tennessee, and Florida the non-signers escaped electoral retribution. The essay examines the complex of local issues and racial reaction that led to two of the three nonsigners in North Carolina being defeated in Democratic primaries within two months of their refusal to sign.

In "The White Reaction" I examine why noted southern moderates like J. William Fulbright and Brooks Hays, from a state, Arkansas, which prided itself on its progressive racial image, nevertheless signed the Manifesto. Both political calculation and personal racial conservatism led Fulbright to defy the advice of his liberal aides and sign. Brooks Hays and James W. Trimble were persuaded by Governor Faubus to sign. I argue that Faubus was convinced by the events of early 1956 that it was political suicide to defy mass white segregationist sentiment, but that he, himself, helped create that segregationist sentiment, which he later claimed to be the prisoner of at the time of the Little Rock crisis in 1957. I conclude that in 1956 Arkansas moderate politicians had already displayed the fatalism and caution that rendered them ineffective in Little Rock in 1957–58.

"Closet Moderates" develops these ideas on a regional basis to explain why white liberal politicians were not the force of the future in the South, why they were not at the helm during the region's racial convulsions of the 1950s and 1960s. I suggest that conservative leaders in the South, confronted by the pressure for racial change in the 1950s, were determined to convince ordinary southern whites that segregation could be preserved. White liberal politicians by contrast were paralyzed by their belief that mass white segregationist sentiment was overwhelming. Because their own commitment to racial change was so limited and their awareness of African American demands so second-hand, they could not devise a strategy for gradual racial change that could deliver substantive change to the African Americans who supported them in the 1950s variant of biracial politics. When African Americans opted for direct action protest in the 1960s, and the federal government mandated racial change in the South, it was not southern liberal politicians who guided the region into acceptance of racial change but southern businessmen.

"From Defiance to Moderation" examines the process of racial change in South Carolina. Massive Resistance in South Carolina was a "top-down" phenomenon. The state's leaders, far from dousing the fire of popular racist sentiment, sought to fan the flames. Massive Resistance in the state was neither as peaceful or restrained as South Carolinian politicians like to recall. But South Carolina's business and political leaders, led by Fritz Hollings, did see the eventual inevitability of racial change and the dire economic cost of continued resistance. They invested no little political courage in persuading their followers to support economic development and racial moderation.

The final essays look at the long-term political consequences of the collapse of segregation and the extension of black political participation. V. O. Key Jr. in 1949 predicted that the collapse of the four pillars of the Old South—the one-party system, rural overrepresentation in state legislatures, segregation, and black disfranchisement—would greatly strengthen the forces of southern liberalism. The essays explain why biracial politics in the modern South have tended to favor lily-white, conservative Republicans rather than liberals.

"When I Took the Oath of Office" traces the history of welfare liberalism in Louisiana from Huey Long to Edwin Edwards that combined high spending, corruption, and racial moderation. Good government reformers from Sam Houston Jones to David Treen combined retrenchment and racial conservatism and could only briefly overcome the potent electoral appeal of spending and services. The collapse of oil and gas revenues in the 1980s spelt the end of high spending and exposed the cost of corruption. Republicans appealed to the cultural and racial conservatism of lower- and middle-income whites who struggled in a declining economy. David Duke exemplified that appeal but his high-profile extremism suggested potentially damaging economic consequences. Republicans not handicapped by his Nazi and Klan baggage succeeded where Duke failed. But there was little in the quality of the state's governance to suggest that the state could benefit, like other southern states, from a diversified, high-tech economy or that the poverty of the state's "have-nots," black and white would be alleviated.

In "The Dilemma of Biracial Politics" I examine the consequences of increased black political participation after the Voting Rights Act of 1965. The essay pays due attention to the policy gains that come from African American voting but notes the limitations of the business progressive, New South governors of the 1970s. It traces the rise of the Republican Party, particularly in the 1990s, and weighs the impact of race, rather than the Christian Right and anti-tax sentiment, in the creation of the modern lily-white GOP. Finally it shows how difficult it is for Democrats to secure the 35 to 40 percent of white voters and still mobilize the black vote and the unpalatable choices, local power and patronage against statewide liberal influence, that face African American politicians.

Two quintessential members of Roosevelt's new generation of southerners were Lyndon Johnson and Albert Gore Sr. Their careers started in the localized, patronage-oriented politics of the one-party South of the 1930s and ended in the two-party, issue-driven, nationally oriented politics of the modern South. They passionately believed in the power of the federal government to modernize the South through investing in its infrastructure roads, atomic energy, cheap power, and water resource development. They shared a common desire to eliminate poverty in the South. They were racial moderates and internationalists. "Southern New Dealers Confront the World" describes the personal rivalry between Johnson and Gore that led to a bitter break over Vietnam. Where Johnson envisaged reconstructing Vietnam as FDR had reconstructed the South, Gore saw an endless, and hopeless, war of attrition that would imperil relations with both Russia and China. Vietnam ended the political career of both men.

The forces that led to the rise of the modern Republican Party in the South were present in Albert Gore's defeat in 1970. "The Anti-Gore Campaign of 1970" shows how Gore's challenger in the Democratic primary rehearsed the same arguments that the Republican candidate, William E. Brock, successfully deployed in the general election. Gore's opposition to the war and to Richard Nixon's southern nominees to the Supreme Court was used to amplify an argument that Gore was out of touch with his constituents. His stance on busing and gun control rounded out the picture in carefully crafted TV ads. But what was indicative of the future of Republican Party success in the South was the injection of religion into the campaign and the failure of Gore to support prayer in schools.

1

Huey Long and the New Deal

Politicians who combined demagogic appeals to lower-income white farmers, bitter denunciations of large corporations and Wall Street, and vitriolic personal abuse of their opponents were a familiar sight in the twentieth-century South. In a one-party system where the key election was the Democratic Party primary, candidates had to mobilize voters without the benefit of a party organization. Large-scale campaign finance from conservative economic interests offered one means of getting out the vote. Support from county elites who manipulated local power offered another. To a candidate who could rely on neither campaign wealth nor the endorsement of local power brokers, the only alternative path to power was a colorful and dramatic personal campaign to arouse the electorate.[1]

Among these southern demagogues, Huey Long of Louisiana was *sui generis* in three respects. First, most southern demagogues, once elected, either quickly shelved their reform rhetoric, substituted appeals to racial prejudice for substantive reform, or found themselves stymied by conservative legislatures. Long largely eschewed racial appeals and translated his electoral promises to the poor whites of Louisiana into real legislative achievement in the fields of highways, health, and education between his election as governor in 1928 and his assassination in 1935. Second, few southern demagogues showed any appetite for the hard work of long-term political organization. But Long, once he had survived an impeachment attempt in 1929, built himself an almost impregnable power base in Louisiana, maintaining ruthless control of the state legislature not only while he was governor, but also while he was a United States senator. Third, most southern demagogues did not travel well: their appeal was parochial, regional at best. Long, however, bitterly attacked Roosevelt's New Deal, launched his own program massively to redistribute the nation's wealth, and set out from Louisiana to proclaim his analysis of the

1

nation's ills to western farmers and northern industrial workers. He threatened to wreak havoc in the 1936 presidential election by picking up, so a poll for the Democratic National Committee indicated, as many as six or seven million votes as a third-party candidate. He was arguably the only plausible presidential candidate to emerge from the Deep South in the twentieth century until George Wallace and Jimmy Carter thirty years later.

This phenomenon aroused massive interest in the 1930s. Liberal observers, struck by the unashamedly dictatorial nature of Long's control of his own state, sometimes saw parallels between Long and the contemporary European fascist dictators. Such a picture fitted in well with the concerns of social scientists of the 1950s who were investigating the sources of right-wing extremism in America. In the same tradition as Joe McCarthy and George Wallace, Long was portrayed as a leader who aroused the status resentments of an irrational mass movement.[2] Political scientist Allan P. Sindler and New Deal historian Arthur M. Schlesinger Jr., however, correctly identified the sources of Long's power in the very real economic grievances of the politically powerless lower-income rural whites of Louisiana. Although both Sindler and Schlesinger stressed Long's positive achievements at the state level, both saw Long ultimately as a demagogue, cynically exploiting the real grievances of the dispossessed while seducing them with fraudulent remedies. Sindler was doubtful that Long's state reforms benefited the masses of Louisiana. Schlesinger saw Long's national share-our-wealth scheme as simply a glib panacea designed to delude the helpless.[3]

To T. Harry Williams, in his prize-winning biography, Long was neither an incipient fascist nor a cynical demagogue, but a genuine radical who injected a much-needed dose of realism into southern politics. Williams succeeded in persuading a formidable number of Louisiana politicians to unburden themselves with remarkable frankness in oral history interviews. The result was an unsurpassed and vivid account of the free-wheeling reality of the state's politics. Williams argued that while most southern politicians, both conservatives and demagogues, made an essentially romantic and backward-looking appeal to Civil War loyalties and white supremacy, Long offered a realistic analysis of the economic plight of poor southerners and a realistic assessment of what was needed to bring about change. His sometimes corrupt and ruthless tactics were, Williams contended, essential to overcome the power of the entrenched conservative oligarchy in Louisiana and successfully to enact a reform program. At the national level Williams portrayed Long as a sincere "mass leader" who correctly pointed to the inadequacies of the New Deal and offered a genuine challenge to the New Deal, not from the right but from the left. Shrewdly recognizing that threat, another master politician, Franklin Roosevelt, moved quickly to defuse the danger by unscrupulously manipulating patronage and income-tax investigations in Louisiana. Unable to defeat Long by those methods, Roosevelt acted to "steal Huey's thunder" in 1935 by shifting to the left himself.[4] Williams's analysis coincided with the views of revisionist historians of the New Deal in the late 1960s who saw Long's popularity in 1935 as evidence of the essentially conservative nature of the New Deal and as an indication that there existed popular support for more radical options, if only Roosevelt had chosen to tap such potential.[5]

Recently more sober assessments of Long have been presented, summed up by Alan Brinkley's conclusion that Long was "neither monster nor messiah." Both Glen Jeansonne and Brinkley are unconvinced by Williams's uncritical justification of Long's methods in Louisiana, both point to the precisely circumscribed nature of his reforms there, both see the "share our wealth" scheme as an unworkable panacea, and Brinkley points to the "softness" of much of Long's apparent national support in 1935.[6]

In the light of this considerable body of secondary literature, I wish to examine four areas of Long's career which offer the chance to draw conclusions about the reform achievements and limitations of both Long and the New Deal. First, a look at Long's local record can explain why he was so much more effective than other southern demagogues and can test Williams's contention that his reforms were fundamental and his methods unavoidable. Second, an examination of the operation of the New Deal, in particular the political reprisals directed at Long, raises questions about the effectiveness of the New Deal at the local level, the degree of the New Deal's commitment to reform, and the potential for federal intervention to restructure local Democratic parties. Third, an analysis of Long's critique of the New Deal and the alternatives he proposed can test the extent to which he offered a genuinely radical challenge to Roosevelt. Finally, an estimate of the strength of his national support in 1935 offers a measure of popular dissatisfaction with the New Deal and the extent to which there was potential support available to the New Deal for more radical options if Roosevelt had chosen to appeal to it.

Conservative forces dominated the politics of Louisiana, as of other southern states, in the early twentieth century. Power rested in an alliance of large planters of the black-belt cotton and sugar parishes in the south of the state, the city machine of New Orleans, and the industrialists, preeminent among whom was Standard Oil, who had been attracted by the state's natural resources and cheap labor. The conservative elite had finally made safe its hegemony by defeating through fraud and violence the Populist-Republican challenge in 1896. The massive disfranchisement of both black and lower-income white voters that followed ensured that the white farmers of the northern hill parishes would not be able to repeat that Populist onslaught on the status quo. A one-party system and disfranchisement enabled conservative

forces to ignore the welfare needs of lower socioeconomic groups, made corruption easier, and strengthened the power of organized economic interest
groups. Ethnocultural divisions between the Protestant north and the
Catholic south further lessened the chance of a successful mobilization of
lower-income voters. What distinguished Louisiana from other southern
states was the degree of toleration of corruption and the extent of the unre-
sponsiveness to popular needs on the part of the conservative oligarchy.
Taxation was minimal, as was state spending. The state provided neither
effective regulation of corporations, nor social welfare programs, nor substantial public services. As a result, even before the Depression, Louisiana ranked
with its resource-starved neighbor Mississippi in the grinding poverty that
faced the overwhelming mass of its population. In 1929 the state actually
ranked above other southern states in real *per capita* income, but that
reflected its industrial base. The real quality of life of its overwhelmingly rural
population was illustrated by its ranking of forty-third in the value of farm
property, forty-fifth in the number of farms served by electricity, and forty-
seventh in the percentage of adult illiterates.[7]

From Long's first campaign for the Railroad Commission (later the
Public Service Commission) in 1919 to his election as governor in 1928,
there was no doubt which path he planned to follow to political power: identification with the hitherto excluded poor whites against the corporate oligarchy. He campaigned tirelessly in the rural areas, seeking the support of
farmers to whom he had once peddled patent medicines, margarine, and the
Bible. To mobilize this support he pioneered the use in the state of cars,
sound trucks, radio speeches, and the distribution of circulars. He even dictated the quality of paper on which the circulars were to be printed: "Don't
use any of that damn smooth stuff. Use some that they can use on their back-
sides after they get through reading it." The enemy was always the same. As
he said in his 1924 campaign for governor, "Standard Oil Company and
other predatory corporations will not be permitted to rule Louisiana." On
the Public Service Commission he relentlessly worked to lower the rates that
utilities charged the consumer. In his 1924 campaign, however, he had been
unable successfully to straddle the dominant cultural issues of the Klan and
Prohibition and failed to pick up Catholic support in the south. What Long
was able to do in 1928 was, for the first time since the Populist challenge of
the 1890s, to bring class and economic issues to the fore in Louisiana. He
promised much-needed government services to his lower-income supporters,
improved roads, schools, and hospitals, and long overdue regulation of the
corporations and public utilities. To a large extent he also avoided the race
issue, the stock-in-trade of so many southern politicians who sought to divert
the attention of the electorate away from economic grievances.[8]

What distinguished Long was not his espousal of the poor white cause, but the way in which he translated his promises into reality when he became governor. He dragged the state's road system out of the mud and into the twentieth century, doubling the mileage of highways and increasing sixfold the mileage of concrete roads. He provided free school textbooks to children at both state and parochial schools and centralized the whole school system: the state took over the tax burden of supporting schools and established an equalization fund to help poorer parishes. To combat adult illiteracy he launched an innovative night-school program. For college students he transformed Louisiana State University into a major regional university. To remedy the shortage of doctors in the state, he dramatically expanded medical education with the building of a new medical school at LSU and he doubled the number of patients in the state's hospital for the indigent. He brought changes to the state's prisons and mental asylums, secured the supply of natural gas to New Orleans, and, far from surrendering to the power of the corporations, he substantially increased the severance tax on oil companies, introduced a tax on carbon black, and a state income tax.[9]

By the standards of any southern state government in the 1920s and 1930s it was an impressive record. By the standard of a demagogue with reform pretensions, like Theodore Bilbo in Mississippi, it represented a stunning expansion of state government services. But the achievement had limitations that cannot be ignored. For all his anti-corporation rhetoric, Long's record was very much in the mould, as George Tindall has pointed out, of "business-progressivism." A number of southern governors, particularly in the 1920s, had instituted reforms to facilitate the modernization of their states: the reorganization of state governments into efficient and honest instruments, the provision of roads, education, and health care. But such reforms were meant to attract middle-class, not lower-income, voters and to attract, not deter, outside investors. Thus, business-progressive governors did nothing to upset established relations between employers and a cowed labor force, did little to increase the corporate tax burden, and did little to promote social welfare legislation. Long's emphasis on roads, education, and health fit neatly into this pattern, even if cheap and honest government was not one of his aims.[10] Much of his reform was made possible by the constitutional reforms and the changes in the tax base brought in by the archetypal, if rather ineffective, "business-progressive" administration of Governor John Parker, 1920–1924.[11]

Long's stated goal was a "modern efficient commonwealth." He worked with the Commercial Affairs Committee, a group of business leaders in New Orleans, to modernize the port. Sixty-six percent of his spending in 1931 was on highways.[12] A road-building program offered Long many advantages:

campaign contributions from highway contractors, considerable largesse with which to reward faithful legislators, and real benefit to the state's industrialists, small-town businessmen, and commercial farmers. Such a program offered only incidental benefits to the mass of tenants and sharecroppers, whose horizons, in the absence of increased cash income, would be as limited as ever. Indeed, nothing in Long's proposals in Louisiana suggested that he envisaged any change in the basic structure of the state's agriculture. His concern was with the owner-operator who voted for him, not with the disenfranchised tenants and sharecroppers. Similarly, the benefits for rural Louisiana of his educational and health reforms were likely to be long term: in the short term, the increased opportunities for students at LSU and the increase in the number of doctors trained at Medical School would have little meaning for the poorer sections of the rural community. Even the state takeover of financial responsibility for the school system did not immediately lead to more money for the schools since the Depression cut into potential tax revenues.[13] Two educational reforms, however—the provision of free textbooks and the adult illiteracy program—had an immediate effect right down the social scale.

For all his rhetorical denunciations of the corporations, there is no evidence that Long intended to drive them out of Louisiana. On the contrary, his taxation and labor policies were consistent with the business-progressive model of securing economic growth through a favorable tax environment for business and a low-wage and docile labor force. Long lessened the dependence of the state on local property taxes which had certainly borne most heavily on taxpayers of average and below-average means. He reduced assessments and exempted lower-income families. He did increase the tax burden on corporations and, after an abortive attempt which led to his impeachment, introduced an occupational licensing tax on the refining of oil. Nevertheless, these steps toward a more progressive tax structure were limited. The tax burden on corporations was still relatively light: the discretionary rate of the occupational tax set by the Long administration was low and the new state income tax provided a very narrow band between lower- and higher-income payers. Long relied heavily on consumer taxes on cigarettes and gasoline, and it was the taxpayers of the future who would have to pay off the bonded debt he incurred for his state spending.[14] It should be noted, nevertheless, that the impact of Long's rhetoric lingered. State promoters of Louisiana's industrial development were still haunted and handicapped by the state's reputation as an anti-corporation state in the 1970s.[15]

As far as labor was concerned, Long showed little sign of impinging on corporate authority over their employees. He refused to send the militia into New Orleans to break a strike of street railway employees and he opposed the yellow-dog contract. But he passed no labor legislation of note, and he did nothing to establish the right of collective bargaining in the state, or to raise minimum wages. Indeed, his supporters killed a bill to regulate the hours of work of female labor, and he reportedly told a labor delegation that "The prevailing wage is as low as we can get men to take it." He opposed legislation against child labor by arguing that "picking cotton is fun for kids anyway." As for welfare legislation, he resisted the idea of old-age pensions put forward by an anti-Long gubernatorial candidate in 1932, refused to appropriate money for mothers' pensions, and provided nothing for unemployment relief during his control of state politics.[16]

Long, therefore, seems to have responded to conventional rural and conservative constituency pressures in Louisiana despite his almost total control of the state legislature. Long's prescriptions for economic growth in the state were much the same as those put forward by business progressive and conservative advocates of industrial development. Growth would come from above—from the trickle down of benefits as industries were attracted by the state's cheap labor—rather than from below—from demand stimulated by increases in mass purchasing power. Long's program did not match the liberalism of the remedies put forward by New Deal supporters in the South later in the decade when they founded the Southern Conference for Human Welfare. The elimination of southern poverty, they argued, would only come through measures designed to raise the purchasing power of tenant farmers and industrial workers. The methods they advocated—tenant protection through well-funded rural poverty programs, minimum-wage legislation, and protection of trade unions' civil liberties—were not foreshadowed in Huey Long's Louisiana.[17]

Long has been praised for his achievements in two areas in which he could not possibly accrue any political benefit: prison reform and provision for blacks. Long, however, did little to improve Louisiana's notorious prisons, indeed he probably made conditions worse for the inmates. He did appoint an honest and effective general manager of the prison system, but, as Mark T. Carleton has pointed out, R. L. Himes was only appointed after Long's first political appointee had proved hopelessly incompetent. Himes was appointed solely for his ability to run the prison system as cheaply as possible. As Long himself boasted when he appointed the former business manager of Louisiana State University, "I have appointed him because of the close manner in which he has guarded every fund and property of the University. His careful manner of handling the university business has earned him the name of "tighty" on the campus and that is the kind of man we need at the penitentiary." Far from making the system more humane or introducing some rehabilitative component, Himes made the system more brutal in his efforts to make it self-supporting. He intensified the usual regime of flogging and long convict work hours, and the number of deaths annually between 1931 and 1935 were the highest since the days of the old convict lease system.[18]

Long, as Williams emphasizes, usually avoided appeals to racism. His negro-baiting references were the small change of campaign rhetoric rather than the core of his appeal, unlike such contemporaries as Theodore Bilbo, Eugene Talmadge, and Tom Heflin. While not challenging segregation, Long routinely claimed that blacks should benefit alongside whites in his programs.[19] He criticized New Deal crop-control policies for their effect on black tenant farmers and attacked the federal-state operation of social security because of the likely local exclusion of blacks from old-age assistance programs.[20]

Yet, there is no evidence that blacks benefited from Long's public works and educational programs. He certainly had no intention of positively aiding blacks. When, for example, he abolished the poll tax in 1934, it was with the specific aim of increasing white voter registration. White registration rose by almost 200,000 between 1932 and 1934 while only 500 more blacks registered, blacks who in any case could not vote in the Democratic primaries.[21] When Long was under political pressure he did not hesitate to use the race issue. In 1932 "Coozan Dudley" LeBlanc, whose skills on the stump and appeal to rural audiences stemmed from the same background as a traveling salesman as Long, challenged Long's handpicked gubernatorial candidate, O. K. Allen. LeBlanc's potentially vote-winning issue was his advocacy of a $30-a-month old-age pension. Long's response was to condemn LeBlanc's burial insurance business as "a nigger burial and coffin club," to circulate pictures of LeBlanc surrounded by black officers of the Thibodeax Benevolent Association, and to headline that under LeBlanc's pension scheme "Some 60,000 Negroes would get $30 per month."[22] Later, Long denounced both old-age and unemployment benefits on the grounds that blacks would benefit from them.[23]

Even in the context of Louisianan and southern politics, therefore, there were precise limits to Long's innovations. Nevertheless, he achieved far more than most southern politicians elected on the basis of lower-income white support. How did Long manage to achieve the power that most demagogues, and indeed later southern liberals, failed to attain? How crucial was the fraud, corruption, and violence that were part of his methods?

Long's victory in 1928 was essentially a personal one: his supporters in the state legislature fell far short of a majority. Yet he transformed this ephemeral personal support into a powerful and permanent political organization. Not only was Long able to overcome a determined drive by conservative opponents to impeach him in 1929, but he went on to achieve virtually dictatorial power in the state. He was able to go off to Washington in 1931 as a United States senator, yet still exercise day to day control over the governor's office and run the state legislature. At the height of his control, the legislature passed and discussed under his personal supervision 46 bills in twenty-two minutes and enacted 463 bills in six months. Legislators often had very little idea what they were voting for. One lawmaker asked, "When will we know what these bills are all about?" "Tuesday, when they are passed," replied Long. As he told a lone opposition senator, "I'm the constitution round here."[24] Slates of candidates endorsed by Long ran as an identifiable ticket, with the result that Louisiana developed a bifactional, Long/anti-Long political structure that gave the state something of the characteristics of a two-party system. That factional divide outlasted Long and was still a salient political factor in the 1960s.

However much contemporaries may have seen Long's dictatorship as a model of European fascism, his power was based on the familiar tools of American machine politics: patronage, corruption, electoral fraud, and violence. Long simply used these tools more systematically and ruthlessly than most southern politicians. Yet, as with other machine politicians, the ultimate base of Long's power was his popular support. In return for the services he provided, Louisiana voters gave him enthusiastic and loyal backing.

Patronage at the start gave Long the opportunity to build up his following. As he built up this legislative support, so he moved further to expand his control of patronage, with the result that in the end he had virtually cut off the lifeblood of any organized opposition. As a starting point, the governor of Louisiana had more appointive positions at his disposal than many governors. Then Long maneuvered quickly to control Boards with large payrolls and political influence: the New Orleans Dock Board, the Levee Board, the Highway Commission, the Conservation Commission, and the Board of Health. In order to control politicians whose loyalty was doubtful, he often made appointees sign undated letters of resignation. To perpetuate his control he next moved to control the judiciary and the election machinery in the state. Finally, his compliant legislature took away from local and municipal government much of their appointive powers and vested them in the state. In the case of an anti-Long center like New Orleans, one observer noted that it was left with not "enough patronage to support the government of an unincorporated village." Another center of opposition suddenly found that the legislature had declared its elective offices to be vacant, with the governor having the power to fill temporary vacancies.[25]

Williams estimates that Long had as many as 25,000 jobs at his disposal by the time he finished—a formidable head start for any political organization.[26] What made Long's control of patronage so notable was that no job was too small or unimportant to be filled by a Long supporter or his friends or relatives. Similarly what distinguished Long was his determination that no opponent, no matter how weak or ineffective, should have a public position.[27] Long reached down into the state university, the Charity Hospital in New Orleans, and into local school boards to ensure that no public critic of his administration stayed in a state job. Academic freedom went by the board as far as the state university was concerned. Long regarded it as his property and would not tolerate any faculty member publicly opposing him. He went to inordinate lengths to pursue insignificant and powerless opponents. John Minor Wisdom, who was to become a distinguished judge on the Fifth Circuit Court of Appeals, recalled that as a Republican law student at Tulane in 1932 he bet $15 against Long, who had publicly bet $50,000 at 2–1 odds, that Allen would win the gubernatorial primary. The *New Orleans States-Item* carried the next morning a banner headline, "Lone GOP Takes $15 of $50,000 Wager." The publisher, a close personal friend of Wisdom's and a political ally of Long's, explained to Wisdom that he had ordered the story as a compromise to Long's demand of him that Wisdom be humiliated. Long then attempted to get Wisdom's brother fired from a public relations position with an insurance company.[28] Long's ruthless pursuit of defeated opponents was shown the following year. Having already ensured that Dudley LeBlanc's political power was demolished by supervising his defeat both for governor and for reelection to the Public Service Commission, Long determined to ruin LeBlanc financially as well. The legislature passed a law designed specifically and solely to put his burial insurance association out of business.[29] As an opposition leader noted, "If you were for him [Long] you could have anything you wanted. If you were against him, God help you unless you were an extraordinary man."[30]

The line between patronage and corruption is a narrow one. That distinction between offering jobs and favors in return for support and an outright bribe of a legislator was certainly blurred at the time of the impeachment crisis. Cash payments certainly secured the signatures of at least some of the state senators who signed the decisive "round robin," which stated that they would not in any circumstance vote for the governor's impeachment. The signatories were also rewarded later by lucrative appointments, contracts, and legal fees. Businessmen dealing with the state, notably road contractors, definitely made kickback payments to Long and his henchmen, which both lined Long's pockets and, more importantly, funded his campaigns. His most important backer, Bob Maestri, a furniture dealer on the fringe of the red light district of New Orleans, who allegedly made his fortune selling beds to brothels, became chairman of the Conservation Commission and later mayor of New Orleans. State employees at various times were required to contribute "voluntarily" 10 percent of their salaries to the Long organization or to take out subscriptions to Long's newspapers. The deduct box containing these contributions was never discovered, despite the frantic efforts of his friends to find out at Long's deathbed where he had put it. Some of Long's most trusted associates, like Seymour Weiss, faced incometax evasion indictments and later went to jail.[31]

Long's own attitude to this corruption was dismissive. Challenged on graft in the road-building program, he replied, "We got the roads in Louisiana, haven't we? In some states they only have the graft."[32] Williams has defended the corruption of the Long regime by arguing that Long kept corruption in check—he did not want graft to get in the way of the accomplishments that he was so proud of. It was Long's successors who let corruption run riot, with the result that both the governor of the state and the president of the state university ended up in jail. Williams asserts that, in any case, illegal contributions to the Long machine did not serve a corrupt purpose, since Long never allowed his independence to be compromised: he was beholden to no one. According to this reasoning, no matter how large Long's illegal fortune, he could not be considered corrupt since he did not allow corrupt payments to influence his decisions. Finally, Williams maintains that Long was aware of the problem and was planning to root out corruption in his organization before his death. This contention rests on the uncorroborated hearsay evidence of one of Long's associates. There were no signs of Long actually taking any steps against corruption, and he appeared to think that his close associates were simply being persecuted by the Internal Revenue Service.[33]

Corruption was not, of course, new in Louisiana and Long's conservative opponents were as guilty as anyone. Long may have bribed legislators to stave off his own impeachment, but several legislators testified that the pro-impeachment forces attempted to bribe them. Before the impeachment, legislators also recalled that they could pick up as much as $20,000 in the evening at the Heidelberg Hotel from the Standard Oil lobbyist, who was anxious to defeat the proposed occupational tax.[34]

Election fraud was rife in Long's Louisiana. In 1932 the state legislature killed a bill providing for specific penalties for anyone convicted of fraudulent election practices. Fixing elections became a crime without a punishment. The most blatant vote-fixing occurred in St. Bernard's parish, where Leander Perez, boss of Plaquemines Parish, regularly returned majorities for Long's candidates that were twice the total number of registered white voters in the parish.[35] But it must be conceded that election fraud was endemic in Louisiana. Perez had been piling up such majorities before Long came to power and would continue to do so until the 1960s. Electoral corruption was also an integral part of the New Orleans city machine politics. Nor did Long's frauds match the bloated majorities piled up in the state's black-belt counties by the conservative elite in order to defeat the Populists in the 1890s. Again, what was distinctive about Long was not the fraud itself but the fact that through his control of the judiciary and the local boards of election supervisors, with the occasional help of the state militia, there was little chance of any effective challenge by opposing factions.

Some of the more hysterical accusations of Long's opponents about the violence of the regime were probably untrue, notably the impeachment article stating that he ordered the murder of a state representative. Yet routinely Long's bodyguards beat up hecklers, there were some still unexplained abductions of politically embarrassing witnesses, and opposition printing presses burned to the ground. Violence in turn drove Long's opponents to violence. In 1934 Long attempted to circumvent a Democratic primary election in an opposition district when the congressman died. He ordered the congressman's widow nominated as the Democratic candidate for the meaningless general election. A local anti-Long judge enjoined the general election in his own judicial district. Specially sworn-in deputies burnt the ballots and fired on the state police in order to prevent the election taking place. Hodding Carter, a courageous newspaperman who had personal experience of the rough-house tactics of Long's guards, recalled, "The real importance of the episode is its indication of the desperation to which his [Long's] tactics could drive otherwise law-abiding men. Our role as special deputies was specious. And it was no fun to feel like an outlaw, especially when the other side had the militia, the state police, most of the judges, and a majority of the voters in the state at large." [36]

As Hodding Carter found, to be an opponent of Long in Louisiana was akin to being a civil rights activist in the Deep South of the 1950s and 1960s. One risked physical assault and the loss of one's livelihood with the frustrating knowledge that there was nowhere to seek redress—not from the police, nor in the state courts, nor at the ballot box. This was the testimony not just of died-in-the-wool reactionaries, but also of liberals who had shared many of Long's reform aspirations.

The ultimate frustration for the opposition, or for its more liberal and intelligent advocates like Carter, was the knowledge that Long's power rested, in the final analysis, on popular support. Like all good machine politicians, Long had delivered tangible and long-overdue benefits to the voters and he was rewarded by their support. His steadily increasing majorities could not be accounted for simply by fraud and coercion. By abolishing the poll tax Long stimulated even greater participation in politics by the hitherto excluded lower-income whites. The period of intraparty competition between pro- and anti-Long factions, which Long's regime heralded, guaranteed that both sides would have to compete for the support of those lower-income voters in the future. Whenever Long was in political trouble, he may have resorted to corruption, but he always took his case to the people. By pointing to the very tangible benefits of Longism that they saw all around them and by lambasting their common enemies, Long won an intensely loyal following. In the impeachment crisis he may have bribed some legislators, but his major defense was to demonstrate that the people supported him. He addressed rallies all over the state and saturated the electorate with circulars: "The Same Old Fight Again Standard Oil Company versus Huey Long. How it became a crime for the Governor to fight for the cause of suffering and destitute humanity." It was Long's demonstrated ability to convince their constituents that persuaded the wavering key legislators to stand by Long in that crisis.[37]

This popular support made much of the fraud, corruption, and violence gratuitous. It may well have taken a certain ruthlessness to break the back of the conservative opposition, but, once he had done so, Long let his insatiable taste for absolute power take over. No opposition, however liberal, well meaning, or ineffective, could be tolerated. The consequence in Louisiana was that, although Long stimulated the forms of democracy in many ways, he also bequeathed a massive cynicism about the democratic process; an opposition that had been driven to vigilantism and an electorate that would come to expect corruption among its elected officials as a matter of course.

It was not simply Long's record of achievement that made him unusual in the South: it was the fact that this record was established during the Depression. Indeed, he justified his spending program precisely because there was an economic downturn: there was no better time to launch a building program than when labor and materials were cheap. In September 1930 he argued that "Louisiana's plan and forward step, if followed immediately by all other states, will solve all problems of unemployment and depression for two years to come."[38]

Yet the reaction of every other southern government was not to spend money, but desperately to seek means of retrenchment. Spending cuts and regressive sales taxes to offset declining property tax revenues were the main strategies for balancing the state budgets. In part, southern states were paying the price of earlier spending programs. States that had launched bond issues to finance road programs in the early 1920s now found themselves in a time of deflation burdened with massive debt charges. The timing of Louisiana's bond issues, however, meant that they would be paid for in a period of returning prosperity and inflation. But the reaction of most southern governors was not just a reaction against past profligacy, but mirrored the time-honored views of local conservative elites and followed also the path of state governors throughout the country.[39]

Even when voters elsewhere in the South expressed their discontent with the existing conservative political establishments after 1929, they often elected colorful and demagogic politicians who, for all their rhetorical denunciations of the corporations and Wall Street, offered conservative remedies for economic ills. William "Alfalfa Bill" Murray in Oklahoma was prepared to use the National Guard to curb the overproduction of oil, but was hostile to the very idea of unemployment relief. Robert Reynolds in North Carolina was elected to the Senate preaching a doctrine allegedly "so strange that it had never been heard before by this generation in North Carolina," but his program simply called for the repeal of Prohibition, the insurance of bank deposits, and the payments of the veterans' bonus. Eugene Talmadge in Georgia rejoiced in the title "The Wild Man from Sugar Creek" and vowed "Sure I'm wild and I'm going to stay wild," but his appeal to the small farmers was for rigid economy against high taxation and high government spending. In this context of the Depression South Long's record shone out brightly.[40]

The Depression gave Long the chance not only to put his ideas into practice in Louisiana, but also to expound his beliefs on the national stage. Elected to the Senate in 1930, Long had been unable to take his seat immediately since his lieutenant-governor had become a bitter enemy. By 1932, however, Long had maneuvered him out of office, installed a tame governor in Baton Rouge, and could go to Washington without relinquishing day-to-day control of the state. As a senator he always aroused the interest of the curious and the media, but from the start he also reiterated his basic thesis that a fundamental maldistribution of wealth was the cause of the nation's difficulties. A major redistribution of that wealth was the only remedy that would sufficiently restore mass purchasing power to bring back economic recovery. His ideas culminated in the "share-our-wealth" scheme, which he launched in February 1934. Long visualized an America in which every family would have an allowance of $5,000 to establish a home and would be guaranteed an annual income of at least $2,500. No personal fortunes would exceed $5 million and no income exceed $18 million a year. Annual capital levies and income taxes would ensure this redistribution.

At first, Long had convenient targets to attack: Hoover and the conservative leadership of his own Democratic Party. No task afforded him greater pleasure than to deride majority leader, Joseph T. Robinson of Arkansas, as a tool of the corporate interests represented by Robinson's law firm in Little Rock. Long found congenial company in the Senate in the small group of Progressive dissidents who challenged the bipartisan conservative orthodoxy. To his death he remained on good terms with men like George Norns and Burton K. Wheeler.[41]

How would Long react to Roosevelt and the New Deal? Despite their different backgrounds, the patrician from New York and the hillbilly from Louisiana had common interests. For all its inconsistencies, the New Deal ultimately held to the view that there had to be structural reforms in the United States to ensure the return of a sound and real prosperity. The root of the economic problem was underconsumption; the solution, the restoration of mass purchasing power. The New Deal launched large-scale spending programs, moved finally toward more progressive taxation, sought to restrain the abuses of Wall Street and incurred the bitter hostility of the financial and business community. Long supported Roosevelt for the Democratic nomination in 1932 and at the Chicago convention probably played the decisive role in keeping the wavering Mississippi delegation in line between the second and third ballots. He campaigned effectively for Roosevelt in the Western farm states.[42] In the first hundred days he supported the administration when it spent money, agreed to currency inflation, and protected smaller banks, but opposed it when businessmen and bankers appeared to wield too much influence (as in industrial recovery and emergency banking legislation) or when measures were deflationary (like the Economy Act).[43]

Long was not alone in his concern about the restrictionist tendencies of the New Deal and the possible malign influence of large corporations. Many progressives, particularly in the Middle West, shared his doubts. The progressive bloc in Congress, nevertheless, largely remained loyal to the New Deal through 1936.[44] Long, on the contrary, split with Roosevelt in the summer of 1933 when Roosevelt made it clear that Long would not be receiving federal patronage. This left the senator free to become more and more vehement in his denunciations of the New Deal, and the president increasingly attempted to undermine Long's position in Louisiana by the systematic denial of patronage and by the reactivation of Treasury investigations of the income-tax returns of Long and his associates. The ostensible New Deal justification for its actions was the need to prevent the corrupt use of federal funds and the politicization of New Deal programs in the state. To Long and to T. Harry Williams, the Roosevelt moves were simply a politically motivated attempt to destroy the power base in Louisiana of a dangerous rival and to build up Long's political enemies, even to the detriment of New Deal principles.[45] New Deal policy in fact was neither as disingenuous as its supporters sometimes liked to claim nor as cynical and ruthless as Long and Williams believed.

There were three options open to Roosevelt and the New Deal in distributing jobs and running programs in Louisiana. First, the New Deal could have cooperated with Long. This was not out of the question. After all Long fulfilled both conditions that usually guided the distribution of New Deal patronage: he had supported Roosevelt before the Chicago convention and his was the established Democratic political organization in Louisiana. Progressives like Norris and Philip LaFollette, friendly to both Long and the president, believed Roosevelt could have worked more closely with the senator and lamented his failure to do so.[46] In some government programs there was actually close cooperation between New Deal agencies and the Long forces. Agricultural Adjustment Administration (AAA) crop control programs were administered at the local level by the county agents of the State Extension Service, which was controlled by Long. There appear to have been no problems with this arrangement. The Louisiana director of the National Re-employment Service, though a Republican, was a friend of Long's and his agency was responsible for providing half the work force for the Civil Works Administration and all the workers for the Public Works Administration (PWA). When its functions were taken over by the State Employment Service appointed by Governor Allen, a Washington investigation, prompted by the accusations of Long's opponents in New Orleans, found no evidence of political favoritism in work assignments.[47]

The second option available to Roosevelt was to adopt a policy of strict neutrality between Long and his opponents. This was the option chosen by the Resettlement Administration (RA) in 1935 when it established its programs of rehabilitation loans and grants to poorer farmers. The director for Louisiana, Pete Hudgens, successfully argued that the RA should avoid being the tool of either Long or anti-Long factions. As Hudgens predicted, the outcry over this scrupulously nonpolitical policy came not from Huey Long but from his opponents. As one anti-Long congressman fulminated, "My God, here he [Hudgens] sits with the most powerful patronage weapon in Louisiana, and he's not going to do a Goddamn thing about it." Long, in contrast, reassured Hudgens that as long as the RA kept its policy of neutrality, he would not interfere or obstruct the program: "All I'm concerned about is that you help these poor people. As long as you stick to that job, I'll never bother you. The first time I catch you appointing somebody because one of those sons of bitches tells you to I'll drive you out of Louisiana." As one of Hudgens's aides recalled, "He was sent down there to keep Huey from wrecking it, and found that what he had to do was to keep Huey's political *opponents* from wrecking it too."[48]

Similarly, Harry Hopkins, in order to keep his relief program out of political hands in Louisiana, insisted on the appointment of someone from outside the state with no ties to either faction as the state director of the Emergency Relief Administration. Governor Allen and the Long forces accepted this and on the whole did what the director, Harry Early, asked them to. They were happy to pass the buck of unemployment relief to the federal government and wash their hands of the business. It was Long's opponents who consistently and relentlessly pressurized Early and Hopkins for a more political program.

For the most part, the New Deal adopted the third option of actively directing patronage to Long's opponents. To Alan Brinkley, the explanation was that in the summer of 1933 Roosevelt needed to distance himself from Long to avoid giving any impression that "share-the-wealth" was any part of the New Deal philosophy.[49] To T. Harry Williams, "two great politicians had come into unavoidable conflict. Each was so constructed that he had to dominate other and lesser men. Neither could yield to the other without submerging himself and dimming his destiny. And instinctively each recognised the other's greatness, and feared it." In due course, according to Williams, Roosevelt in 1934 became increasingly alarmed by the threat Long posed and personally masterminded the moves to destroy him politically.[50] The explanation of New Deal policy seems in fact to be both less calculated and more prosaic.

New Deal fears about the misuse of federal funds by the Long forces were not entirely groundless. Louisiana's overheads for the Unemployment Relief Commission, which distributed the relief money loaned by Hoover's Reconstruction Finance Corporation (RFC), were two to three times the average elsewhere. Some $200,000 of RFC money was frozen because Alice Lee Grosjean, Long's secretary and state supervisor of public accounts, had secretly deposited it in a pro-Long bank, which was closed after the banking holiday pending reorganization.[51] Aubrey Williams recalls visiting the Relief Commission headquarters as Hopkins's assistant and finding a luxurious suite of rooms, a number of Long henchmen drawing large salaries, and no obvious work for them to do. Williams never did find out what they were supposed to be doing. It is likely that if Long's followers had been given a free hand by New Deal agencies this sort of routine corruption would have been common. However, as Williams also noted, a strictly neutral policy by the New Deal was respected by Long where it occurred. What he could not tolerate was the New Deal rewarding his opponents.[52]

New Deal decisions on patronage were taken against the background of a barrage of complaints that Jim Farley had received about Long from his opponents in Louisiana. Whatever the views of Roosevelt and his postmaster-general about Long, it was difficult for them to ignore these complaints because they came from men whom leading administration officials knew well. Former governor J. Y. Sanders Sr., for example, was an old friend of Secretary of Commerce Dan Roper and Secretary of State Cordell Hull. John P. Sullivan was a leading Elk and thus knew Farley well. Former governor John Parker had worked with Harold Ickes in the old Progressive Party. Former senator Edwin Broussard, who was challenging Longite John

Overton's election in 1932 to the Senate, was, unlike Long, respected by his gentlemanly Senate colleagues. Five of the state's congressmen, led by John Sandlin and Cleveland Dear, had thrown in their lot with the New Deal, rather than Long, and were proudly proclaiming their fidelity to Roosevelt. Farley and Roosevelt were bound to be impressed by the repeated litany from these established politicians that Long and his associates were unfit to govern. That message was reinforced by southern congressional leaders and cabinet members, who were fearful that Long could unleash popular political forces in the South that could upset the carefully controlled patterns of deference and dependence that underpinned conservative control of the region's politics.[53]

Thus, the patronage plums in Louisiana, like the post of collector of Internal Revenue, federal judgeships, federal attorneys, and marshals, went to candidates endorsed by the anti-Long leaders, Sanders, Sullivan, Parker, and Ed Rightor, an ally of Sullivan and an attorney for Broussard in the hearings investigating Overton's election. The PWA advisory board and the state and district committees overseeing the local implementation of the National Recovery Administration (NRA) were dominated by outspoken critics of Long. Not satisfied with this, the opposition pressed continually against the nonpolitical handling of relief. As Long's criticisms of the New Deal intensified, so Roosevelt became increasingly receptive to these demands of Long's opponents. He made it clear in early 1935, both in cabinet and at the National Emergency Council, that no one associated with the senator was to be placed in office. In April 1935, an avowedly anti-Long state senator was appointed to replace the non-political Early as ERA director. Frank Peterman then went on to head the Works Progress Administration (WPA) in Louisiana. In both organizations he created new divisions of personnel, with a director for each congressional district, to select administrators and supervisors and he stuffed the divisions with anti-Long appointees. Washington allowed this to happen, despite the fact that Peterman proved to be guilty of "inefficiency from every angle from which a job could be viewed."[54]

Long had good reason to be skeptical of the purity of the New Deal's motives. He complained that the New Deal was rewarding "the most rebuked, repudiated, conscienceless characters known to either the public or the private life of Louisiana or any other state."[55] Long may have been wrong in his deep-rooted assumption that all his opponents were corrupt opportunists, but Roosevelt was wrong if he thought he was fostering embryonic New Deal liberalism in the state by his appointments. On the one hand, the opposition to Long which the New Deal was rewarding coalesced round old-time, routinely corrupt political bosses such as Sanders, attorney and lobbyist for special interests like Standard Oil, or Sullivan, with his brewery and racetrack interests in New Orleans. On the other, it represented rather aristocratic elite reform groups who, while they favored clean government, were irredeemably conservative on economic and social welfare issues. On the whole both groups had opposed Roosevelt's nomination. Similarly the anti-Long congressmen who backed the New Deal had little sympathy with or understanding of New Deal liberalism; they had simply jumped on the New Deal bandwagon because Roosevelt offered them both an issue and the means with which to challenge Long. Anti-Long forces as a whole joyously latched onto the New Deal because it seemed to offer them a chance to be rescued from political oblivion. Federal patronage and the benefits derived from New Deal programs could be used to offset Long's control of state and local government in the battle to win over the Louisiana electorate.

If Roosevelt also believed that by channeling federal patronage and largesse he could destroy Long's power base, he was mistaken. Long's *American Progress* advised its unemployed readers to "get all the relief they could and then vote right."[56] As Hodding Carter recalled that is precisely what happened: "The poor jobless devils took the work orders readily enough but they didn't vote WPA."[57] Long's popular appeal in Louisiana could not be bought off by patronage or New Deal benefits.

When the Long machine, backing Richard Leche, overwhelmed anti-Long congressman Cleveland Dear in the 1936 gubernatorial primary after Long's death, the New Deal finally acknowledged defeat. In doing so, the administration signaled the limitations of its commitment to honesty and efficiency. In return for the Long organization dropping its opposition to Roosevelt, federal funds started flowing once more into Louisiana through the agency of the state government. A cornucopia of graft with WPA money was tolerated at least until the scandals became too public in 1939. Long's opponents, hitherto so well rewarded, were cast aside. Most of them showed their true colors by becoming conservative opponents of New Deal economic regulation. What New Deal liberalism survived in the state, survived within the Long organization, notably in the administrations of Huey Long's brother, Earl, after the war.[58]

What New Deal policy revealed was less a carefully calculated master plan to destroy Long, more an opportunistic strategy that fed on differing impulses: part a genuine concern about corruption and misuse of federal funds, part a willingness to believe allegations and complaints about Long because of the sort of people who made them; part a lack of understanding of the local interests of Long's opponents, and part a willingness to turn a blind eye to the political misuse of the New Deal if the target also represented a serious political threat to Roosevelt. A blind eye to political coercion at the local level was not solely a New Deal failing in Louisiana: Illinois and

Pennsylvania were but two examples of Washington's willingness to tolerate use of the WPA in particular blatantly to build up pro-New Deal machines.[59] Louisiana, however, also revealed one of the major obstacles that time and again in the 1930s bedeviled Roosevelt's efforts at intervention in local politics in order to build up genuinely liberal local Democratic parties: the difficulty of identifying correctly from Washington politicians at the local level who were both notably liberal and possessed of genuine local political strength.[60]

Whatever political considerations distorted the actions of New Dealers in Louisiana, the fact remains that the New Deal directly and tangibly benefited the underprivileged in Louisiana far more than did the Long machine. Long's reforms in the state had done almost nothing for the poorest sections of the community—the able-bodied unemployed, unemployables, and the rural poor. The New Deal, for all its many limitations, revolutionized provision for these groups.

Before the New Deal, relief in Louisiana was the responsibility of the parishes. Apart from the widely varying, but always inadequate, nature of the aid they gave, there was a further restriction, in that their police juries were only allowed to aid unemployables. They were specifically forbidden to assist the able-bodied unemployed, the very people hit by the Depression. Before 1933 no state or local appropriations had been made for unemployment relief, aside from a $750,000 bond issue floated by New Orleans. In 1932, however, Governor Allen had established an Unemployment Relief Commission (URC) to qualify for loans from the Reconstruction Finance Corporation for unemployment relief. The pressing need for such relief was highlighted by the URC's average caseload of 115,000 per month between October 1932 and May 1933. In contrast, the Federal Emergency Relief Administration (FERA), which the New Deal established in 1933, aided for two years on average 274,397 Louisianans a month, about 12 percent of the population. Of the $49 million that the FERA spent in the state, $47.5 million came from the federal government, nothing from the state government, and only $1.5 million from local sources. It was true that most southern states contributed little to FERA spending and relied far more than states elsewhere on federal funds, but even in the South only South Carolina equaled Louisiana in the miserliness of local contributions to relief.[61]

When it came to providing jobs for the unemployed, Long's road-building program at its peak employed only 22,000 men. In the winter of 1934 the New Deal's Civil Works Administration (CWA) put 80,372 men to work. The major work relief program of the federal government, the Works Progress Administration, employed on average 40,143 a month in 1936; 27,107 in 1937; 39,312 in 1938; and 40,189 in 1940. In March of that year it was providing employment for one-third of the unemployed in the state.[62]

As for the longer-term provisions of welfare, the Social Security Act of 1935 transformed and modernized at a stroke the provision of welfare in the state. The act made Louisianans eligible for old-age insurance, made it worth the state's while to introduce an unemployment compensation scheme, and used the incentive of matching funds to improve categorical assistance for the indigent aged, the blind, and mothers with dependent children. In the latter provisions, Long's legacy and the New Deal interacted. Long's successors had no qualms about seeking out matching federal money and the traditions of state spending which he had established meant that Louisiana's provision of categorical assistance after 1935 was easily the most generous in the South.[63]

The New Deal's agricultural recovery programs rescued the state's commercial cotton, rice, and sugar planters. By 1938 cash farm income had risen 114 percent from its 1932 low. Both the rise in cash income and the increase in farm real-estate values substantially exceeded the national average. Essentially, the price rises prompted by the Agricultural Adjustment Administration, together with the government rental and benefit payments and easier credit, enabled Louisianan farmers to stay on the land in the 1930s so that in the 1940s they could enjoy the benefits of mechanization and a dramatically expanded domestic market. But what of the rural poor, that section of the rural population who remained poor no matter how prosperous the rural sector of the economy became? The limitations of the New Deal's efforts to help tenant farmers are well enough known. In Louisiana between 1937 and 1941 the Farm Security Administration (FSA) made loans to only 941 of the state's more than 100,000 tenant farmers to enable them to purchase their own farms. Nevertheless, almost half of the state's tenant farmers received rehabilitation loans or grants from New Deal agencies in the 1930s, in striking contrast to the total absence of any program to aid tenant farmers sponsored by the Long regime or his successors.[64]

The New Deal also haltingly moved into areas of reform in the state that, for all his dictatorial control of the legislature, Huey Long had never tried to introduce: low-cost urban housing, rural electrification, minimum-wage legislation, and guarantees of the right of workers to collective bargaining. At the state level, there is no doubt that the benefits of New Deal liberalism were both more generous and spread more widely than those of Long's business progressivism.[65]

How valid were Long's criticisms of the New Deal at the national level and how radical were the policy alternatives that he put forward? Few areas of New Deal policy escaped Long's scathing attacks. Agricultural production control and the destruction of surplus crops were wasteful and immoral. The New Deal, argued Long, failed to protect tenant farmers. The AAA's cotton program drove tenants from the land and proposals for tenancy purchase legislation in 1935 were principally designed to profit existing landowners anxious to sell poor land.[66] Wall Street, he alleged, shaped New Deal financial and banking legislation. The NRA was the product of too much business influence, it would foster monopoly and its bureaucracy, which would be under the thumb of the large corporations, had been given too much power. The Social Security Act was an "abortion': its benefits were inadequate and the provision of federal matching of state funds for categorical assistance would produce variations in benefits, penalize poorer states and discriminate against blacks. He favored a purely federal scheme. Above all, he lambasted the New Deal for failing to redistribute wealth: "Not a single dime of concentrated bloated pompous wealth, massed in the hands of a few people, has been raked down to relieve the masses." He rejoiced in Roosevelt's sudden move in 1935 to secure "soak the rich" taxation but the results disappointed him: he would have drafted a bill to yield $165 billion a year, he claimed, rather than the $340 million that the bill sought.[67]

The limitations that he focused on in his comprehensive indictment—a restrictionist farm policy geared to the needs of commercial farmers, excessive business dominance of the NRA, the ramshackle federal-state system of social security, the lack of redistributive taxation—were limitations that New Dealers often acknowledged, that progressive critics lamented in the 1930s and revisionist historians highlighted in the 1960s. What of the policy alternatives proposed by Long? To the senator the issue was simple. He was a radical critic of the New Deal, challenging it from the left for failing to go far enough in its reforms. "Whenever this administration had gone to the left I have voted with it, and whenever it has gone to the right I have voted against it."[68]

But Long was not offering a thoroughgoing radical alternative to the New Deal. As Alan Brinkley has pointed out, Long's proposals reflected many of the strengths and weaknesses of American agrarian radicalism.[69] He was advocating measures to alleviate the very real economic plight of millions of Americans, particularly small landowners, but without challenging their individualistic values or threatening capitalism. Above all, he did not want to increase the apparatus of the modern state. No aspect of the New Deal aroused Long's anger more than the trend to increased bureaucracy. Government bureaucracy took away from individuals the power of decision making in their day-to-day economic lives and was unaccountable to the people, responding instead only to organized interest groups. Long ultimately wanted to restore individual control over economic destinies, control that was during the New Deal thwarted not only by the forces of great wealth but also by the federal government. As a result, Long often advocated desirable goals but scorned the means that might in practical terms attain them. For all the radical denunciation of distant plutocrats, Long did not envisage a basic change in the structure of American society. Long's proposals were a mixture of the conventional, the contradictory, the glib, and the impractical.

Agriculture highlighted the basically conservative and contradictory nature of Long's ideas. The core of Long's prescription for agriculture was the government purchase of surplus commodities and their storage for years when food supplies fell short. This was essentially the solution offered by the price support loans of the Commodity Credit Corporation set up by the New Deal in 1933, and later incorporated as the heart of the 1938 Farm Act. Long's proposal was clearly open to the same objections that were levied at the New Deal farm program: it was aimed at commercial farmers, it promised no change in the basic structure of farming and landownership, it offered no solution to the problem of ever-increasing surpluses in government hands, and did nothing to tackle the problem of underconsumption. Exactly the same criticisms could be levied at the other plank of Long's farm platform. This was currency inflation, a panacea designed simply to raise the prices paid to farmers, that proposed no restructuring of agriculture, and offered no means by which consumers could pay higher food prices.

No one was more dismissive than Long of the production control ideas of Henry Wallace and his advisers. Yet Long's most original solution to the farm problem called for a degree of production control and government intervention that even AAA planners never dreamed of. In 1931, as cotton prices fell precipitously, Long advocated a total ban on the planting of cotton in 1932. In August a special session of his legislature passed legislation to implement such a "Cotton Holiday." It was to go into effect if states representing three-quarters of the nation's cotton acreage passed similar legislation. The crucial state was Texas. Most southern governors deflected pressure from their cotton-planting constituents to act by calling on Texas to act first. No amount of pressure from Long could persuade Governor Sterling and the Texas legislature to do more than call for a reduction of acreage in 1932 if one-third of other southern states agreed.[70]

T. Harry Williams praised Long's plan as a "bold—even revolutionary action." In contrast to voluntary acreage reduction, which was "useless," Long "alone among the southern executives had shown vision and courage." Yet, as Williams admitted, the plan had been sold to Long by the large cotton planters in Louisiana.[71] For all the concern which Long later professed, the scheme offered nothing to tenants and sharecroppers. On the contrary, if implemented it would have resulted in their displacement on a scale far greater than was caused by the AAA. H. L. Mitchell, the future leader of the

Southern Tenant Farmers' Union, recalled that the plan took no account of how tenants were to survive in 1932 with neither credit nor cash income.[72]

How was Long's plan to be implemented? What sort of police force and government bureaucracy would be needed to ensure that over a million cotton farmers did not produce any cotton? It was precisely a practical question like this that was solved for cotton by the AAA's voluntary domestic allotment plan, which combined crop control, voluntarism, and local administration by the farmers themselves. Yet it was such schemes that Long himself denounced so bitterly. It was the bureaucracy of the AAA compelling "the farmer and the farmer's wife and the farmer's boy to take cognizance and have knowledge of every ruling that is made by the various and sundry agencies through the Secretary of Agriculture" that aroused his special wrath.[73]

Such practical questions and contradictions did not trouble Long. The Cotton Holiday plan was almost a perfect vehicle for him. He could pose as a bold champion of cotton farmers, it offered no challenge to the basic power structure of cotton planting, there was never any danger of it being put into action, and yet the failure to act could be blamed on the southern conservatives, notably the governor of Texas.

It was no coincidence that Long received such an enthusiastic reception at conventions of the Farm Holiday Association (FHA) in the Midwest in 1934 and 1935. His farm program combined the same apparent radicalism and basic conservatism as Milo Reno's organization.[74] On the one hand, the New Deal could be denounced passionately for not doing enough for farmers; for example, not guaranteeing the cost of production. On the other, the New Deal could equally passionately be denounced for doing too much, for allowing bureaucrats to trample on the individual rights of farmers. In its place, Long and the FHA could offer simple, apparently self-sustaining remedies of government price guarantees and currency inflation, which allegedly required no elaborate bureaucracy, and certainly did not threaten the existing structure of power in rural America.

As for nonagricultural recovery, Long advocated a ten billion dollar public works program, though he condemned the New Deal's own public works scheme as a "dole mill." [75] But the creation of the requisite mass purchasing power for recovery would obviously come from Long's most radical proposal the substantial redistribution of wealth.

However real the problem Long was addressing, there were major flaws in his share-our-wealth scheme. First, it was one thing to redistribute income through taxation, it was another to redistribute wealth, much of which was not in the form of money. Long could give no clear idea how nonmonetary wealth could be redistributed. Second, Long's figures did not add up. There were simply not enough millionaires and too many poor families for the benefits that Long envisaged from dissolving a few fortunes to materialize. One estimate suggested that by eliminating fortunes of over $1 million (more drastic than Long proposed) each family would receive $400, far short of the $5,000 allowance that Long promised. To ensure that each family received that $5,000 allowance, no family would be able to retain more than $7,000 in wealth. Then to ensure that each family received an income annually of $2,500, no family would be able to retain more than $3,000 of its annual income, in contrast to the $1 million which Long was prepared to allow. To achieve the sort of benefits from redistribution that Long wanted, there would have to be a massive overall expansion of the American economy. Long, like most of his contemporaries, had little idea how to engineer that scale of economic growth. Third, the great virtue of Long's scheme was its simplicity. Redistribution would occur through the straightforward application of the tax codes. There would be no great expansion of the federal bureaucracy. Yet Long himself admitted on other occasions that a giant federal "Share-Our-Wealth" corporation would have to supervise and administer wealth redistribution.[76]

Long's proposals highlighted the fact that the strength of his appeal lay not in a pitch to the people at the bottom of the pile in America—the tenants and sharecroppers, blacks, the urban unemployed, industrial workers—but to more substantial citizens who had been laid low by the Depression.[77] The homeowner threatened by foreclosure, the farm owner-operator paralyzed by debt, the small-town merchant unable to fight off the chain stores, the old people whose savings had been wiped out during the slump, the small businessman unable to cut costs like his larger competitors—these were the people who welcomed Long's promise to remedy their plight without destroying their traditional individualistic values. The secret of Long's success was summed up in his assertion that "I can take this Roosevelt. He's scared of me. I can out-promise him and he knows it." Long could out-promise Roosevelt and yet, at the same time appeal to conservative suspicion of the bureaucratic, collectivist, and dictatorial nature of the New Deal. As in agriculture, so in industry and welfare, the New Deal could be attacked at one and the same time for not doing enough and for doing too much. Long denounced the New Deal for bribing voters with welfare and spending payments, and then criticized the Social Security Act for not being generous enough. He bitterly criticized bureaucrats for attempting to dictate to states how federal funds should be spent, then scorned the Security Act for not introducing a purely federal system with all the bureaucracy that that would inevitably entail. Long could out-promise Roosevelt in the areas of farm prices, minimum incomes, and welfare payments, at the same time as reassuring his supporters that the familiar economic structures in which they conducted their day-to-day lives would not be radically changed.

Long was not anti-capitalist. His targets of attack were distant Wall Street financiers and men of great wealth like the Rockefellers, not local employers or small town bankers, merchants, and landlords—the elites who constituted the economic and social power structure at the local level.[78] This thrust was consistent with the business progressivism of his state reforms. In time the relationship of Long and his successors with local corporations and businessmen became almost cosy. Long himself established his own successful oil company, the Win or Lose Corporation, which seems never to have lost since it leased to other oil companies oil lands that it had originally leased from the state of Louisiana on the favorable terms that only inside information could bring.[79] It was entirely consistent that Long's son Russell should be such a diligent protector of the interests of the oil companies on the Senate Finance Committee. It was understandable that Long's cronies, when they succeeded him, showed no interest in redistributing wealth except into their own pockets. It was also consistent that Long and his closest disciple in the Share-Our-Wealth movement, G. L. K. Smith, should accuse Roosevelt of communism. Long once suggested that Roosevelt hold the Communist Party convention and the Democratic Party convention at the same time to save money.[80] Smith, a man who ended up on the fascist, antisemitic fringes of the latter-day Christian right, yet never lost his personal and absolute devotion to Long and his share-the-wealth ideas, remained convinced that Roosevelt "was completely captured by the Marxist, Socialist elements, even down to the brazen self-confessed Communists."[81] Long's challenge to the New Deal was scarcely therefore a radical challenge from the left. The problems that Long was trying to solve and the grievances he was trying to remedy were real enough. What he was offering as solutions were glib panaceas, designed to reassure the discontented that the necessary changes could be brought about without radical or painful measures.

How popular a threat did Long pose to the New Deal? In the absence of systematic public opinion polling, Long's assassination makes the question one that Roosevelt would have described as "iffy," since Long never faced Roosevelt, or the issue of the New Deal, head on in an election. Yet some clues remain: Long's political forays outside his own state, his network of Share-Our-Wealth clubs, a poll conducted for the Democratic National Committee in 1935, and the showing of the Union Party in 1936.

Long's barnstorming campaigns on Roosevelt's behalf in 1932 certainly convinced Jim Farley of Long's appeal in the northern plains states. The ecstatic receptions given Long at Farm Holiday Association conventions in Iowa in 1934 and 1935 testified to his continued appeal to western farmers.

Long himself drew the conclusion that he could take Iowa by storm any time.[82] In the South he demonstrated his power to invade conservative strongholds in 1932 when he launched a successful whirlwind campaign in Arkansas, the home of majority leader Joe Robinson. Long's campaign almost singlehandedly won the Senate primary for the hitherto unregarded Hattie Carraway, widow of the previous senator.[83] In 1935 Long and G. L. K. Smith returned from a visit to South Carolina convinced by their reception in Columbia that they could capture even that bastion of conservatism. They might have been less confident if they had known that a United Textile Workers' organizer had followed Smith from mill village to mill village distributing anti-Long propaganda supplied by Senator Jimmy Byrnes.[84] In neighboring Mississippi, Long threw his weight behind Governor Conner's successful candidacy in 1931, though Conner then proceeded to implement extreme retrenchment and imposed a sales tax. Theodore Bilbo was sufficiently conscious of the support the Louisiana senator wielded in Mississippi that he was publicly very cautious in his references both to Long and the share-our-wealth movement, even though he hated Long and had promised to take care of him when he was elected to the Senate in 1934.[85]

Support for Long was not confined to the South or the western farm states if his network of Share-Our-Wealth clubs was a reliable guide. There were over 27,000 SOW clubs nationwide with possibly 8 million members. The clubs were particularly strong in the Far West, a region Long never visited and never displayed much interest in. Alarmist reports of the strength of the clubs' appeal reached Jim Farley in 1934 and early 1935 from a wide variety of places. At the very least the clubs constituted a superb mailing list whose value was emphasized by the zeal with which Long's successors, notably Earle Christenberry and G. L. K. Smith, fought for its control after Long's death. Were the clubs more than that? Did they represent a genuine grass-roots organization? The evidence suggests that where the clubs were more than simply a collection of names on paper, their activity and strength was the result of unauthorized activity by local entrepreneurs and politicians anxious to use the Share-Our-Wealth movement for their own particular ambitions. Thus, in California the clubs fell into the hands of a disgruntled local politico who had fallen out with the End Poverty in California (EPIC) organization and was using the clubs to claw his way back into influence. In other areas, particularly the cities, the clubs offered sharp-eyed operators the chance to exploit Long's popularity and make some money selling material which they had received free from the Long organization and collecting and pocketing subscriptions.[86]

More substantial testimony to Long's support came in the poll conducted by Emil Hurja in 1935 for the Democratic National Committee. The poll suggested that at that stage Long would pick up 12 percent of the popular vote as a third-party candidate in a presidential election. The poll was taken by Jim Farley to indicate that Long might poll as many as six million votes in 1936, a performance that might throw the election to the Republicans. Hurja's poll indicated that Long's votes would cause the Democrats to lose New York, Illinois, Indiana, Ohio, and Colorado to the Republicans, and that his support was greater than the projected Democrat majority in Maryland, Michigan, Washington, Minnesota, and Iowa. A Republican victory caused by Long's intervention seemed to be the scenario envisaged by the senator himself. The election of a reactionary Republican would lead to an economic collapse and pave the way for a Long triumph in 1940. Hurja's poll was primitive; it was also taken well over a year before the presidential election and at a time when the New Deal appeared to be floundering. But the pollster did try to use basic sampling techniques, and his results revealed that Long drew support equally from urban and rural areas and that he received backing from all regions, though less so in the Northeastern and Mid-Atlantic states.[87]

What gave Long's threat to the New Deal added weight was the possibility of his linking up with other leaders in 1935 who were fanning the flames of discontent with the New Deal. Like Long, Father Coughlin, the radio priest from Detroit, combined charismatic personal appeal with denunciations of big business and big government. Dr. Francis Townsend, crusader for a $200-a-month revolving pension, similarly linked bold action on behalf of the aged with the defense of traditional values. All three advocated some form of currency manipulation as a prerequisite for reform. All three condemned New Deal bureaucracy and dictatorship. Speculation about a possible coalition was inevitable. At the same time, in the Midwest, the apparent difficulties of the New Deal in early 1935 revived interest in the idea of an independent Progressive or Farmer-Labor challenge in 1936.

Despite Roosevelt's fear that progressive Republicans might favor a Long candidacy, it seems unlikely in retrospect that the LaFollettes in Wisconsin or Floyd Olson in Minnesota, on whom third-party activists pinned their hopes in the Midwest, would ever have endorsed a Long challenge. They interpreted the real danger in 1936 as a reactionary Republican victory, bankrolled by big business, and that fear was likely to deter them from third-party endorsements.[88] A coalition between Long, Coughlin, and Townsend was much more probable. Whatever Long's private views of his fellow demagogues, he did endorse Coughlin's proposals for banking reform and liberalized his old-age pension proposals to move more in line with Townsend. He held at least one secret meeting with Coughlin.[89] Given the bitter hatred with which all three increasingly regarded Roosevelt, it is difficult to imagine that they would not have joined forces as an independent political grouping in 1936.

After Long's death, of course, Coughlin, Townsend, and Long's Share-Our-Wealth successor, G. L. K. Smith, joined together to endorse the Union Party candidacy of William Lemke. The derisory showing of the Union Party in 1936 is not a very satisfactory test of Long's potential support as a third-party candidate for three reasons. First, Lemke, a congressman from North Dakota, totally lacked the charismatic appeal of Long. He had, recalled G. L. K. Smith, the "charisma of a deserted telephone booth."[90] Second, the Union Party made no headway in the cities where Hurja's poll pointed to significant Long strength. Finally, it made no headway in the South where surely Long's appeal would have been considerable. Nevertheless, the campaign did illustrate the obstacles that would have faced Long as a third-party candidate in 1936. There were problems of organization, not only in getting a candidate's name on the ballot but also in turning groups like SOW clubs and Townsend clubs into effective vote mobilizers. There were also powerful personal jealousies between the demagogues. In 1936 both Coughlin and Townsend had second thoughts about sharing the limelight with each other, and even greater doubts about playing second fiddle to Gerald Smith, a masterly rabble-rouser.[91] But the most important obstacle was the ability of Roosevelt to attract lower-income voters with the very tangible benefits that the New Deal had provided farmers, the unemployed, and trade union members. Alan Brinkley has argued convincingly for the "soft" nature of Long's support outside Louisiana. The fact that Long could appeal to so many dissatisfied elements in 1935, and appeal to the followers of other dissident leaders, was a source of strength. But though this support may have been widespread, it may not have been intense. What so many dissident leaders found in the 1930s was that though they hated Roosevelt, their followers did not necessarily do so. It was the susceptibility of the followers of dissident leaders to Roosevelt's blandishments that would have proven a powerful obstacle to a Long candidacy in 1936 outside Louisiana.[92]

Huey Long was a remarkable figure. He built a record of substantive reform in the teeth of bitter opposition in one of the most backward states in the country. It was a record of reform unmatched by any other southern politician who built his support primarily on the support of lower-income whites. It was a record of reform unmatched by most governors in the Depression, whether in the South or in the nation. As a national politician, he made a powerful appeal to those whose fortunes the New Deal had not yet restored after the disasters of the Depression. His denunciations of the New Deal highlighted the very real limitations of Roosevelt's reforms. The political response of the New Deal in Long's own state, far from fostering a pro–New Deal liberalism, rewarded some of the most corrupt and conservative politicians in the state simply because they opposed Huey Long. Long offered a plan for the redistribution of wealth that promised to make New Deal measures seem mere pale palliatives. He drew support from all over the nation.

Yet in the final analysis, Long did not represent a radical challenge to Roosevelt from the left, nor did his record and support indicate that there was in the America of the 1930s a constituency hungry for radical leadership, if only Roosevelt had been willing to provide it. Long's reforms in Louisiana were essentially of the business-progressive variety. They were reforms designed to provide the essential services that a modern commonwealth seeking economic growth required. His reforms did not benefit the poorest sections of the population; the New Deal, for all its limitations, did. At the national level, Long's appeal illustrated the conservative constraints under which all reform movements, including the New Deal, labored in the 1930s: the persistent faith in individualism and traditional values that survived for so many Americans despite the trauma of the Depression. Long stressed the dangers that the New Deal posed to such individualism. The policy alternatives he proposed promised Utopian goals, but eschewed the mechanisms of state power that might have attained those goals. His radical rhetoric was directed against distant scapegoats, rather than the pressing inequities in the distribution of local economic and social power. In the end, his national support had precise limits. The evidence of Long's ideology, and of what we know of the social background of his followers, suggest that he lacked the support of the very groups—the unemployed and the mass production industrial workers—that gave the urban liberalism of the New Deal its powerful reforming thrust.

2

How Did the New Deal
Change the South?

In the late 1960s the focus of New Deal historiography shifted away from Washington to the states and the localities, away from national policy making to the implementation and impact of particular New Deal programs at the local level. These studies have established as a historical truism that the New Deal was not imposed on the states by policy makers in Washington through an army of federal officials loyal only to their New Deal masters. At every turn New Dealers had to defer to state power, to rely on state officials, and to tailor their programs to local community norms. My first task is to try to make some sense of all the case studies of the New Deal in operation in the South. My second task is to try to measure the overall effectiveness of the New Deal by testing its impact on the nation's poorest and most racially backward region. In answering that question it is all too easy to get trapped into the cycle of lamentation and celebration that characterizes so much New Deal historiography. The New Deal is recurrently lambasted for missing golden radical opportunities, disparaged for decisively distorting the free market through the dead hand of government bureaucracy, or praised for rescuing American democracy by safeguarding the economic security of ordinary Americans. It has been much easier to denounce or to champion Roosevelt than it has been to *explain* the relationship between New Deal reform and the longer-term changes in American society. My final aim is to try to identify what role, if any, the New Deal played in the amazing transformation of the South over the last fifty years from a stagnant, permanently poor, rural, rigidly segregated society to a fast-growing, increasingly prosperous, urban, racial democracy.[1]

31

I

At first sight the New Deal could not fail to have a profound impact on the South. The federal government intervened directly in the daily lives of almost every southerner. It told farmers what they could and could not grow. It told employers what they could and could not pay their workers and limited their ability to hire and fire at will. The Tennessee Valley Authority rejuvenated an entire river basin. What the *Progressive Farmer* called the power revolution brought electrification for the first time to the countryside. The New Deal introduced unemployment compensation and old-age insurance. It provided undreamt of levels of welfare assistance to the poor. In the cities federal public works programs left a lasting physical imprint on the community by building the capital facilities which in the North had been constructed by private investors.

Most communities in the South still bear the traces of the New Deal in a school, a housing project, a library, a park, or a historic building restored—all provided by the federal government in the 1930s. In Memphis the Works Progress Administration constructed a $25,000 building that was modernistic in design, with curtained windows, shower baths, spacious runways, individual rooms, and offering a daily change of bedding. This was the municipal dogpound.[2]

Yet the New Deal left the basic economic, social, racial, and political structure of the region largely untouched. In 1930 the South was a poor, rural, one-crop society in which too many people chased too little farm income. In 1940 the South was still a poor, rural, one-crop society in which too many people chased too little farm income. In 1930 the South was a bastion of the open shop. In 1940 it was still an anti-union stronghold. In 1930 the South was rigidly segregated and blacks were economically and politically powerless. In 1940 blacks were still economically dependent, politically impotent, and rigidly segregated. In 1930 southern politics were dominated by a conservative alliance of county seat elites, planters, and industrialists, largely immune to popular pressure because of their economic dominance and the restricted nature of the electorate. In 1940 those same political leaders still controlled the South. As V. O. Key Jr., noted, the have-nots continued to lose out in the region's disorganized politics.[3]

II

The New Deal rescued cotton and tobacco farmers. Josiah Bailey wrote in December 1933, "Eastern North Carolina, a very large section devoted to agriculture has been prostrated for five years. This year the people are really prosperous . . . with one accord they give the credit to the President." A Mississippi banker told Turner Cartledge in 1935 about his county's cotton farmers, "I can show you papers in our current portfolio that had been cancelled as uncollectable years ago. People come in here and ask to pay back interest on notes we literally have to fish out of the waste basket." The Agricultural Adjustment Administration established the mechanisms of production control, price support loans, and ample credit that would enable those farmers who stayed on the land to work in a relatively risk-free environment and to enjoy prosperity when it returned during World War II. The AAA also established the political processes whereby organized commodity groups could guarantee favorable government responses in the future.[4]

But New Deal planners had more ambitious plans to modernize southern agriculture. Recognizing that high-cost American cotton could not compete on the glutted world market, they wanted to subsidize the gradual switch of southern agriculture from high-cost cotton production to a more diversified farming. Recognizing that there were too many farmers in the South working on submarginal land in too small units they wanted to resettle those farmers on better land in new communities with model housing, ready credit, supervision, and cooperative services. Both goals failed. The Farm Bureau, the pressure group that had been rescued by the New Deal, resisted any efforts to subsidize cotton agriculture other than by rigging a fair price in the marketplace. The Resettlement communities aroused bitter congressional opposition and catered to a very small number of farmers. In any case farmers were reluctant to move; they resented the obstacles placed in the way of acquiring their own farms; the individual units were too small to be viable; and the turnover of clients was high. Economic forces during the war and after would ultimately achieve the diversification and reorganization of southern agriculture, not government planners.[5]

What of the rural poor, the tenants, and the sharecroppers? David Conrad described them as the forgotten farmers of the New Deal. The works of Conrad himself, Donald Grubbs, Sidney Baldwin, Louis Cantor, and Paul Mertz have ensured that any neglect in the 1930s has been amply offset by the attention of historians since 1965. The story is now familiar enough: initial indifference to the tenants' plight on the part of the Cotton Section and the landlord-dominated local committees of the AAA; the discrimination against tenants in the allocation of rental and benefit payments; the lack of any guarantees that tenants received the payments due to them; the eviction of tenants in defiance of the Cotton Contract, particularly in the western part of the region; the remarkable, but ultimately doomed, desperation militancy of the biracial, socialist-led Southern Tenant Farmers' Union; and the belated and ineffective assault on rural poverty by the Farm Security Administration.[6]

Three qualifications need to be made. The AAA undoubtedly displaced tenants, as the analysis of the origins of the Arkansas and Oklahoma migrants who ended up in California shows all too clearly. But while many tenants were displaced by low cotton prices before the New Deal, others were displaced when the government protection of tenant rights was much more stringent in the late 1930s. And the 1930s were not nearly as important as the 1920s or the 1940s for tenant migration off the land.[7]

Second, the relationship between the AAA and mechanization of cotton agriculture was complex. It was not simply that government payments enabled the landlords to mechanize and thus dispense with tenants. The great investment in cotton harvesters was a product of the high prices and the labor scarcity of the 1940s. What happened in the plantation areas in the late 1930s, as Warren Whatley and Gavin Wright have shown, is that planters rushed to buy tractors to mechanize their pre-harvest operations. They could do so because they now had the pool of the wage labor available to do the cotton picking and therefore did not have to rely so heavily on farm tenancy for all-the-year-round labor.[8] Finally, it is not clear what policies the New Deal ought to have followed instead. The encouragement to tenants to buy their own small farms was anachronistic when mechanization increasingly dictated economies of scale. The STFU acknowledged that its own members did not want the union's preferred alternative: collective and cooperative farms. Pete Daniel, the most sophisticated analyst of the relationship between government programs and technological change, has argued that the New Deal should have rehabilitated tenant farmers in an old-fashioned barter relationship and subsistence farming. This solution ignores the fact that farmers themselves wanted a cash income in order to share, for example, in the consumer benefits of electrification, which thanks to the TVA and the REA they were beginning to enjoy in the 1930s. Daniel argues nostalgically that it was better to survive in poverty on the land than to move to the cities: "At the centre of this (farm) life was a natural harmony—the season of planting, hoeing, harvesting and settlement. It was a primitive way of life, a struggle for survival, but the human race has found grim satisfaction in living as close to the margins of absolute failure as possible." But most southern farmers had been living close enough to absolute failure for too long. They wanted a substantial cash income like other Americans. In the end the New Deal for the rural South was essentially a holding operation. It enabled cotton and tobacco farmers to survive the Depression and allowed an underemployed surplus labor force to remain on the land when there were no economic opportunities elsewhere. When wartime prosperity came both black and white tenants and sharecroppers could at last move to the defense industries and the cities.[9]

III

In the North in the 1930s the combination of worker militancy and the federal government protection of trade union rights under the Wagner Act produced the great breakthrough in union organization as labor organized mass production workers and moved from the fringes of the economy to the centrally important industries. In the South that combination of rank-and-file protest and government assistance failed to shake the power of anti-union employers. There was no breakthrough in labor organization.

The worker militancy was certainly there. Southern workers in the 1930s were not conservative, individualistic rural migrants hostile to collective action. Weary of paternalism, angry at wage cuts and stretch outs, hopeful of help from Roosevelt, they demonstrated unaccustomed determination in flocking to the union banner. In the depths of the Depression miners waged a futile battle against wage cuts and evictions in Harlan County, Kentucky. Inspired by Section 7a of the NRA, 20,000 Alabama coal miners joined the UMW in 1933–34. In a massive explosion of frustration, Piedmont textile workers joined the moribund United Textile Workers, at the same time forcing their leaders into a disastrous and premature strike in September 1934. Rubber workers in Gadsden, Alabama, made repeated efforts to organize in the face of violent repression. Steel workers in Birmingham unionized the Tennessee Coal and Iron subsidiary of U.S. Steel in 1937.[10]

But determined protest was not enough. Nor could the new federal protections always help. In the case of steel economic circumstances—the prospect of rapidly filling order books—might persuade a national corporation like U.S. Steel to sign a union contract to ensure continuous production and order its southern subsidiaries to do likewise. Even in Birmingham, however, other employers saw no need to do likewise. The final employer to sign a union contract did not do so until 1974. In textiles employers had absolutely no incentive to concede to union demands. In 1934 at the time of the great textile strike the industry was already producing in excess of demand. In 1937–38 when the Textile Workers Organizing Committee launched its campaign, recession had once again gripped the industry.[11]

Where employers were determined to resist they could utilize local community sentiment to defeat the unions. Rubber is the classic example. When the URW attempted to organize Goodyear in Akron, Ohio, Goodyear found that they could not sustain a vigilante strikebreaking organization in the face of local community hostility. In Gadsden, Alabama, on the contrary, the local press denounced outside agitators, and local law enforcement officers co-operated in beating up and kidnapping union organizers and breaking up picket lines. (Employers also used more mundane tactics: they held a strip-tease show in the local YMCA to attract workers away from a union meeting.) In the South labor was too politically powerless to impose its will on local sheriffs, on state legislatures, which passed a host of anti-labor laws after 1937, and on state governors who would usually be prepared to call out the National Guard to help break strikes. (Bibb Graves of Alabama and Olin Johnston of South Carolina were two exceptions to the general rule in the 1930s: they both turned down at least once employer requests to call out the Guard.)[12]

The workers' political impotence was starkly illustrated in Birmingham, Alabama. The poll tax disenfranchised so many in Birmingham that 20,000 votes in a voting-age population of half a million in Jefferson County were enough to win local elections. There were 57,000 potential union members, half of them black. At most only 5,000 CIO members could vote. Political weakness like this meant that unions were unable to offset traditional anti-union tactics by the employers. As a result neither rank-and-file militancy nor federal protection was enough to break down the long-standing pattern of worker dependency in industrial relations.[13]

IV

Before the New Deal, welfare provision in the South was firmly ensconced in the old Poor Law traditions. No state made any provision for relief for the able-bodied unemployed. Nor did most counties. Birmingham had abolished its welfare department in 1924. Until 1933 most southern efforts to alleviate the plight of the unemployed were confined to coordinating private charity efforts. In 1932 RFC aid forced southern states to adopt some form of welfare organization. But it was Harry Hopkins's Federal Emergency Relief Administration that revolutionized relief provision in the South. Ninety percent of relief spending under the FERA in the South was provided by federal money, compared to 62 percent in the rest of the country. To qualify for such aid, states had dramatically to professionalize their welfare organizations. As Michael Holmes noted, "Many counties in Georgia that had never seen a social worker now had one permanently stationed within their borders." Later, to qualify for federal matching funds for categorical assistance to the old, the blind, and dependent children, southern states had to maintain that revolution in professionalism. Southern cities established departments of public welfare for the first time. Southern states were forced to develop unemployment compensation programs. Old-age insurance for southerners became a federal responsibility .[14]

But this welfare revolution was plagued by two persistent problems: local administration and joint federal state responsibility. It was difficult to find qualified staff to run relief programs in the South. Those in South Carolina were described as "conscientious, hard working, sincere and incompetent." Hostility to women appointments and to nonpartisan appointments was widespread. So too was traditional local hostility to the whole idea of relief. State legislatures were reluctant to make appropriations. Governor Eugene Talmadge of Georgia simply believed that castor oil was all the unemployed needed. Everywhere FERA and WPA operations were curtailed at harvest time to ensure the availability of as large a force as possible for cotton picking. Later in the 1930s assistance for the unemployed who were not given WPA jobs was patchy. At least five South Carolina counties, for example, made no relief provision for them at all.[15]

The federal state operation of Social Security not only meant that states varied considerably in the generosity of the benefits they offered and the conditions they imposed on recipients, but also that many southern states could scarcely afford to participate in the system at all. The principle of matching funds meant that the poor southern states received less per capita from New Deal spending than any other region. It was not only Huey Long who called for a purely federal system of social security to offset southern poverty and southern discrimination against blacks. William Colmer, later one of the most reactionary, and states rights Mississippi congressmen, also called for a federal social security system because his state was simply too poor to take advantage of matching funds. Mississippi was the last state in the union to enter the Aid to Dependent Children Program. The ramshackle nature of the New Deal's welfare state was compounded by the exclusion of farm laborers from Social Security. Lee Alston and Joseph Ferrie have argued that southern landlords opposed the inclusion of farm laborers and lobbied to keep benefit payments low in the South because they did not want to see government welfare undermine their own paternalist in-kind benefits. They feared government benefits would loosen the control over their tenants which in-kind benefits enabled them to maintain. Thus the impact of the New Deal's welfare revolution on the South was severely restricted by local poverty and entrenched conservative hostility.[16]

V

As is well known, the New Deal, conscious of the need to maintain southern congressional support, did little for southern black civil rights. Roosevelt did not wholeheartedly commit himself to the fight for anti-lynching legislation or to abolish the poll tax. New Deal programs in the South routinely discriminated against blacks and perpetuated segregation. At best, as in the tenant purchase schemes and in the rehabilitation grants of the FSA, blacks received assistance in proportion to their share of the population, not in proportion to their need. Blacks, so many of whom were sharecroppers and farm laborers, disproportionately suffered from the failure of the New Deal rural poverty programs. Southern employers routinely solved the problem of higher costs resulting from the NRA and minimum-wage legislation by discharging black workers.[17]

Southern blacks were, nevertheless, grateful to Roosevelt because what aid they did receive from the New Deal was vastly greater than any assistance they had received in the past or were likely to receive from white state and local governments. Discriminated against they may have been, but southern blacks were not excluded as they had so often been before. In New Orleans, for example, at the outset of the Depression, the city council had restricted employment on public works projects entirely to poll tax payers—that is, whites—and even tried to make the same stipulation for employment on the municipal dock wharves. New Deal officials fairly quickly stamped out any similar efforts to exclude blacks from FERA and CCC programs in 1933 and 1934. Similarly FERA and WPA spending both on school building and on emergency teachers virtually rescued black education in the South, which had been the first target of economy-minded school boards and state legislatures.[18]

Southerners such as Will Alexander, Aubrey Williams, Clark Foreman, Brooks Hays, Frank Graham, C. B. "Beanie" Baldwin, and Clifford Durr were all radicalized by their service in Washington in New Deal agencies. They began to look critically at traditional patterns of race relations in the South and began to envisage the end of segregation. But, as Morton Sosna and John Kneebone have shown, southern liberals who remained in the South, notably the much-celebrated liberal newspapermen, clung tenaciously to the doctrines of paternalism and gradualism and to the hostility to federal intervention which demanded the maintenance of segregation. Jonathan Daniels neatly illustrates the distinction as Charles Eagles has demonstrated. As editor of the *Raleigh News and Observer,* Daniels was a persistent critic of New Deal discrimination against blacks and of police racial brutality. But he expected blacks to stay in their accustomed place either on the land or as servants; he opposed black voting and strongly defended segregation. Only when he went to Washington during the war as presidential assistant did his racial views begin to change. More aggressive liberals like Foreman, Baldwin, and Williams were sacrificed by Roosevelt during the war to assuage outraged southern conservatives. When New Dealers like Williams, Alexander, and

Durr returned to the South after the war they found themselves treated as outcasts.[19]

There was an even smaller group of southern white radicals who openly defied the racial dividing line in the South in the 1930s. Tony Dunbar has shown how they were influenced by the social gospel to put interracialism into practice in organizing the unemployed, tenant farmers, and industrial workers, and attempting to educate a new generation of community workers at Highlander Folk School and Commonwealth College. But they were a tiny minority and their activities opened them up to ferocious red-baiting assaults and unrestrained vigilante violence.[20]

VI

New Dealers hoped they could avoid the divisive racial issue by concentrating on the economic needs of the South. New Deal relief agencies first uncovered the full, hitherto unsuspected, dimensions of rural poverty. Social scientists at Chapel Hill and southerners in federal agencies in Washington pulled this data together to proclaim the South in 1938 as the nation's number-one economic problem. Capitalizing on this diagnosis New Dealers formed the Southern Conference for Human Welfare to lobby for a dramatically new way of modernizing the South. The key was the creation of mass purchasing power through federal intervention. Minimum-wage legislation, welfare legislation, the extension of social security, and a farm tenancy program were to be the economic core of this strategy. But to attain this goal there would have to be a political transformation. Economic democracy would require the protection of the civil liberties of trade union organizers and the abolition of the poll tax. But whereas the New Dealers saw Washington as the region's salvation, conservative leaders saw "Washington as the South's No 1 economic problem." Conservatives preferred the traditional model for securing economic growth in the South: the attraction of low-wage industry by the promise of a sympathetic context of cheap government and a cheap docile labor force. There was never much doubt that southern conservatives would win this argument. Ironically, they were forced to be more active in the search for low-wage industry because existing industries in the South had had to raise wages in response to federal legislation. Consequently, starting with Mississippi, southern states began actively seeking outside investment by promising attractive tax concessions and subsidies. James C. Cobb in *The Selling of the South* shows that this conservative modernization strategy was the policy followed by southern governments right through the 1940s and 1950s. The strategy had an additional advantage. The sort of businessmen likely to be attracted to the South were perfectly happy with the existing pattern of traditional race relations in the region.[21]

VII

The triumph of the conservative modernization strategy and the failure of the Southern Conference for Human Welfare highlighted the persistence of political conservatism in the South.

At first sight, Roosevelt had reason to be optimistic about the future of southern liberalism. He could look at the liberal southerners in his own administration. He could look over to Capitol Hill and see the implacable Hugo Black from Alabama calling for a minimum-wage legislation; or Maury Maverick from Texas crusading for civil liberties and major economic change; or Lister Hill and Claude Pepper elected to the Senate from Alabama and Florida in 1938, despite supporting minimum-wage legislation; or Lyndon Johnson elected to Congress from Texas, despite supporting Supreme Court reform. Together with what John Sparkman called "TVA liberals" these younger politicians who met regularly in Washington to discuss southern problems appeared to be the force of the future in the South.[22]

In addition, southern congressional leaders had loyally backed the president throughout his first term. As with almost all southern representatives, any qualms they had about the vast new powers of the federal government were outweighed by the constituents' desperate need for economic assistance and by their delight at the New Deal challenge to forces of economic privilege outside the region. Few politicians in the South, even the irreconcilably conservative Josiah Bailey, dared oppose FDR on the stump before 1936. Southern congressional leaders retained a dogged personal loyalty to FDR which survived many frustrations. They also continued to rejoice in New Deal farm programs and in measures aimed at out-of-state financial interests such as holding companies, national banks, and the New York stock exchange.[23]

Nevertheless, southern political liberalism was precisely circumscribed among the region's established politicians. Southern industrialists, particularly in Texas, Louisiana, and Alabama, were bitter early opponents of Roosevelt. Harvard Sitkoff has shown just how soon they raised the racial issue to frighten voters away from the New Deal. They found a receptive audience in the black belts of Alabama, Georgia, and Mississippi. As one Georgia registrar noted, "You ask any nigger in the street who's the greatest man in the world. Nine out of ten will tell you Franklin Roosevelt. That's why I think he's so dangerous." This potent brew of economic and racial conservatism led directly to the Dixiecrat states' rights revolt of 1948.[24]

Even politicians who did not harbor this animus toward Roosevelt were often privately lukewarm about the New Deal. As the saying went, "as thin as the liberalism of a Texas congressman." Few southern governors or state legislatures showed any inclination to enact "Little New Deals" in their states. Those who did, often did not know what they were doing. Eurith D. Rivers was elected on a pro-New Deal ticket in 1936 in Georgia. In reality he was an office-hungry former ally of rabid Roosevelt hater Eugene Talmadge. Imperial Wizard of the Ku Klux Klan, Hiram Evans was on his staff. An adviser recalled that Rivers rang him one morning after the election to say, "I got elected because I said I was going to provide for an old-age pension and a lot of other welfare programs, but I don't know a damn thing about it. How about fixing me up a "welfare program." [25]

Above all, most southern congressmen became increasingly alarmed by the nonemergency direction of the New Deal. Vast spending, large welfare programs, and support for organized labor might have been tolerable in an economic emergency, but once a semblance of agricultural recovery had been secured by 1937 congressmen began to resent the increasingly northern, urban orientation of the New Deal. Closer to home, local county seat elites in the South feared the threat the New Deal posed to existing patterns of dependence in the region. The traditional power of landlords and employers was threatened by labor organizers, rural poverty programs, and minimum-wage legislation [26]

In this climate southern liberals became increasingly vulnerable. If they did not compromise they were beaten like Maury Maverick in Texas. Even if they did compromise they might still be beaten like Luther Patrick. Most carefully tempered their enthusiasm for the New Deal in deference to their constituents. Ironically, one of the most vociferous supporters of aggressive New Deal urban liberalism in the late 1930s was the notorious racist Theodore Bilbo. Chester Morgan has shown that the Mississippi senator grew even more ardent in his support of labor and welfare legislation designed to benefit lower-income voters in the northern cities just at the time his southern colleagues were running for cover.[27]

The fundamental problem was that the New Deal had scarcely touched the basic political structure of the South. Most potential beneficiaries and supporters of the New Deal were effectively disenfranchised. When Lister Hill was elected to the Senate in 1938 less than 10 percent of Alabama's voting-age population voted. Hill summed up his dilemma to Virginia Durr, who advocated the abolition of the poll tax as a solution to the problems of southern liberals: "If you will guarantee that this thing will pass, I'll vote for it, because the kind of people that will be voting after the poll tax is off, they'll be the kind of people that will be voting for me. But unless you guarantee it's going to pass the House and the Senate, I can't do it." Here was the classic statement of the attitude that would plague southern liberals in the postwar world as well. They lamented that they operated in a conservative political structure. But they would not lift a finger to change that structure. They willed the end but not the means. Change could only be imposed by federal authority, but supporting such change might imperil their political careers. Instead, they counseled caution and moderation in order to preserve their influence. This influence, which they so assiduously protected, was of no avail when the racial crises of the 1950s and 1960s finally came. Moderates like Lister Hill and John Sparkman were completely unable to influence events or to dictate the timetable of change [28]

VIII

In contrast to this emphasis on the limited short-term impact of the New Deal, commentators have recently stressed the longer-term forces unleashed by the New Deal. Gavin Wright has argued that "the economic underpinnings and social glue that had kept the regional economy isolated were no longer present in 1940." Numan Bartley has contended that a "growth oriented metropolitan elite replaced a county-seat elite committed to traditional social structures." Douglas Smith has identified a decisive growth in urban consciousness during the 1930s. I have in contrast been more impressed by the way in which ruling elites responded to the threat of the New Deal by reaffirming their commitment to traditional patterns of economic growth, traditional patterns of dependence, and traditional patterns of race relations.[29]

There were some longer-term changes in the South fashioned by the New Deal. Outside the South the transfer of political allegiance of urban blacks to the Democrats strengthened the hand of a new civil rights coalition whose formation has been so clearly delineated by Harvard Sitkoff. The coalition which developed during the thirties of black pressure groups, labor, the radical Left, and New Deal liberals now had increasing political leverage over both the national Democratic Party and the Supreme Court. Over the next thirty years this pressure would yield the federal intervention which would eventually dismantle segregation.[30]

We still lack studies, particularly community-level studies, of the southern black response in the 1930s. But for all the New Deal's limitations, relief and recovery programs did give slightly more breathing space to southern blacks. The right to vote in crop-control elections and the availability of alternative sources of credit or relief lessened a little their overwhelming dependence on white landlords and merchants. Oral history interviews suggest that southern black community leaders for the first time saw the federal government as a potential saviour: the federal government had intervened to attempt to solve the region's economic problems—perhaps, black leaders dared to hope, federal government might step in to solve the South's racial problems.[31]

There was also a time-lag in Roosevelts's political impact on the South: it was in the 1940s that younger politicians influenced by him came to the fore. Liberals were able to put together an electoral alliance of lower-income whites and black voters who were being registered in small but steadily increasing numbers in the southern cities. Politicians like Jim Folsom, Sid McMath, and Kerr Scott stressed New Deal-style economic policies that would have a common appeal across racial lines to lower-income voters. At the same time, relative prosperity in the 1940s enabled even the poorest southern states like Mississippi to make welfare advances. Mississippi could now afford to participate in federal welfare programs that required matching state government appropriations.[32]

What brought dramatic change to the South, however, was not the New Deal but the war. World War II was the juggernaut that ran over southern society. Jobs in defense industries at last enabled a surplus rural population to leave the land. Soaring farm prices gave southern farmers the means to mechanize: a potential labor shortage gave them the incentive to do so. Southern agriculture was about to be modernized.[33]

The wartime and postwar boom enabled blacks to move into southern cities where they would have a degree of economic independence and living space—essential pre-conditions of the civil rights movements of the 1950s and 1960s. World War II permanently heightened black expectations.[34]

Federal spending in the South on defense, and later on space, in both the war and the cold war was the catalyst that enabled the southern economy to take off into self-sustaining economic growth. Low wages and rural poverty persisted but the South was to become also a region of high-tech industry and diversified agriculture that would attract in-migration from affluent whites and, eventually, from returning blacks.[35]

IX

New Dealers dreamt ambitious dreams of a modernized South in which small farmers prospered, low-wage industry was eliminated, workers were unionized, and the federal government guaranteed adequate wages and welfare. It was to be a democratized South in which the have-nots would at last have political power. For the more ambitious among the reformers, the advent of economic democracy in the region would also herald the breaking down of traditional patterns of race relations. Such dreams were unrealized. In the economic emergency of 1933 the federal government lacked the bureaucratic and administrative capacity to impose radical change on the South. New Dealers had to work with, not against, southern congressmen, the economic interests that were to be regulated, and local state government agencies. Inevitably these institutions were buttressed. By the time New Dealers had developed plans to transform the South, these conservative forces which the New Deal had rescued would be in a position to stifle New Deal aspirations. The unanticipated consequences of the New Deal were the strengthening of the position of large planters, the triumph of conservative strategies of securing economic growth, and the hardening of resistance to changes in race relations. The New Deal shored up the traditional structures of southern society. Consequently, when economic modernization came to the South in the aftermath of World War II, the destiny of the South was not in the hands of New Deal–style reformers but of the familiar local elites who were determined that economic growth should not undermine traditional patterns of dependency and deference and of white supremacy. It would take two forces that New Dealers had not envisaged to break that control: coercive intervention in race relations by the federal judiciary on the one hand, and a massive popular protest from below by the civil rights movement on the other. It was World War II and these later unexpected phenomena, not the ambitious federal plans of the New Dealers, that eventually transformed the South.

3

The Modernization of the South:
The Lament for Rural Worlds Lost

I

The outlines of the modernization of the South since 1930 are clear enough. A poor, rural, and small-town South has become a booming industrial and urban region. Government price supports and prosperity have enabled farmers to dispense with their tenant and sharecropper labor force, to mechanize, to consolidate their land holdings, and to diversify their crops. The sharecropper shack has disappeared; soybeans and chickens have replaced cotton as the South's main agricultural income earners. In the process some eight to nine million southerners left the land, finding jobs not only in the northern cities but in the new urban South. The number of black farmers fell from almost a million in 1930 to a mere sixty thousand in 1978. The South's industrial economy took off into self-sustaining economic growth after the federal government pumped billions of dollars into the region during World War II and the cold war. Garment and textile sweatshops have been joined by electronic component plants, tire factories, research parks, aircraft factories, and space flight centers as millions of new nonfarm jobs have been created in the New South.

Seldom has modernization of a traditional rural economy occurred so quickly. In a generation, the small labor-intensive cotton farms worked by mules have been replaced by capital-intensive, diversified, mechanized agribusinesses. In the past ten years this revolution has drawn the attention of some remarkably gifted and sensitive historians. Gilbert Fite has shown how, on the one hand, the availability of capital and technological and scientific

45

advances enabled southern farmers to mechanize and consolidate and then how, on the other, the growth of a prosperous urban South created the market and the infrastructure to pull them away from cotton to the diversified farming which southern agrarian reformers had for so long unfailingly advocated. Pete Daniel has shown how the differing technologies in cotton, tobacco, and rice combined with federal farm policy to dictate the varying pace of structural change in those commodities. Jack Temple Kirby has shown how the fragmented, unmechanized plantations were transformed into "neoplantations" that first used hired labor, but were ultimately able to replace even that with machines. More than anyone else, Jack Kirby has shown us how the very diverse parts of the South—not just the plantations but also the highland South, the wiregrass and hill farms and the truck farming South—were modernized and opened up to the cash nexus. He has also richly captured the culture of that old rural world.[1] At the urban and industrial end of the process, Gavin Wright has shown how the low-wage economy of the South that allowed its leaders successfully to isolate it from the national economy was undermined by the New Deal policies and World War II. Finally, James Cobb has shown how southerners deliberately set out to attract industry to the South that would disturb traditional relationships between employer and employee and between black and white as little as possible.[2]

I want to raise three questions about this process of modernization: first, to query whether the 1930s and the New Deal were the decisive turning points; second, to ask if there was a "road not taken" in the 1930s that would have produced a modernized South without the massive dislocation of the old rural world; and third, to query the nostalgia for rural worlds lost. In the final part of this chapter, I want to look at the views of John Shelton Reed, that traditional, distinctively southern cultural values survived the collapse of the old rural order, and to examine the links between southern distinctiveness and racial change.

II

In a paper on "How Did the New Deal Change the South?" which I gave at the meeting of the European Southern Studies Forum in Berlin in 1988, I argued for the essentially limited impact of the New Deal on the rural South. "In the end," I concluded:

> the New Deal for the rural South was essentially a holding operation. It enabled cotton and tobacco farmers to survive the Depression and allowed an underemployed surplus labor force to remain on the land when there were no economic opportunities elsewhere. When wartime

prosperity came, both black and white tenants and sharecroppers could
at last move to the defense industries and the cities.

Most of the writers on the modernization of the rural South disagree and see
the New Deal and the 1930s as the decisive time which put the South on
"the federal road" and shaped the large-scale and mechanized agriculture that
ensued. Jack Kirby has laid out the argument succinctly. The old unmechanized plantation system rested on abundant labor and scarce capital. The
New Deal gave the planters capital. Rental and benefit payments under the
AAA, which went overwhelmingly to the landlords, gave planters the chance
to buy tractors and thus mechanize the pre-harvest cotton production.
Acreage reduction gave them the excuse to evict tenants. They could replace
them with hired laborers. No longer did planters have to support tenants all
year round to ensure that they had an adequate labor force for the still non-
mechanized harvesting. Now New Deal welfare programs could support the
surplus labor force through the winter and early summer. Then, with the
assistance of sympathetic relief administrators, the planters could simply hire
that labor for the harvest. The New Deal was, in Gavin Wright's phrase, a
"planter's heaven."[3]

I have to say that I was probably wrong in my assessment of the New
Deal's role. I have probably been too influenced by my work on tobacco
where the AAA program served to freeze the existing structure of tobacco
farming in the 1930s. I was also probably guilty of what I have criticized historians of the New Deal for doing—that is, I was too concerned to defend or
justify New Deal policies and their intent, rather than examine the dispas-
sionate economic consequences of such policies.

Nevertheless, I retain some residual doubts about the current interpretation of the decisive role of the New Deal. First, as Jack Kirby acknowledges,
the start of the mechanization of the southwestern cotton plantations predated
the New Deal and reflected relatively high cotton prices in the 1920s.[4] Second,
the acquisition of tractors in the 1930s was a very limited process in the southeast. Even in Mississippi, only 2.7 percent of farm operators owned tractors by
the 1940s. Third, more people left the land in the 1920s and in the 1940s and
1950s than in the 1930s. The number of sharecroppers in the Mississippi
Delta declined by 9.4 percent in the 1930s, by 70 percent in the 1950s.[5] It was
during the war and after that the Delta Pine and Land Corporation—the classic modern neoplantation—started pulling down its tenant shacks. What were
surely the decisive stimuli to modernization were the high cotton prices of
World War II that gave the planters the capital to mechanize; the defense-
related jobs that took the surplus labor force off the land and gave the stimulus to bring in the cotton harvester; and the revolution in agricultural chem-
istry that enabled planters to eradicate weeds and defoliate cotton plants without hired labor. These were wartime and postwar developments.

III

Was there a road not taken in the 1930s: alternative policies that might have averted the painful dislocation in the lives of millions of farmers and led to a more equitable and healthy rural society? Jack Kirby rightly reminds us that modernization is not inevitable, nor is the form it takes.

New Dealers of course had alternative, or rather subsidiary and long-term, policies. Urban liberals in the AAA wanted to give tenants a fairer deal in 1934–35; the Farm Security Administration aimed to rehabilitate poor farmers, to resettle marginal farmers on good land in communities where they could be supervised and take advantage of collective facilities, and to loan money to tenants to buy their own farms; the Bureau of Agricultural Economics wanted to phase out high-cost cotton production and to shift wartime agricultural production to small farms; the New Deal liberal modernization scenario laid out in the TNEC Report on the South in 1938 saw the poverty of the South eliminated by raising the income and protecting the political, civil, and economic rights of both southern workers and the rural poor. All these alternatives were doomed to defeat; they threatened the pre-eminent local dominance of the planter elite and that elite was in a position to thwart unwanted policy initiatives by its congressional power and by its position in the farm policy-making apparatus secured in 1933. The need that year to secure the consent of the planters themselves to implement the cotton plow-up bolstered the power of the groups that would block longer-term New Deal reform aspirations. As James Cobb neatly put it, the New Deal, in opting for rapid recovery, settled for social peace in its time.[6]

Were the alternatives feasible? Were there opportunities missed? Jack Kirby in *Rural Worlds Lost* reluctantly thinks not: "By 1933 Southern farmers ... had but one question before them: would they accept expensive, but labor-saving, agricultural science, government regulation and subsidies, or would they perish? It was no question at all."[7]

John L. Thomas in his 1986 Commonwealth Fund Lecture, "'The Road Not Taken': Perspectives on Post-Frontier America, 1920–1940," implicitly thought there *was* an opportunity for a different route forward. He was looking at those who advocated what he called a regionalist vision, who sought a middle way between large-scale corporate capitalism and bureaucratic statism. He found such a vision in many places including the early TVA; but, above all in the South, he found it in the ideas of Rupert Vance. Thomas pointed to his advocacy of a small-scale diversified agriculture. He quoted Vance's contention that "perhaps life in the rural South is capable of being lived to the fullest with much less devotion to the money economy than elsewhere."[8]

Similarly, Pete Daniel believes that the road not taken was the one of sta-
bilizing and upgrading tenancy and sharecropping. This road "could have
preserved the rural culture and absorbed integration and welfare." He cites
the FERA experiment in Franklin County, North Carolina, where two hundred farm families were encouraged to grow corn, peas, and sorghum and to
barter with the surplus they produced. This older form of economic relationship and noncommercial subsistence farming showed "how little experience
farmers needed to succeed in the country."[9]

Irrespective of the unavoidable political realities of the New Deal's relationship with the existing political elites in the South, which would have
inhibited such alternatives, were they feasible solutions to the long-term
problems of southern rural poverty? Could southern farmers be denied a cash
farm income? How would such farmers view rural electrification, which
would open up new consumer possibilities for the rural South but which
would also need cash? The New Deal surely needed to raise total farm
income in the region: schemes of subsistence or semi-subsistence agriculture
were irrelevant to that goal. In the end there were also simply too many
people on the land in the South. The solutions to the South's rural poverty
ultimately had to lie in the southern cities: in jobs for the tenants and sharecroppers and in an urban market for the products of a diversified agriculture.

IV

There are those who lament the failure of those alternatives and lament the
loss of that rural world. For Pete Daniel, the rural existence may have been
grim but it "was made bearable by church services, family visits, schools, con-
versations at the cross-roads store, and any number of singings, drinkings,
marryings, and, if the literature is any guide, fornications and adulteries. At
the center of this life was a natural harmony—the seasonal plowing, planting, hoeing, harvesting and settlement." It may have been a primitive life,
"but the human race has often found grim satisfaction in living as close to
the margin of absolute failure as possible." Could those tenant farmers really
be better off in the city? "Does television substitute for the gallery of Will
Varner's store at Frenchman's Bend? Is any pavement as solid as the soil?"[10]

Ferrol Sams opens his novel *Run with the Horsemen* with the boy's recognition of the solidity of that soil:

> The father owned the land. He plowed it, harvested it, timbered it and
> hunted over it. It was his. ... he also knew that in turn the land owned his
> father. Everything the father did eventually revolved around the nurture
> of the land. Without the land here would be no family. The ungodly were

not so and lived in town. They were like chaff which bloweth away. Their feet were not rooted in the soil, and they were therefore of little consequence in the scheme of things.[11]

Sams went on to give a marvelously evocative account of all the tasks done by hand in pre-mechanization cotton cultivation and of the symbiotic relationship between man and mule.

In black novelist Ernest J. Gaines's *A Gathering of Old Men,* the villain is Fix Boutan, who brought the tractors in: Tucker regales Sheriff Mapes with the heroic and tragic tale of his brother Silas,

> ". . . the last black man round here trying to sharecrop on this place. The last one to fight against that tractor out there". . . ."How can a man beat a machine?" he asked. . . ."Well, my brother did. With them two little mules, he beat that tractor to the derrick."[12]

Harry Crews in *Childhood: A Biography of a Place*[13] recalls the lasting impact of Bacon County and the old way of life:

> I have always known, though, that part of me never left, could never leave, the place where I was born and, further, that what has been most significant in my life had all taken place by the time I was six years old. . . . the biography of a childhood which necessarily is the biography of a place, a way of life gone forever out of the world.

But is this a real lament for those rural worlds lost? In *Run with the Horsemen,* the horrific climax is provided by Porter Osborne's father who puts out the eye of Porter's black friend Buddy. Buddy had dared to try to persuade one of the father's tenants to move to another landlord. The old men gathered in Ernest Gaines's novel are there to recount the horrors perpetrated on them by whites—horrors which meant that they all had reason to murder Beau Boutan, who was killed at the start of the book. The ultimate importance of Bacon County for Harry Crews is that he left it at the age of seventeen and never returned there.

There may be white nostalgia for the rural worlds lost, but you will not find that same yearning in black autobiographies. There is no nostalgia in the recollections of Maya Angelou or Pauli Murray or Anne Moody or Charlie Evers. Nor is there in the oral history interviews of former sharecroppers. Neil McMillen observed in his study of black Mississippians that "sharecropper accounts—particularly oral histories gathered by black interviewers in recent decades—contain little nostalgia for 'dem olden times' found in some WPA slave narratives dictated to whites in the 1930s." In narrative after narrative, the image of tenantry as latter-day bondage recurs: "'I call it slavery'. . . . 'It was just like slavery time'. . . . 'Nothing but slavery.'" As one interviewee recalled, when asked to compare her life in 1970 to her life as a Clay County field hand, "I would consider we was [now] living in Heaven, considering from the time we was living in Hell."[14]

What there is, is a celebration of the strength of character of ordinary black men and women, particularly kin folk, who provided assertive role models for the young blacks growing up—Maya Angelou's grandmother, Pauli Murray's aunt, Anne Moody's schoolteacher who secretly taught her about the NAACP, Charles Evers's drunken, womanizing and politically apathetic father who nevertheless taught his sons the importance of not being short-changed by white men. What can be mistaken for wistful nostalgia is the detailed and proud recreation of the old methods of cultivation and production, of the physical strength and the skill which the old methods required. They may not have stood up to the white men but they do not want it to be forgotten that they made the old system work. Their craft gave them some value and self-esteem which helped them survive. As Yank tells Sheriff Mapes in *A Gathering of Old Men,*

> They ain't got no more horses to break no more. The tractors, the cane cutters—and I ain't been nothing ever since. They look at you today and they call you trifling, cause they see you sitting there all the time doing nothing. They can't remember when you used to break all the horses and break all the mules.[15]

Nate Shaw wants the past to be recorded to show that he counted for something even if his family no longer seem to know or care.[16] Communist union organizer Hosea Hudson was no romantic about the South of the 1930s and he had no lack of self-esteem, but nevertheless he insisted that his interviewer Nell Painter faithfully record in massive, even wearisome, detail the mechanics of steel production.[17] Jack Kirby is surely right to conclude that

> [s]ome migrants and commuters mourned the loss of local relations and the homier life of the semisubsistence economy, but most (especially black folk) were happy to be free of the oppression of the old system. No romantics were they.[18]

The rural world described by Harry Crews, Ferrol Sams, and Ernest J. Gaines was violent. Harry Crews described Bacon County in terms that historians of the culture of honor like Edward Ayers and Bertram Wyatt-Brown would recognize:

> In Bacon County, the Sheriff was the man who tried to keep the peace, but if you had any real trouble, you did not go to him for help to make it right. You made it right for yourself or else you became known in the county as a man who was defenseless without the sheriff at his back. If

that ever happened, you would be brutalized and savaged endlessly because of it. Men killed other men oftentimes not because there had been some offense that merited death, but simply because there had been some offense, any offense. As many men have been killed over bird dogs and fence lines in South Georgia as anything else.

It was also a world in which the family was central. Harry Crews again:

> Families were important then, and they were important not because the children were useful in the fields. . . . No, they were important because a large family was the only thing a man could be sure of having. Nothing else was certain. . . . a man didn't need good land or stands of hardwood trees to have babies. All he needed was balls and the inclination.

A religious world, as Ferrol Sams wrote of Brewton County:

> Everyone believed. No one was fool enough to put any desire ahead of being saved. It was just as important to be Raised Right. The child who had been Raised Right was not only Saved but had spent a large part of his formative years in the House of the Lord.

And finally a local world. As Porter Osborne Sr. told his son: "All of a sudden it hit me. I'd never be able to live happily in a place where I didn't recognize every name on all the tombstones and know which one were mine."[19] Would these underlying values survive modernization or would they be as ruthlessly bulldozed away as the sharecropper shacks had been?

V

As "the bulldozer revolution" proceeded remorselessly, as a national mass media enveloped the South, as suburbs sprawled anonymously, so observers saw the region lose its distinctiveness. The *New York Times* journalist Tom Wicker, who grew up in Hamlet, North Carolina, returned to "the new, prosperous, progressive, homogeneous South, with its concrete arteries and shrieking jets and piercing neon." Each time he went back, it seemed "more nearly an interchangeable part of the vast, grim sameness of a nation that has discovered in mobility that no one need ever leave home because everything and every place can be made to look, taste, feel and sound like every other thing and place." Another returning *New York Times* journalist, Fred Powledge, took particular exception to the spread of K Marts everywhere. These mass-market, standardized, low-price chain stores symbolized for him the forces of homogenization and the erosion of a distinctive South.[20] John Egerton labeled it "the Americanization of Dixie":

> The modern acquisitive, urban, industrial, post-segregationist, on-the-make South, its vices nationalized, its virtues evaporating if not already

dissipated, is coming back to the Mother Country, coming back with a bounce in its step, like a new salesman on the route, eager to please, intent on making it.[21]

But at the same time in the 1970s historians argued for a persistent southern identity that survived modernization. In *Place over Time,* Carl Degler argued for the continuity of a southern distinctiveness. The region remained more rural, more poor, more violent, more religious, and more black than the rest of the nation.[22] In his essay on "The Ethnic Southerners," George Tindall compared southerners to immigrant groups. No longer did historians see immigrants as the "uprooted," traumatized and alienated when wrenched from their peasant cultures to be set down in America. Rather, immigrants were "transplanted" with strong ethnic ties and cultural identities that enabled them to survive the dislocation of the transatlantic upheaval. So the millions of southerners who had just undergone an equally painful transition from the old rural world were sustained by a cultural baggage that they brought with them.[23]

In making that suggestion George Tindall drew on the work of the sociologist John Shelton Reed. In *The Enduring South* in 1974, Reed used survey data to demonstrate that traditional distinctive southern cultural traits had survived urbanization and industrialization. The rural world described by Ferrol Sams and Harry Crews might have disappeared, but southerners were still characterized by their attachment to family and local place, by their religiosity, and by their culture of violence. Since then Reed has continued to find more and more indicators of southern distinctiveness: the absence of high-quality sociologists, the existence of more identifiable regional social types than in any other part of the country (though California is catching up), and the disproportionately large number of southerners who believe that they live in the best state in the country. The middle-class suburban southerner who subscribes to *Southern Living* is, Reed argues, just as distinctive and committed to many of the old values as the redneck and the good ole boy.[24]

VI

One aspect of southern distinctiveness that was increasingly celebrated in the 1970s was the southern pattern of race relations. White southerners had of course long claimed that in practice race relations were better in the South than in the North. Writers like William Alexander Percy unashamedly contended that southerners, whatever their views on the racial capabilities of blacks, treated them well because they knew and understood them. Northerners, whatever their abstract views on black rights, treated blacks impersonally and cruelly. Percy professed to be shocked by the callous way blacks were treated in northern cities. Katharine DuPre Lumpkin was appalled by how many southern racist views she encountered in the North. It was also long a tenet of southern liberals that they knew better than northern integrationists how to bring about racial change in the South. In the 1950s and 1960s such assertions took on a defensive, tentative quality in the face of black protest and federal intervention; it was southern white supremacists who aggressively proclaimed that they knew their Negroes, that they were happy, that the only problem was outside agitators and that liberal northerners were hypocrites. Southern liberals had in the meantime to bite their tongues and suppress their suspicion of northern smugness and condescension.[25]

Vann Woodward told Willie Morris of the March to Montgomery from Selma. At one point he and several fellow historians had gathered in a circle and given three cheers for Martin Luther King. "There we were," Woodward said, "walking down the highway to Montgomery. I looked over to the side of the road, and I saw the red-necks lined up, hate all over their faces, distrust and misunderstanding in their eyes. And I'll have to admit something. A little part of me was there with 'em."[26]

Then, suddenly it was all different. Some southern white liberals, like Leslie Dunbar, and some black leaders, like Andrew Young, had claimed that if radical change were imposed on the South, southerners would surprise the rest of the nation with the speed and accord with which they adjusted to the new racial reality. A shared cultural and religious heritage and a shared land would foster an accommodation. In the 1970s the South did seem to have peacefully accepted dramatic racial change: the dismantling of the physical attributes of segregation, large-scale black voting, black officeholders, particularly in law enforcement, visible jobs in government and business for middle-class blacks, massive integration of the schools, the transmogrification of "good ole' boy" segregationist politicians into old-style Populists, and the election of a new breed of "New South" politicians who combined racial moderation with efficient government. No longer did southerners have to be apologetic about their distinctive race relations, they could point to greater integration than in the residentially segregated North and to the fact that in 1976 black southern votes put a white peanut farmer into the presidency.

Once more John Shelton Reed was there to sum it up. In his article "Up from Segregation" he highlighted standard indices of this substantial racial change. He was particularly keen to do so since in 1970 he had asked in an article "Can the South Show the Way?" and replied affirmatively. In his 1984 lecture he could point to the standard indices of dramatic racial changes: the net in-migration of blacks returning to the region; the declining percentage of poor black families; the 1981 figure that Mississippi had more elected black officials than any other state in the nation. But what most impressed him was survey data on white attitudes and his perception of what had happened to racial etiquette and what it meant in terms of *respect* for black southerners:

> Manners *have* changed. More and more, in places like courthouses and stores and schools, Southern whites seem disposed to treat black Southerners as sort of honorary white folks—and by and large, whatever their private opinions of one another, white Southerners treat each other with courtesy and at least the appearance of good-natured respect. Southern blacks, for their part, seem willing to return the favor. The upshot is that on a day-to-day basis (which is how most of us lead our lives, after all) black-white relations in the South seem more cordial, less prickly, than black-white relations in the cities in the North.

He was optimistic about the future because he believed that modernization—education, urbanization, and exposure to the outside world—would eradicate two distinctive southern traditional values: racism and authoritarianism.[27]

VII

Reed ended his 1984 summing-up by hoping that the South might yet give the world what Leslie Dunbar had hoped for, "its first grand example of two races of men living together in equality and with mutual respect." How did that hope for distinctive southern race relations look in 1992?

It is difficult to draw up a balance sheet. It is a South in which a white politician can be elected governor of Mississippi despite well-publicized sworn affidavits that he had slept with three black transvestites, where George Wallace can be given an honorary degree at Tuskegee, where the first black to attend Clemson University can be elected mayor of Charlotte and almost senator for North Carolina, where Doug Wilder can be elected governor of Virginia with endorsements from old stalwarts of the Byrd machine like Watkins Abbitt. But it is also a South where Doug Wilder's main achievement is to slash government spending and not raise taxes, where exit polls in Mississippi in 1988 appeared to show that there were no white Democrats under the age of thirty-five, where the Moral Majority demands of politicians moral and religious conformity but really wants economic conservatism and racial bigotry, where black mayors get elected at a time when their cities increasingly lack the resources to solve their constituents' problems. The racism and authoritarianism which Reed expected to be eroded by modernization have not disappeared.

It is a South where school desegregation works in a city like Charlotte, but not in Atlanta; where Georgia senators can lead a march against racial hate in Forsyth County, but where the Klan revives and racial bombings multiply; where continued middle-class black economic gains are offset by industry's determination to shun counties with large black populations, and where the cities develop an underclass little different from the ghettos of the North.

Reed relied on survey data. One problem highlighted by the 1989 election results was that white voters lied about their voting intentions when racial issues were involved. Both Wilder's narrow victory in Virginia and Helms's triumph the following year in North Carolina showed that whites who said they were going to vote for a black candidate actually did no such thing. Perhaps an interesting reversal has actually taken place. In 1971 black writer Albert Murray returned *South to a Very Old Place.* In Atlanta he had lunch with *Newsweek's* Joe Cummings, a white who was skeptical about southern white acceptance of racial change. They were served by a white waitress fresh, as Murray said, from Tobacco Road. Murray was sure if she were interviewed at home she would have negative views on desegregation but in the cafe she was more concerned with serving both of them and getting the order right. "Is," Murray asked, "what she says when interviewed on desegregation as a specific issue really more significant than the way she is acting right now with me sitting right here?"[28] Here was an example of Martin Luther King's aphorism, "Laws may not change hearts and minds, but they sure as hell change the way people act." Yet twenty years later I suspect the relationship between action and words has changed right round. White southerners are reluctant to admit racially prejudiced views to opinion pollsters, they are unwilling to vent publicly racist sentiments, but they will act in ways that will sustain re-segregation and the election of men like Jesse Helms, and—almost—David Duke. The early 1980s now look like a lost golden age of racial optimism.

However, I want to end on an ambiguous note about the relationship between modernization, traditional values, and regional distinctiveness. One of John Shelton Reed's indicators of southern distinctiveness was the disproportionate number of professional footballers in the NFL who came from the South. As Jack Kirby notes, college football became the southern passion play in the 1930s.[29] At strait-laced southern Baptist Willingham University created by Ferrol Sams, it is explained to Porter Osborne that the football players are different from all other students: "The coach ships 'em in here on scholarship from Pennsylvania and Ohio on account of their muscles, and they're sumpin else. They're all Dagoes or Hunkies or Polacks or something like that. Anyhow, they're all Catholics." Not only that but they had not heard of the

War Between the States.[30] Times change but the imperative to win does not. In the 1970s, legendary Alabama coach Bear Bryant had to watch his Crimson Tide get torn to shreds by the black running backs of the University of Southern California, black footballers recruited from black high schools in rural Alabama. A drunken Bryant went on television to say that those running blacks should be playing for Alabama and the university football team was integrated. In 1991 the national college football center of gravity had moved from California, the Midwest, even Texas and Alabama. In one week's national rankings three of the nation's top five football teams came from Florida: FSU at Tallahassee, University of Florida at Gainesville, and Miami, which had won three national championships in the last ten years. They do so largely with home-grown footballers. Why are they so successful?

To answer this question we have to look at the demographics of modernization. Between census counts in 1980 and 1990, Florida jumped seventh to fourth place among the fifty states in population. Said one coach: "It doesn't take a genius to figure out what happens when the population explodes. When Disney bought the land in Florida for Disney World, the population in this state in the '70s and '80s just went haywire. I noticed the prospects and the talent were increasing by leaps and bounds." In part, the answer lies in the national phenomenon of street-hardened ghetto schoolboys from urban ghettos seeing football as the way out of crime and poverty. Miami provides one quarter of the state's high schools. But in part, the answer also lies in the traditional vales of the farms. An FSU assistant coach said: "People look at Florida and think of palm trees and beaches, and we've got some pretty ones. But this is also an agricultural state. We've got three kids on our team who used to cut sugar cane. And if you've ever done that all day in the Florida sun, you know for a fact that there's nothing we can ask of them on the football field that will be any tougher." Perhaps there's life in those rural worlds lost still.[31]

4

Whatever Happened to Roosevelt's New Generation of Southerners?

In 1934 Carl Elliott borrowed twenty-five dollars from a grocer in Vina and traveled to Tuscaloosa to study at the University of Alabama. Thrown out by the curmudgeonly president, George Denny, Elliott surreptitiously managed to register, slept under a truck the first night, and then managed to squat in the university boiler house. Eventually he became Denny's houseboy. Two years later, Elliott was president of the student body. Senator Hugo Black, on the look-out for progressive political talent, arranged for him to meet the President in Washington. Elliott never forgot that private meeting with "the man who was, and also remains, a political god for me—Franklin D. Roosevelt." Returning home, Elliott started a law practice in Jasper. Faced with acute distress among the farmers and miners, he invoked an ancient Alabama statute and halted a train, commandeered its coal and potatoes, and distributed them to the needy. In 1948 Elliott was elected to Congress. For sixteen years he was part of the most liberal congressional delegation in the South, joining his House colleagues Robert Jones, Kenneth Roberts, and Albert Rains, and Alabama's senators, Lister Hill and John Sparkman. During that time, back home, Big Jim Folsom served two terms in the governor's mansion as a champion of the common man and foe of the Big Mules of Birmingham and planters of the black belt.

Increasingly targeted by segregationist forces, Elliott was finally squeezed out of Congress in the at-large congressional election of 1964 that followed re-districting. Hoping to check Alabama's slide into dictatorship and racial isolation, Elliott challenged the Wallace forces again in the 1966 gubernatorial election. Elliott's final defeat left him devastated financially. Ostracized in Jasper, Elliott lost his home and his health and eked out a miserable existence

58

in the very years that Alabama finally made the adjustments to the racial change and economic progress that Elliott had devoted his career to securing.[1]

Carl Elliott and his colleagues in the Alabama delegation were precisely the sort of southerners that Roosevelt had in mind when he counseled patience to Norman Thomas in 1936. FDR attempted to defuse the socialist leader's concern about the plight of southern sharecroppers by assuring him that he knew the South and there was arising a "new generation of leaders" in the region.[2]

The history of conservatism in the postwar South and the region's often violent resistance to racial change make it tempting to dismiss Roosevelt's optimism as characteristic wishful thinking. The main thrust of New Deal historiography has been to stress the role of southern conservatism from the late 1930s onwards. Southerners were the key figures in the conservative bipartisan coalition that checked New Deal reform aspirations after 1936. Roosevelt was unable to "purge" those conservatives in the primary elections of 1938. During the war, southern congressmen took the lead in dismantling emergency New Deal agencies and blocking plans for the extension of the welfare state. After the war, hostility to the Truman administration's civil rights stance led to the Dixecrat states' rights' revolt of 1948. In examining local southern politics in the late 1930s, I myself have argued that there was a "lack of the electoral raw material in the South to sustain an ideologically clearly defined liberal party."[3]

Southern politicians had enthusiastically supported the New Deal throughout 1936 because, whatever their ideological doubts about federal power and federal spending, they were acutely aware that their constituents were desperate for the jobs, credit, and rising farm income that New Deal relief and recovery programs brought them. But, whereas constituency pressure before 1936 demanded support for the New Deal, after 1936 that pressure counseled caution. To the rural elites who had been so grateful for assistance in the economic emergency of the Depression, the nonemergency agenda of the New Deal seemed geared to northern and urban needs. The rural, small-town elites who dominated so much of southern politics saw traditional patterns of paternalism, deference, and dependence threatened: welfare programs and union organization seemed to undermine employer control in the workplace; welfare and rural poverty programs challenged the customary dominance of landlords and merchants over tenants and sharecroppers.[4]

The failure of the purge in 1938 seemed to confirm that the New Deal had not liberalized the South. The race issue had been used by conservative opponents from the start of the New Deal to whip up popular support for their opposition to Roosevelt's economic policies. As late as 1936, for example, when Eugene Talmadge race-baited Richard Russell, the tactic did not seem to work. Yet in 1938 it did. In 1936 men like Russell could effectively argue that the race issue was settled: in 1938 southerners, their sectional sensibilities aroused by the nonemergency New Deal, were fearful of federal intervention by a government responsive to newly Democratic black voters in the northern cities. What the failure of the purge suggested was that the New Deal had alarmed political elites by threatening traditional patterns of dependency in the region, but could not make good the threat because it had left the structure of southern politics untouched: it had failed to extend the electorate. Most potential lower-income supporters of the New Deal were effectively disfranchised. The restricted electorate, which eliminated the likelihood of sustained constituency pressure for social welfare or labor legislation, seemed to set very precise limits to the potential liberalization of the Democratic Party. Roger Biles in *The South and the New Deal* concluded: "The small band of New Deal liberals in the South constituted a tiny minority...Overshadowed by their more powerful conservative colleagues, these highly vulnerable New Dealers generally survived on the political scene for only a short time." A politician who did not compromise like the unapologetic radical Maury Maverick in San Antonio would be red-baited to defeat. Even a cautious moderate who did compromise and try prudently to avoid the race issue like Luther Patrick in Birmingham would also be eventually beaten. The war, of course, gave southern conservatives in Congress the excuse to eliminate New Deal reform programs on the grounds that they were hampering the war effort. Alan Brinkley in his brilliant study of New Deal liberalism in the late 1930s and during the war fails to find or mention any southern liberals.[5]

Two excellent recent books have painted a very different picture. They have drawn attention to the alternative radical strategy of modernizing the South from the bottom up: extending the benefits of the New Deal to lower-income southerners and protecting their civil rights at the same time. These southern New Dealers aimed to solve the nation's number one economic problem through federal underpinning of living standards and by sustaining the basic civil liberties of both African Americans and union organizers.

Patricia Sullivan, in *Days of Hope: Race and Democracy in the New Deal Era* (1996), has systematically delineated a coalition in the South of New Deal liberals, labor organizers, Communist Party workers, and black activists who espoused, on the one hand, a national New Deal policy for creating mass purchasing power in the region, and, on the other, a local strategy of organizing at the community level. Identifying this radical moment, she writes:

> For a time, southerners had reached across racial boundaries to advance
> political and economic democracy in the region, with the support of the

federal government and a strong national labour movement. The central lesson was the power of segregation to undermine all efforts to establish a healthy democracy in the region.

If progressives in the South were to be a force for change, they required the moral, political and financial support of democratically minded people throughout the region . . . They [the activists] created legal precedents, experimented with new political forms, and organized round issues of social and economic justice. Such eclectic and improvisational efforts collectively expanded the possibilities of democracy in a racially fractured civic landscape.

Sullivan's work is particularly valuable in four respects. First, she shows how Charles Houston and Thurgood Marshall took the National Association for the Advancement of Colored People "home" to the South in the 1930s, crisscrossing the region seeking plaintiffs to sustain a litigative strategy to challenge, or at least equalize segregated facilities. They also encouraged the formation of local NAACP branches and exhorted community leaders to register to vote. Second, Sullivan demonstrates that, despite the inaction of the New Deal in many areas of civil rights, southern African American leaders saw the potential for federal government action in the South, for if the federal government could solve the region's economic problems in the way it did in the 1930s, then the government might intervene to solve the region's racial problems. Third, Sullivan became the first historian to show how African Americans launched voter registration drives in the 1940s through campaigns that were not academic exercises to secure civil rights for the small number of middle-class blacks, but real responses to community grievances about police brutality or egregious discrimination.[6]

Finally, Sullivan identifies an opportunity for this New Deal alliance after *Smith v. Allwright* in 1944. Black voter registration drives were underwritten by the Congress of Industrial Organizations' Political Action Committee and became part of an effort to secure the election of liberal southern candidates in the 1946 elections. Sullivan places this southern liberal upsurge in the context of a national struggle, epitomized by Henry Wallace, to secure the extension of the New Deal in the face of southern Democratic obstructionism. Bob Korstad and Nelson Lichtenstein identify a lost opportunity in the alliance of left-led unions and black workers in some southern cities. Adam Fairclough, directly complementing Sullivan's work on voter registration, has shown that in Louisiana revitalized NAACP activity was not merely a litigative middle-class strategy, but was crucially linked to voter registration, community organization against police brutality, and local labor radicalism. He concludes that the 1940s in Louisiana was the first act in the two-act play that constitutes the modern civil rights movement. Historians, he argues, have slighted "the scope of popular involvement during the 1940s and early 1950s...in much of Louisiana and much of the South, voter registration was tantamount to direct action."[7]

John Egerton in *Speak Now against the Day: The Generation before the Civil Rights Movement in the South* (1994) takes as his starting point the fact that the 1930s was a remarkable decade of self-criticism in the South. "It seems fair to say," he writes, "that self-examination of the region was more advanced and more extensive than ever before." Coupled with the changes unleashed by the New Deal and the war, this critical spirit created an opportunity for change that Egerton believes was spurned:

> One of the things I have come to see in retrospect is how favourable the conditions were for substantive social change in the four or five years right after World War II. It appears to have been the last and best time —perhaps the only time—when the South might have moved boldly and decisively to heal itself voluntarily. But it didn't act, and the moment passed, and all that has happened in the tumultuous days since...has followed from that inability to seize the time and do the right thing, not simply because it was right, but because it was also in our own best interest.

Though the Birmingham conference of 1938, which founded the Southern Conference for Human Welfare, was Egerton's centerpiece, his account largely features a mix of intellectuals, academics, writers, newspapermen, and black and white radicals. Politicians, for whom Egerton had little respect, find little room in his 627 pages, as "they were conspicuously absent from the ranks of the critics and the reformers." Trying to think of senators or congressmen or governors who were advocates of, or spokesmen for, reform, Egerton found that "Hugo Black is just about the only one who springs to mind...in the Deep South progressive or moderate or even mildly conservative congressmen were as scarce as hen's teeth." In the Senate, he saw a "depressingly familiar picture of negative leadership" matched by the House of Representatives which was equally "as devoid of southern statesmen, a few honest plodders notwithstanding."[8]

There was, however, a new generation of New Deal southern politicians as well. Just as in the North issue-oriented politicians came to replace patronage-oriented politicians in the Democratic Party, so in the South, younger politicians ideologically committed to New Deal economic goals came to replace patronage-hungry congressmen who had only supported FDR in the economic emergency of the 1930s. This new generation of white, usually younger, politicians in the South was actually elected to office, drawing on the support of an alliance of lower-income whites, organized labor, veterans, women, and the small but slowly increasing African American electorate. They espoused economically liberal and racially moderate policies. They constituted a significant part of the South's representation in Congress. They contributed to what Ira Katznelson, Kim Geiger, and Daniel Kryder (following in the footsteps of V. O. Key Jr.) have recently identified on the basis of roll call analyses: a party-based liberal coalition of nonsouthern and southern Democrats on welfare state, fiscal, regulatory, and planning issues.[9]

In Alabama, Lister Hill moved from the House to the Senate in 1937 and Sparkman followed him in 1946. Albert Rains was elected in 1944, Robert Jones in 1946, and Carl Elliott in 1948. In Tennessee, Albert Gore Sr. was elected to the House in 1938, Estes Kefauver in 1940, and J. Percy Priest in 1942. Kefauver and Gore would, in 1948 and 1952 respectively, go to the Senate. In Arkansas, Clyde Ellis was elected from the Fourth District in 1938. J. William Fulbright took over from him four years later and James Trimble would succeed Fulbright when he was elected to the Senate in 1944. Former New Deal official Brooks Hays was elected from Little Rock in 1942. In Texas, Albert Thomas was elected in 1936, Lyndon Johnson in 1937, and Lindley Beckworth in 1938. North Carolina produced Charles Deane in 1946 and Mississippi elected Frank Smith from the heart of the Delta in 1950. Katznelson concluded they "supported much of the party's social Democratic agenda with a level of enthusiasm appropriate to a poor region with a heritage of opposition to big business and a history of support for regulation and redistribution." Meanwhile, in the state houses, Folsom in 1946 was followed by Sid McMath from Arkansas, Kerr Scott from North Carolina, and Earl Long from Louisiana in 1948—all of them elected while excoriating the political establishments and entrenched economic interests in their respective states.[10]

The success of these issue-oriented politicians was founded on a number of factors whose importance has only recently, and sometimes only partially, been acknowledged. These include infrastructure politics; a common-man, popular appeal, the relative prosperity of southern states and their newfound ability to match New Deal spending; the wartime success of southern labor, and the impact of the war on white southerners—both those who stayed at home and those who served in the armed forces.

New Deal programs built up the region's infrastructure. Relief and public works programs rescued the South's education system. In southern cities the Works Progress Administration and Public Works Administration built roads and airports, developed ports, and funded the capital projects that in the North, a generation earlier, had been funded by private enterprise. Tennessee Valley Authority–inspired cheap power made possible industrial development. Federal spending in World War II dramatically quickened the pace of change: the billions of dollars on defense contracts and training facilities kick-started the region into self-sustaining economic growth for the first time. New jobs absorbed the rural surplus population; high prices, new urban markets, and electrification enabled southern farmers to mechanize and diversify.[11]

John Sparkman described himself as a "TVA liberal." What southern New Dealers learned from infrastructure politics was that the federal government, through an agency like the TVA, could regenerate an entire region, and they drew from the New Deal experience the lesson that the South could not prosper on its own. Federal government assistance was to be the answer to the region's problems of education, hospital construction, medical research, vaccination provision, electrification, and the provision of rural library services and telephones.[12]

Jordan Schwarz has shown how some southern politicians saw particular personal, political, and regional opportunities arising from New Deal policies, policies that would not only bring much-needed assistance to deprived areas but also would foster the dynamic economic growth that would create the Sunbelt. TVA provided the cheap power to facilitate industrial development, while great water resource projects—usually neglected by historians—not only provided flood control but made available essential water for industrial locations. The Reconstruction Finance Corporation, under the Houston banker Jesse Jones, broke the eastern monopoly on credit and made capital available for thrusting regional entrepreneurs. Public works projects provided lucrative contracts for politically connected businessmen who in turn funded helpful congressmen. Lyndon Johnson was one of those congressmen who saw the possibilities. As his backer, George Brown, head of a construction and engineering firm, recalled, "Lyndon Johnson would take me to these meetings of the Southern congressmen and that's the way they'd be talking. That the South would get these dams and these other projects and it would come out of the other fellow's pockets."[13]

This emphasis, and the efforts of liberal governors to attract industry and to invest in the infrastructure of roads and schools, has led them sometimes to be described as "business progressives" or "Whigs." But their strategy was not simply a top-down conservative economic approach designed to attract industry at any cost. They brought welfare benefits to their constituents that had long been denied them by conservative elites. They certainly sought industry but they did so defending the rights of organized labor and fighting for substantial increases in state minimum wages. They championed cheap power, particularly through rural electrification cooperatives and the state development of water resources. These rights put them on a bitter collision course with the major utility companies like Arkansas Power and Light and the Duke Power Company. Their policies did have a genuinely reformist, social welfare, redistributionist element.[14]

This new generation of southern candidates espoused a common-man, popular appeal. They took their electoral case directly to the people, circumventing the local county seat elites who usually brokered their localities' votes. Lyndon Johnson's campaign for Congress in 1937, in which he reached out to voters in the tiniest and most isolated communities and completely overturned "the leisurely pace normal in Texas elections," is well known. Robert Caro has also shown how well financed that campaign was. Less well known is the successful campaign for Congress the following year by Texan Lindley Beckworth. Beckworth modeled his campaign on LBJ's in terms of reaching every voter through ten speeches a day, but he did so without LBJ's money. He had $1,100 from a note signed by twenty-five of his townsfolk. His headquarters was a room in his father's house with no telephone. He had no money for newspaper advertisements and could only afford hand-painted signs. He used two cars with crude public address systems: one borrowed, and one bought on installment. A more unlikely common-man candidate was the Rhodes scholar, Anglophile and former university president, J. William Fulbright. In 1942 he campaigned for the seat vacated by the rural electrification champion, Clyde Ellis, by wearing a check shirt and reaching every nook and cranny of his hilly, 175-mile-long and 50-mile-wide district. No one ran a more basic campaign than Jim Folsom for governor in Alabama in 1946. His headquarters was a payphone in a barber's shop, and he made speeches at every crossroads in the state, attracting an audience with his country band, the Strawberry Pickers, and denouncing the established interests in Alabama—the Black Belt planters and the Big Mules of Birmingham.[15]

The South's relative prosperity in World War II gave southern governors the opportunity to participate in New Deal welfare programs that required states to match federal money. In the 1930s revenue-starved southern states often could not afford to take part, but in the 1940s they could. Even Mississippi, the poorest state in the nation, could afford to join the Aid to Families with Dependent Children programs. The 1940s witnessed the greatest advances in state welfare provision for children in Mississippi's history.[16]

The war enabled organized labor to play a greater part in the region's politics, a role obscured by the region's anti-union reputation. Wartime prosperity, the prospects of defense contracts and federal government protection under the War Labor Board enabled unions to make dramatic gains, even in bastions of the open-shop such as textiles. Textile unions broke into some of the industry's most important chains and won 436 contracts over a three-year period covering 100,000 workers. Southern textile workers received eight separate pay increases between 1941 and 1946, increasing their wartime pay in percentage terms more than any other group of mass production workers. Said one union official: "It has been in the last four years a relatively simple matter to organize plants and to get them under contract...there can't be much wrong with a union like that." Unions used their political power to defeat some traditional enemies. Rubber workers helped Albert Rains defeat Joe Starnes in Gadsen in 1944. Textile workers in Rome, Georgia, helped Henderson Lanham defeat Malcolm Tarver in 1946.[17]

World War II's role in stimulating African American expectations has been amply documented. Only recently has attention been given to the war's impact on white southerners. Some white southerners, even in Mississippi, saw the connection between the nation's democratic war aims and the need for a different domestic and international order. Keith Frazier Somerville wrote a fortnightly column in the *Bolivar Commercial* aimed at the Delta county's boys serving in the armed forces. Much of it was devoted to news about their hometown of Cleveland, such as births, deaths, and marriages, and news of their fellow servicemen. In the columns, however, Somerville was at pains to stress the wartime contribution of all the county's ethnic and racial groups, in particular the black participation in the war effort. In Mound Bayou, the all-black community:

> I found America dreaming again. Dreaming of the day her sons will come marching home, dreaming of better housing and hospitalization...dreaming too of absolute fairness. And here in Bolivar County, there are many Southern white men and women, descendants of men and women who for eighty years have had their problems close to their hearts, who are dreaming with them that when our boys of all races, creeds, and color come home again to peaceful years, we may all work together to make our dreams come true.[18]

A white Alabaman who had moved from his farm to work in the Mobile shipyards wrote in a laboriously scrawled pencil letter to his conservative home congressman, that African Americans should have the vote:

> After all we are taking a stand in world affairs as a nation against oppression and it looks to me as though it is high time we as southerners had better take the lead and solve that much-kicked Republican football...it seems that the old tradition of a damn nigger has gone and must be remedied by an enlightened and liberal stand by our own party...I am as you know not what is called a "nigger lover." It is just something that has come out and I think we should do it before it explodes under us.[19]

Service overseas could make the ideological imperatives of the war seem even more powerful to white southerners. David Reynolds in *Rich Relations* has documented with great clarity the way in which service in Britain broke down local and traditional attitudes among GIs. White southerners constituted one-third of the nation's servicemen. Whereas the British and the Canadians determined that their soldiers should not receive privileged treatment in comparison with local civilian populations, the Americans insisted that living conditions should be good enough for the GIs to allay any possible discontent with war service. As a result, many southerners experienced a standard of living in the military that comfortably exceeded the standards they were used to in the Depression. But service abroad posed more fundamental questions. Claude Ramsey, a future Mississippi labor organizer, remembered being stationed outside Rennes where his unit of white southerners adopted a French Moroccan who had got detached from his unit:

> [He] became the favorite of everybody. Everybody really liked him. I got to thinking about it. I said, "This is a hell of a thing. We've got a black man from Morocco, French Morocco, who is the real favorite of a bunch of white guys from the South. I'm just wondering what would happen if this was going on in Mississippi."

Rowan Thomas, from Boyle, a small town near Cleveland in the Delta, wrote a nationally reviewed book describing his service round the world with his air squadron. Poverty in India prompted him to assert:

> Here is another war we have got to win after this war is over: the war against misery and poverty. This world cannot long endure dazzling jewels on the perfumed body of one lady, and only sparkling tears in the eyes of the hungry millions. [The servicemen] felt we were an integral part of a world revolution... Soldiers everywhere agreed that we can no longer exist behind our own walls, that the peoples of the earth are our neighbors, and we must live and work with them in peace and security. [They pronounced] "If we can't help every man, woman, and child to have the simple necessities of life, then we're wasting our time and our lives."[20]

It is not surprising, therefore, that John Stennis, before running against rabid racist John Rankin to succeed Bilbo in the Senate from Mississippi in 1947, should make passionate speeches in favor of the United Nations. He argued that the United States should be prepared to give up some of its national sovereignty to the international organization. In 1948 Frank Smith, his publicity director, joined thirty to forty veterans in the Mississippi legislature and recollected that, "I knew either directly or indirectly that most of them were idealists who hoped to have a part in making a better day." Smith went to Congress in 1950.[21]

Like Smith, Jim Wright in Texas identified the Depression and World War II as the formative influences on his political development. Like many

returning veterans, he was anxious to challenge the old guard on his return from service overseas. At the University of Texas Law School, he reorganized the Young Democrats, who in December 1945 called for anti-lynching legislation, an end to the poll tax, and the admission of black students to the Law School. In 1946 he went to the state legislature in a group of veterans who were determined to change the shape of Texas politics. Stuart Long recalled that legislature:

> As a result, the kids came home with the feeling, "By Golly, we've saved democracy. Now let's make it work at home." I saw this pop out in so many places. Candidates for the legislature in 1946, the ones elected in '46. I think we had 85 or 90 house seats, something like that, who were veterans, and a large number of Senators who were. There was a great injection of youth in Texas, youthful idealism, which is another name for liberalism.[22]

Across the South there were GI revolts in which returning soldiers aimed to overthrow traditional local power structures. Sid McMath came to prominence in one such revolt in Garland County, Arkansas, in 1946. McMath, who was only thirty-four, had won a silver star serving with the marines in the Pacific. Backed by other young veterans he ran for prosecuting attorney against the local boss of the gambling resort of Hot Springs, Leo P. McLaughlin. McMath labeled the boss "his majesty Der Fuehrer of Hot Springs" and placed words from *Mein Kampf* alongside McLaughlin's in campaign advertisements. "The voice," McMath alleged, "was the voice of Leo, but the words are the words of Hitler." In that election McMath organized armed platoons at service stations ready to go anywhere they thought there was likely to be trouble. They cut the telephone wires to the neighboring county so that their opponents there could not find out by how many votes the opposition was behind and therefore how many ballots would have to be stuffed in that county to create a majority.[23]

In Florida, Dante Fascell's political world was also shaped by the New Deal and World War II. As a northern migrant he had fought Klan-type gangs in his Coconut Grove school when he was a small boy. After the war he returned home determined to take a full part in political life. In Miami's version of a GI revolt—Fascell's first political campaign and "the damnedest political fight I have ever seen"—he crusaded for the recall of the corrupt and conservative Miami City Commission. By 1947 he was president of the Miami Junior Chamber of Commerce, the Italian-American Club, and the Young Democrats. He then worked to get his commanding officer elected to the state legislature. Fascell, like Jim Wright, was elected to Congress in 1954. They consciously saw themselves as a new "revolutionary" intake in the House.[24]

However, this new generation of southerners was not to be the force of the future in the South. In the 1950s and 1960s the South seemed increasingly in the grip of conservative, segregationist forces and, when racial change came, it was conservative businessmen and their allies who usually brokered the South's adaptation to new realities. What went wrong for Roosevelt's acolytes? It was clear that many of the factors that paved the way for liberal success were ambiguous in their impact.

A common-man appeal capitalizing on lower-income white resentment of established economic and political forces was not the monopoly of liberal politicians. Such an appeal could also be made by rabid segregationists like Eugene Talmadge and Theodore "The Man" Bilbo, both elected in 1946 pandering to lower-income white suspicion of outside interests and distant government and their competitive hatred of blacks. Similarly, infrastructure politics did not always have a redistributionist social-justice element. Such politics were equally compatible with "business progressive" Whig moves to encourage investment from industries attracted to the region's cheap labor and hostility to unions.[25]

The South's new relative affluence blunted the challenges of the union movement. As southern textile firms sold off company houses to their workers, and their employees pocketed higher wages, so textile workers were increasingly tied into credit commitments both for house repayments and the purchase of consumer goods that they had come to enjoy. They were reluctant to jeopardize these purchases by losing income through strike action. As long as non-union firms matched the wages paid by unionized plants, so workers wondered if strike action to secure a union contract was worthwhile. The optimism of union organizers proved to be false.[26]

The war increased racial tension and violence in the region as much as it opened the minds of southern whites and heightened African American expectations. Whites reacted with alarm to examples of black assertiveness and mobility. The presence of so many northern black troops in military bases near small towns, who were unwilling to comply with the established etiquette of southern race relations, fuelled the fears of local whites and law enforcement officials and stretched to breaking point overcrowded and inadequate recreational facilities and public services. In the shipyards, the presence of black workers aroused white fears of job competition. The result, as James Burran has shown, was an upsurge of lynchings, murders, and assaults, often by local police, followed by retaliatory race riots. The violence continued after the war, aimed at returning black veterans who dared to step out of line.[27]

The political activity of returning white veterans was not always geared to promoting racial change. Jennifer Brooks's definitive study of GI revolts concluded that returning politically active veterans espoused a "definition of progress that was quintessentially a southern white one." Strom Thurmond and Herman Talmadge returned from the war to campaign for progressive reform at the state level. As Talmadge recalled, "When I came along it was after World War II, and I knew the people of Georgia had made up their minds that they wanted to see more progress in state government. So I advocated what my father would've thought was a progressive platform." But Thurmond and Talmadge were equally determined to defend white supremacy, and they appealed to wartime sentiment to do so. Talmadge asserted that the choice in 1946 would "determine whether or not we will fight to preserve our southern traditions and heritage as we fought on ships at sea and as we fought on foreign soil."[28]

It is now commonplace to cite the role of anti-communism in marginalizing Roosevelt's new generation of southerners. Adam Fairclough argued in his study of Louisiana that "the Cold War had produced an ideological chilling effect that made criticism of the social order, so commonplace during the Roosevelt era, unfashionable, un-patriotic and politically dangerous." There is no doubt that the use of the anti-communist issue played a major part in marginalizing and excluding white radicals who openly espoused the end of segregation: the Southern Conference, the Progressive Party, the left-led unions, and radical black allies such as the Civil Rights Congress in Louisiana. No one can doubt the profound impact of social and political ostracism on New Deal liberals like Aubrey Williams, Clifford and Virginia Durr, and Will Alexander. But as Michael Heale's study of McCarthyism in the hinterland shows, opponents of racial change, for example in Georgia, did not need anti-communism to justify violent racial repression in the 1940s. It was later, during Massive Resistance, that southern anti-communism really flourished and stifled dissent. Most of the new generation of issue-oriented liberal politicians were red-baited in the 1940s and with the notable exceptions of Frank Graham and Claude Pepper, they survived.[29]

Like John Egerton and Patricia Sullivan, I believe that the new generation of southern liberal politicians was undone by the race issue. But I believe that these politicians had a somewhat longer shelf-life and were not marginalized by the race issue until the mid- to late 1950s. Even after the *Brown* school desegregation decision of 1954 and the backlash which that provoked, liberals could still get elected in parts of the South. What defeated the southern liberal politicians was, in part, the sheer weight of the white commitment to segregation in the South revealed in Massive Resistance, and also, as I have argued elsewhere at length, the liberals' own fatalism. Roosevelt's new generation was undone by its own commitment to gradualism in racial change and its faith that long-term economic change would gradually erode the institution of white supremacy. As Frank Smith commented, "Large-scale economic progress was the only avenue likely to lead to a solution of the race problem in Mississippi." When African Americans demanded immediate, rather than gradual, change in the 1950s and the Supreme Court mandated desegregation, southern liberals were paralyzed by their conviction that mass white sentiment in the South would not tolerate such imposed, dramatic change. The fatalistic liberals retreated into a resigned silence and left a political vacuum which conservative advocates of Massive Resistance gleefully filled.[30]

Nevertheless, there was life in the Roosevelt legacy even after the 1950s. Elliot Janeway recalled that:

> Ickes told me Roosevelt had said that he was frustrated about that boy, that if he hadn't gone to Harvard, that's the kind of uninhibited young man he'd like to be—that in the next generation the balance of power would shift south and west and this boy could well be the first Southern President.

The southern boy of whom Roosevelt was so enamoured was Lyndon Johnson. FDR's new generation of southerners may have been marginalized by the dynamics of the race issue and often by their own fearful caution, but in the end it was a southern New Dealer who, in the Civil Rights Act of 1964 and Voting Rights Act of 1965, would impose immediate, federally mandated racial change on the South.[31]

5

Southerners Who Refused to Sign the Southern Manifesto

On Monday, March 12, 1956, Georgia's senior senator, Walter F. George, rose in the Senate to read a manifesto blasting the Supreme Court for its decision in the *Brown* school desegregation case. The Manifesto condemned the Court's "unwarranted decision" as a "clear abuse of judicial power" and commended the motives of "those States which have declared the intention to resist forced integration by any lawful means." The signers of the Manifesto pledged "to use all lawful means to bring about a reversal of this decision which is contrary to the Constitution." By this time, white southerners could not avoid confronting the issue of school desegregation. Black plaintiffs were in courts demanding that local school boards comply with the *Brown* decision: southern states were passing a barrage of anti-desegregation statutes to prevent compliance. One of the aims of those initiating and drafting the Manifesto—principally Richard Russell of Georgia and Strom Thurmond and Harry Byrd of Virginia—was to ensure that all white southerners united behind moves to defy the Supreme Court. Richard Russell, the most influential southern senator, lamented that there were five or six southern senators who were prepared to agree with the *Brown* school desegregation decision. Russell and his colleagues aimed to make those waverers publicly proclaim their determination to resist the Supreme Court. If the South could "obtain a unity of action" then that evidence of united resistance would force northern politicians and the Court itself to reconsider imposing desegregation on the South.[1]

For the most part the sponsors of the Manifesto succeeded. Southern moderate or liberal congressmen felt that they had no alternative but to sign, given their perception of the overwhelming popular commitment to segregation. Alabama's Lister Hill, facing a primary challenge from a right-wing, states' rights fanatic apparently signed the Manifesto without even reading it. The most liberal of the Alabama house delegation, Carl Elliott, for whom Franklin Roosevelt was and remains his political god, remembered that there was no way he could survive unless he signed. He had not yet achieved what he wanted to achieve on economic and social issues in Congress. He concluded that he'd "probably make the same decision again."[2]

Others moved reluctantly. In Arkansas Fulbright's staff even prepared a statement explaining why he was not going to sign, but then he decided that he had secured enough changes toning down the document to allow him to sign. Kerr Scott of North Carolina rang his aide Bill Cochrane on the morning the Manifesto was issued asking him to take his name off the document, but it was too late. Little Rock congressman Brooks Hays had refused to sign, but Governor Orval Faubus came to Washington and spent two or three hours at James Trimble's hospital bedside persuading Hays and Trimble, the two most moderate members of the Arkansas delegation, to sign. Faubus convinced them that they needed to do something to "quiet the people down," otherwise the Klan would take over.[3]

Despite this perception of overwhelming segregationist constituency pressure, three southern senators did not sign, as well as twenty-two southern members of the House (one each from Tennessee and Florida, three from North Carolina, and seventeen from Texas). In this paper, I want to try and identify the sources of the nonsigners' racial moderation and to examine their political fate. Did they face electoral retribution or did their careers suggest that there was a political alternative to massive resistance, a road not taken by most southern moderates in the 1950s?

I

In Texas, presidential aspirations, the demands of national party leadership, and a local factional battle for control of the Texas party combined to put Lyndon Johnson and the majority of the state's congressional delegation in the moderate camp.

The drafters of the Manifesto asked neither Johnson nor House speaker Sam Rayburn to sign. They argued that they did not want to compromise LBJ's position as majority leader. As John Stennis, a member with Richard Russell of the subcommittee that originally drafted the document, recalled:

> Well on a personal basis and just Senator to Senator, of course we wanted him [LBJ] to sign it, but at the same time we recognized that he wasn't just a Senator from Texas, he was a leader and he had a different responsibility

in that degree. It wasn't held against him, I'll put it that way, by the
Southerners that he didn't sign it.

Johnson was following a delicate balancing act keeping his power base in
Texas, retaining the support of the southern senators, yet trying to establish
a record on civil rights that might win him northern support for a presidential bid. Whatever personal sympathy Johnson had for poor African Americans, shown in his efforts as Texas National Youth Administration director,
he had largely employed conventional, even extreme, segregationist rhetoric
in order to win and retain his Senate seat. But he managed to convey to
northern liberals that he would not have signed the Manifesto even if it had
been presented to him. The act of not signing impressed some northern liberals as an act of great political courage: Hubert Humphrey remembered the
"many times" LBJ mentioned his refusal to sign.[4]

But Johnson, like his mentor Sam Rayburn, also feared for the unity of
the national Democratic Party in election year. To his mind, the Manifesto
unnecessarily brought to the surface a divisive sectional issue that would gra-
tuitously antagonize northern Democrats. The oratory surrounding the
Manifesto was reported "distasteful" to Johnson who "didn't want national
party unity disturbed by fights over highly controversial issues." Johnson
worked to convince northerners that the Manifesto was largely designed for
home consumption, an effort to reelect Walter George, who was facing a
tough reelection battle against segregationist Herman Talmadge. As George
Reedy explained, "George had become somewhat a hero to many Northerners
and they were willing to go pretty far to do anything that would strengthen
his prospects over Herman Talmadge." So Johnson defused the issue in the
North, yet at the same time, kept the confidence of the southerners. When a
correspondent quoted an alleged Johnson comment dismissing the Manifesto
as a piece for home consumption, Richard Russell angrily retorted in capital
letters "I DO NOT THINK LYNDON JOHNSON MADE ANY SUCH
STATEMENT." Harry Byrd and Russell both endorsed Johnson as a presidential candidate.[5]

Why were so many Texas congressmen prepared to join Johnson and
Rayburn in refusing to sign the Manifesto? A convenient answer, of course,
was that race simply was not as much of an issue in Texas as in other southern states with larger African American populations. The *Beaumont
Enterprise,* whose editor in fact supported the Manifesto, argued:

> There has been less interest on the part of Texas national lawmakers in
> such vehicles of protest as congressional manifestoes than has been the
> case in other areas of the South. This situation is undoubtedly due to the
> fact that many sections of the state have very few Negroes...it is hard to
> get excited about a problem what does not exist on the local level.[6]

But race *was* a major issue in Texas politics in March 1956, at least as much as in Florida, Arkansas, and North Carolina. States' rights was a powerful doctrine reflecting concern about federal control of the Tidelands oil, and about Supreme Court decisions on both segregation and anti-communist state legislation. Governor Shivers intended to "'paramount'" the re-declaration of states' rights as the top political issue in Texas." He regarded interposition as a "basic fundamental right" and secured a referendum on maintaining school segregation that passed comfortably that summer. Senator Price Daniel was deciding whether or not to run for governor to succeed Shivers at the very time he signed the Manifesto. He decided to run and defeated Ralph Yarborough, whom he denounced as the candidate of the National Association for the Advancement of Colored People (NAACP) and of the labor leader, Walter Reuther. Rabid segregationist and anti-communist Martin Dies signed the Manifesto, ran for reelection for the statewide at-large congressional seat and won overwhelmingly.[7]

In the east Texas First District, Wright Patman, populist scourge of bankers and financiers, was opposed from the start in 1956 by a candidate who aimed to "beat him on the segregation question," capitalizing on the fact that allegedly Patman was supported by "99 per cent of the Negro vote... and had refused to take any stand on the segregation issue." Despite his resolute support of all segregation measures, Patman had consistently faced such opposition. Patman signed the Manifesto, released it in advance to newspaper editors in his district, and made a central plank in his speeches, press releases, and campaign literature that he had signed the Manifesto, which had been, he noted, "so severely criticized by communists and fellow-travellers." His opponent nevertheless did not surrender the issue: segregation-related issues constituted the overwhelming bulk of his TV speeches and newsletters. Patman bolstered his staunch defense of segregation and his record on public works, water projects, and industrial development by securing information on his opponent's wild drinking, insurance scams, and faked heart attacks. Patman won comfortably.[8]

The majority of Texan congressmen, however, refused to sign the Manifesto. They were a very disparate group in terms of age, personality, political ideology, and constituency. Some, like Jack Brooks in the Second District and Jim Wright from Fort Worth, represented a new breed of younger liberal politicians who constituted the "new generation" of southerners Franklin Roosevelt had expectantly awaited. The Depression and World War II shaped their philosophy. Wright, like many returning veterans, was anxious to challenge the old guard on his return from service overseas. At the University of Texas Law School, he reorganized the Young Democrats who in December 1945 called for anti-lynching legislation, an end to the poll tax, and the admission of black students to the Law School. In the state legislature, he was in a group of eighty or ninety veterans who were determined to change the shape of Texas politics. As mayor of Mansfield he worked to improve black schools. In 1954 he ran for Congress, challenging the powerful Amon Carter and the *Fort Worth Star Telegram*. In 1956 his father warned him about the "damn NAACP getting out of hand." Such activities would lead to a revival of the Klan, and he reminded his son of the damage done in the 1920s by such appeal to prejudices. Nevertheless, when the Manifesto was issued, Wright believed that both prudential considerations and Christian principles demanded that he not sign: not only was the Supreme Court decision the law of the land but "hatred is evil in the sight of God. The Negro is a child of God, as am I and as are my kinsmen. He possesses an immortal soul, as do we." He applauded resolutions of the Texas Council of Churches and the Canterbury Association in Austin in favor of desegregation.[9]

There were older liberals, like Albert Thomas, who also refused to sign. Thomas prided himself on the projects and developments he brought to Houston, but he was also still proud of his role in the passage of the Fair Labor Standards Act of 1938. But there were a number of less liberal voices. Joe Kilgore had voted for Eisenhower in 1952 but was a new congressman with significant numbers of Hispanic voters in his border constituency. Hispanic voters were also a factor for the anti-radical San Antonio machine politician Paul Kilday. But there were also a number of stalwart conservative senior figures with powerful committee assignments—George Mahon, Omar Burleson, Olin Teague, and Bob Poage—who refused to sign the Manifesto, together with wealthy socialite Clark Thompson. At the far right, was Dallas Republican Bruce Alger. Alger was a prototype of Goldwater Republicanism. A property developer who had exploited Dallas's postwar boom, Alger was a fervent apostle of individualism: he opposed the income tax and social security, and was proud of his claim to be the only congressman to vote against free school milk. Yet Alger was the only southern Republican not to sign the Manifesto. He detested southern Democrats, who were masterminding the Manifesto, as much as he detested socialists. Indeed, he lamented that it was the Democratic Supreme Court in *Brown* that overturned the correct doctrines enunciated by a Republican Supreme Court sixty years earlier. He had also spent much of his early life outside the South, had been educated at Princeton, and claimed to be friendly with Albert Einstein. Despite their ideological differences, it is possible to suggest some common threads among the Texan nonsigners. Unlike those who signed, most of the nonsigners had served overseas in World War II and, between them, they represented all the major urban centers in Texas—Austin, Beaumont, Corpus Christi, Dallas, Fort Worth, Houston, Lubbock, and San Antonio.[10]

But the one indisputable common thread amongst the nonsigners was Sam Rayburn. Of the Texans who signed, Rayburn was friendly only with Patman. Of the others, Walter Rogers was simply not part of his circle, Fisher had long since parted company with the Speaker on most policy issues, and Rayburn despised Dies and Dowdy. The rest of the Texas delegation (with the exception of Republican Bruce Alger) was the most cohesive and powerful in the South; its members were numerous enough to ensure that Texas had one representative on every major committee in which the state had a vital interest, and each member deferred to his representative in those specialist areas. They met for lunch every Wednesday to raise matters of common concern, and they looked to Rayburn both for leadership and protection. In turn, Rayburn looked after their interests: even the most senior Texas congressional figures like Poage, Mahon, Thomas, and Kilday deferred to a man who had been in the House almost a quarter of a century longer than they had. As for the younger representatives, Rayburn took a particular paternal interest in the fortunes of some of them, notably Frank Ikard, Homer Thornberry, and Joe Kilgore. On the issue of the Manifesto, these men would follow Rayburn's lead, whatever their private feelings.[11]

Rayburn himself regretted the *Brown* decision and hoped that Texas could "delay it coming into operation for as long a time as possible," but it was the law of the land. Like Johnson, he did not like divisive sectional issues being raised in such a way that they could not in some way be brokered into compromise within the Democratic Party. The Manifesto made such compromise difficult. In any case, he believed that "any congressman worth his salt can lead his district" and thus encouraged his fellow Texans to avoid signing the Manifesto.[12]

Rayburn's stand is also intimately wrapped up in the fight for control of the Texas party in 1956 which was in turn inextricably linked to the race issue. Rayburn claimed not to "have hated anybody," but he grudgingly admitted that "there are a couple of shitasses I loathe." Richard Nixon was one, Bruce Alger another, but he reserved special venom for Governor Allan Shivers. The hatred was mutual. On Shivers's side it dated back to his disappointment that Rayburn had not delivered more from Congress or president on Tidelands oil. On Rayburn's part, it dated back to what he believed was his betrayal by Shivers over the 1952 presidential campaign. Rayburn was determined that in 1956 the Texas party would not be led by those who supported Eisenhower in 1952 and who clearly intended to back the general again. He forced Lyndon Johnson to mobilize the "loyalist" forces to fight at the precinct and district conventions to take control of the State Democratic Executive Committee and to control the delegation to the National Convention. Rayburn was making the first steps in this campaign as the Manifesto was drafted. The fight between the "loyalists" and the Shivers forces was firmly drawn on the race issue. The nonsigners were the forces of moderation; the Shivers faction was the faction of interposition and massive resistance. George Reedy complained that Shivers "played on the emotions of race hatred, anti-northern hatred and any other hatred that were available." No attack got under Rayburn's skin more than Shivers's jibe that LBJ's speech on great Texans "From Sam Houston to Sam Rayburn" should be reworded "From Santa Anna to Sam Rayburn." The Texas congressmen loyal to Rayburn were drafted in to campaign in their districts. The Johnson-Rayburn forces, consciously claiming the moderate ground against the extremists, routed the opposition.[13]

Some of the nonsigners, nevertheless, heard from their constituents. Mississippi segregationist John Bell Williams made a favorable reference to the "splendid" local Fort Worth congressman at a meeting of the Tarrant County Citizens' Council on March 16. The audience greeted this reference to Jim Wright with "thunderous boos." Disappointed by Wright's failure to sign, a Cleburne couple expected him to tell them where he also stood on "the *infamous* United Nations, the States of the Forces treaty, the Bricker amendment and the so-called Alaska Mental Health bill." A Fort Worth evangelist was certain that Wright did not want "your daughter to attend school where every ninth child had syphilis or gonorrhea." A write-in candidate materialized against Wright in the primary. Bob Poage faced no opposition but had to defend himself against those who expected him to sign. He argued that segregated schools could best be kept by keeping quiet about the issue: the confrontations in Alabama showed the wisdom of not "hollering and shouting" on the issue. Jack Brooks wrote in August that he had just endured a "rough campaign... about the manifesto. In fact, it was the meanest, most vicious that I was ever in." Bruce Alger in the general election campaign found that his Democratic opponent, Dallas district attorney Henry Wade, hammered away at Alger's failure to sign.[14]

Nonetheless, all these incumbents survived. Wright has forgotten about his write-in opponent, Brooks defeated the son of his congressional predecessor by a 2-to-1 margin, and Alger saw the Democratic challenge off comfortably. Poage in retrospect noted "I don't recall hearing as much complaint as some other people say we heard at that time. I doubt that the district approved of it [the *Brown* decision], but neither did I think that our district was getting up in arms about it."[15]

Race was a vital issue in Texas politics in 1956 and Texans as a whole endorsed segregation and elected segregationist state officials. Yet they also reelected those who did not sign the Southern Manifesto. National and local imperatives drove the majority of Texas congressmen safely to ignore segregationist constituency sentiment.

II

In Tennessee a similar mix of national presidential ambitions and state leadership shaped the parameters within which leading politicians could afford not to sign the Southern Manifesto. The Manifesto was issued in the midst of Estes Kefauver's battle in the Democratic primaries for the 1956 presidential nomination. As a southerner chasing national office, he had little choice but to denounce the Manifesto. The drafters did not even bother to ask him to sign it. He reiterated his 1954 stand that the *Brown* decision was the law of the land and had to be obeyed. He regarded as pure deceit "any attempt to lead the people into believing Congress could change the court's ruling." "People of goodwill" should be left to seek solutions at the local level. The federal government had an obligation to help much more vigorously to facilitate such solutions. He also saw the issue in an international dimension in the cold war: "people all over the world with skin that is not white are restive."[16]

Albert Gore had a different power base in Tennessee to Kefauver: he was widely regarded as a more down-to-earth politician and he was well regarded by his fellow southern senators. But he shared Kefauver's economic liberalism: his hostility to big business, his championing of public power, and his support of progressive taxation. Gore also had national ambitions. He was hankering after the vice presidential nomination in 1956, as was the governor of Tennessee, Frank Clement. It was said in Tennessee that year, "in America it is possible for any man to run for president. In Tennessee they all are." Gore had been rather less emphatic than Kefauver in his endorsement of the *Brown* decision: it was the law of the land, but he stressed that the decision was fortunately not for immediate implementation and that it had been taken out of the hands of Congress. He was at pains to point out to constituents that these views did not mean that he agreed with the decision. Gore now recalls that he was always "upfront" on the race issue. He dates his awareness of the moral dimension of civil rights to his first trip from his constituency to Washington in 1937. On the long drive he could find no restrooms that the black nanny, who was looking after their baby, could use. That first trip he had to make a long detour to his cousin's house in the mountains to stay the night. Subsequently, he made an arrangement with a motel in eastern Tennessee. The family and the nanny could stay, provided they arrived after dark and left before the other guests in the morning.[17]

Gore regarded the Manifesto as "the most spurious, inane, insulting document of a political nature claiming to be legally founded I had ever seen." It represented an act of secession. It was "utterly incomprehensible and unsupportable." Thurmond invited Gore to sign it on the floor of the Senate, waving the sheet with all the southern signatures in front of him and jabbing him in the chest. After Gore replied, "Hell, no," he looked up to see that all the southern pressmen, obviously primed in advance, were in the gallery. In Tennessee he soon heard from chapters of the Federation for Constitutional Government. As his wife's old classmate, Sims Crownover, threatened him, Gore faced "almost certain defeat in 1958." Crownover repeated a familiar theme: voters expected Kefauver not to sign. One correspondent claimed, Kefauver "has made it quite clear from the outset that he would sell the entire South to the NAACP in return for a few votes" but, Crownover said they felt Gore had "actually betrayed the South because people felt that you were on their side."[18]

Gore received plenty of mail to weigh against the segregationist protests. A month after the Manifesto was issued, he claimed that mail on the subject had almost stopped. The race issue had been used against Kefauver in the 1954 Tennessee primary and would be again in 1960. Gore's opponent in 1958, Prentice Cooper, specifically campaigned on the issue of the Manifesto and waved a copy of the Declaration at every opportunity on the stump. But both Gore and Kefauver successfully fought off such well-financed challengers, and Gore later claimed that in Tennessee the race issue was not as divisive as the Vietnam War when people would cross the street rather than shake hands with him. Veteran Nashville congressman and staunch Baptist Percy Priest also had little trouble gaining reelection after not signing the Manifesto. Two Tennessee congressmen who did sign, Ross Bass and Joe Evins, went out of their way to claim that the Manifesto was meaningless.[19]

The path of racial moderation was easier in Tennessee than in some southern states: a greater percentage of voting-age blacks were registered, organized labor was a force to be counted, the Tennessee Valley Authority had a liberalizing impact, and there were newspapers who supported compliance with the Supreme Court. But in these respects Tennessee was not so very different from North Carolina and Arkansas at least. What distinguished Tennessee was that both senators and the governor chose to seek public support for compliance with the law of the land. In such circumstances when the three leading politicians ("you and coon-skin and pretty-boy" in the words of one of Gore's less friendly constituents), despite their rivalry, set the terms of the political debate in a particular way, racial moderation had a chance of success.[20]

III

In Florida Spessard Holland had sufficient doubts about the Manifesto to work with Fulbright and Price Daniel to tone it down, but he eventually signed and George Smathers as a matter of reflex followed suit. Several Florida congressmen were reported to be reluctant to sign, but rabid segregationist Bob Sikes removed their doubts.[21]

Dante Fascell from Miami was unmoved by this pressure. Like Jim Wright and Frank Smith, Fascell's political world was shaped by the New Deal and World War II and after the war he returned home determined to take a full part in political life. As a northern migrant with boyhood experience of Klan-type groups in school, Fascell always reacted to Klan-style bullying. Anticipating the *Brown* decision, he addressed public meetings in Dade County with the principal of the black high school urging the community to take steps to prepare for change. As a candidate for Congress he sought black support through traditional means—surreptitiously through local black ministers and with the help of a former sheriff and current state senator, who had originally thought Fascell could not win because he was too short, the wrong race and voters could not pronounce his name. But he also became the first candidate in Miami to seek black support "in daylight" taking his three-piece band into black neighborhoods and actively canvassing the black community. He announced that he considered the Manifesto a "piece of chest-thumping"—he was one of the few nonsigners immediately to issue a statement explaining his decision, a feisty unapologetic statement remorselessly demonstrating the futility of the Declaration. The reaction was strong from his constituents: "Man," he recalled, "that was like jumping off the Brooklyn Bridge at high noon. I took my life in my hands." But he survived: he already knew that the filing date had passed and that he would face no opposition in the Democratic primary.[22]

IV

The evidence from Texas, Tennessee, and Florida suggests that there might have been more room for maneuver than southern moderates were prepared to credit. The evidence from North Carolina is more ambiguous. First, it highlights what an idiosyncratic and personal matter taking a moderate stand on racial matters was. Second, the fate of the congressmen who did not sign suggests that the political perils were not imaginary.

There was considerable unease in the North Carolina congressional delegation about signing the Manifesto. At first, only Herbert Bonner and Graham Barden from the rural East signed. In the end, however, only three congressmen refused to sign. All faced immediate primary battles for reelection in which their failure to sign was a salient issue. Two of the three were defeated.[23] It is difficult to imagine three more disparate congressmen than

Charles Deane, Harold Cooley, and Thurmond Chatham and three more diverse routes to racial moderation.

Harold Cooley had not entirely lost the vestiges of liberalism which saw him elected to the House as a New Dealer in 1934. As chairman of the House Agriculture Committee, he saw himself as part of the national Democratic leadership; he had to work with northern and western representatives of other farm commodities to ensure favorable treatment for tobacco; and he may have had thoughts of his own of the vice presidential nomination in 1956. Not lacking in the sense of his own importance, Cooley resented being presented with the Manifesto by the senators as a sort of *fait accompli*, when House members had been kept out of the discussions that led to its drafting.[24]

Thurmond Chatham was the millionaire chairman of the board of directors of the family Chatham mills. In the 1930s he was a Roosevelt-hating member of the Liberty League. In 1940 he supported Republican Wendell Willkie. Elected to Congress on an anti-union platform in 1948, he remained firmly opposed to unionization, particularly of his own mill, and he opposed raising the minimum wage. As a student at Yale, however, in 1916 he had sat next to a black student in two of his classes and become friendly with him; in the navy in World War II he had seen desegregation in operation; on the House Foreign Affairs committee he had become friendly with younger liberals, Abraham Ribicoff and Lloyd Bentsen. His support for national Democrats on foreign policy began to spill over into the domestic field. He favored recognition of Red China. When the Supreme Court decision came in 1954 he said he had been expecting it, he was confident that the South would take it in its stride, and he was pleased that the decision was out of the way. America would be able to turn its attention to "the greater problems which face us in the international sphere."[25]

By contrast, Charles B. Deane was an unequivocal liberal on domestic economic and social affairs. He had been elected in 1946 with the backing of the textile and railroad unions in his Eighth District. He could be relied on by both the national Democratic leadership and by national union leaders. He was also a staunch Baptist and former secretary of the state Baptist Convention.[26]

Both Deane's religion and his economic liberalism led him to a liberal stand on civil rights. But there was another compelling impetus. Deane had become a member of Moral ReArmament (MRA), the movement for moral uplift known earlier as the Oxford Movement and led by Frank Buchman. In 1951 Deane had been to one of MRA's plays in Washington. As he told a former congressman, the consequences were startling, "revolutionary things have taken place in our family...I saw myself as I really was, wrapped up in a cloud of self-righteousness going round with a mask and there were a good many iron curtains within the family circle." His daughter sacrificed a legacy that was to pay her way through college, gave it to MRA, went to work for MRA full time and went round the world as part of the integrated cast of "The Vanishing Island," a musical in rhyming verse written by Peter Howard. Deane himself accompanied the play part of the time.[27]

The message MRA put across was one of absolute personal standards: absolute honesty, absolute purity, absolute unselfishness, absolute love. People imbued with these standards could resolve all the conflicts in society either in the international sphere, in labor relations, or in racial matters.[28]

MRA was wholeheartedly anti-communist, but it was convinced that military spending could not contain communism, especially in the Third World. Rather, as Deane himself passionately believed, Americans needed to win the battle for hearts and minds. The battle could not be won by the picture of American capitalism as "half-dressed women, debased youth, effeminate heroes, gangsters and cowboys." It could not be won by "Big talk coupled with low living." Victory needed young people "as thoroughly trained and disciplined in living the ideology of freedom" as the communists and "honest about the places where change will come if the faith of our fathers is to be fulfilled."[29]

Race relations was one of the areas where change would have to come. Deane's religious and political concern for the dispossessed reinforced his conviction that racial change at home was essential if America was to have success overseas. This conviction was strengthened by an MRA visit to Kenya where he visited the prison camps for the Mau Mau fighting the British. He was acutely conscious of the potential black hatred for the white race.[30]

In the primaries that followed it is difficult to disentangle the race issue from other local issues. But the issue was unambiguously joined in Charles Deane's case. Deane had not faced serious opposition in 1952 and 1954. No opponent filed against him in 1956 until he failed to sign the Manifesto. Two days later a local school superintendent told him "it is clear to a number of people that if any average candidate ran against you, you would not be able to secure 30 per cent of the votes in your district at the present time." Then a retired FBI agent and law partner of a former lieutenant-governor announced against Deane. The first two items in all Paul Kitchen's literature were that the candidate would have signed the Manifesto and that he opposed race mixing. Deane's daughter was smeared by the distribution of a cropped photograph showing her at an MRA camp next to two blacks. Blacks were paid to ring up white voters and ask them to support Deane. A textile union leader sadly reported that his members would no longer support the congressman. As a result a congressman who had had powerful support in his district and had assiduously catered to his constituents' patronage and pork-barrel needs found himself comfortably beaten. He lost all the counties bordering on the South Carolina black belt with the highest percentage of blacks in their population. He even lost his home county of Richmond by a 3-to-1 vote, with the opposition forces, including black voters, marshalled by the local sheriff.[31]

In the case of Chatham and Cooley the evidence is more mixed. The first letter Chatham received after refusing to sign the Manifesto told the congressman, "you express yourself like a Damn Yankee. If you like the Negro you can have him but I think you are a dead duck." Two days after not signing the Manifesto, Chatham was told "your not signing, along with the rest of the Southern congressmen in opposition of [*sic*] desegregation (mongrelizing) will I'm sure place you in favor with senator [*sic*] Hubert Humphrey and his Negro worshippers." The North Carolina Patriots targeted Chatham for special opposition with particular success in two counties in his district.[32]

Cooley had no opposition until he refused to sign the Declaration. Then he was opposed by local broadcaster Waldemar Eros Debnam, who had written the popular racist tract *Then My Old Kentucky Home, Good Night*. Debnam labeled Cooley the NAACP candidate. Debnam claims he resisted attempts to buy his candidacy off. "I regarded the Manifesto as a recall issue and it was my intention to play the fact that Cooley had attacked the document to the hilt, letting the people draw their own conclusions...I made it plain that I regard this segregation business as of tremendous importance to our people and the duty of every man to stand up and fight by every legal means forced racial integration."[33]

But there were local and personal factors in the elections as well. Chatham had faced surprisingly stiff opposition in 1952 and 1954 from political unknowns who had capitalized on his absentee record in Congress. In 1956, irrespective of the Manifesto, he was going to face opposition from a substantial local politician, a county solicitor who represented part of the constituency that felt that it had been overlooked historically in terms of congressional representation. Chatham's opponent stressed his absenteeism, his foreign trips, and his earlier support of Republican candidates. There was also a whispering campaign about Chatham's alcoholism (and, indeed, Chatham died of cirrhosis of the liver in 1957).[34]

Cooley had long since ceased to keep his political fences mended, and he too enjoyed foreign junkets. He was attacked as the "globe-trotting gadfly." Voters were told "the district needs a full time congressman." There were even deeper personal factors. The first person to denounce Cooley for not signing the Manifesto, and to consider running himself, was Pou Bailey, the man who later persuaded Jesse Helms to run for the Senate. Bailey's cousin was the man Cooley defeated to get into Congress twenty-two years earlier:

Bailey's uncle had defeated Cooley's father for the same congressional seat in 1916.[35]

Chatham remained unapologetic for his refusal to sign the Manifesto. He ran best in high-income wards and in black wards in Winston-Salem, an early forerunner of the cross-class, biracial alliance that would play an important part in southern politics in the 1960s. Cooley won—but he race-baited the race-baiter to do so. He started off the campaign by stressing the false hopes that the Manifesto aroused and the fact that as a lawyer he could not attack the Court in the language of the Manifesto. While he still asserted that he was proud of his decision not to sign, by the end of the campaign he was proclaiming that he hated and despised the *Brown* decision. Then he counterattacked by accusing Debnam of advocating desegregation of public transport and for having eaten a meal with the NAACP's Roy Wilkins in Wilkins's home in New York City. His opponent, said Cooley, had said, "let the Negro eat where he pleases, sit where he pleases and sleep where he pleases. This is exactly what Debnam's friend Roy Wilkins has been advocating for years." Flanked by Senator Sam Ervin, Cooley flooded the district with his segregationist propaganda and overwhelmed Debnam by a 2-to-1 margin.[36]

V

The wide diversity of political opinion among the nonsigners—from New Deal liberal to Democratic Party stalwart to right-wing ideologue—highlights the personal and fragmented nature of the forces of southern racial moderation in the 1950s. A variety of factors led to their decision not to bow to segregationist pressure in 1956: experience in World War, national political ambitions, concerns for party unity, cold war fears, religious belief, an urban political base. But all these factors were also compatible with the defense of white supremacy.

Did their experience suggest there was an alternative to defiance, a road not taken by most of their moderate and liberal colleagues in the South in the mid-1950s? None of these politicians came from the Deep South, black majority districts. A historian second-guesses a Frank Smith, a Hale Boggs, or a Carl Elliott at his peril. In the absence of detailed public opinion polls, a historian needs to be careful about confident assertions about what their constituents might have tolerated in the 1950s. The fate, outside the Deep South, of Chatham and Deane in their primary elections is, in any case, enough to give the presumptuous historian pause. It is important, however, to note that conservatives at the time were much less confident than their moderate protagonists that public opinion was overwhelmingly in the massive resistance camp. The irony was that conservatives and liberals both believed that public opinion was on the other side. Most moderates believed that whites were so stirred up on the race issues that they had no alternative but to retreat and become "closet moderates." Conservatives such as the drafters of the Southern Manifesto, by contrast, believed that public opinion was insufficiently aroused on the race issue, that white southerners were entirely too likely to accept the inevitability of compliance with the Supreme Court decision. The difference was that the conservatives were prepared to use instruments like the Manifesto as part of a righteous crusade to change public opinion, to convince white southerners that desegregation was not inevitable, that white supremacy could be protected. Most southern moderates were not prepared to take their case to the people.

Did congressional moderates have to be so supine? The case of the nonsigners does suggest that there might have been some room for maneuver. In both Texas and Tennessee significant elements of the state political leadership defined the parameters for debate in such a way that racial moderates enjoyed a measure of protection from electoral retribution. It is difficult to believe that that alternative was not available in Arkansas, Florida, and Virginia. Mississippi, South Carolina, and Louisiana may not have offered such scope. (Even there, Frank Smith has suggested that he always hoped that an agreement among political and business leaders for a united stand in favor of compliance with the Court could have carried the day against segregationist demagogues.)[37] But surely Alabama offered the possibility of a compliance alternative: a state where the governor and both senators were economic liberals and racial moderates and which boasted the most liberal House delegation in the South. Instead, personal incompetence on the part of the governor and personal caution on the part of the congressional politicians paved the way for a segregationist triumph.

But if there was a road not taken in the South in the mid-1950s what direction was the road going in?

If most of the nonsigners recognized that the *Brown* decision was inevitable, that it was the law of the land, and outright defiance was futile, few of them were in any hurry to give up the privileges of segregation and, like other moderates, they feared the power of white public segregationist opinion. They were therefore gradualists, like the moderates who signed the Manifesto, like the Eisenhower administration, like the Court, and indeed, as Walter Jackson has shown, like most northern white liberals.[38] They all feared an aroused white citizenry. What Lyndon Johnson, Estes Kefauver, Albert Gore, Jim Wright, and Charles Deane objected to in the Manifesto was the fact that it stirred up that white sentiment and created the false hope that the court could be defied. What they wanted instead was token compliance, to leave the matter to local men and women of goodwill of both races.

Their strategy begged the question of what would happen if these local men and women of goodwill would not agree to compliance, since these moderates also set their face firmly against what they called "forced integration." They seemed to believe that if no one stirred up the issue, segregation would slip in without arousing mass white outrage. Indeed, for someone like Bob Poage, the reasoning seemed to be that if no one stirred up the issue, segregated schools could continue indefinitely. This stealth-like approach, and the repeated calls for a "cooling off period," was one reason why they denounced the NAACP as extremists, because NAACP action inevitably brought the issue to center stage. The southern moderate politicians had a vivid sense of the opinions of their white constituents, but they had no equal sense of the opinions of southern African Americans. Even those moderates who courted black support mostly did so at a distance, relying on black leaders and intermediaries to deliver the black vote, rather than coming face to face with black voters. Those black leaders were often, as Numan Bartley has described them, "racial diplomats" who told the white politicians what they wanted to hear.[39] It was not surprising that Albert Gore, Jim Wright, and Dante Fascell could refuse to sign the Southern Manifesto, vote for the 1957 Civil Rights Act, but vote against the 1964 Civil Rights Act.

The gradualist strategy espoused by the nonsigners of the Manifesto might have spared the South some of the bitter racial turmoil of the late 1950s and early 1960s. But the strategy they advocated contained a considerable amount of wishful thinking. It was almost a strategy based on *not* campaigning to persuade ordinary white southerners of the merits of gradualism. It was not a strategy likely to succeed in the face of conservative segregationists who were determined to take their case to the people, to mount a righteous crusade to convince white southerners that the Supreme Court could be defied.

6

The White Reaction to *Brown*

ARKANSAS, THE SOUTHERN MANIFESTO,
AND MASSIVE RESISTANCE

When the Supreme Court handed down the *Brown* decision, knocking out the constitutional basis for segregated education, the justices were under no illusions about the enormity of the change they were asking of the South. The southern judges, notably Hugo Black, left their colleagues in no doubt as to the extent and pervasiveness of the white South's commitment to segregation. Black conjured up apocalyptic visions of blood in the streets and predicted the destruction of the forces of southern liberalism.[1]

That perception on the part of the Court of mass white segregationist sentiment in the region underpinned its decree in May 1955 laying down how *Brown* was to be implemented, how school desegregation was to be accomplished. The Court placed its faith in local community initiatives, monitored by local federal district judges. To avoid stirring up angry white popular resistance through immediate change imposed from outside, the Court placed its confidence in moderate, law-abiding leaders across the region who would be given the opportunity to lead their communities into voluntary and gradual compliance with the law of the land.[2]

Arkansas appeared to be just the sort of southern state to justify the Court's optimism. It boasted two of the leading practitioners of biracial politics in the region. Governors Sid McMath and Orval Faubus had combined liberal economic policies aimed at lower-income whites and blacks with the active solicitation of support from the steadily increasing black electorate. They had fought for increased appropriations for African American institutions, appointed African Americans to both state and Democratic Party positions, and had taken public stands against both lynching and the poll tax. In 1948, 1950, and 1954 they had defeated segregationist opponents—in contrast to those southern states where race-baiting had already eliminated liberal politicians. McMath attributed neither of his defeats—for reelection as governor in 1952 and for the Senate against John McClellan in 1954—to the race issue. He considered McCarthyism and the role of labor unions to be more important.[3]

In Washington, the state was represented by three of the most liberal southerners in Congress—Brooks Hays, James Trimble, and the fervent internationalist J. William Fulbright. Together with Harry Ashmore, editor of the leading newspaper in the state, the *Arkansas Gazette,* they had actually attempted in the years before *Brown* to establish the ground rules for a regional compromise on race, which they called the Arkansas Plan. According to this plan the South would make good its commitment to gradual racial change by eliminating lynching, removing the obstacles to full political participation by African Americans, and striving for genuine equality in the provision of black education. In return, the national government would be patient and back off counterproductive demands for immediate desegregation. To a certain extent, the administrations of McMath and Faubus had indeed been taking the steps to meet Arkansas's part of such a regional bargain. Even before *Brown,* the University of Arkansas had integrated both its medical and law schools.[4]

What went wrong? How did Arkansas become the southern state that resisted school desegregation so violently that federal troops were sent in to enforce Court orders and impose school desegregation, precisely the outcome that Arkansas moderates, the president, and the Supreme Court itself so fervently hoped to avoid?

Little Rock white leaders at the time were both bewildered and surprised by the outcome. How had it happened here? as school superintendent Virgil Blossom put it. How could a city that was enjoying unprecedented economic growth, had quietly desegregated its buses, parks, and hospitals, and had received national acclaim for its own voluntary school desegregation plan become a symbol of massive resistance, the subject of national and international opprobrium?[5]

From the start, Little Rock leaders blamed outsiders—whites from outside Little Rock—for their troubles. But the most convenient scapegoat, who offered the Little Rock leaders the easiest way of absolving themselves of responsibility, was Governor Faubus, who, the leaders argued, undermined their own responsible position by stirring up the forces of mass popular resentment. In 1990 Sid McMath laid out this position bluntly in an interview with John Egerton:

> You know custom dies hard. But there were people, intelligent people
> and educated people, and people in positions of leadership, that knew it

[desegregation] was inevitable. The *Brown* decisions, you know, and that it's just a matter of time.... You know Virgil Blossom had this plan which he had taken to all the civic clubs and the labor organizations and various groups in Little Rock, and had their approval. It was an integration, but people were willing to accept, you know, people are law-abiding. They were willing to accept it as the law of the land. They didn't like it. 'Course, they would welcome an alternative, and Faubus gave it to them. The Virgil Blossom plan, if Faubus had stayed out of it, would have gone in and worked...if they'd had proper leadership at the time the Central High School thing never would have happened.[6]

It is not my concern at this point to argue how partial and self-serving this statement was. What I want to look at is the reaction to the *Brown* decision in white Arkansas up to the Southern Manifesto of March 1956, when the entire congressional delegation, liberals and conservatives, signed that blast of defiance at the Supreme Court and pledged to resist the *Brown* decision. What I want to argue is that there was no reason to be surprised by the Little Rock crisis in 1957: the political dynamics of the race issue, which inhibited an effective policy of compliance with desegregation, were already in place by March 1956. Specifically, I will argue (1) that Faubus was convinced by the events of early 1956 that it was political suicide to defy mass white segregationist sentiment; (2) that Faubus himself helped create that segregationist sentiment, which he later claimed to be the prisoner of in 1957; and (3) that racially moderate politicians at the national level had already displayed the fatalism and caution that rendered them ineffective when the crisis developed in Little Rock in 1957–58.

In March 1956 Sam Harris argued in the *Arkansas Gazette* that the state had, until recently, been fulfilling the hopes that moderate, responsible leaders would maintain a "balanced stand" on integration. He said that "despite the best efforts of extremists in the integration versus segregation argument" the volatile subject had not become an important item in the political field until a few weeks before.[7]

Up to the end of 1955, Arkansas did indeed look as if it were moving responsibly in the way the Supreme Court hoped. In 1954 conservative governor Cherry announced simply that the law would be obeyed. By 1955 three of the state's school districts had desegregated; the university town of Fayetteville in northwestern Arkansas claimed to be the first community in the South to announce its intention of desegregating its schools, and desegregation followed peacefully in September 1954 under the leadership of Superintendent Virgil T. Blossom, who moved soon thereafter to Little Rock as superintendent of the Little Rock School District. The Charleston School District, also in the west, had in fact opened its schools on an integrated basis the month before Fayetteville. Both school districts had very small black populations and the costs of busing blacks to all-black high schools were crippling. In northeastern Arkansas, Hoxie followed suit in 1955. The Little Rock school board announced its intention in 1954 of desegregating in the fall of 1957. Governor Faubus, perceived as a racial moderate, showed little desire to interfere in the decisions of these local school boards.[8]

The state legislature in 1955 failed to pass a pupil assignment law, which would have circumvented the *Brown* decision. Segregationist pressure groups like the White Citizens' Councils of Arkansas and White America, Inc., lacked, as historian Neil McMillen has shown, both the popular support and the elite leadership that characterized groups in states like Mississippi and Alabama. They campaigned against desegregation in Hoxie, but they failed in the face of determined Court opposition and the refusal of Faubus to intervene.[9]

This picture of moderation has to be qualified. Undoubtedly most white Arkansans favored the continuation of segregation, if possible. Even those who now believed segregation to be wrong were in no hurry to give up the privileges that the system brought to whites. Some had undoubtedly come to the conclusion that segregation was wrong from a Christian and moral point of view, but such decisions were often uncertain and individual. State and regional church groups were more likely than local congregations to make such decisions public. More whites, including church people, put a premium on obedience to the law. Neither of these stances was going to produce a campaign or crusade for compliance with school desegregation. The *New York Times* surveying Arkansas identified the Arkansas Council on Human Relations, the churches, and lawyers as groups advocating compliance. But, the *Times* noted, "for the most part they speak softly."[10]

In eastern Arkansas in the areas of large black populations, the commitment to segregation was very different. In Hughes the school board had built two new black schools. "I would never let my two daughters," said one resident, "attend a school with two Negroes to one white. It will not work." Said the mayor, "There's just not going to be any nigger kids going to white schools here. They've got to come a long way first. We wouldn't be building these two nigger schools if we were going to integrate." "It will be twenty-five years before widespread integration is undertaken in southern Arkansas," predicted the state commissioner of education.[11]

In eastern Arkansas segregation functioned as a source of labor control for Arkansas planters. It was also a source of negative stereotypes, for it was difficult for east Arkansas planters to view as equals a dependent and subordinate group whom they saw performing nothing but menial jobs. Finally, segregation functioned to ameliorate fears: what, whites worried endlessly, would African Americans do if they were not under the strict control of segregation?[12]

It was here in eastern Arkansas in early 1956 that white supremacy pressure groups appeared to be whipping up segregationist passion. In Hoxie, Little Rock attorney Amis Guthridge, a former opponent of Brooks Hays, and state senator James D. Johnson combined as attorneys for the Hoxie Citizens' Council. They then launched a campaign to secure enough petitions to put an interposition amendment on the ballot. A rally at England, on the edge of the delta, on February 24 drew an audience of two thousand. They heard Guthridge call for three hundred thousand signatures for the interposition amendment, which, according to Johnson, would nullify the "illegal action" of the Supreme Court. Roy Harris reported on the steps Georgia was taking to avoid compliance.[13]

At the end of the England rally, former governor and Dixiecrat Ben Laney warned: "We have had some sanctimonious politicians in Arkansas who couldn't open their mouths on this issue before. After a few more meetings like this, they will reconsider." Jim Johnson was clearly planning to challenge Faubus, and there was speculation that Laney might challenge J. William Fulbright for his Senate seat. Faubus, for one, adjusted his position accordingly. In January he reported that "85 per cent of all the people in the state are opposed to integration of the races at the present time. I cannot be a party to any attempt to force acceptance of a change to which the people are so overwhelmingly opposed."[14]

Faubus also sent a committee of legislators with the chairman of the state Board of Education Marvin Byrd to Virginia to examine Virginia's massive resistance tactics. All the lawmakers were from eastern Arkansas; four had attended the England Citizens' Council rally. On their return, they reported that an emergency existed in Arkansas. Faubus endorsed their findings in favor of an interposition resolution in the state legislature (as distinct from a constitutional amendment) and a pupil placement law. While he left open the question of whether a special session of the legislature would be needed and still expressed faith in local efforts as the best way to handle the issue, the governor made it clear that he was "ready to resist all efforts to completely integrate Arkansas's public schools." Thus, Faubus moved to break Jim Johnson's monopoly on segregationist sentiments.[15]

What was happening in eastern Arkansas was not happening in a vacuum. Whites across the region in 1954 and 1955 might content themselves that school desegregation might never happen—that intimidation of black plaintiffs and decisions of local white judges might delay integration indefinitely. But by early 1956 it was clear that determined black plaintiffs would eventually get to court and some school boards would comply. Whites in the

Deep South flocked to join the Citizens' Council. At the same time African Americans stepped up their activism: in Alabama, Montgomery blacks boycotted the buses and Autherine Lucy attempted to enter the state university; in Arkansas, the NAACP, impatient at the timetable allowed in the Blossom Plan, attempted to secure the admission of black schoolchildren at Little Rock Central High School on January 22, 1956, and, failing in this effort, filed suit in the federal district court in Little Rock on February 7.[16]

It was against this background that the document known as the Southern Manifesto pledged its signers from the U.S. Congress to "use all lawful means to bring about a reversal of this decision [*Brown*] which is contrary to the Constitution and to prevent the use of force in its implementation." The drafters of the manifesto were not marginal men but the most senior southern senators. They aimed above all to persuade white southerners that school desegregation could be prevented, for they were concerned that white southerners were too fatalistic on the race issue; they believed that if doubtful southerners could be convinced that the Supreme Court could be defied, then the North might be persuaded to go slow on the enforcement of desegregation.[17]

When the manifesto was proposed in February 1956, the majority of Arkansas congressmen welcomed the opportunity to reemphasize their segregationist credentials. Conservative senator John McClellan had already joined Representative Howard Smith and Senator Willis Robertson of Virginia in sponsoring legislation to restrict the appellate powers of the Supreme Court and to protect explicitly the right of states to operate segregated schools. Congressman E. C. "Took" Gathings from the Arkansas delta had recently demanded a congressional investigation of communist influence in the NAACP, using the information on its officers and board members supplied by the House Un-American Activities Committee.[18]

Congressman William Norrell, whose district included England, Arkansas, was virtually incapacitated. Facing a tough reelection battle in 1956 but unable to return to his district to campaign, he was later advised to publicize his signing of the manifesto to bolster support in his constituency. Oren Harris in southern Arkansas was a political ally of McClellan and Ben Laney and had not been averse to using the race issue against challengers for his seat. He was the Arkansas representative on the committee chaired by William Colmer of Mississippi, which served to coordinate southern congressional resistance to civil rights legislation. In this role, Harris actually circulated the manifesto to his fellow Arkansas congressmen for their signatures.[19]

Wilbur Mills, as second-ranking Democrat on the Ways and Means Committee, was a close ally of Speaker Sam Rayburn, who, like Lyndon Johnson, saw the manifesto as a gratuitous airing of an emotional sectional issue that was bound to divide the national Democratic Party and could not be brokered by the usual compromises. Mills also had the national leadership aspirations that prompted some other southerners to eschew the manifesto's extreme rhetoric. But Mills kept closely in touch with political developments in Hoxie and was in no doubt about the strength of segregationist sentiment in his district. He was also a close ally of Faubus. On this issue, unlike most controversial issues, he did not consult Rayburn:

> But I had to sign it, I felt like. I didn't talk to Mr. Rayburn about it but if I hadn't signed it, I'd have been beaten on that. That thing in Little Rock was so explosive that they would have beat me about the least, any little thing that you might have done or not done that indicated that you weren't on their side in maintaining segregation. So it helped me at the time, you see.[20]

The alacrity with which congressmen from southern and eastern Arkansas signed the manifesto testified to their own segregationist views and their perceptions of their constituents' commitment to traditional patterns of race relations. The test of the success, however, of the authors of the manifesto in obtaining "unity of action" in the South and bringing wavering politicians into line was not their capture of the conservative faithful but rather their ability to bring into the segregationist camp the internationalist, progressive senator J. William Fulbright and the two most liberal members of the House delegation, Brooks Hays from Little Rock and James W. Trimble, Fulbright's successor in Congress from his northwest Arkansas district.

The news that Fulbright had signed the manifesto disappointed many of those in the North and outside the United States who admired his internationalist politics and his courageous stand against Joe McCarthy. Many Fulbright scholars expressed their dismay at the damage done by the manifesto to America's image in the very countries to which the senator's international exchange program had sent them. Fulbright's initial response to critical correspondents was that the "matter is much too involved to treat adequately in a letter." But in the long run, his explanation, which he never disavowed, was, first, that he had signed reluctantly and only after securing changes to the manifesto that toned down the initial intemperate drafts; second, that he had no political alternative but to sign, otherwise he would have faced certain defeat; third, that he was no racist and that the manifesto was consistent with his doctrine of gradualism, promoting change in race relations through gradual economic and educational change, rather than through legislative or judicial fiat.[21]

Unlike the most respected southern liberal senator, Lister Hill of Alabama, who allegedly signed the manifesto without reading it, Fulbright was reluctant to sign the first draft presented to the southern senators. Indeed, his aides, who were keen that he not be associated with such a defiant document, prepared a statement explaining why he was not going to sign. The statement was cast very much in the same mold as the statements of southerners like Lyndon Johnson and Albert Gore, who did not sign. Like the public pronouncements of most southern political moderates in the 1950s, the aides' proposed statement did not indicate approval of the Supreme Court decision; indeed, it deplored attempts to force integration on the South. But it argued that intemperate pronouncements like the manifesto, by alienating nonsoutherners, would make the task of resisting forcible federal intervention more difficult.[22]

Fulbright's aides argued that the problem of school desegregation was best left to local officials. Their proposed statement expressed the view that Governor Faubus had been maintaining through 1955: that the wisest course for a state was to "give its local communities and school boards the widest possible discretion to do what they wish and what they can. For this is a problem which is peculiarly local in the strictest sense of that word. Local autonomous school boards can deal with it far more wisely and effectively than we, the Congress, or perhaps even the states." What was particularly disturbing about the manifesto to Fulbright's aides, as it was to all those who did not sign, was that it held out "the false illusion" to southerners that the Supreme Court decision could be overturned and gave a "false hope" that state measures designed to avoid the impact of the decision would be successful. Instead, the duty of southern leaders, the proposed Fulbright statement argued, was one of "candor and realism. It is simply unrealistic to say that a decision of the Supreme Court is 'illegal and unconstitutional' and to imply, thereby, that it can be overturned by some higher tribunal."[23]

Fulbright rejected the advice of his aides. Instead, he worked with Senators Holland (Florida), Daniel (Texas), and Sparkman (Alabama) in a subcommittee to tone down the revised version of Thurmond's original draft that had been prepared by Richard Russell, John Stennis, and Sam Ervin. Moderates who had signed, like Lister Hill, were anxious not to be left out on a limb and put pressure on the nonsigners to come up with acceptable language that would ensure a united front. Indeed, as Price Daniel remembered it, Fulbright was one of those who had signed and he only worked to revise the draft when he realized that Holland and Daniel would not otherwise sign.[24]

The changes that Fulbright and the subcommittee secured were largely cosmetic. It was true that the *Brown* decision was no longer denounced as "illegal and unconstitutional," but it was still "unwarranted" and "a clear abuse of judicial power" and an exercise of "naked judicial power." The manifesto did promise to use lawful means to resist, and it appealed to southerners to refrain from disorder and lawlessness, but so did the Russell draft. It did eschew an explicit commendation of interposition, but the Russell draft had already eliminated an endorsement of interposition and it commended the motives of states "who have declared their intention to resist forced integration [as distinct from the *Brown* decision itself] by any lawful means."[25]

"I don't think anything has happened to shake my belief that I wouldn't have survived politically if I hadn't taken the course I did," Fulbright told his biographer, Randall Woods. This perception of overwhelming mass white segregationist sentiment had led Fulbright in the past to advocate voluntary and gradual racial change. He had supported the admission of a black graduate student to the University of Arkansas Law School, but he argued at the time against legislation in race relations which "may in fact create such antagonisms as to destroy much of the progress we have made during the last several years." Economic prosperity and education, not laws, he believed, would bring peaceful racial change in the South. This progress was now threatened by the *Brown* decision. As he stated after the manifesto was issued, "the whole theory of revolutionizing racial relations by fiat is wrong. You can't pass laws to make men be good to each other." The Supreme Court decision had confirmed his worst fears because it had merely stirred up groups like White America, Inc. Fulbright felt that the popular response left him no option but to sign the manifesto.[26]

Certainly Fulbright's friends in eastern Arkansas feared that Dixiecrat Ben Laney would exploit racial passions to run against the senator in 1956. When Fulbright signed the manifesto they felt, as Jim Hale in West Memphis told him, that Laney would not now run. Fulbright's aide John Erickson told him of a conversation between Liz Carpenter and *Arkansas Gazette* reporter Sam Harris: "Sam thinks your signing the Manifesto pretty well takes care of Laney."[27]

It is difficult to see that Fulbright needed to have been so cautious. John Erickson liked to drive off potential opposition by depriving potential candidates of possible sources of campaign funds in the fall before a reelection year. In 1956 Fulbright was already assured of the backing of the single most powerful source of funds in Arkansas, Witt Stephens, whose investment firm now controlled Arkansas Louisiana Gas Company. The senator remained on close terms with the Faubus administration. It did not seem that political necessity demanded that he sign the manifesto.[28]

Certainly, many of Senator Fulbright's Arkansas supporters were disappointed. Racial moderates in a state that prided itself on its progress in race relations felt that Fulbright had let them down and undercut their position. Nowhere was this felt more strongly than in his hometown of Fayetteville, where, after all, his brother-in-law, Hal Douglas, had been chairman of the school board that had presided over school desegregation. As Gordon McNeil from the university history department put it:

> Might not the man whose name is given to a scholarship program designed to win us friends abroad, and the former law professor who knows the possible consequences of intemperate attacks on the court, also have declined to sign? . . . You have given aid and comfort to the extremists who reject our fundamental democratic and Christian principles. Did you really mean to do this? Did you really want to stir up the die-hards here in your own community of Fayetteville, where the adjustments to more equal educational opportunities are being made peacefully?

As one among a number of Little Rock lawyers and churchmen noted, "You yourself know that Arkansas has experienced very little trouble during the outset of this program and surely as integration moves into the Little Rock system, the majority of the state will follow the pattern with little opposition." Fulbright, lamented the wife of a Little Rock teacher, could "have given encouragement to the mass of the people who are not vocal, but who want to see our state progress." Many were opposed to integration "but those people are law-abiding citizens and have only been waiting for the leadership from the right sources."[29]

The disappointment of racial moderates in Little Rock and northwest Arkansas might have been expected. What was especially poignant was the disappointment of churchmen in eastern Arkansas who now felt abandoned and isolated. As a West Helena minister noted, "I am not writing McClellan or any of the other representatives of our state for I more or less expected such from them. I am writing you only because your assent to this attitude is a truly disturbing thing. I would never have believed that you would be party to such."[30]

To the end, Fulbright argued that he had been right to sign the manifesto. He did, however, note wistfully that he did not "think that the gradualist school that I belonged to, looking back from now, will receive the approval of history." However, it was not Fulbright's gradualism that was flawed, but the fact that he did not speak up for gradualism at the time. As a perplexed former Fulbright scholar and Presbyterian minister in Jim Johnson's hometown of Crossett complained, the manifesto was not advocating gradualism: "I am fully aware of the difficulties that will accompany integration. But I look on it not as an evil to be avoided, but a good which is worth the price it costs. If you had said 'slow down' I could have understood your position even if I did not agree with it, but when you said 'stop' I am left wondering."[31]

It is difficult to avoid Randall Woods's stark conclusion that "indisputably" Fulbright was a racist. There are many gradations of racism, and certainly Fulbright was no race-baiting demagogue. But, unlike many of his correspondents, Fulbright had not come to see segregation as a moral evil or unchristian. Fulbright was not uneasy with the patrician prejudices of his eastern Arkansas planter friends, and he did not see desegregation as an important enough issue to stand up against what he perceived to be the deeply held sentiments of the mass of his constituents.[32]

Fulbright acknowledged the passion of the segregationists' beliefs—"You had a hell of a chance of persuading them that it's a good thing for their daughter to go to school with a black man"—but he had no similar feel for the impatience of his African American constituents. He had little personal understanding of the poverty and daily humiliation of their lives, and, like most liberal politicians in the South in the 1950s, he campaigned for black votes at a distance through his aides who dealt with particular community leaders. These leaders—"racial diplomats," as Numan Bartley calls them— were used to telling white politicians what those white politicians wanted to hear. As a result Fulbright was shielded from the growing sense of grievance in the Arkansas African American community. Leaders of that community, like Lawrence Davis and I. S. McClinton, whatever their private thoughts, reassured Fulbright that they understood the political realities of his position. Fulbright's signing of the manifesto, underpinned by his certainty of the strength of mass white segregationist sentiment, was entirely consistent with his political philosophy and with his later inaction during the Little Rock crisis.[33]

Fulbright never regretted signing the Southern Manifesto. Brooks Hays regretted signing almost immediately after he had done so. Hays had been a prominent moderate on racial matters and a prominent Baptist, a New Deal–style liberal on domestic policy, and a committed internationalist on foreign affairs, with many northern congressional contacts. In 1949 he had proposed, at the instigation of Fulbright and Harry Ashmore, the Arkansas Plan for racial progress: support for federal action on antilynching and against the poll tax in return for the South maintaining segregation. He described himself as a states' rights liberal who favored positive action by the southern states to fend off federal intervention. He did not approve the *Brown* decision, but he had initially refused to sign the manifesto because it approved interposition and because it had no appeal to the people to pursue legal and constitutional methods for change. He still held out even after the changes engineered by Fulbright, Holland, and Daniel had met those objections. But as more and more southern representatives signed, Hays found himself under pressure from other moderates not to break ranks.[34]

Orval Faubus was in Washington in the spring of 1956, and he set himself the task of securing the signatures of the two holdouts, the two most liberal members of the delegation: Hays and James W. Trimble. With Oren Harris, who was collecting the Arkansas delegation signatures, Faubus accompanied Hays to the Bethesda Hospital where Trimble was ill. Faubus spent three hours at Trimble's bedside persuading the two liberals to sign. As Hays recalled:

> Faubus...confronted the two of us...with the idea that if we did not do something to allay the hysteria and the fears that had been generated of his being forced all of a sudden conceivably through military action on the part of the federal government, if we did not do something along that line to quiet the people down, that we would find what he called the Ku Klux Klan and the extreme Citizens' Council groups taking over the political life of the state, and that the racists and the radicals would displace the moderates. Faubus was known as a moderate.

When Trimble eventually agreed to sign, Hays felt that he was obliged to follow suit. He was not proud of his action: "in the present context I can see that I shouldn't have done it because it didn't spare us much. I think we could still have saved the political leadership of the state from those extremists but the threat was powerful enough that I was influenced."[35]

In 1976 John Ward, editor of the *Conway Log Cabin Democrat* brought together two of the principal actors in the Little Rock crisis: Orval Faubus and Brooks Hays. Hays had paid for his failed 1957 efforts to mediate between Faubus and President Eisenhower by losing his congressional seat in the general election of 1958, defeated after a last-minute write-in campaign by segregationist forces. Hays was willing to believe the best of people and in the 1976 interview he appeared to accept Faubus's assurance that he "didn't do anything against Brooks" in that 1958 race, indeed that Faubus had "discouraged... everyway in the world" his secretary, who masterminded the write-in campaign. Faubus was anxious to show that "a man in public life then" had to act pragmatically and was keen to argue that he and Hays had adopted much the same pragmatic stance. To make his point he turned the conversation to the Southern Manifesto, identifying it as "the forerunner of our opposition... signed by every member of the Congress from all the Southern States except two... and one of them got beat and the other had strong opposition and the only way he saved himself, he said, 'I didn't sign it because it wasn't strong enough.' And he survived. Do you see, in all that situation, for the federal government to issue an order like that and place all the burden on the state authorities or local authorities and say, 'Go ahead, and (looking at it from the pragmatic standpoint) commit political suicide now. We're aloof from it.' I didn't think it was proper. I didn't think it was honest. I didn't think it was courageous."[36]

In 1992 Faubus told John Kirk:

> So then up in Washington, they get the pressure. What do they do? They devise and proclaim the Southern Manifesto...even Fulbright, the great liberal, became the first man to sign it. Brooks Hays went up and signed it, all from Arkansas. So the handwriting was on the wall for everybody in that time, in that situation. So the congressmen, they'd say "Oh we've done all we can, now it's up to the state administration."[37]

Faubus believed that the mass white segregationist public opinion that forced people to sign the manifesto left him no alternative but to defy the courts in 1957. What he conveniently ignored was the role he himself played in creating that pressure. What Faubus and the conservatives were aiming to do was to stir up white public opinion, to convince the people that token compliance was not inevitable and that the Court could be defied. They then hoped that wavering politicians who might have accepted the inevitability of gradual change would be coerced back into the massive resistance camp.[38]

This conservative strategy worked in Arkansas. Fulbright and Hays appear to have been paralyzed by their conviction that the mass of white public opinion was overwhelmingly hostile to any desegregation. They were not prepared to campaign for the gradualism they espoused, nor were they prepared to campaign to persuade the people to accept the inevitable. Instead, Fulbright and Hays, egged on by Faubus, signed a document which, as Fulbright's aides acknowledged, gave the "false illusion" to white Arkansans that the Supreme Court could be successfully defied.

This fatalism by the state's leading politicians reflected a fatalism among southern moderates generally in the 1950s, a reluctance to attempt to build up public support for compliance. It was as if they believed that public agitation would unnecessarily stir up the forces of white popular racism, whereas if no fuss was made gradual racial change and desegregation could quietly be implemented almost unnoticed: a strategy seemingly followed by Little Rock community leaders in the summer of 1957.

What the Southern Manifesto demonstrated in Arkansas was that if you disavowed compliance with the Supreme Court, you were in no position to control the segregationist pressure groups that resolutely opposed any compromise with desegregation. Faubus's strategy in 1956 was predicated on the notion that concessions to segregationist pressure would enable moderates like himself to stay in office and defuse the extremist threat. Instead, he found that in a battle where one side is prepared to mount a righteous crusade to defy the Supreme Court, and the other wants to keep quiet, the segregationists were going to win.

Fulbright's moderate correspondents who were so disappointed by the senator in 1956, and who felt that their positions in their communities as advocates of compliance with the law of the land had been undermined, were right to be apprehensive. The experience of March 1956 suggested that if the choice came between obeying Court orders and bowing to segregationist mob pressure, moderates at the community level could look in vain for help from leading politicians like Fulbright and Faubus. It was difficult to convince people that there was no alternative but to obey the law of the land, that they should accept the inevitable, when leading politicians in the state were proclaiming that there was an alternative, that desegregation could be avoided.

Reviewing the apparently polarized racial and political scene in March 1956, newspaperman Sam Harris predicted that fame awaited the Arkansas politician in the next two years who resisted demagoguery and exercised some courage. Fame would come to an Arkansas politician, as Harris foretold, but it was a demagogue who was to achieve it.[39]

7

"Closet Moderates": Why White Liberals Failed, 1940–1970

I

Kerr Scott was the most liberal governor of North Carolina in the twentieth century. He was elected in 1948 in an upset victory over the state treasurer, Charles Johnson. The blunt uncompromising Scott campaigned for his "branchhead boys"—isolated rural voters who lived not at the heads of the rivers but at the ends of the tributaries—and against "lawyer-business" rule. Johnson was supported by most members of the General Assembly, and by most state officials and county commissioners. Scott put together a coalition of lower-income, especially rural, whites and blacks to defeat him. For the first time for years, noted one observer, you did not know who was going to be governor. Johnson had been so confident of winning that allegedly he had ordered a new Cadillac with special hubcaps. Edwin Gill, protégé of Max Gardner, and later state treasurer himself, was so surprised, it was said, that he tried to jump out of his second-floor office window.[1]

In office, Scott rewarded his liberal coalition. He built 12,000 miles of farm-to-market roads, paving the dirt roads of rural North Carolina, and lifting the state out of the mud. He stimulated a dramatic increase in the provision of rural electrification and telephones. He improved teachers' salaries and pensions and increased spending on school construction. He raised welfare benefits and widened unemployment compensation coverage. For African Americans, he defused a proposed march on Raleigh by consulting black leaders, fought for increased appropriations for black institutions, monitored black efforts to register to vote, especially in eastern North Carolina, and appointed blacks to state government positions. Above all, he appointed Harold Trigg, president of St. Augustine's College, as the first African American to serve on the state Board of Education.[2]

For organized labor, Scott attempted to repeal the state's anti-closed shop law and to raise the minimum wage. Unlike his predecessors and successors, he intervened in strikes on behalf of the strikers, not the employers: he did not call out the National Guard to break strikes. When textile workers struck Hart Mills in Tarboro and spent most of 1949 on strike, Scott condemned the owners. He complained that the company "doesn't believe in unions," that they were inflexible, and set on busting the union.[3]

When Scott had campaigned for commissioner of Agriculture he had criticized the lack of representation for the interests of thousands of farmwomen: it was a repeated theme. He appointed the first woman, Jane McKimmon, to the state Board of Agriculture. As governor, he attempted to secure more representation for women in state appointments and appointed North Carolina's first female superior court judge, Suzie Sharp, later chief justice of the state supreme court. Scott also appointed women campaign managers, notably in critical counties like Forsyth.[4]

Scott sought the economic modernization of the state but it was a New Deal–style modernization strategy, aimed not at attracting low-wage industry through cheap labor and tax incentives, but at creating economic growth through the creation of mass purchasing power, and by sustaining and increasing the income of black and white lower-income voters. There was a liberal cutting edge to Scott's policies: he confronted the state's bankers over state financial deposits and revenue; the oil companies over an increased gasoline tax; the utility companies over rural electrification and water resources; and employers over union rights, strikes, and the minimum wage. He recognized the essential ingredient of federal aid if the state were to solve its long-term economic problems: he supported federal aid to education, federal development of water resources, federal aid for hospital construction and low-cost housing, and some form of national health insurance. He was a southern politician firmly in sympathy with the economic policies of a liberal Democratic national administration, a sympathy emphasized when he appointed the former press secretary to FDR and Truman, Jonathan Daniels, as Democratic National committeeman. He confirmed that liberalism by appointing the state's most advanced New Dealer, UNC president Frank Graham, to the United States Senate. Scott was one of the last North Carolina politicians to be proud of the adjective *liberal.* As he praised Frank Graham to one audience, "You haven't got a better liberal in America than the Senator you've got."[5]

And there were North Carolinians who responded with zeal to this liberal politics. On September 16, 1949, one admirer wrote to Scott that he was, "as far as I am concerned, . . . the first North Carolinian in my lifetime who has had the vision and the ability to become President of the United States." The admirer encouraged Scott "to set his cap for that accomplishment. This is the political era of the 'Little Man.' You have a way of getting along with that Little Man, make the most of it." That enthusiastic admirer of North Carolina's most liberal governor was a young Jesse Helms.[6]

Almost twenty years later, Kerr Scott's son, Robert, set his sights on the governor's mansion. In 1967 in a speech in Dunn he blasted "the civil disobedience movement and its demonstrators," "hippies," "Black Power advocates," "coddlers of criminals," "the United States Supreme Court and the federal establishment," "peaceniks" and "free-wheeling academics," and blamed them for disorder in America. In 1968 Scott won a narrow election victory over Republican Jim Gardner by taking a tough "law and order stance" and distancing himself from the Johnson administration and the Hubert Humphrey campaign. As governor, he used the National Guard and state troopers to quell disturbances in Oxford and Wilmington and to end student occupations in Greensboro and Chapel Hill.[7]

In 1969–70 I was a graduate student supporting my research by teaching the History of Western Civilization to textile majors at North Carolina State University. On February 23, 1970, I wrote pretentiously to my parents:

> On the Saturday I went to see *Un Homme et une Femme* at the Union. A beautiful and sensitive film which had been inexplicably banned by the owner of the local TV network. This man, a Nixon supporter with Wallaceite tendencies, who rather cleverly exploits anti-intellectual prejudices, would no doubt have apoplexy if he watched BBC2 for an evening.

That television owner, Jesse Helms, announced that month that he had become a Republican. It was, wrote Thad Stem to Jonathan Daniels, no great surprise: "The next big surprise will be Raquel Welch's announcement that she has big tits. Maybe Harry Golden will confirm the fact that he is Jewish." In 1972 Helms defeated Democrat Nick Galifianakis for the Senate, implying that Galifianakis was neither American nor Christian, and like the Democratic candidate George McGovern, was soft on drugs. Helms won by gaining the support of the Wallace Democrats from rural Eastern North Carolina. That same year, Kerr Scott's campaign manager from 1954 and the former governor, Terry Sanford, was overwhelmingly defeated in his effort to stop George Wallace in the state's presidential primary.[8]

The purpose of this lecture is to ask how the South got from liberal hope to a conservative reality, how the liberal "politics of the Little Man" championed by Jesse Helms in 1949 became the reactionary "politics of the Little Man" espoused by Jesse Helms in 1972.

II

Kerr Scott was not an isolated figure for change when he was elected in 1948. He was part of a liberal window of opportunity that opened up for the South in the 1940s from the economic and social changes unleashed by the New Deal and World War II. Historians have identified a class-based civil rights movement focusing on economic issues in left-led unions. They have vividly recaptured the dynamic biracial faith of New Deal radicals in the Southern Conference for Human Welfare. They have chronicled the strenuous efforts of postwar unions both to organize workers and to elect sympathetic politicians. They have shown how returning GIs and women acted to clean up local politics and how the NAACP organized voter registration drives.[9]

White liberal politicians like Kerr Scott and his fellow governors, Jim Folsom, Sid McMath, and Earl Long, capitalized, as I argued in chapter 4, on these popular forces to forge lower-income, biracial electoral coalitions. The voters supported the provision of long-overdue public services for the "have-nots," services that conservatives elites and the poverty of southern governments had previously denied them. They were racially moderate supporting the rights of blacks to vote, protecting spending on black institutions, especially schools, and appointing the first African Americans to state boards. In Washington, southerners were elected who believed that the New Deal has shown how federal spending and federal government projects could rescue the region from poverty. Elections to the Senate, from Lister Hill and Claude Pepper in 1938 to Albert Gore in 1952, and to the House, from Lyndon Johnson in 1937 to Frank Smith in 1950, showed how lower-income black and white southern voters could support candidates who advocated investment in the region's infrastructure and redistributive social welfare measures. Finally at the local level, men like Jim Wright in Fort Worth, Jack Brooks in Beaumont, Frank Smith in Sidon, Terry Sanford in Fayetteville, Dante Fascell in Miami, and Joe Langan in Mobile came back from the war, went to graduate school, took control of the Young Democrats in their city and state, and got elected to their state legislatures, joining other veterans determined, in Smith's words, to "have a part in making a better day." Smith would go to Congress in 1950, Wright, Brooks, and Fascell in 1954.[10]

III

These liberal and racially moderate politicians were not the force of the future in the South, despite the hopes of successive presidents and the Supreme Court. Their civil rights strategies until 1963 were predicated on the willingness of

responsible southern leaders to lead their communities into voluntary acceptance of racial change. Instead, southern voters increasingly supported conservative candidates who most vociferously protested their loyalty to segregation
and their determination to resist racial change. When racial change was eventually imposed on the South in the 1960s the adjustment to that change was
engineered not by the old liberals and racial moderates but by transmogrified
segregationists, business leaders, and, after 1970, a new generation of business progressive New South politicians. The scene of liberal successes was also
the scene of the most violent and vigorous segregationist resistance. It was
under Jim Folsom that a mob would prevent Autherine Lucy from entering
the University of Alabama. It was his liberal protégé George Wallace who
would stand at the schoolhouse door and defy the federal government. It was
Sid McMath's liberal protégé, Orval Faubus, who would use the National
Guard to prevent the desegregation of Central High School. Two years after
Kerr Scott's election to the Senate in 1954 when one observer contended that
race "will never again raise its ugly head" in North Carolina politics, Scott
had signed the Southern Manifesto and endorsed the Pearsall Plan, North
Carolina's version of Massive Resistance. It was the racially moderate mayor
DeLesseps Morrison who allowed mobs to roam the streets of New Orleans
to enforce a boycott of desegregated schools in 1960.[11]

What had gone wrong?

One argument clearly is that the liberal window of opportunity never
existed, that racial and economic liberals were neither sizable nor liberal enough
seriously to threaten conservative hegemony and the established racial and
economic status quo.

First, organized labor failed in its bid to undermine the South as a bastion of the open shop. Textile unions, according to Tim Minchin, never solved
the free rider question: if employers of nonunion plants matched the wages
of those plants which were under contract, why should nonunion workers
risk strike action to secure a contract that would not bring them any economic benefits but would threaten their ability to keep up the mortgage and
credit payments that they now made as homeowning consumers? Were white
workers interested in interracial cooperation? Time and again, the answer
seemed no. As Bryant Simon argued in South Carolina, in response to black
activism, even as early as 1938, millhands had "emerged as a reactionary
political force."[12]

Second, returning veterans were as likely to believe that their wartime sac-
rifice had been in order to maintain white supremacy as to establish a new
racial order. As Jim Cobb and Jennifer Brooks have pointed out, returning veterans were the perpetrators of postwar racial violence, founders of the Citizens'
Council and core members of a reinvigorated Klan. Herman Talmadge, Strom

Thurmond, and George Smathers were prominent among candidates who parlayed successful war records into postwar political success as defenders of the racial status quo. As Thad Stem noted about Klan members in eastern North Carolina in the 1960s, they were not just "malcontents, freaks and oddballs," they were also financially successful men who were "as hot for the Klan as they were hell on Hitler, all the way from Libya to the Rhine."[13]

Third, "the political era of the 'Little Man'" was not necessarily conducive to liberal politics, either in racial or economic affairs. The common man, good ol' boy style of politics of a Jim Folsom was equally a style used by reactionary politicians like Eugene Talmadge. Populist suspicion of elites and special financial interests could equally be tapped as anti-statist sentiments, that fueled resentment of government spending and taxation and hatred of African Americans. Folsom himself noted the discrepancy:

> Gene Talmadge...got elected in 1946. I got elected cookin' turnip greens and he got elected on the race issue. That was his personal preservation, and I never did use it. The same time right in adjoining states—the same background—ethnic background...He got elected just raisin' hell about the race question. Negro, Negro, Negro, Negro, and I never mentioned the thing. And I shook hands with the Negro.

Conversely, economic liberalism did not automatically go with racial moderation, as the records of politicians like New Deal supporters and race-baiters Theodore Bilbo and John Rankin indicated, or as the resolute refusal of union-backing Olin Johnston to betray any public hint of racial moderation testified. Equally the ranks of racial moderates included economic conservatives. An analysis, for example, of those who did not sign the Southern Manifesto reveals conservative Texas congressmen, loyal to Sam Rayburn, a right-wing Republican and future Goldwater loyalist, and a union-busting, Liberty League, textile millionaire from North Carolina.[14]

Finally, women may have been influential in the churches, in interracial groups, and in the later campaigns to keep public schools open, but much of this activity for a long time scarcely entered the public space. White women were arguably more prominent in support groups for the Dixiecrats and in vocal segregationist groups like the Mothers' League for Central High in Little Rock and the Women for Constitutional Government in Mississippi. Gladys Tillett might proclaim that "Women Will Win This Election" for Frank Graham in 1950 but she was wrong.[15]

The second argument is that the liberal window of opportunity had always been closed by the race issue. The forces of popular white racism made it politically suicidal after World War II for any politician to deviate from a staunch defense of white supremacy. To survive and preserve his influence, the aspiring liberal politician had to suppress any sentiments for racial moderation. Carl Elliott, courageous North Alabaman liberal congressman, for whom Franklin Roosevelt was, and remained, a political god, recalled the inexorable process:

> There was no room left in the middle for anyone . . . you had to do what you could to somehow connect with the people, to find some way of appeasing them without sacrificing your principles . . . When that [Southern] Manifesto came along, neither these [Deep South] colleagues nor my constituents back in Alabama cared about moderation. You were either with them or against them. And if you were against them, you were gone. Voted out. Politically excommunicated . . . I knew there was no way I could survive and I hadn't yet achieved what I came to Congress to do.

Politicians like Elliott and the rest of the Alabama House delegation followed the lead of their liberal senators Hill and Sparkman and ran for cover. They became in Hodding Carter's words "closet moderates." It was a pattern repeated all over the South. Historians differ over the date when the race issue apparently closed the liberal window. Pat Sullivan puts it as early as 1946 and the defeat of CIOPAC candidates in those elections and the subsequent travails of the Southern Conference and the failure of the efforts of Henry Wallace and the Progressive Party in 1948. For Morton Sosna, 1950 was the time when liberalism on race was fatal to political careers in the region, as the defeats of Claude Pepper and Frank Graham indicated. For Michael Klarman, the decisive moment comes with the violent backlash after *Brown,* which in turn stimulated black protest. Southern moderates were irrelevant in the ensuing battle between the southern conservatives and the federal government. "By propelling southern politics towards racial fanaticism, *Brown* set the stage for the violent suppression of civil rights demonstrations in the early 1960s, which in turn aroused previously indifferent northern whites to demand federal legislative intervention to inter Jim Crow."[16]

Anti-communism has been seen as part and parcel of the conservative resistance to racial change and liberal failure. For Pat Sullivan the new national liberalism largely abandoned a bold civil rights strategy, and the anti-communist issue, remorselessly exploited by southern conservatives, fatally divided the Popular Front coalition in the South. For Korstad and Lichtenstein, anti-communism was used to break up the alliance of left-led unions and black workers. In Louisiana, Adam Fairclough wrote,

> The impact of McCarthyism was so profound that one could argue that a fundamental discontinuity separated the period 1940–54 from the following decade. Well before 1950 the Cold War had produced an ideological chilling effect that made criticism of the social order, so common-

place during the Roosevelt era, unfashionable, unpatriotic, and politically dangerous.

The dynamics of the potent mix of pervasive white racism and anti-communism were read differently by Numan Bartley. For Bartley, unlike Sullivan, national liberals were not too cautious on civil rights but too radical. Bartley blames the failure of postwar southern liberalism squarely on national cold war liberals. American liberalism, Bartley argues, abandoned its vision of economic reform and redistribution aimed at the biracial lower-income coalition in the South, and instead embraced the politics of anti-racism and desegregation. It substituted a moralistic concern for symbolic opportunity and the elimination of *de jure* segregation for the substance of a drive to tackle the problem of black and white disadvantage. Liberalism "became increasingly fixated on race relations," it lost "most of its substance and direction" and left white workers with "little aside from contempt and the right to compete for scarce jobs with black workers."[17]

According to Bartley, the civil rights movement chose the wrong target —*de jure* segregation, especially in education, where white fears for their children were so profound. The movement should have concentrated on voting rights and economic gains. Similarly Michael Klarman sees the litigative strategy on education, seeking redress from outside the region, undercutting southern moderates' efforts at gradual, internal change in the areas of interest that engaged southern blacks before 1954. Korstad and Lichtenstein also lament this direction away from issues of economic equality and working-class empowerment which Martin Luther King would vainly try to resurrect after 1965. This line of argument has clear contemporary resonance. In 1998 Jim Sleeper contrasted Vice President Albert Gore's "racial moralism" unfavorably with "the honorable but more grounded approach of his father." Gore Sr. "favored government intervention in economic relations rather than in racial ones." His was a more authentically "progressive" emphasis on economic redistribution.[18]

IV

All these analyses have a great deal of truth in them. But I want to argue for a different dynamic of the issues of race, class, and anti-communism, one in which liberal possibilities persisted past 1954 only to be undermined in part by the liberals' own fatalism. The particular biracial politics of the 1950s failed to deliver what African Americans wanted, driving them to eschew politics for direct action protest. This protest marginalized southern liberals.

On the one hand, it was transmogrified segregationists and business leaders who mediated the acceptance by southern communities of federally mandated racial change. On the other, black assertiveness, together with economic and cultural dislocation for lower-income and middle-income whites, provoked conservative southern Republican success.

It is obviously prudent not to overstate the political strength of postwar southern liberals. The structural obstacles which V. O. Key identified as perpetuating conservative hegemony and inhibiting the interests of the "have-nots" were, even with the slowly increasing black electorate, still formidable. In a state like Mississippi the short-lived collaboration of a maverick newspaper editor, a university chaplain, and a detached Nobel laureate in a spoof parody of Citizen Council magazines can scarcely be portrayed as a major threat to established interests. But, nevertheless, I do believe that the existence of a southern New Deal–style postwar political liberalism has been underestimated. Recently, I believe this reflects the persuasive case made brilliantly by Alan Brinkley in *The End of Reform*. Brinkley, who does not mention any southern liberals, argues that the New Deal legacy was for the next generation a national liberalism, aimed at consumers, not producers, committed to economic growth, not redistribution, and championing a limited, not interventionist, state in economic affairs. National liberalism had become, in Arthur Schlesinger's well-known formulation, qualitative, rather than quantitative. But this view of national liberalism in itself underestimates the extent that this "consensus" was contested and problematic in the 1950s. It also virtually ignores the South where the time-lagged impact of the New Deal ensured that a redistributionist liberalism surfaced and struggled through the 1940s and 1950s. Most southern states saw a vigorous competition between liberals and conservatives over the appropriate modernization strategy for the region. The conservatives triumphed more often than not, and ultimately won, but that should not obscure the persistent conflict through these years.[19]

When William Colmer could seriously warn fellow Mississippi congressman Frank Smith to steer clear of hawk Henry "Scoop" Jackson of Washington on the grounds that Scoop Jackson was a communist, one clearly should not underestimate the power of anti-communism in the South. Indeed, Maury Maverick Jr. recalled that in the South liberals were in favor of filibusters as the only weapon to stop anti-communist excesses. He recalled that in Texas,

> There was a bill for awhile to give anyone the death penalty who belonged to the Communist Party. I remember that I had a hand in reducing that to life imprisonment. That was a great liberal move at the time. (*laughter*)

Well, hell, it sounds silly today, but you know, God Almighty, I was at least trying to keep the Reds from being put in the electric chair and now, I feel like a damn fool even talking about it.

There is no doubt that anti-communism, exploited by conservative elites, destroyed southern radicals in the 1940s—the Southern Conference, left-led unions, the Civil Rights Congress's work in Louisiana. Red scare politics played a major factor in the defeat of Claude Pepper and Frank Graham in 1950, though both incumbents were unusually vulnerable to guilt-by-association cold war fears. But anti-communism had been a staple of some southern conservatives, particularly some southern industrialists, since the early New Deal. Anti-communism was part of the staple of some southern politicians, the small change of the rhetoric of politicians like Herman Talmadge. It was not a major theme in the 1940s. Opponents of racial change in Georgia at that time did not need anti-communism to justify violent racial repression. It was later, as Michael Heale's study of state versions of the House Un-American Activities Committee indicates, that southern anti-communism really flourished and stifled dissent. Massive resistance and black activism fueled anti-communism, rather than anti-communism fueling massive resistance. Many of the southern liberal politicians who espoused biracial politics in the 1940s and early 1950s were routinely red-baited, but equally routinely survived. Later, black activism, then student anti-war protests in the 1960s, fed anti-communism in southern states, as Warren Billingsley's new study of the Speaker Ban law in North Carolina, passed in 1963, demonstrates, and the career of Jesse Helms exemplifies.[20]

Race was the issue that overwhelmed southern liberals. But how did the mix of personal ideology and constituency pressure play out?

The standard reminiscence of southern politicians, from Governor John Patterson of Alabama to William Fulbright, is that whatever their rhetoric at the time, they were merely paying necessary obeisance to racist popular sentiment and, in reality, were working to moderate white responses and pave the way for inevitable racial change. As a black attorney ruefully noted to Calvin Trillin in 1960, if all the white politicians who said they were working backstage for racial justice actually were, "it must be pretty crowded there behind the scenes."[21]

For the most part southern liberal politicians were supporters of segregation after World War II. As David Chappell has pointed out, most southerners were. Few politicians publicly espoused the opposition to segregation that the radical New Dealers and labor leaders of the Southern Conference endorsed or that the academics and community leaders in the Southern Regional Council belatedly supported. But, as Chappell and Mills Thornton

have reminded us, there are important gradations in the support of segregation which can dictate substantially different political action. Explicit racial
appeals were not the stock in trade of the southern liberals. They did not
always resist the temptation aggressively to use such appeals—Earl Long in
1939, Claude Pepper in 1944 were notable examples—but for the most part
they eschewed violent racial appeals in favor of a preemptive strike to establish their segregationist credentials and then a rapid move on to advocacy of a
substantive liberal economic agenda. On the whole they did not come from
the black belt and they lacked the personal investment in status, the negative
racial stereotypes, and the fear of a no-longer subservient black labor force that
wedded black-belt whites to the determined maintenance of segregation.[22]

What most liberals felt was a Jacksonian sense of fairness that blacks
should neither suffer the inexcusable excesses of segregation, nor be denied
the basic right to vote. Some had supported the Claude Pepper campaign
against the poll tax and backed federal legislation in 1942. Governors like
McMath and Folsom resisted attempts by conservatives to reverse the effects
of the *Smith v. Allwright* decision and appointed registrars committed to
black voting rights. Earl Long sought to prevent New Orleans black voters
being purged from the rolls—they were, he said, his niggers and he wanted
their votes. Most southerners who did not sign the Southern Manifesto in
1956 went on to support the Civil Rights Act of 1957, seen by them as a
measure against voting discrimination, and the younger ones went on to support the 1965 Voting Rights Act.[23]

The right to vote was intimately linked to education and economic
growth. Education and economic opportunity was to be the key to gradual
progress in racial matters. As Frank Smith said, "Large-scale economic progress
was the only avenue likely to lead to a solution of the race problem in Mississippi." As he told Hodding Carter in 1949, outsiders had to understand
"why the southern liberal or any southerner of progressive stripe must primarily concern himself with trying to improve the *economic* position of his
people." Just as the solution to the region's racial problems lay in increasing
prosperity for black and white southerners, so the region's economic problems could not be solved while southern blacks were mired in poverty. The
keys to solving the region's racial problems were first, political rights for
blacks to extend the electorate and make the system more responsive to the
welfare needs of lower-income voters; second, federal economic assistance for
the region to raise the living standards of both blacks and whites; and third,
education to enable African Americans in particular to take advantage of the
economic opportunities created by liberal policies. Southern liberal governors
saw federal aid to education as essential to meet this last objective. This policy was clearly prudential: it served the needs of the liberals' biracial coalition

of supporters without driving a wedge in that alliance by raising the issue of segregation. But it also reflected a good deal of contemporary academic optimism that economic modernization would inevitably bring racial change, since segregation would be too inflexible and expensive for a modern society and higher incomes would lessen the competitive racism and insecurities of poor whites.[24]

It is this southern liberal agenda which Numan Bartley believes was undermined by the racial moralism and symbolic posturing of national liberals. It is easy to sympathize with Bartley's irritation at Truman's policy of "after the bang, the backtrack," the bold demand for legislation which embarrassed southern liberals but which he knew had no chance of passage. Demands for a permanent Fair Employment Practices Committee and the issue of the Powell amendment to proposals for federal aid to education were undoubtedly awkward for southern liberals. But I think that Bartley underestimates the extent to which social democratic redistributionist politics persisted among mainstream southern politicians into the 1950s. The popular front liberalism of the Southern Conference for Human Welfare was not an economic reform program undermined by the imposition of a national civil rights agenda. The SCHW was race-baited and red-baited because of its own indigenous racial radicalism. The argument that the targeting of *de jure* segregation, particularly segregated education, was misguided, seems to be misplaced on two grounds. First, it assumes that tackling *de jure* segregation was somehow a goal that had nothing to do with the aspirations of southern blacks active in the voter-registration and union-organizing drives of the 1940s. Second, it assumes that a concentration on extending the franchise would not have aroused the same powerful opposition that desegregating the schools provoked. The violent resistance to extending voting rights in Mississippi throughout this period rather belies that assumption. As Jeff Norrell showed in Macon County, Alabama, black-belt leaders like Sam Engelhardt realized that school desegregation was probably inevitable. What they did not want to see was black voting. As Engelhardt recalled, "Everybody has an angle when they get in [politics]. I was worried...about the tax assessor...because of all our holdings. That was my angle—to protect ourselves. Not only me, but my family. My aunts, uncles, and cousins owned land." Black voting would mean black tax assessors: "If you have a nigger tax assessor what would he do to you?" he asked a journalist in 1956.[25]

The gradualist liberal agenda presupposed a regional compromise on race: the South would put its own racial house in order, the federal government would back off its civil rights agenda. Harry Ashmore, the editor of the *Arkansas Gazette,* and liberal Arkansas representatives Brooks Hays and James Trimble, with William Fulbright's encouragement, attempted to establish the ground rules for this compromise in 1949. The South would make good its commitment to gradual racial change by eliminating lynching, by removing the obstacles to full political participation by African Americans, and by striving for genuine equality in the provision of black education. In return the national government would be patient and back off counterproductive demands for immediate desegregation.[26]

The Arkansas Plan received little support in either the North or the South. Southern liberals may have espoused the necessity for gradual racial change, but they did little in the run-up to the *Brown* decision to lay out a strategy for achieving that gradual change. They continued piecemeal to protect black votes, fight for increased appropriations for black institutions, and appoint some African Americans to government office and to state Democratic Party positions. The coherent strategy in these years came from conservatives in Mississippi and South Carolina who mounted a massive drive genuinely to equalize school facilities in an effort to forestall a school desegregation decision. Liberal politicians were inhibited from that sort of program by the nagging realization that the Supreme Court would not necessarily protect separate but equal.

V

If the liberals anticipated Brown, which in retrospect most of them did, they did not share this knowledge with their constituents. Their standard response was that they thought that segregated schooling was the best for both races and that the Court had not ruled yet. In many ways they remained in control of the race issue in the years after 1950, even through 1955. Sid McMath attributed neither of his two defeats—for governor in 1952, for the senate in 1954—to the race issue, but rather to McCarthyism and the issue of unions. His liberal protégé, Orval Faubus, won election as the racially moderate candidate in both 1954 and 1956. John Sparkman was reelected in 1954 without significant opposition, just as Lister Hill had been in 1950. Jim Folsom secured a second term as governor with the highest first primary vote in Alabama history. He enjoyed unprecedented success with the state legislature in 1955. Earl Long was elected to a third term as governor in Louisiana in 1955. Earl Black indeed has noted how rarely race surfaced as a major issue in gubernatorial elections in the south as a whole, 1950–1954. Albert Gore was elected to the Senate in 1952 and Estes Kefauver reelected in Tennessee in 1954 against conservative, segregationist opposition.[27]

Kerr Scott was elected to the Senate after the *Brown* decision in 1954 despite a last-minute racial smear by his opponent, when eastern North

Carolina was flooded with a forged advertisement in which a Winston-Salem black leader endorsed Scott for his stand on non-segregation. As Terry Sanford, his campaign manager recalled, the vicious race-baiting campaign against Frank Graham four years earlier had seared minds in North Carolina:

> The lesson to those who would heed it, [was] that the race issue is a terrible weapon and can be used with overwhelming effectiveness . . . I learned a great deal out of that. I started keeping a notebook of how to deal with the racist campaign. In fact, I kept that notebook in a bureau in my bedroom and every time I'd have a little thought about how to gig somebody and get around the issue, I'd make a note of it . . . I may have had twenty-five or thirty pages of notes in there. But I learned one thing and that is don't ever let them off the defensive.

Sanford put that lesson to good effect in 1954. He exposed the fraud, called in the SBI and the FBI, secured confessions from one of the perpetrators and gave every possible publicity to the tactic.[28]

But Scott's success in fighting off that smear illustrated the dilemma southern liberals faced after the *Brown* decision. Sanford's anger at the smear was not because the statement by the Winston-Salem black was false—it was not: the African American was a genuine supporter of Scott. The anger was at the implication that Scott was not a supporter of segregation. What Scott had said when *Brown* was announced was that, "I have always opposed, and still am opposed, to Negro and white children going to school together." Scott, as did all southern liberals, called for compliance with the law of the land, but also made it clear that he did not intend to run against popular sentiment. Other liberals, like Albert Gore, endorsed the decision more explicitly, but were still careful to point out that advocating compliance did not mean that they approved of the decision. Lyndon Johnson and Estes Kefauver both argued that people of goodwill at the local level should best resolve the matter.[29]

In 1954 and 1955 the contradictions in these stances were not exposed. In 1956 the liberals found it harder to square the political circle. In 1954 and 1955 it may have been, as Albert Gore recalled, that white southerners still did not think that school desegregation would actually happen. By 1956 they could be under no such illusion. The *Brown II* implementation decree, the petitions of African American parents to local school boards, for example in Dallas County, Alabama, and the appearance of black plaintiffs in court as in Little Rock, indicated that desegregation would eventually get underway. Conservative leaders throughout the South moved to alert white southerners of the danger and to impose conformity in defense of segregation. Citizens' Council leaders attempted to coerce local dissenters into silence. Black Belt leaders in the state legislatures attempted to prevent any local school board stepping out of line and voluntarily complying with court-ordered school desegregation. The authors of the Southern Manifesto, notably Harry Byrd, Strom Thurmond, and Richard Russell, aimed to impose a regional "unity of action" and force the five or six southerners in the Senate who Russell lamented were prepared to agree with the *Brown* decision to get off the fence and proclaim their determination to resist the Supreme Court.[30]

Most southern liberal politicians ran for cover. Lister Hill, facing opposition from right-wing zealot John Crommelin, almost fell over himself in the rush to sign the Southern Manifesto. Indeed, Fulbright claimed that Hill signed without even reading it. Sparkman and the Alabama congressional delegation followed suit. Sparkman was soon being praised by Citizens' Council leader Sam Engelhardt for his part in bringing about "a unified effort ... in Congress by all the Southerners to uphold our traditions of segregation." William Fulbright claimed to have signed more reluctantly after changes were made in the draft of the manifesto. His aides, anxious to disassociate him from the intemperate document, drafted a statement explaining why he would not sign: the manifesto held out the "false illusion" that the Supreme Court decision could be overturned and would merely alienate non-southerners and make the task of resisting forcible federal intervention more difficult. Fulbright rejected their advice and remained convinced "that I wouldn't have survived politically if I hadn't taken the course I did." Kerr Scott in North Carolina made the same move, even more reluctantly. He had been deluged with mail from the North Carolina Patriots in early 1956 and did "not intend to run counter to the majority of our people in North Carolina which is against integration." He changed his mind and attempted to take his name off the list of signers but he was too late. Brooks Hays, like Scott, regretted signing. He only signed when Faubus came to Washington and persuaded Hays and James Trimble, at Trimble's hospital bedside, to sign, "if we did not do something along that line to quiet the people down, that we would find what he called the Ku Klux Klan and the extreme Citizens' Council groups taking over the political life of the state, and that the racists and the radicals would displace the moderates."[31]

It was a decisive move for men like Hill, Scott, and Fulbright. Hill cut himself from contact with anybody that might taint him with racial liberalism. As his old campaign manager Richard Rives started making landmark decisions protecting black rights on the Fifth Circuit Court, so Hill disowned him. They had offices in the same federal building in Montgomery, yet Hill never talked to Rives from 1956 to the time he retired from the Senate in 1968. He cut off all personal and public contact with Supreme Court justice Hugo Black, the man to whom Hill owed his Senate seat. He even took a portrait of Black off the wall in his own home, lest any visitor suspect that he had any sympathy with the judge's views. Even as Virginia Durr voted for Hill in 1962, she noted sadly that she had not talked to her old family friend for eight years.[32]

Fulbright continued to appoint liberal staff who attempted to push him toward a more moderate stand on civil rights, but he refused to divert from his opposition to any federally inspired racial change. During the Little Rock school crisis, Sid McMath pleaded with Fulbright to return to the state and make a television address to call for compliance with the law but he failed to do so. His staff urged him to return from an Interparliamentary Union meeting in London and make a statement but Fulbright used his absence in London as a justification for refusing to comment. He never abandoned his belief that hypocritical neo-abolitionists in the North were attempting to impose alien change on the South. He fully participated in the filibusters against civil rights legislation in 1964 and 1965 and voted against the open housing act in 1968. He did this despite the fact that his assistants believed in 1964 that they had persuaded him to vote for a closure motion to end the filibuster. He did this despite LBJ's entreaties. He did this despite the mounting evidence that business interests and even conservative religious groups in Arkansas by the mid-1960s were prepared to accept the desegregation of public accommodations and the protection of black voting.[33]

Kerr Scott's aide, Bill Cochrane, was always sad that he had not been able to take the senator's name off the list of signatories of the manifesto. Scott, he recalled, never believed in that kind of "strong stuff." But North Carolina leaders had brought forward the Pearsall Plan, the state's own version of massive resistance which would allow local schools to close rather than desegregate. The state's leaders aimed to stir up segregationist sentiment, to persuade whites in eastern North Carolina that school desegregation could be avoided in the foreseeable future. Scott endorsed the Pearsall Plan. His protégé, Terry Sanford, would continue to support the plan right through 1964. North Carolina's resistance succeeded so well that fewer African American children were attending white schools in 1964 than in any other southern state.[34]

Liberals who took a bolder line nevertheless offered a precisely circumscribed alternative. Sid McMath recalled, "there were people, intelligent and educated people, and people in positions of leadership that knew it [desegregation] was inevitable." People in Little Rock were prepared, he said, to accept the Blossom plan for school desegregation in 1957. "The Virgil Blossom plan, if Faubus had stayed out of it, would have gone in and worked...if they'd had proper leadership at the time the Central High School thing never would have happened." But McMath himself admits that the Little Rock crisis caught him unawares: too late did he and Winthrop Rockefeller go round to see Faubus to try and dissuade him from his strategy of defiance. Community leaders in Little Rock had cooperated with Blossom in winning over elite opinion: they had made no effort to win over the support of lower-income whites whose children would attend Central High. It was as if they thought that by keeping quiet, school desegregation would slip in without arousing mass white outrage.[35]

Similarly in Alabama, Folsom proved incapable of devising a successful strategy to confront the three challenges he faced in 1956: the barrage of anti-desegregation measures that were going to pass the state legislature, what to do about the bus boycott in his own state capital, and what to do about the court-ordered entry of Autherine Lucy to the University of Alabama. He might denounce the legislature's interposition resolution as futile but he persisted in his public belief that you could maintain segregation *and* uphold the Supreme Court decision, and he advanced no alternative strategy for facilitating gradual desegregation. In Montgomery, secret meetings with black leaders seemed to convince him of their steadfast intent; indeed, he may have encouraged them to step up their demands to call for the complete dismantling of segregation on the buses. But his call for a biracial commission to solve the problem was irrelevant and ineffectual when white leaders were simply not prepared to negotiate. As the mob gathered, determined to prevent Autherine Lucy from enrolling at the university, Folsom was on a drinking and fishing spree. By the time he sobered up and rang his office from a payphone in a country store, the mob had won. It would take another seven years of increasingly racist politics before the federal courts would finally end Alabama's massive resistance.[36]

The congressmen who refused to sign the Southern Manifesto also offered a cautious strategy for racial change. What they wanted was token compliance whereby the issue of school desegregation could be left to local men and women of goodwill of both races. This was an important argument against the massive resisters who were determined not to let local school boards have the discretion to desegregate. But there was a substantial element of wishful thinking in the liberals' approach. The moderate strategy begged the question of what would happen if local white men and women of goodwill would not agree to desegregate, because the liberals had also set their face firmly against what they called "forced integration." Their faith that economic growth would produce gradual racial change also involved a good deal of wishful thinking. Southern business leaders, as Jim Cobb has shown, were prepared for the longest time to believe that they could have economic modernization and preserve traditional patterns of race relations at the same time. They were prepared to tolerate very considerable damage to the region and their communities before they decided that the cost of resistance was too high. Finally, southern liberal politicians, like southern conservatives, could not really envisage African Americans dictating the timetable of racial change. It was not surprising that Albert Gore, Jim Wright, and Dante Fascell could refuse to sign the Southern Manifesto, vote for the 1957 and 1965 Civil Rights Acts which dealt with the right to vote, but vote against the 1964 Civil Rights Act.[37]

VI

Did the white southern liberal politicians have to be so cautious? Did they have to be so deferential to white segregationist sentiment?

A historian should not lightly second-guess the conclusions of a Frank Smith, a Carl Elliott, or a Hale Boggs from Deep South states, who decided that they could not afford to take a public stand in favor of black civil rights or school desegregation. The fate of two North Carolinian nonsigners of the Southern Manifesto, Charles Deane and Thurmond Chatham, particularly the conscientious constituency servant Deane, shows that the perils of electoral retribution were real enough. It is difficult to see that there was much room for maneuver in Mississippi, in South Carolina, or perhaps in Louisiana. But the survival of Estes Kefauver and Albert Gore in Tennesssee suggests that liberals could survive where a significant part of the state political leadership defined the parameters for debate in such a way that racial moderates earned a measure of protection.[38]

In Arkansas, where his own brother-in-law had presided over school desegregation in Fayetteville, it is difficult to see why William Fulbright had to be so cautious. Fulbright's chief assistant liked to drive off potential opposition by depriving possible candidates of any sources of campaign funds in the fall before a reelection year. When Fulbright signed the manifesto in 1956 he was already assured of the backing of the single most powerful source of funds in the state. Witt Stephens was firmly behind Fulbright because of the senator's support for the Arkansas Louisiana Gas Company. Fulbright was still on close terms with the Faubus administration.[39] In Alabama, where the state's three leading elected politicians were all liberals and where the state House delegation was the most liberal in the South, it seems that politicians could have afforded a more moderate racial stance. Hill faced no serious opposition in 1950. In 1956 his supporters assured him that he had nothing to worry about. Sparkman admitted that the "only really hard" campaign he ever had was in his first race for the House of Representatives in the 1930s. Subsequently, he was never forced into a run-off in the whole of his political career.[40]

Closet moderates justified their racial caution by maintaining that they needed to stay in office to reserve their influence for racial moderation and economic liberalism. Yet they faced more and more right-wing segregation-ist opponents, some of whom would see to Frank Smith and Carl Elliott's defeats in 1962 and 1964. And increasingly they had to moderate their eco-nomic liberalism as their constituents responded more and more favorably to the anti-government rhetoric of the segregationists.[41]

Most southern liberal politicians found it difficult to envisage the end of segregation. Even those who believed that segregation was wrong were under-standably in no hurry to give up the privileges that the system brought to them as whites. Some, like Charles Deane, had undoubtedly come to the conclusion that segregation was wrong from a Christian and moral point of view, at least once the Supreme Court had pointed the way. Such decisions were, on the whole, guarded and individual: they secured support from state and regional church groups, but much less often from local congregations. Most put a premium on obedience to the law. But such views were not likely to lead politicians to risk a crusade or campaign for compliance with school desegregation in the 1950s as long as they believed that the mass of white sentiment was opposed to racial change.

But, as David Chappell points out, staunch segregationists were by no means equally convinced that the majority of whites were zealously deter-mined to defend segregation. Most liberal politicians believed that whites were so stirred up on the race issue that politicians had either to retreat and become "closet moderates" or to adopt a stealth-like approach to racial change. Conservative leaders, by contrast, feared that public opinion was insuffi-ciently aroused on the race issue, that most southerners were too likely to accept the inevitability of compliance with the Supreme Court. The difference was that in the 1950s, conservatives passionately committed to segregation were prepared to mount a righteous crusade to convince white southerners that desegregation was not inevitable, that white supremacy could be pro-tected. Liberal and moderate politicians, personally much less passionate about the issue of desegregation, were not prepared to take their case to the people. In a battle between politicians prepared to take their case for massive resistance to the people and politicians who were reluctant to campaign for gradualism, there could only be one winner.[42]

One reason why southern liberal politicians were so resigned was that they were much more attuned to the passions of their white constituents than to the impatience of their black supporters. White liberals were unable to penetrate the ritual of condescension and deference that characterized their relations with black leaders. Their relationships with the African American community were conducted at a distance. We do not yet know enough about how politicians secured black support in the politics of the 1940s and 1950s.

They rarely campaigned directly for black support. Instead they approached, usually through intermediaries, local leaders in the black community who delivered their community's vote as a bloc. Kerr Scott used a funeral director in Winston-Salem and a janitor at East Carolina Teacher's College. Folsom used his chauffeur, Winston Craig. When Charles Deane, perhaps the most liberal southern congressman, faced a tough primary battle after refusing to sign the Southern Manifesto, he had to write to James Taylor at North Carolina College in Durham to check out the names of African Americans in his own district whom he could contact. To no avail, the black vote in Rockingham was delivered to his opponent by the sheriff's contacts in the black community. Revealingly, Sid McMath, when interviewed by John Egerton, could barely remember the names of the African American leaders he dealt with. When Terry Sanford ran for governor in 1960, he claims to have turned down the offer of the black vote in Durham in the first primary. Instead ,he arranged for the vote to go to another candidate. He knew he was going to need a second primary and he did not want his opponent to be able to identify him as a recipient of the black bloc vote. By contrast, when a younger politician like Dante Fascell ran for Congress in 1954 he recalled that he was the first candidate in Miami to campaign for the black vote "in daylight."[43]

African American leaders understood the system and the limitations of their leverage. In 1950, when Strom Thurmond ran against Olin Johnston for the Senate, the Reverend I. DeQuincy Newman explained that "It was a matter of choosing between a rattler and a moccasin." Johnston campaigned by attacking Thurmond for appointing a black doctor, a "nigger physician," said Johnston, to the state medical board. But African Americans remembered, as Modjeska Simkins put it, that "Strom vilified Negroes in 1948... and we swore vengeance." An estimated 50,000 African Americans voted overwhelmingly for Johnston, who won by fewer than 28,000 votes. Sometimes politicians unexpectedly came up against undiluted African American sentiment. Ed Dunaway recalls taking Sid McMath in 1949 to a meeting of the Urban League in Little Rock. Harry Bass gave the secretary's report. According to Dunaway, "he got up there and started haranguing and waving his arms and he said that there—this had nothing to do with any report of activities—he said, 'there is absolutely nothing wrong with intermarriage between Blacks and whites'... Well, I thought Sid was very uneasy as you can imagine, and I was absolutely, almost purple and finally said, he just kept on, finally Sid said, 'Ed, I can't sit here and listen to this.' So we got up and walked out of the damn meeting."[44]

But more often prudent black leaders, "racial diplomats" as Numan Bartley describes them, told white politicians what they thought the white politicians wanted to hear. In 1956, for example, I. S. McClinton in Arkansas assured Fulbright's aide that the black community recognized that the Arkansas senator had no alternative but to sign the Southern Manifesto. Most white politicians were shielded from the growing sense of grievance in the black community: they did not have the same personal feel for the humiliations and impatience of the black community that they had for the fears of the white community.[45]

As a result this first postwar system of biracial politics simply could not satisfy the demands of black voters. Montgomery provided an early example of how politics failed to yield results and pushed African Americans into direct action. As Mills Thornton showed, black voters constituted 7.5 percent of the electorate and held the balance of power between two white factions. They used this leverage to secure concessions from white politicians on the appointment of black policemen, for representatives on the parks board, and for better treatment on the buses. When Mrs. Parks was arrested, black leaders intended to use the boycott simply as a temporary method of increasing that leverage. It was the intransigence of the white community that negated that form of political negotiation and drove the black leaders to the courts to seek the complete overthrow of bus segregation and a sustained boycott. By contrast in Mobile Joseph Langan actively solicited black support in his race for the state legislature in 1946 and worked closely with NAACP leader, John LeFlore, to protect black voters and to equalize teachers' salaries. In 1953 he was elected to the city commission with black support which he publicly welcomed. In office he worked with LeFlore and the Non-Partisan Voters' League to secure urban renewal, desegregate public accommodations, schools, and the University of South Alabama. Because the system was responsive, African Americans in Mobile eschewed direct-action protest.[46]

In most communities, however, biracial politics in its 1950s variant increasingly could not deliver the changes in segregation that black community leaders and their supporters wanted. Direct action, rather than electoral politics and negotiation, and demands for the immediate, rather than gradual, end of segregation increasingly became the tactics of the black community.

This is a process of racial protest and political change that is rather different from that outlined by Michael Klarman and David Chappell. Klarman sees the violent white supremacist backlash after *Brown* as producing ultimate federal intervention. Chappell sees the divisions in the white community over the best way to defend segregation being shrewdly exploited by the civil rights movement. My interpretation is that white conservative aggression and white liberal fatalism ensured that the system of biracial politics failed to deliver the changes that African Americans wanted. African Americans, rather than exploiting white divisions, were forced into direct-action tactics by white unity. The white backlash to these protests generated the political dynamic of the 1960s where federal intervention mandated racial change and whites had to come to terms, belatedly, with the implications of inevitable racial change.

VII

No white southerner could dictate the timetable of racial change in the 1960s. The civil rights movement from below and the federal government from outside executed a squeeze play on the South. One southern liberal was, however, a key player in this exercise, Lyndon B. Johnson. In moves that brought joy to his old radical New Deal friends from the South, Aubrey Williams and Virginia Durr, Johnson secured the passage of coercive federal legislation, rather than voluntary local agreements, to provide for immediate, rather than gradual, change in public accommodations and voting in the Civil Rights Acts of 1964. Johnson's Great Society also produced the economic and welfare reforms that southern liberals had been pushing for in the 1940s and federal aid to education, another southern liberal article of faith. Kerr Scott's former campaign manager, Terry Sanford, saw his creation, the North Carolina Fund, serve as both a model and an ally of the war on poverty.[47]

In the politics produced by civil rights protest on the one hand and white backlash on the other, the white southern liberal politicians had little role to play. The dominant figures of the 1960s were the good ol' boy segregationists and business leaders.[48]

The short-term consequence of the failure of the system of biracial politics was that the lower-income whites who potentially supported liberal candidates on economic issues, increasingly supported segregationists in the late 1950s and 1960s who combined a "common man good ol' boy appeal" with the staunchest rhetorical defense of white supremacy: men like Orval Faubus, Ross Barnett, Lester Maddox, and, preeminently, George Wallace. The attempts by old southern liberals—McMath and Folsom in 1962, Carl Elliott and Ellis Arnall in 1966—to halt the tide were doomed.[49]

The leaders who finally recognized the inevitability of federally imposed racial change were business leaders who belatedly saw the damage to their community's economies that massive resistance was causing. As Jim Cobb showed years ago, southern business leaders moved to help their communities to take the first steps toward integration. As Sanford Brookshire, president of the Chamber of Commerce and then mayor of Charlotte recalled, "It seems odd now that . . . I, and I think the rest of the white community throughout the South were overlooking the legal and moral aspects of the problem . . . the Chamber was aware and concerned about the boycotts and disruption of business in [other cities], apprehensive that Charlotte might suffer in a like manner unless the protest movement could be contained here." As Harry Golden acidly noted, Charlotte's business leaders "would elect Martin Luther King or Malcolm X mayor if somehow one of them could give them a guarantee of no labor unions and no minimum wage for laundry workers." Two white leaders were crucial in negotiating a settlement to the racial crisis in Birmingham in 1963. One was the reform mayor Albert Boutwell, elected after David Vann and other young professionals had swept out the old city commission government. The other was Sid Smyer of the Senior Citizens Committee. What had these two leaders been doing when liberal Jim Folsom was confronting the racial crisis in Alabama in 1956? Boutwell had been the mastermind behind the massive resistance in the state legislature. Sid Smyer, a leading former Dixiecrat, was busy in the North Alabama Methodist Conference. He was making sure that the Conference did not unite with another jurisdiction that was integrated, and he was orchestrating lay pressure on any Methodist minister who showed signs of departing from racial orthodoxy.[50]

The passage of the 1965 Voting Rights Act and the dramatic extension of black voter registration led to a biracial coalition very different from the lower-income alliance that southern liberal politicians had put together in the 1940s and 1950s. Now affluent whites and blacks formed a cross-class biracial coalition based on shared interests in peaceful racial change. In the 1970s there were new young faces adept at coalition building—moderate enough on racial issues to satisfy their black constituency, conservative enough on social and economic issues to appeal to white voters. Racial moderation was allied to business progressivism. That combination was too powerful for William Fulbright. When Dale Bumpers challenged the senator in 1974 the 125,000 registered black voters in Arkansas voted 4 to 1 to retire Fulbright from office.[51]

But alongside the bright New South politicians and the transmogrification of old-style segregationists like Wallace and Thurmond who now had to adjust to the reality of African American voting, there was another shift, a shift that put the final nail in the southern liberal coffin. Lower-income white voters who had been conservative and anti-government on race now became conservative and anti-government on economic issues as well.

Whites in eastern North Carolina had been the backbone of the liberal wing of the Democratic Party in the state since the New Deal. In 1964 whites in eastern Carolina resisted the blandishments of Barry Goldwater, no doubt because of the threat he posed to tobacco price supports. African American assertiveness had not yet impinged on their daily lives. But after 1964, school desegregation finally came to the East, albeit in token form. It was one thing for the affluent whites of the Piedmont to tolerate racial change when they could retreat to their white suburbs or send their children to private schools. These options were not open to whites in eastern Carolina. African American assertiveness was even more threatening in areas where large black populations would be competing with whites for scarce economic resources. White taxpayers lost sympathy with the redistributionist spending and welfare programs of the Great Society which seemed to them to reward lawlessness and rioting. They saw traditional cultural and religious values undermined by rioters, privileged students at Chapel Hill who protested the Vietnam War and burned the flag, and a Supreme Court which banned school prayer and opposed segregated schools, yet sanctioned pornography and protected the rights of criminals. The whites confronted these changes when the tobacco economy they depended on was being revolutionized by mechanization. Driven from the land, they had to adjust to new work disciplines in low-wage sewing factories, pickle plants, and poultry-processing facilities. As Linda Flowers noted, "That they were all the victims of an utterly impersonal concentration of trends and forces, of history in fact, was not so satisfying an explanation as that somebody was in charge and caused the bottom to drop out." The scapegoats were easy to find: a liberal federal government, the national Democratic Party, and blacks.[52]

The first response was to join the Klan. Between 1964 and 1967 North Carolina had the largest Klan outside of Alabama and Mississippi. In 1968 they would vote for George Wallace. But no man was better positioned to tap their anger at the liberal media, communists in Chapel Hill, and Martin Luther King than Jesse Helms, who had been addressing their concerns daily first on the radio, then on WRAL TV 5. As Frank Rouse, Helms's ally in the Republican Party noted, "these Eastern North Carolina Democrats were rednecks...country...rural...extremely honest...plainspoken and ultraconservative...if not religious on a day to day basis...he would be inherent Southern Baptist...he may not go to church and Sunday School every week and go to choir practice on Thursday night, but because of his environment and because of his family, he would be religious." These rednecks compromised their political morality a bit by voting for Wallace in 1968, said Rouse, and that broke the bond. By 1972 they were ready to vote for Jesse Helms. That religious conservatism and economic insecurity was but a forerunner of what would happen in the South as a whole with the rise of the Christian Right and the economic insecurities of ordinary whites whose median income declined from the 1970s.[53]

So Jesse Helms, the supporter of the liberal Kerr Scott who had fostered a coalition of lower-income whites and blacks in the 1940s, had become the lily-white conservative Republican of the 1970s.

VIII

The Texas-born political scientist V. O. Key had confidently predicted that the collapse of the main institutional supports of conservative power, which duly took place, and the extension of political participation and competition, which also duly took place, would substitute the politics of economics for the politics of race. The forces of southern liberalism would be greatly strengthened and the "have-nots" who lost out in traditional southern politics would at last receive tangible benefits from the distribution of government largesse.

The politics of race did not disappear. The extension of political participation and competition did not in the long-run produce the liberal, class-based, biracial coalition of lower-income blacks and whites that Key expected. Instead, it produced a political system which pitted an all-white Republican Party against a Democratic Party that secured 90 percent of the African American vote but which to win sufficient white support to gain power had to espouse conservative economic policies.[54]

This polarization, as Numan Bartley rightly asserts, did not come about because in some immutable fashion "the font of southern racism was [always] poor and working-class whites." It came about because, confronted by the pressure for racial change in the 1950s, conservative leaders in the South were determined to convince ordinary southern whites that segregation could be preserved. White liberal politicians by contrast were paralyzed by their belief that mass white segregationist sentiment was overwhelming. Because their own commitment to racial change was so limited and their awareness of African American demands so second-hand, they could not devise a strategy for gradual racial change that could deliver substantive change to the African Americans who supported them in the 1950s variant of biracial politics.[55]

African Americans eschewed politics therefore for direct action. The pincer movement of the civil rights movement from below and the federal government from above imposed immediate and rapid racial change on the South. The calm with which the South reacted to these changes gave lie to the dire warnings of the segregationists. It was, of course, lower-income whites who bore the brunt of the physical reality of desegregation on a day-to-day basis in the South and they did not face it in a major way until the late 1960s, when their own economic future was uncertain. Their frustration with a government that imposed racial change and failed to halt cultural change spilled over into a hostility to government intervention in the economic sphere.

The dream of a liberal biracial politics was over.

8

From Defiance to Moderation: South Carolina Governors and Racial Change

It is a great privilege to share the platform tonight with two of the men, Senator Fritz Hollings and Governor John West, who did most among the white leadership to guide South Carolina into acceptance of the end of segregation and the embrace of dynamic and diversified economic growth, the state's move from defiance to moderation. It is also a daunting task, as I am not a historian of South Carolina, although I have done some work on the state's congressmen and the Southern Manifesto. I am not attempting tonight to add freshly researched material to the wonderfully nuanced studies of South Carolina's response to racial change by Marcia Synott and John G. Sproat, the comprehensive dissertation on 1963 by Ron Cox, the overview by Walter Edgar in his remarkable *South Carolina: A History,* or the fine study by Gordon Harvey of New South governors and education that features John West.[1] What I believe the organizers of the event want me to do, instead, is to put the established narrative of white South Carolina's response to racial change into a regional context, to see what was distinctive and what was not about the state's reaction.

I

It may be a measure of British provincialism but unfortunately South Carolina does not feature in the news in Britain very often. Even the hundredth birthday of Senator Strom Thurmond might not have broken that pattern of neglect. But the BBC's Washington correspondent, Nick Bryant, was a Cambridge historian who went to Oxford to write a rather good Ph.D. dissertation on the Kennedy administration and civil rights. He was also a great admirer of Dan Carter's biography of George Wallace. So, well before the furor over Trent Lott's comments, British viewers and listeners had the benefit of listening to Professor Carter give his views at some length on the then-senior senator. At the same time, the *Economist* reminded its British readers of Olin Johnston's comment, handed on by Harry Ashmore, on listening to one of Senator Thurmond's diatribes on the subject of civil rights, "Listen to ol' Strom. He really believes all that shit."[2]

Johnston's implication that South Carolina politicians, unlike Thurmond, did not believe their segregationist rhetoric has been widely accepted. Johnston himself warned a young Dick Riley that segregation was on its way out—and should be. William Jennings Bryan Dorn remembered, "We did not really believe what we said back then." For that matter, Thurmond himself always denied the Dixiecrat movement was about race. Leading political figures told John Sproat, off the record, in the early 1980s that they had known from the start that segregation was doomed. The argument was that the forces of popular mass white racism were so powerful that no politician could challenge them and be reelected. Harriet Keyserling from a later generation of reformers accepted that argument in her memoirs. The linked argument was that precipitate desegregation would unleash a tidal force of white violence and pave the way for racial demagoguery of the Tillman and Cole Blease variety. Rembert Dennis argued that the Gressette School Committee, the legal fountain spring of South Carolina's massive resistance legislation, "was more of a delaying procedure, a maneuver because of the finance involved than it was any real effort to forever thwart it [desegregation]. Everybody recognized it couldn't be done. It was just a delaying proposition, until the state could take on the full responsibility, principally in education, of full integration."[3]

These views are not merely the comfortable efforts of veteran politicians to reassure themselves. They are closely linked to two important strands in current historiography. The first is Michael Klarman's argument that the *Brown* decision "temporarily destroyed racial moderation in the South and it halted the incipient amelioration of Jim Crow practices that had been occurring in much of the South in the late 1940s and early 1950s." It propelled "southern politics towards racial fanaticism" because it "decreed that racial change take place first in an area of life—grade school education—where white southerners were certain to be most resistant." Similarly, Numan Bartley argues that the civil rights movement was wrong to target education, it should have targeted voting rights where resistance would have been less. Bartley also blames national liberals and the Truman administration, in the same terms that Olin Johnston did, for substituting a moralistic concern for symbolic opportunity and the elimination of *de jure* segregation for the substance of a drive to tackle the economic problems of lower-income blacks and whites.[4]

These views constitute what I call the "self-exculpatory model" of massive resistance in South Carolina. The responsibility for massive resistance lies with everybody *except* the white political leaders of the state. The blame is placed on racist white workers in the state, the NAACP, the Supreme Court, and northern liberals. In the face of the obstacles placed by these irresponsible forces, the leadership of the state acted with as much restraint as it could.

If the model of South Carolina in the 1950s is self-exculpatory, the model of the state in the 1960s is "self-congratulatory." From the peaceful integration of Clemson in 1963, anticipated and orchestrated by Governor Hollings, to the collapse of "freedom of choice" schemes and the acceptance of substantial school integration under the watchful eye of Governors Robert McNair and John West, South Carolina surprised observers by the peaceful nature of racial change in contrast to the violent confrontations that wracked Alabama and Mississippi. The state's responsible leadership received high praise from the Kennedy administration. Its governors attracted national media attention and commendation. And historians have concurred. The titles themselves convey the essence, "Firm Flexibility," "Integration with Dignity," "Pragmatic Conservatism," "Calm and Exemplary."

What had happened? Gordon Harvey saw John West as one in "a long line of moderate governors who have steered South Carolina to safety through the swirling waters of Civil Rights without major violence." According to Walter Edgar, following Numan Bartley, the new growth-oriented metropolitan elites had triumphed over the old traditional county elites. They did so by championing "moderation and social stability," and thus used "an old and venerated South Carolina tradition." These elites and the governors of the 1960s had realized that order and harmony were crucial to economic growth and that was more important than preserving the racial status quo.[5]

There is some force to the self-exculpatory model of defiance and the self-congratulatory model of moderation. But let me try and tease them out a little and ask some questions about the context, and try to make explicit the implicit comparisons which often underpin them.

II

The self-exculpatory account of the years of defiance up to 1963 plays down the coherence and proactive quality of the massive resistance strategy in

South Carolina and underestimates just how pioneering and successful the strategy was in a regional context.

Fritz Hollings and John West were together here at the Citadel before the war. World War II was a formative experience. As West recalls:

> We spent four years in public service of a very special but very demanding kind. And we realized that there were satisfactions in public service. The four years that we spent many of us had opportunities—Fritz Hollings for example in North Africa, I in the Pacific, including Japan with the occupation forces [and] you were then on a mission that was an unselfish mission in terms of you weren't working for yourself. You were working for a bigger cause, a cause that transcended any selfish motives. The only selfish motive was trying to survive of course. So, I think that our class, and I look back at the group that came into our university law school in 1946, many of them entered public service, and a lot of political people: Jim Mann, Hugo Sims in the Congress, innumerable people in the legislature and, of course, Hollings himself.[6]

Throughout the South white veterans were coming back determined to construct a better South.

They went to law school under the GI bill, they dominated the legislatures, for example, of Texas in 1946 and Mississippi in 1948, they organized GI revolts against local political machines and rings, they supported candidates for statewide office who were putting together coalitions of lower-income whites and the small, but increasing black electorates, candidates who promised the long-overdue investment in public services that had been denied so long by conservative elites, candidates like war hero Sid McMath in Arkansas.[7]

In South Carolina such a candidate was Strom Thurmond, war hero, injured when his glider crashed behind enemy lines of D Day. When Thurmond ran for governor in 1946 and promised a "progressive outlook, a progressive program, a progressive leadership," when he called in his inaugural for greater attention to Negro education and equal rights to women, he sounded like so many of the New Deal–style southern liberals elected in the late 1940s. When he claimed "the solution of our economic problems" would cause racial problems to disappear, he sounded like a Hodding Carter or a Frank Smith. When he explicitly equated ridding the state of the influence of the Barnwell ring with ridding Europe of the Nazis—"I was willing to stamp out such gangs in Europe"—he sounded for everything like a Sid McMath in Arkansas or a Delesseps Morrison in New Orleans.[8]

But like fellow veteran Herman Talmadge in Georgia, Thurmond argued that the freedom he had fought for in Europe was the freedom to fight for traditional patterns of race relations. Thurmond took the state not down the liberal GI route but the Dixiecrat route. Whatever he claimed later, race, of course, was at the core of the Dixiecrat challenge. It was important to tell the nation that "there's not enough troops in the army to force the southern people to break down segregation and admit the Negro race into our theaters, into our swimming pools, into our homes, and into our churches."[9]

Thurmond's presidential run in 1948 may have been a quixotic gesture, born of opportunism and ambition. But it was fundamentally a preemptive strike against civil rights legislation. And, as such, had the overwhelming support of most of the South Carolina political establishment, especially the congressional delegation in the House, if not Senator Johnston. It was, as the *Spartanburg Herald* complained, a "top-heavy organization." If the national Democrats were competing for the black vote, then the independence of the South manifested by the revolt in 1948 would either put a Republican in the White House or would force the Democrats to make concessions in the future. The convoluted stance of the national Democrats on civil rights and party loyalty later in 1952 and 1956 suggest this tactic did have an effect. Thurmond's successor in the governer's mansion in Columbia, his local friend James F. Byrnes, "knew that third parties were never going anywhere." Instead, he adapted Thurmond's strategy into, first, attempts to mobilize regional solidarity in the Democratic Party, to reinstitute Calhoun's doctrine of a concurrent majority so that the South could thwart federal civil rights initiatives, then second, into support for Republicans—for Eisenhower in 1952 and later for Richard Nixon.[10]

Byrnes returned to South Carolina as governor with immense prestige in the state with both the traditional county and new metropolitan elites. He came back with unparalleled international exposure and experience at the highest echelons of the country's legislative, executive, and judicial branches. No one was better placed to lead South Carolina into a realistic acceptance of racial change. As the future superintendent of education, C. B. Busbee, recalled, "whatever the problem was," the universal assumption was that Byrnes "could solve it."[11]

Byrnes instead took the lead in masterminding the region's resistance to racial change. First, Byrnes and attorney Robert Figg conceded that the schools in Clarendon County, the subject of the *Briggs v. Elliott* case, were not equal. Then he put before the legislature a massive school equalization program and secured the passage of a three-cent sales tax to fund it. The aim was to render "separate but equal" genuinely equal and to forestall court-ordered desegregation. No other state mounted such a massive program. It was a remarkable achievement and had a short-term success in persuading the local federal court, over Judge Waring's passionate objection, to give the state time to make good its commitment to equalization. The dramatic improvement in black schools may possibly have lessened the African American leadership's desire to push school desegregation cases in the state. It is also important to stress that this coherent preemptive strategy meant that conservatives had the only coherent strategy on offer in the region in the years before the *Brown* decision. Southern liberals, as I have argued elsewhere, may have espoused the necessity for gradual racial change, but they did not lay out a strategy for achieving that change. Liberals may have believed that eventual desegregation was inevitable, but they did not share that insight with the voters. The Byrnes strategy had the field to itself before 1954.[12]

The second strand of Byrnes's strategy was to take charge of the legal defense in the school desegregation cases: first, to persuade legendary lawyer John W. Davis to take the case; then to lobby his old Supreme Court colleagues, Fred Vinson and Felix Frankfurter; next, to persuade his political ally, Dwight Eisenhower, to prevent the Justice Department filing an *amicus curiae* brief on the part of the plaintiffs; and finally, to persuade the attorney-general of Kansas, a state in which facilities were genuinely equal, to join the case. This personal tour de force, of course, came to naught to Byrnes's bitter disappointment and surprise. But I believe Byrnes's efforts made an important contribution to the short-term success of massive resistance. His warnings of bloodshed and demagoguery in the event of precipitate desegregation may not have finally swayed the justices in the first *Brown* decision. But Byrnes's warnings, his reputation among the judges and with the president, must have influenced the implementation decree the following year. It also shaped Eisenhower's refusal to put his massive personal authority behind the *Brown* decision, and the Court's subsequent reluctance in the 1950s to assert its authority in school desegregation cases. As the Court bent over backward to accommodate the South, the argument of moderates and liberals that white southerners had no alternative but to comply with the law of the land was undercut. It was patently obvious that the Court could be defied. The Clarendon County case highlighted that result. After *Brown II*, Judge Parker ruled that the decision did not mandate integration, only non-segregation, paving the way for pupil placement laws. The reason the NAACP did not commit resources to appeal that decision was that they feared that a Supreme Court, influenced by its faith in the reasonableness of southerners like Jimmy Byrnes, would formally accept that the Parker interpretation was adequate.[13]

Byrnes had spurned the opportunity to provide moderate regional leadership before 1954. In 1954 there was another opportunity. He might have led South Carolina into accepting *Brown* as the law of the land and mediated the transition to some form of gradual compliance with the decision. That prospect for Byrnes was held out by historian Arthur Schlesinger, who communicated with Byrnes via the old New Dealer, Ben Cohen, who had worked with Byrnes at the State Department. For Schlesinger, the "greatest challenge to constructive statesmanship that we have had in this country" was for responsible southerners to bring forward plans that fully took into account local conditions—but "honestly directed to the abolition of segregation in the schools"—provided "responsible northerners" did "not insist on abrupt or precipitate changes." Might, Schlesinger asked Cohen, Byrnes "now accept the inevitable and dedicate these last years to an earnest attempt to work the thing out?"[14]

Schlesinger's query reflected how much prestige Byrnes enjoyed in the North. One can only speculate on what might have happened if Byrnes, who had so much political power and prestige in rural and metropolitan South Carolina, who was as comfortable with farmers as with business giants, and Eisenhower, with his immense status as a military hero and his reputation particularly among southern businessmen, had invested their prestige in making it clear to white southerners that the Supreme Court had to be obeyed. One reason why Eisenhower would not was because of the respect he had for Byrnes. What Byrnes and other conservatives in the South failed to realize was just how much understanding and leeway that northerners, including ADA liberals like Schlesinger, were prepared to show the South. As Walter Jackson has shown, northern liberals were as gradualist as their southern counterparts. They accepted the southern argument that precipitate change would lead to violence and demagoguery. They were no more anxious to secure speedy compliance than white southerners.[15]

Instead of compliance, the General Assembly, under the grim leadership of George Bell Timmerman, passed just about every massive resistance measure known to man. Timmerman himself was determined that "segregation would not end in a 1000 years." By the time the Gressette committee had done its work, the state had deleted its constitutional provision for public schools, taken the power to withdraw state funds from any schools to and from which courts had ordered a student transferred, given local school board rules the force of law, screened library books, investigated the NAACP at State college, banned NAACP members from government employment, closed Edisto State Beach, and reaffirmed bus segregation. In 1956, in Howard Quint's words, the General Assembly passed segregation measures at a mass production rate.[16]

South Carolina's version of massive resistance worked. It created a closed society, just as closed as Mississippi, in which dissent was not tolerated. Fear, said an Episcopal minister, covered the state like a frost. Dissenting academics, both black and white, at the University of South Carolina, Benedict, Allen, and South Carolina State College were fired. Dissenting clergy were driven out by their congregations. Jack O'Dowd from the *Florence Morning News* left the state. What happened to Will Campbell and Hazel Brannon Smith in Mississippi happened to their counterparts in South Carolina. Public advocacy of moderation was restricted to the publication, organized by Episcopalian ministers, of *South Carolina Speaks: A Moderate Approach to Race,* itself a tortured and defensive volume, to the occasional church resolution, to the few chapters of the South Carolina Council for Human Relations led by the redoubtable Alice Norwood Spearman, and to the defense of public schools by women's clubs.[17]

This climate of conformity was not created simply by persuasion or even social ostracism. It was created by blatant economic pressure and by violence. [One of the abiding impressions of this conference in both papers and personal testimony is the countless examples of violence and economic intimidation, often unacknowledged in the records, directed especially at African Americans.] Black plaintiffs like Harry Briggs and his wife were fired. Other black activists, like Joseph Delaine, were fired on and his church burned. An African American candidate for the Gaffney City Council in 1952 withdrew because of death threats. Whites who helped blacks were flogged and beaten. As the Klan revived in the Piedmont in 1957 so, as Tim Tyson has vividly described, Klansmen on three occasions attempted to dynamite the house of Claudia Thomas Sanders, who contributed one of the less tortured essays to *South Carolina Speaks.* Sanders was ostracized by her friends and extended family. As Tyson concluded, "No public figure of any stature uttered one public word against either the attempt to kill Claudia Sanders and her family or the acquittal of her assailants. The silence was louder than the dynamite."[18]

Defiance in South Carolina, then, was not a restrained response by a leadership anxious to channel popular white supremacist thought into safe channels until an accommodation with inevitable change could be worked out. If there were politicians who saw the writing on the wall, they were silent. As a black minister once wryly observed to Calvin Trillin in 1960, if all the white politicians who said they were working backstage for racial justice actually were, "it must be pretty crowded there behind the scenes." What white leaders were concerned about was not that whites in the state or the region were too fired up on the race issue, rather they worried that they were too quiescent and resigned. Conservative journalist W. D. Workman bemoaned a "blight of submissiveness," the "cry of surrender." Citizens' Council leader Farley Smith complained of "the apathy of the average white citizen." Alice Spearman described the Committee of 52, leading clergy, businessmen and professional, who called for maintaining segregation and interposition, as a "revolt in high places." When the South Carolina Association of Citizens'

Councils gathered to hear James Eastland in early 1956, the entire political leadership of the state was on the platform. When Strom Thurmond drafted the Southern Manifesto, his aim was not to assuage popular racism, his aim was to stir up popular segregationist feeling by convincing wavering politicians and their constituents that the Supreme Court could, and should, be defied. Defiance in South Carolina was a top-down phenomenon.[19]

Would the defiance have been any less if the NAACP had not made education its primary target? The immediate postwar violence in response to any signs of black assertiveness do not suggest an alternative strategy would have provoked less opposition. If the NAACP had concentrated on voting, progress would not have been quick. The hysterical reaction to the end of the white primary, and the fact that only 10,000 additional blacks were able to register in the fifteen years, 1946–1961, did not suggest a calm reaction to an emphasis on voting. As in the rest of the South, violence was as likely to be the response to voter registration as it was to school desegregation drives.[20]

South Carolina leaders united for the long haul to defend segregation and white supremacy. Thurmond and Byrnes, in particular in 1948, 1950, and 1954, had separate opportunities to lead their state in a different direction. They chose not to. Instead, the leaders worked to convince white South Carolinians that the Supreme Court could be defied. The leaders did nothing to disabuse ordinary South Carolinians of that notion. White South Carolinians, like their leaders, saw no reason voluntarily to give up the privileges of whiteness if they did not have to, even if they had doubts about segregation, and South Carolina's leaders were telling them that they did not have to.

III

Fritz Hollings, both as a member of the General Assembly and as lieutenant governor, had been part of the inner circle masterminding South Carolina's strategy of defiance. He believed that most blacks favored segregation: "If there's one thing against our way of life in the South, it's the NAACP. And if the U.S. Supreme Court can declare certain organizations as subversive, I believe South Carolina can declare the NAACP both subversive and illegal." The NAACP was part of a conspiracy with the Congress of Industrial Organizations (CIO) and New England politicians to "cut off the flow of industry to the South." When he ran for governor in 1958 he race-baited his opponent, Donald Russell. Hollings maintained he was the candidate best qualified to "defend the southern way of life," in contrast to his opponent who had been prepared to entertain the possibility of integration at the University of South Carolina. Hollings promised to "resist the demands of a power-hungry federal government." Hollings's supporters would race-bait Russell again in the Senate race in 1966, distributing among textile mill workers photographs of Russell shaking hands with black civil rights leader Deke Newman at his integrated inaugural.[21]

But the context of that latter incident is revealing. The Hollings supporters had the photograph because Newman himself had given it to them, anxious to help Hollings win. Hollings had from the late 1940s spoken passionately about the appalling state of South Carolina schools. He had made it clear that, "it's foolish to even consider for a moment that abolishing public education is the solution, we can never abandon our public school system." South Carolina needed jobs and to get jobs it needed an educated work force, black and white. Hollings brought in John West and other powerful legislators to strengthen the State Development Board and to kick-start the industrial recruitment program. He continued spending on school education, attempted to turn the state universities into the equivalent of the North Carolina Research Triangle (a move thwarted by the lack of imagination of the University of South Carolina leadership), and instituted a major program of technical institutes that would provide the necessary skilled work force. Fifty-seven thousand new jobs came in four years. The economic progress Hollings and his allies sought would eventually come into conflict with the requirements of white supremacy and segregation.[22]

But first, Hollings had to confront civil rights demonstrations in 1960. It has been suggested that a moderate civil rights leadership in South Carolina tended to eschew direct-action protest and that this helped moderate white leadership in the state. But that is certainly not how Hollings experienced it:

> We had the first cases...I was on the scene. I was either out in front of Trinity Church, I was either out down the hill, I was over in Sumter, there was a competition thing. CORE would demonstrate in Charleston, time you got down there the NAACP had demonstrated in Columbia, then you came back to Columbia, then they'd break out with CORE in Rock Hill, and time you'd turn up at Rock Hill they'd try to put one down in Sumter.

What has not been much commented on is how Hollings handled these demonstrations in order to avoid violence. Just as Laurie Pritchett in 1961–62 in Albany, Georgia, realized that police and mob violence would give great leverage to the black protesters, so Hollings worked to avoid violence and he prided himself that no one got hurt at the South Carolina demonstrations. He understood that badly trained local police would make mistakes. Instead, he brought in black deputies from the State Law Enforcement Division (SLED), black policemen from Columbia, Charleston, the State College campus, and used them to police the demonstrations:

> We had black policemen policing the streets and the incidents, and when one of them [the demonstrators] stepped out of line there was a black policeman leading him to the paddy wagon and they then put away their cameras. They said this isn't what we wanted. So they started in this state but they didn't get the news story and the impact that they thought was necessary and we just stayed out there ahead of them every time.

Hollings believed that black leaders understood that he was enforcing the law impartially for blacks and whites. At the same time J. P. Strom, head of SLED, who did a "magnificent job" according to Hollings, was infiltrating the Klan and controlling white extremists. Hollings like his contemporary and fellow World War II veteran and ally in the Kennedy campaign of 1960, Terry Sanford, also kept open lines of communication with the black leadership.[23]

But it is important to remember that a corollary of the Laurie Pritchett approach was an uncompromising refusal to negotiate with the protesters. Similarly, Hollings's strategy made possible mass arrests and enabled local communities to refuse to negotiate with the sit-in demonstrators. As a result, communities in South Carolina in 1960 and 1961 did not make the concessions on the desegregation of lunch counters and public accommodations that cities in the North Carolina and Tennessee Piedmont did.[24]

When Hollings toured the state in 1961 he recalled, "People thought I ought to have some magic to stop the monster that was about to gobble us up, or else they expected me to go to jail. It looked to me like it was high time that we started sobering people up, before it turned out to be too late." One might note in parenthesis that it was the South Carolina leadership that had given people the drinks in the first place.[25]

In 1962 Hollings set about educating people that change would have to come. He told newspaper editors that they should prepare their readership for eventual defeat in the courts, that legal defenses would fall "like a house of cards," and that inevitable desegregation would follow. Benjamin Muse, traveling the state for the Southern Regional Council in 1961 and 1962, detected a note of change. All over the South southern businessmen had heeded the dreadful warning of what had happened at Little Rock and the loss of investment that had followed the violence and the school closings there. Representatives of the Little Rock Chamber of Commerce had made it their business to travel round the South warning communities not to go down the Little Rock route. In 1961 Atlanta businessmen had taken that warning to heart and paved the way for the desegregation of the University of Georgia and Atlanta schools. Alabama businessmen had started to react after the violence inflicted on the Freedom Riders in May 1961. Mississippi businessmen would respond more slowly. It would be the Ole Miss crisis that in retrospect convinced them that they were "whistling in the wind," "fighting a cannon with a pea shooter." In South Carolina in 1961 and 1962 construction magnate Charles Daniel and the textile manufacturers association chief executive John Cauthen were working to convince businessmen that they needed to support compliance with eventual Court decisions.[26]

It was the handling of the integration of Clemson at the start of 1963, the peaceful admission of Harvey Gantt, that really showed that South Carolina might avoid the violence that bedeviled other massive resistance states. "The conspiracy for peace" involved in that incident has been amply documented. But I just want to make three observations about the crisis.

First, the actual admission of Harvey Gantt took place on Governor Russell's watch, and Russell and his staff always claimed that "Hollings had little to do with it," that there was "no big planning," that Russell never talked to Hollings about it. "People may have drawn up a plan," said Russell, "but I don't think any particular plan like that was followed." This interpretation clearly flies in the face of all the evidence of the meetings of businessmen, newspapermen, and the Clemson administration that took place in the twelve months preceding desegregation. It also ignores the importance of Hollings's farewell address to the General Assembly, when he remarked that *Brown* was, "the fact of the land," that "South Carolina was running out of courts," that they operated under a "government of laws," "law and order would be maintained," and the state would conduct itself with "dignity." As John West recalls:

> The legislature was all white of course. It was very tense. If Hollings had said, "Go to War," the legislature would have done just that. They had all sorts of ideas of massive resistance...Then he departed from his text. He said to Pete Strom of SLED, "Pete, you make sure nothing happens up there." Well, that was a turning point and it was a stupid political move for the immediate situation, because there was no black voting in those days. It was really one of the most courageous and one of the most dramatic things I've seen in public life....And that speech simply deflated the strong pro-segregationist sentiment.[27]

Second, it has been argued that South Carolina would have complied with the courts irrespective of what had happened at Ole Miss in the fall of 1962.

Certainly, the planning, and university and government acceptance that they would have to comply with the courts, was already there. But Ole Miss clearly concentrated minds. Hollings refused to send a motorcade in support of Barnett. Instead, he sent Pete Strom to observe and that visit informed the detailed plan for Clemson they drew up, drawing on the lessons of Ole Miss: law enforcement control of the entire area around the university and, particularly, careful management of the press, giving them defined access and information on a controlled basis, but not allowing a free for all, "so they wouldn't roam around for a week ahead of time."[28]

Third, the Kennedy administration was as anxious to avoid another Little Rock as were South Carolina businessmen and, as Marcia Synott notes, harried federal officials fretting over crises in states like Alabama and Mississippi must have been relieved to see responsible leadership in South Carolina and were clearly prepared to cut the state a good deal of slack. John Seigenthaler, assistant to Bobby Kennedy, confirmed that faith in responsible local leaders. He recalled that there were three southern states where the administration believed, "there was a comfort level with the leadership": Oklahoma, North Carolina, and South Carolina. In each state there were governors—Howard Edmondson, Terry Sanford, and Fritz Hollings—who had worked for the Kennedy campaign in 1960. "But you had the feeling that Fritz and Howard and Terry had a handle on the politics of their own state. And that didn't mean they wouldn't whistle Dixie, it just means that they were going to make sure that progress was made." These were the responsible local leaders that the Kennedy executive civil rights strategy relied on. After Ole Miss, an understandably nervous administration was reluctant to trust southern assurances that troops would not be needed to enforce court orders, but they were, in the end, prepared to trust assurances they received from South Carolina: from William Jennings Bryan Dorn and the congressional delegation and from Governors Hollings and Russell.[29]

As Ron Cox has shown, Clemson was the model for the desegregation of the University of South Carolina and the desegregation of Charleston schools in 1963. In both cases, the state appealed Court decisions as far as it could in order to demonstrate that all avenues of protest had been exhausted. Meanwhile, the governor, the university officials, and the local officials made careful plans for peaceful desegregation.[30]

If Ole Miss had concentrated the minds of South Carolina's business and political leaders, so the violence in Birmingham in May 1963 concentrated the minds of local leaders as they confronted planned demonstrations and sit-ins to desegregate public accommodations in eight cities in June 1963. They had seen the appalling national publicity that Bull Connor's dogs had provoked. What happened, instead, in South Carolina was what had happened

earlier in upper South cities in 1960. Local business leaders worked feverishly to establish biracial committees that would negotiate a peaceful desegregation of public facilities. It was often a tortuous process. It involved riots and mass arrests in Charleston and no progress was made in Orangeburg and Sumter, which had to wait for the 1964 Act to compel the desegregation of local facilities. But, on the whole, urban South Carolina desegregated in 1963.[31]

Despite his integrated inaugural, Governor Donald Russell was as grudging a mediator of racial change as one might expect a protégé of the unrepentant and bitter Jimmy Byrnes to be. But his successor, Robert McNair, worked much harder so that the industrial development drive would not be derailed by racial violence. McNair had to confront the initial token compliance desegregation of most South Carolina school systems, the effects of the 1964 and 1965 civil rights acts, a new generation of more assertive African American leaders, and the eventual impatience of the courts with the slow pace of desegregation under freedom of choice plans and the requirement for full-scale integration. McNair worked tirelessly to keep lines of communications open with black leaders and developed an informal alliance with Deke Newman. He set up a fifteen-man advisory board that worked with community leaders and businessmen to facilitate peaceful school desegregation and, like Hollings, he made it clear that "when we run out of courts, then we must adapt to the circumstances": at all costs law and order must be maintained. His hands-on approach generally enabled him to exercise control over events. His attention strayed disastrously at Orangeburg in 1968. But generally, he played a very similar role to that played by Bob Scott in North Carolina at a time when other states were in the hands of good ole boy segregationists like Governor Wallace, Claude Kirk, and Lester Maddox.[32]

In 1970 mobs in Lamar overturned two school buses, crowded with schoolchildren, while a Republican gubernatorial candidate ran a white backlash campaign. Stirred by this violence, suburban Republican whites and an overwhelming percentage of black voters put Lieutenant Governor John West in the statehouse. West had stood up to the Klan in the 1950s after the beating of a white Camden band teacher. West's response to the death threats, on J. P. Strom's advice, was to carry a gun for two or three years. His wife's response was to go round to the local Klan leader and promise that if any harm came to her husband she would personally come round and kill him. While West "probably couldn't hit anything at ten feet," his wife was an excellent shot. West was part of the Hollings industrial development team, and as lieutenant governor he had arranged for the grievances of Orangeburg students to be published in the *Senate Journal* and to investigate those grievances.[33]

In his inaugural he promised a "color-blind" administration and like other New South governors elected in 1970 received favorable national media attention. He liked to think, "the election of 1970 hopefully will be the last in which race was the dominant factor." West worked to ensure that the massive school integration that came to Deep South states after 1970 worked smoothly at the local level. To that end, and to eliminate discrimination in government agencies, he established the Human Affairs Commission. He recalled with pride:

> I guess, if I had to single out any one thing for which I've gotten the most satisfaction [it] is the race relations thing. That was a crucial area when I was elected we passed the Human Affairs Commission and I like to think that we broke that color blinders…It's disturbing to see the polarization of the states now, black and white. At least in a fairly critical period we made a transition and changed a lot of attitudes.

He explained how the Commission worked:

> We selected the blacks as the problem spotters and the whites as the problem solvers. That meant we got a lot of the very active, almost militant blacks who could spot the problems, and who had the support with the blacks who weren't militant. The whites were establishment people who had judgment and concern, and who could change public attitudes and change things that ought to be changed.

He had his critics. Hayes Mizell complained that West's emphasis on "quality education" was a sop to law and order whites. But he managed palpably to lessen racial tensions and to secure general black and white support for the process of change.[34]

At the same time his drive to secure outside investment was spectacularly successful, bringing in over 40,000 new jobs in two years. African Americans benefited. First the booming textile industry integrated. In 1964, 5 percent of mill workers in South Carolina were black; by 1976, one-third were. Second, international investors brought industry below the fall line. In 1972 foreign investment in South Carolina was over 10 percent of all foreign investment in the United States. Firms from outside the United States did not share the stereotypes of managers, north and south, in the United States that African American workers were lazy, uneducable, and militant unionists. Overseas investors were prepared to locate industries in areas of high black populations. What the investors were interested in was not that the work force might be black, but that it was nonunion and well educated in the technical institutes that Fritz Hollings had established. Most dramatically, Koyosako located in Orangeburg because their managers were impressed by the good race relations in the community, which had been so wracked by racial tension from 1955 to the aftermath of the Massacre.[35]

Self-congratulation seems therefore to be justified in no small measure. The state at the heart of defiance of the federal government had responded to court decisions, legislation, and the opportunities of economic growth by desegregating without the turmoil of other massive resistance states. But nagging doubts remain about this model.

First, defiance continued. No sooner had Clemson integrated than Governor Russell called for the provision of tuition grants to enable children to go to private schools and circumvent court-ordered segregation. Private schools flourished and, as the executive director of the South Carolina Independent Schools Association admitted, "everyone knew that our purpose was to set up segregated schools." The state's reaction to the Voting Rights Act was to be the first state to test its constitutionality. Its second response, inspired by segregationist diehards like Micah Jenkins, was to introduce at-large elections in many areas to dilute the black vote. The state's textile industry was one of the most resistant of all southern industries to integration. Tim Minchin has shown that it did not integrate voluntarily or because of a labor shortage, it integrated because of the pressure imposed before 1964 by the federal government in return for government contracts, and after 1964 under the mandate of the EEOC and the pressure mounted by the NAACP's Textile Employment and Advancement of Minorities initiative. Even then, countless EEOC suits indicate the continued discrimination in the industry, especially against black men.[36]

Second, the emphasis on peaceful transition can lead us, Vernon Burton warns, to "understate the occasional horrors and the daily indignities with which African Americans lived." There may not have been the state-sanctioned terrorism that took place in Alabama and Mississippi, or the lawlessness there of the agencies that were supposed to be upholding the law. But there were mass arrests, fire hoses, and countless examples of black activists fleeing for their lives. It is salutary to remember that more protesters were killed at Orangeburg than at Ole Miss, Birmingham, or Selma. There was no incident in the entire South in 1970 to compare with the overturning of the school buses at Lamar.[37]

Third, racial change did not come to South Carolina through the efforts of South Carolina's whites. It did not come gradually or through the inevitable effects of economic modernization. It came through the legal and legislative crises created by white intransigence on the one hand and the combined efforts of the civil rights movement and the federal government on the other. How much congratulation is due the white leadership for eventually and belatedly complying with the law?

Finally, how much credit is due the white leadership for averting the threat of violence, a threat which that leadership had unleashed in the first place?

IV

We may rightly talk of the limitations of today's biracial politics in South Carolina, and of the state's racial polarization, and of the persistence of discrimination and African American poverty. Nevertheless, the collapse of segregation, the end of malapportionment, and the end of black disfranchisement constituted a remarkable transformation in the daily lives of white and black southerners that few in the late 1940s could have predicted.

Historians have started to take segregationist leaders seriously. They are rescuing them from the massive condescension of posterity. The leaders of South Carolina in the massive resistance years were able and conscientious men. It should not surprise us that they were reluctant to relinquish the privileges of white supremacy. Even moderate and liberal white southerners found it difficult to envisage the dismantling of segregation and were certainly reluctant to lay out a strategy for achieving gradual change. It is all too easy for historians, and especially from the safe distance of three thousand miles, to second-guess politicians who failed to take a stand in favor of civil rights or school desegregation.

But to understand the leaders of South Carolina is not to absolve them of responsibility as the self-exculpatory model of the defiance years does. The strategy of defiance was not a holding operation designed to allow racial passions to cool. It was a strategy in which the leadership invested vast resources and energy to try and preserve their own traditional way of life. Far from dousing the fire of popular racist sentiment, the leaders of South Carolina sought to fan the flames. It had chilling consequences for black and white dissenters and for a generation of black schoolchildren and students. It is possible that the policy did in the end act as a safety valve, that exhausting all the means of resistance meant that leaders could demonstrate that there was no alternative but to comply with the courts and legislation in the 1960s, thus undercutting the appeal of a rabid Red Bethea or a John Long. But that argument ignores the fact that it was the leaders of the state who had been remorselessly telling white South Carolinians that segregation could be preserved and who then had to tell them otherwise.

South Carolina leaders marched their followers to the brink. It is to their credit that, having got to the brink, they looked into the abyss and turned round. They had the good fortune to be able to see at Little Rock, Ole Miss, and Birmingham what dire economic and social consequences would follow from continued defiance. They started the slow process of persuading their followers to straggle back. The energy that had been invested in defiance was now invested in moderation. In that situation it took no little courage and no little political skill to reorient the state toward economic development and peaceful racial change. Fritz Hollings, Robert McNair, and John West deserve their measure of self-congratulation.

9

"When I Took the Oath of Office, I Took No Vow of Poverty": Race, Corruption, and Democracy in Louisiana, 1928–2000

I

In James Lee Burke's novel, *A Stained White Radiance,* reformed alcoholic policeman Dave Robicheaux is driving across the bridge that carries I–10 over the Mississippi and into Baton Rouge.

> The river was high and muddy, almost a mile across, and the oil barges far below looked tiny as toys. Huge oil refineries and aluminum plants sprawled along the east bank of the river, but what always struck my eye first when I rolled over the apex of the bridge into Baton Rouge was the spire of the capitol building lifting itself out of the flat maze of trees and green parks in the old downtown area. All the state's political actors since Reconstruction had passed through there: populists in suspenders and clip-on bow ties, demagogues, alcoholic buffoons, virulent racists, a hill-billy singer who would be elected governor twice, another governor who broke out of a mental asylum in order to kill his wife, a recent governor who pardoned a convict in Angola, who repaid the favor by murdering the governor's brother, and the most famous and enigmatic of all the Kingfish, who might have given FDR a run for his money had he not died, along with his supposed assassin, in a spray of eighty-one machine-gun bullets in a hallway of the old capitol building.

My first concern is unashamedly self-indulgent: to look at Long and the color-ful cast of characters described by Dave Robicheaux who have occupied the

Louisiana governor's mansion since. As one observer noted, "Politics plays the role in Louisiana that TV wrestling does in the rest of the nation. It is fixed. It is surreal. It is our spectator sport." I have been a spectator for over forty years, when as a twelve-year-old I first heard of Huey Long.[1]

My second concern is to examine the darker side of that legacy. Dave Robicheaux, who operates a boating dock in New Iberia, lamented:

> Over the years I had seen all the dark players get to southern Louisiana in one form or another: the oil and the chemical companies who drained and polluted the wetlands; the developers who could turn sugarcane acreage and pecan orchards into miles of tract homes and shopping malls that had the aesthetic qualities of a sewer works; and the Mafia, who operated out of New Orleans and brought in prostitution, slot machines, control of at least two big labor unions, and finally narcotics.
>
> They hunted on the game reserve. They came into an area where large numbers of people were poor and illiterate, where many were unable to speak English and the politicians were traditionally inept or corrupt, and they took everything that was best from the Cajun world in which I had grown up, treated it cynically and with contempt, and left us with oil sludge in the oyster beds, Levittown and the abiding knowledge that we had done virtually nothing to stop them.[2]

Put another way, 1995 in Louisiana. The entire membership of the state house of representatives had been subpoenaed by a grand jury examining the FBI's investigation of payments by the gambling interests to state legislators. The payments were designed to secure passage of a bill legalizing gambling, a bill which even its supporters acknowledged could not have passed a referendum of voters. When the bill passed the state senate the president of the senate had walked round the floor openly distributing checks for $2,500 to every legislator. Newspaper investigation of Medicaid showed that by exploiting changes in Medicaid rules, politically well connected developers had set up private psychiatric hospitals: public spending on private psychiatric hospitalization had exploded 9,000 percent in five years. These hospitals were running up profits at ten times the national average. They provided inadequate care that sometimes made patients worse: most of the new beds weren't needed in the first place. Their owners usually included state representatives and their companies invariably made contributions to Governor Edwin Edwards's campaign. Some individual psychiatrists were making almost a million dollars a year treating Medicaid patients. The state Department of Health failed to enforce its accreditation requirements.[3]

An alleged serial killer, believed by the FBI to be responsible for twenty-four murders was at large: you could talk to the suspect by ringing his number at the New Orleans Police Department where Victor Gant still worked as a policeman though he was suspended from patrol duty. Bones were dug up in the garden of a former New Orleans policewoman. She had robbed a restaurant, shot and killed the owners and a fellow officer, and then in response to a 911 call returned to the scene of the crime in uniform to investigate. The bones being dug up were thought to be those of her father, who, it had been assumed, had simply disappeared, but now was presumed to have been murdered by his policewoman daughter. Thirty New Orleans police officers had been convicted and sent to prison in the past three years. In the last eighteen months four officers had been charged with murder, and the chief of the vice squad had been convicted of robbing banks and strip joints. The former head of the Alcoholic Beverage and Control Commission was indicted for receiving $33,000 from Israeli gambling interests in order to return to them thirty-five illicit slot machines that his own officers had confiscated.[4]

On the river, the riverboat casinos which were meant to set sail in order to fulfil the terms of their licences had often failed to do so. Their takings rose by 15–20 percent if they stayed in dock. Their captains justified their failure by arguing, on a November day, that the sun had been too bright and the navigator pilots had been too dazzled by the glare to make it safe to sail. In the city of nearby Slidell, the chief administrative officer admitted that he had falsified his son's birth certificate in order to enable his son to be young enough to play in the under-thirteen soccer league. When league officials challenged him, he threatened to withdraw from use all the city's playing fields which league teams played on. The city manager of Slidell admitted that his assistant had made an error of judgment but argued that he was too valuable an administrator to fire.[5]

Lest anyone think that 1995 was an exceptional year, I'll note some incidents in the three and a half months I was in Louisiana in 2000. The police chief never retracted his statement that police officer Victor Gant was a prime murder suspect in the serial killings. He had finally managed to dismiss him. But the Civil Service Commission reinstated him and ordered him to be paid $106,000 in back pay. In January, the Appeals Court upheld his dismissal but the city had already paid the money and could not get it back. The former Duson police chief was convicted of smuggling marijuana for one of Arcadiana's most notorious drug dealers. He claimed his trips to Houston were merely to pick up supplies for the drug dealer's horse-training business but the jury rejected that plea. A former candidate for sheriff in Sabine Parish pleaded innocent to charges that he had staged an ambush of himself in order to get support in his election bid. Prosecutors alleged that the recently defeated state elections commissioner received more than a million dollars in payoffs for allocating contracts for the supply of voting machines. The secretary of state drove through a police blockade at a road works at midday on Super Bowl day. He admitted being drunk. Having given up his license he expected the state to pay for a car and driver for both personal and public use for the remainder of his term in office. The lead investigator in the Franklinton police department had been charged with bomb making, terrorizing, and attempted aggravated arson. And, of course, in Baton Rouge, four-time governor Edwin Edwards, his son, his former legislative aide, a state senator and brother of one of the state's university presidents, and three others went on trial on charges of extortion, racketeering, and fraud in connection with the granting of the fourteen state gambling licenses. The list of sixty-one unindicted co-conspirators was a who's who of Louisiana politics including the 1995 Democratic gubernatorial candidate, current members of the legislature, former Speaker of the House, and state senate president, some of the most influential African American politicians in the state, and three senior state police officers. The first major witness testified that he threw some of the monthly cash payments, $65,000, in a paper sack through the open window of Stephen Edwards's van. Former Treasure Chest casino owner, Robert Guidry, testified that he generally liked to keep $400,000 cash wrapped in aluminum foil in his freezer. "I shoved it under some deers and ducks I had in there," he said. He also stashed cash in cereal containers stowed beneath a marble lid under his Jacuzzi. It transpired that Edwin Edwards had not written a check or used an ATM machine since 1988.[6]

My second task is to examine the meaning and consequences of this persistent culture of corruption for public governance in Louisiana.

Finally, I want to look at the politics of race in Louisiana, particularly in the light of the rise and eclipse of David Duke and the triumph of white Republicanism. The consequence of both the culture of corruption and a politics that, more than thirty years after the Voting Rights Act, is racially polarized leaves Louisiana particularly ill-equipped compared to other southern states to take advantage of the economic opportunities at the turn of the century.

II

From Reconstruction until 1928 Louisiana was controlled by alliance of planters, the business elites and city machines of New Orleans, and the representatives of the oil and gas corporations that exploited the state's natural resources. Even by southern standards, this alliance was notably conservative and corrupt. It rested on a mutual interest in low taxation and niggardly services for the bulk of the population, leaving Louisiana next to Mississippi as the worst state in the nation in terms of most welfare and quality-of-life indicators. Popular challenges were, if necessary, thwarted by raising the banner of white supremacy or by exploiting the ethnocultural divisions in the state between the Catholic South and the Protestant North.[7]

That conservative hegemony was challenged after 1928 by the freewheeling, high-spending, popular policies of Huey Long that were accompanied also by fraud and corruption. T. Harry Williams, Long's most noted biographer, argued that, for the first time, Long brought recognition and long overdue services to the mass of Louisianans, black and white. Unlike most demagogues he eschewed the race issue. He needed to be ruthless and corrupt because that was the only way to wrest power from the hands of an equally corrupt and ruthless oligarchy. Williams's argument can be developed into a longer-term argument that the Long machine and its successors stayed in power like equivalent machines in the northern cities, not because of corruption but because of popular support and because they performed the latent function of providing order amid factional chaos and provided needed government services for the majority of the population. Reformers, by contrast, the argument would go, were conservative elitists, anxious not to expand but to restrict democracy and economically conservative. The machine politicos were racially tolerant, the reformers staunch segregationists.[8]

How much truth is there in that argument?

Unlike the elite politicians, Huey Long deliberately identified with politically excluded lower-income voters and campaigned tirelessly, particularly at rural crossroads, which established politicians, relying on local power brokers, ignored. He persistently identified himself as a poor white. He deliberately, or maybe unconsciously, cultivated coarse manners—receiving distinguished visitors in his vest or pajamas, wandering round restaurants eating other people's food, drinking prodigiously at least until 1935, attempting to urinate between the legs of people standing in front of him in restrooms. But all the time the message was the same: I'm one of you and "Standard Oil and other predatory corporations will not be permitted to rule Louisiana."[9]

Like Huey, his brother Earl had little difficulty in portraying himself as the common man. He was a biter. Once, during the impeachment crisis he saw a Long supporter talking to an opponent. Enraged, Earl went up and bit the opponent in the neck. Unfortunately, he could not get his teeth out of the man's neck. It took three aides to help extract Long's teeth. As governor, he liked nothing better than to sit in his office with opposition newspapers spread all around him on the floor and to spend the afternoon spitting at them. He much preferred his pea patch farm with its corrugated iron roof, its bare electric light bulbs, wartime bunk beds, and a fifty-five gallon urn of coffee constantly brewing to the delights of the governor's mansion.[10]

He loved spending sprees and couldn't resist a bargain. On one occasion at a supermarket he bought one hundred pounds of potatoes, $300 worth of alarm clocks, 87 dozen goldfish, and two cases of Mogen David wine. At various times he bought ropes, live goats, chickens, seed, hogs, corn, hoes, hats, hams, and earthworms, mostly items for which he had no use and which he promptly gave away. Usually he gave them away at election time. At first it was trinkets, but by the 1955–56 campaign it was hams and televisions. At the Democratic National Convention at Chicago in 1956 he spotted a shoe sale and bought several hundred pairs. When John Kennedy called seeking Long's support for his vice presidential bid, Long made him take off his shoes and put on one of his cheap pairs. To Long's delight, Kennedy left, still wearing "the cheapest pair of shoes that young brat ever put on." And even then he did not endorse him.[11]

A new journalist from New York assigned by the Associated Press to cover the state capitol made an appointment to see Earl Long. The nervous young man was ushered into the governor's office and proceeded to walk up to Lieutenant-Governor Bill Dodd and addressed him as the governor. As Dodd recalled, it was perhaps not a surprising mistake. Dodd had a business suit on and had combed his hair. Long, by contrast was sitting on a couch, barefooted, with one suspender down and one up, his trousers unbuttoned at the top and unzipped halfway down letting his belly hang half in and half out. He was drinking Bud and studying the racing form. When told which one the governor was, the reporter started shaking and could not hold his coffee cup. But Long then proceeded for an hour to give a brilliant interview displaying his complete mastery of the government of the state. By now the reporter was completely relaxed when Long started asking him some questions. Had he grown up in the town or on the farm, Long asked innocently. On the farm, the reporter replied. Then Long asked, "Did you ever screw a mule?" The reporter gasped, turned white, and couldn't talk. Then to round off the humiliation, Long reached down with his right hand and ran his forefinger between his little toe and the next, pulled his hand up to his face, and smelled his finger, then he raised the right cheek of his rear end and badly broke wind. At which point the reporter started running.[12]

Later Edwin Edwards put together a formidable lower-income alliance of Cajuns, blacks, rural whites, and labor to become governor in 1971 and be elected governor four times: the first Cajun and the first Catholic governor of the state in the twentieth century.[13]

On the stump in the old days, Huey and his successors delighted in ridiculing and personally abusing their opponents. For Huey, the bald mayor of New Orleans was "Turkey-head," the old senator Ransdell, a crucial ally for Long in 1928 was "Old feather-duster" in 1932. Earl Long loved to ridicule the elitist pretensions of opponents. Sam Jones was "High Hat Sam, the High Society Kid, the high-kicking High and Mighty Snide Sam, the guy that pumps perfume under his arms." Robert Kennon's blood was "65% champagne, 35% talcum powder," Delesseps Morrison was "Little Boy Blue: The Debutante's Delight." Long so convinced rural audiences that Morrison wore a wig, a tuppy, as Long described it, that Morrison spent time on the platform trying to tear his hair out to persuade the audience that it was real. When Edwin Edwards confronted David Treen, he said that Treen takes an hour and a half to watch *60 Minutes*. Why, Edwards was asked on another occasion, do you talk out of both sides of your mouth at once? So that, he replied, "people like you with nothing between their ears can understand."[14]

The cultivation of a common-man appeal and a colorful, personal campaigning style were stock in trade of any southern politician in a one-party system if those politicians did not have the support of local power brokers or established elites. What distinguished the Longs and their heirs from such demagogues was that, by and large, they delivered what they had promised. They produced the reforms and the government services that the established conservative oligarchy had long denied lower-income voters.

The achievement was particularly notable for Huey Long, who provided the improved roads, schools, hospitals, and long overdue regulation of corporations and utilities during the Depression when most southern governors responded with retrenchment, cutting state services to the bone. After the war, Earl Long once more increased spending on education, notably teachers' pay and free school lunches, substantially improving old-age assistance, investing in hospital construction and farm-to-market roads, responding as in other southern states to the opportunities provided by 1940s prosperity and the demands of returning veterans and organized labor for a new postwar order.[15]

Later, in 1971 Edwards showed himself to be an old-fashioned New Deal liberal who believed a beneficent government could solve people's problems:

> I remember when government made it possible for electricity to be brought to my home. I remember when government made it possible for a bus to pick me up and drive eight miles to school. I remember when government made it possible for me to eat a free lunch at school. I remember when government made books available to me that I otherwise would not have been able to have.

Using the boom in oil and gas revenues of the 1970s Edwards built roads, bridges, hospitals, ports, and schools. He professionalized the state's administration and reduced the 250,000 word state constitution, amended 537 times, to a mere 35,000 words. Probably the ablest governor this century, even a "good government" watchdog conceded that no other politician could have modernized the constitution.[16]

However, two caveats should be made. First, for all the populist rhetoric the spending programs tended to invest in the infrastructure—projects that served to facilitate economic growth. In many ways the reforms of Long and his successors were in the recognized southern tradition of business progressivism. As I have argued, "the New Deal directly and tangibly benefited the underprivileged in Louisiana far more than did the Long machine."[17]

Second, for all the rhetorical denunciations, particularly by Huey, of the large corporations, relations between the Long machine, its successors, and business were fairly cosy. Huey Long may have so frightened the opposition forces that they sought his impeachment, and he raised severance taxes on the oil companies, and introduced a manufacturing licensing tax surreptitiously by tacking it on to a bill which was about something totally different after the oil lobbyists had gone home unaware. But, as William Hair has shown, Long was more interested in power and domination than in substantive policy outcomes. Having demonstrated his power, he immediately moved to reach an agreement with the companies to lower the tax to the smallest rate possible, provided that Standard Oil agreed to refine 80 percent Louisiana oil—not surprisingly given that he himself had major interests in the Win or Lose oil corporation—which always won. Once Long was killed, business interests in Louisiana had no problems coming to terms with his successors. The record of Long's follower, Allen Ellender, and Huey's son, Russell, who between them served for over seventy years in the United States Senate, revealed an unswerving devotion to the needs of the oil and sugar industries, even if there were occasional maverick radical remnants: Ellender's hostility to McCarthyism and initial skepticism on Vietnam, Long's occasional residual support for generous welfare measures, and, for both of them, a firm commitment to social security.[18]

There is little doubt that this record of achievement brought Long and his successors popular support. It was galling to his opponents but even they recognized that Long, for all the fraud and corruption, could ultimately take his case to the people as he did when he was impeached in 1929. In that crisis he bought off the necessary votes to defeat impeachment, but then again legislators were willing enough to be bought. They knew Long was winning over their constituents. Long had addressed rallies all over the state and saturated the electorate with circulars explaining that the impeachment fight was one between Long and suffering humanity on the one side and Standard Oil and the predatory corporations on the other.[19]

But there was more to the power base of Long and his successors than simply popular appeal and government largesse.

Huey Long also relied on the traditional attributes of patronage. He controlled some 25,000 jobs, which if you take each job as worth five votes made a pretty substantial inroad into an electorate of 300,000 voters. What was unusual about Long was that he used this patronage absolutely ruthlessly and systematically. No job was too small to allow an opponent to hold. He required undated letters of resignation from most employees and required that they voluntarily contribute 10 percent of their salaries to the deduct system—a cash reserve which financed both Long's state and national political aspirations. He also moved to strip local elected politicians of power. His tame legislature had by the time of his death given his appointees power over all tax assessments, all police and fire department appointees, all district attorneys, all school teachers. Local Long supporters routinely stuffed ballot boxes under the eyes of compliant election commissioners and, when in doubt, the National Guard could be mobilized to beat down centers of resistance like New Orleans. There was a certain poetic justice that after he was shot, he was operated on by one of his patronage appointees, who in the first operation missed the bullet and the bleeding that caused Long's death.[20]

Corruption was rife and Long routinely bought votes and legislators. His lieutenants lined their pockets too. Despite T. Harry Williams's assertions, it seems almost certain that Long struck a deal with gangster Frank Costello to allow slot machines into the state in return for a fixed share of the proceeds for the Long machine.[21]

Long predicted that his followers would end in prison if they ever used the power he had accumulated. The prediction came true after Long's death. Money was no longer needed to finance their leader's national aspirations. His successors rapidly reached an accommodation with the federal government that led to federal money and projects flowing into the state, opening up the chances of local politicians lining their pockets, using state money for private purposes. The most notable victim was Governor Richard Leche. The president of LSU also made a run for it to the Canadian border after having embezzled half a million dollars. A former high school teacher, appointed by Long as a loyal cipher, he was known as "jingling pockets" Jim Smith because of the illegal cash in his pockets. He used to rewrite minutes of the Board of Trustees to vote himself pay raises. He fell because he used university money to try to corner the international wheat market. A sudden price fall forced him to flee by car, unable to use the university plane because it was being used for an athletic meet. Captured and sentenced to eight to twenty-four years in prison, he became a model prisoner. On his release he was appointed director of rehabilitation for the prison system.[22]

FBI files revealed that after the war Earl Long received kickbacks from insurance companies, racing interests, new car dealers, and the Teamsters Union. He was adept at covering his tracks and explained his technique:

> Don't write anything you can phone, don't phone anything you can talk
> face to face, don't talk anything you can smile, don't smile anything you
> can wink, and don't wink anything you can nod.

Thus, when Governor Edwards allegedly made his extortion demand of San
Francisco 49ers' owner Edie De Bartolo by writing the figure of 400,000
on his paper napkin at the dinner table, he was honoring a well-established
tradition.[23]

In return for allowing untrammelled slot machines in southern Louisiana, Earl Long probably received half a million dollars from Frank Costello
in 1948 and a quarter of a million in 1956, and 120,000 from Carlos Marcello
in 1956.[24]

Persistent allegations about Governor John McKeithen's ties to organized
crime culminated in two *Life* magazine articles in 1967 and 1970 alleging
that Mafia boss Carlos Marcello controlled his administration. While the
State Legislative Mafia Investigation committee argued that there was no evidence of Mafia involvement in the McKeithen administration, even that
committee acknowledged that the Revenue Department had shown great
favoritism to the Mafia boss and that Marcello had benefited from a half-
million-dollar contract to build a levee on his property. Marcello's links to the
State Racing Commission were also undeniable. The race track president
admitted making campaign contributions to McKeithen to enable him "to
be left alone." It would be 1981 before an undercover FBI agent would nail
Marcello. He was convicted of bribing state officials to give him the multi-
million-dollar group insurance contracts for state employees. A former state
commissioner of agriculture and the state commissioner of administration
were also convicted.[25]

Edwin Edwards found himself investigated by IRS agents almost as soon
as he got into office. He admitted accepting campaign contributions from
corporations knowing that the businesses could not legally make those contributions under state law. "That's their business," he said. Louisiana law for-
bade corporations making contributions, it did not, said Edwards, forbid
politicians accepting those contributions. He had more difficulty with allegations in the Koreagate scandal when South Korean lobbyist Tongsun Park
told U.S. investigators that he had made $750,000 in covert gifts to Ameri-
can officials and in campaign contributions, including $200,000 to Louisiana
congressman Otto Passman, a staunch opponent of foreign aid, and $20,000
to Edwin Edwards, a contribution confirmed by Edwards's former aide Clyde
Vidrine. Edwards first argued that any contributions had been made to his
wife as a gift for his children, then that they had been made not by Tongsun
Park but by some other South Korean, who in fact worked for Park's company,

and that in any case he, Edwards, did not know about them until three years after they had been paid. Edwards was also criticized for free airplane trips and hotel accommodations in Las Vegas paid for by the Harrah's Casino. He was also accused of having interests in insurance companies, construction companies, and architecture firms that all won contracts for state projects and from all of which Edwards received a rake-off. Edwards remained upbeat about such accusations. "The only way I can be defeated is if I'm found in bed with a live boy or a dead woman."[26]

The accusations were harder to laugh off in his third term. He was indicted and tried twice on fifty-one counts of racketeering and mail and wire fraud. The prosecution alleged that health care companies paid Edwards $1.9 million before 1983 in return for the granting of licenses for $10 million worth of hospital construction when he became governor. Edwards said he made that from his private law practice for the companies. Prosecutors said that he needed the money to pay off gambling debts of $686,000. The head of Harrah's Casino in Las Vegas testified that, in contrast, Edwards had *won* $562,000 between 1981 and 1984. In a virtuoso performance on the stand Edwards rang rings round the prosecutor, who could never make a New Orleans jury understand the fiendishly complicated arrangements that were allegedly corrupt. He was tried twice, the jury could not reach a verdict the first time, he was acquitted the second.[27]

As for vote rigging, Walker Percy used to argue that Louisianans "cheat with the abandon of Catholics but the efficiency of Protestants." As Earl Long said about voting machines which were intended to eliminate vote fraud, "Give me a Commissioner I can control, and I'll make those machines play 'Home Sweet Home' every time." As late as the 1996 election there were repeated allegations that votes had been bought in New Orleans and that some voters had voted ten or fifteen times, but had complained because they had only been paid once.[28]

A further element in the appeal of Long and his successors was their ability to bridge the ethnocultural gaps that divided the Catholic South from the Protestant North. Prohibition and the Klan had diverted Louisiana voters from economic issues in the 1920s and helped perpetuate conservative control. Long avoided such issues as he tried to concentrate on economic matters. He claimed to have both Catholic and Protestant grandparents. He told a moving story of hitching the horse up to the wagon each Sunday to take the former to mass and the latter to church. When his friends said that they hadn't realized he had grandparents of both creeds, he replied, "Hell no, we didn't even have a horse." Earl Long had a firm rule "no hells or damns north of Alexandria," and in southern Louisiana, he arranged meetings after mass had finished and always gave the parish priest a hundred dollars for church funds. Edwin Edwards straddled the issue equally successfully. Born and raised a Catholic, he converted to Pentecostal Nazarene, and then back to Catholicism.[29]

The final aspect of the appeal of Long and his successors was racial moderation. T. Harry Williams praised Huey Long's racial moderation. Long, he argued, avoided the race issue as an irrelevance and concentrated on economic issues. In the 1930s he could not have done more: both blacks and whites benefited from his programs. Both Alan Brinkley and I modestly questioned this view—noting Long's routine use of racial rhetoric, the lack of black benefit from the education reforms, and Long's criticism of old-age assistance and unemployment relief because blacks would be helped by it. But William Hair, Glen Jeansonne and Adam Fairclough have been devastatingly critical. As Jeansonne argued, Long "can hardly be given credit for not making an issue of a non-issue." They note his racist associates like G. L. K Smith and Leander Perez, his failure to challenge local racists like Perez, the regular use of racial slurs, particularly the accusation of black blood in opponents, the persistence of lynching, and Long's opposition to anti-lynching legislation. "We just lynch an occasional nigger. No federal anti-lynching law would help that." However, Adam Fairclough notes that Long, like FDR, "awakened blacks to the possibility of what an aggressive leader could do." It was perhaps no coincidence that Black Panther Huey P. Newton was named after Huey Long.[30]

As for Earl Long, Adam Fairclough has shown how he plumbed the depths of racism in his 1940 race against reformer Sam Houston Jones. But after the war, Earl Long's basic sense of fairness and appreciation of black voters came to the fore. He was particularly incensed by the callous disregard of black rights by white elites: as he pointed out to a fanatical segregationist, "You got to recognize that niggers is human beings." He fought for increased appropriations for black institutions, ensured that African Americans received over half the benefits of state spending programs, and strove for the equalization of black and white teachers' salaries. He recognized the futility of defiance of the Supreme Court, and he quietly supervised the desegregation of the Louisiana State University campus at New Orleans and the desegregation of the New Orleans buses. Above all, he attempted to protect the rights of blacks to vote. He fought against the efforts of the Citizens' Council after 1956 to purge black voters form the electoral rolls. One of his last acts as governor was to order voting records to be handed over to the U.S. Commission on Civil Rights. As he told the executive secretary of the commission: "You're here to help niggers vote. And I'm for you because they're my niggers and I want their votes. Now we're never gonna talk about my helping you, but I'm gonna get my state registrar to give you the records you need, and after you talk to him, you remember, you never saw me."[31]

It was under intense pressure from the segregationists that Earl Long suffered his famous personal collapse. Earl Long started drinking heavily in 1959 and had a well-publicized affair with French Quarter stripper Blaize Starr. After he had addressed the state legislature incoherently for an hour and a half on live television, swigging whiskey from a coke bottle, his family, including his nephew, the senator for Louisiana, Russell Long, strapped him down in the governor's mansion and committed him to a mental hospital in Texas. Back in Louisiana he was committed to the state mental hospital at Mandeville, but Long got his allies to fire the director of the hospital and replace him with another who declared Long sane and released him.[32]

The heir to the Long machine in the 1960s, John McKeithen, declared himself a 100 percent segregationist but not a hater. Like Earl Long, he recognized both the inevitability of some racial change and the political advantages of winning the support of black voters. In 1963 he ran as a staunch segregationist against Chep Morrison. But he courted black votes to get support for the constitutional amendment to succeed himself. And he overwhelmingly received black support in 1967 when he defeated Klan-backed congressman John Rarick. As Adam Fairclough concluded, McKeithen's metamorphosis from segregationist to moderate helped maintain racial order during the racial flashpoints of the late 1960s, especially as he did not hesitate, when he wanted, to slap down recalcitrant white mayors or police chiefs. He guided the first halting steps of the state to cope with Court-ordered and legislated desegregation. Increasingly, he emphasized the importance of economic growth at the expense of racial confrontation.[33]

His successor, Edwin Edwards, was the first governor unselfconsciously to seek black votes and to reward black supporters with large numbers of appointments to state office and patronage. He espoused genuinely racially moderate politics. The first politician to exploit the full effects of the 1965 Voting Rights Act, he aligned himself with the powerful new black leaders in the Democratic Party, particularly the newly founded black political clubs in New Orleans which aimed to maximize the black vote and offered an entree to black political support to white politicians unfamiliar with that constituency. Many of the New Orleans black political organizations were based on community action projects under the War on Poverty, which gave them jobs and a sound source of patronage. They formed a mutually advantageous alliance with Moon Landrieu, the first overtly racially moderate Mayor of New Orleans who was elected with black support in 1970. Landrieu kept his promise to open up City Hall jobs to African Americans and to appoint blacks to head departments and to his most senior advisory positions. Though Dutch Morial eschewed such close personal links with the Landrieu administration, he won enough white support to get elected as the first black mayor of New Orleans in 1978.[34]

Long and his successors therefore owed their success to their corruption, but also to a common-man appeal and an established popular record of welfare liberalism and racial moderation.

III

What of their opponents?

Huey Long could not take the reform rhetoric of his opponents seriously: his opponents, he believed, were simply representatives of the old established corrupt elite, angry that they no longer controlled the state's politics. There was some truth in his contention. When the New Deal directed patronage to Long's opponents, they directed it to those established figures in the state, usually conservative, who had the ear of men in the Roosevelt administration, like Daniel Roper and James Farley. The lack of New Deal credentials of these conservative anti-Long congressmen were exposed after 1935 when the Long machine came to terms with the New Deal. The anti-Long congressmen who, despite their conservative principles, had backed the New Deal, now became staunch opponents of the New Deal. But there were principled opponents of Long like future Mississippi newspaperman Hodding Carter, and to be a dissenter in Louisiana in the years of Huey Long was very similar, and as dangerous, as being a dissenter from racial orthodoxy or a civil rights activist in later years. When Carter's widow, Betty Carter, died, John Pope's obituary in the *Times Picayune* recalled that when Betty Carter heard that Huey Long had been shot by a man in a white suit, she immediately went to her husband's closet to find to her great relief that his white suit was still there.[35]

Long's most vitriolic criticisms were directed at elite women like Hilda Phelps Hammond, whom he labeled a "tar baby" and an "antique queen." His criticisms were slavishly followed by T. Harry Williams, who dismissed Hammond as a hysterical ranter, who opposed Long because her husband had lost his state job. Pam Tyler, in her brilliant book *Silk Stockings and Ballot Boxes,* has rescued the women who opposed Long from the massive condescension of both Harry Williams and posterity. The women were elitist, but they persisted in their opposition to the Long machine after 1935 when their *bête noire* had gone and when the economic policies of the administration were no longer inimical. The gender dimension was crucial: they saw themselves protecting their children from the corruption, crudity, and immorality of the Long machine. Unlike some women reformers, however, Hilda Hammond, in particular, did not protest with passive feminine charm but with harsh, uncompromising acerbity, which exacerbated traditional male hostility to her.[36]

Economic conservatism lay at the heart of much of the reform opposition. Sam Houston Jones aimed to cut government spending, was at the forefront of southwestern business opposition to the New Deal, and was virulently anti-labor. When he failed to defeat Earl Long in 1948, business interests, appalled at the revival of tax-and-spend policies and the end of "good government reform" in the state set up the Public Affairs Research Council. The council worked closely with Robert Kennon to restore civil service provisions to state government and to secure passage of a constitutional amendment that required a two-thirds' vote in favor of any increased or new tax in both houses of the legislature. The nature of this "good government" organization is perhaps best summed up by the fact that in 1975 its chief executive left to join the Louisiana Association of Business and Industry to lobby successfully for the passage of right-to-work legislation in 1976. That law had originally passed under Kennon, but was repealed by Earl Long. Jimmie Davis, the composer of "You Are My Sunshine," "Organ Grinder Blues," and "I'd Rather Be with Jesus," was tapped by Sam Houston Jones to run for governor in 1944 because Jones was anxious to see continued economic conservatism. Davis stayed out of the state making records and Hollywood films much of the time—in 1946–47 he was out of the state for almost a third of the year. Oilman Buddy Billups in 1959–60 was his chief financial backer, anxious to get favorable treatment for the petrochemical industry. Davis actually vetoed a right-to-work law in his first administration, but subsequent strikes convinced him that had been one of his worst mistakes. Later reformer David Treen was a staunch advocate of retrenchment and an enemy of organized labor.[37]

Linked to economic conservatism was racial conservatism.

Sam Houston Jones was a prominent Dixiecrat. Robert Kennon turned to support Eisenhower in 1952 because of the national Democrats' stance on civil rights, joining forces with the notorious racist Leander Perez. When the *Brown* decision was handed down in 1954, Kennon helped Perez and Willie Rainach to set up the Joint Legislative Committee on Segregation. Jimmie Davis attempted to interpose the state government between the federal courts and the New Orleans School Board in order to prevent school desegregation in New Orleans. Jimmie Davis spent most of his time on the stump in elections singing. He advocated peace and harmony and claimed:

> They're raising Cain about my singing. I've never had regrets about me and my old guitar. It fed me when I was hungry and clothed me when I was ragged. If we had more singing and less fighting, we'd have a lot better world. If anybody in this crowd has ever seen anyone singing and fighting at the same time, I'd like him to raise his hand.

But to win the governorship in the 1959–60 election, Davis made a deal with Citizens' Council leaders Leander Perez and Willie Rainach to give them jobs, a lake at Homer, an appointment on the LSU Board of Supervisors, and control of a state sovereignty commission modelled on Mississippi. Davis accused his opponent of receiving "the appalling bloc of the negro vote." He did nothing to avert the desegregation crisis.[38]

The mayor of New Orleans, Delesseps Morrison, who did get black support, was no racial progressive. As Ed Haas has shown, he dealt with certain black leaders on a clearly defined paternalistic basis which brooked no significant erosion of segregation. He may have been a darling of the Kennedys and he may have been supported by the city's businessmen, but he made no effort to enforce or facilitate the Court-ordered desegregation of New Orleans schools. Instead, he allowed the mob to roam round the streets of New Orleans, to intimidate parents and enforce a boycott of the schools. He defended the mob—booing and jeering were all part of the American way of life, he said. He was determined to establish his segregationist credentials for a future gubernatorial bid. Republican David Treen was by origin an old states' rights ticket supporter in the 1950s and then a member of the elite segregationist Citizen Council groups.[39]

The business elite of New Orleans in 2000 prides itself on its racial moderation and is always sensitive to bad publicity that might deter tourists. Despite that, what is striking is the way the elite sanctioned a school desegregation plan that put all the burden of school desegregation on working-class whites, how much mob violence they were prepared to tolerate before they took steps to secure compliance with the law, and how reluctant they were to desegregate their own private preserves. Tulane University in the heart of Uptown, did not desegregate until 1963, despite the faculty voting to desegregate even before *Brown* and despite the likely damage from the loss of foundation funding of their conservative stance. Tulane was, with the universities of Georgia and Mississippi, the last major southern university to desegregate its football team in 1973. New Orleans did not issue a public accommodations ordinance desegregating bars until 1969. Even as late as 1991, the business elite were reluctant, and in two cases simply refused, to desegregate their Mardi Gras krewes.[40]

The persistent lament of all these reformers was that the Louisiana voters were prepared to abandon them in favor of corrupt politicians who offered their electorate government services and welfare. As Buddy Roemer wistfully acknowledged when Edwin Edwards announced in 1994 that he would not seek a fifth term, "We're last in everything that's good and first in everything that's bad, and he [Edwards] gets elected four times."[41]

IV

By the mid-1980s there appeared to be a sort of equilibrium in Louisiana politics, an equilibrium that was routinely described by political scientists in the 1960s and 1970s. Voters expected a high-spending government and would tolerate a level of corruption in return for government services. The politicians who delivered this cocktail of welfare liberalism and corruption were responsive to their constituents and, because African Americans voted and were a key part of the liberal coalition, these politicians practised and preached racial moderation. Periodically, good government reformers would get elected in reaction to excessive sleaze, but these reformers failed to respond to popular needs, were sometimes as corrupt and machine-minded as the candidates they defeated, and were old-style segregationists, rather than racial moderates. In due course, therefore, the reformers were defeated and the high-spending liberals returned.

That equilibrium was shattered in the mid-1980s, in part by forces peculiar to Louisiana—the cost of corruption in a slumping economy and the rise of Nazi and Klansman David Duke—and in part by regional and national forces—the triumph of white Republicanism manifest in Ronald Reagan.

Voters tolerated corruption as long as the resulting high cost of government services could be met by tax revenues from oil and gas, costs that in effect were met by out-of-state corporations and consumers rather than by Louisiana voters. In the 1980s the chickens came home to roost as oil and gas revenues plummeted. Louisiana would soon have an unemployment rate twice the national average. In a desperate move to avert fiscal chaos Edwards had to drive through a $730 million tax increase and, when that failed to ease the deficit, order cuts in government services, the antithesis of his whole political and economic philosophy. In such circumstances, voters began to find corruption much harder to tolerate. Capitalizing on this discontent was the young, clean-cut congressman Buddy Roemer, who defeated Edwards in the first primary in 1987. Edwards backed out of a second primary battle and conceded defeat.

Roemer promised Louisiana a revolution in politics and to free the state from the grip of corruption. He engineered major improvements in teachers' pay and evaluation and introduced enforcement of tough new environmental standards. But he was unable to secure the fundamental restructuring of the state's tax system that he believed would have permanently solved the state's fiscal crisis and, like so many good government reformers before him, he seemed to be unable to work with the necessary give and take of legislative politics. His separation from his wife and his attraction to New Age philosophy did not impress small-town lawmakers. Courted by national

Republicans he switched from the Democratic Party to the Republican Party, but the state Republican Party was less than enthusiastic about their new recruit.[42]

Roemer described himself as "socially liberal, economically conservative." But that was precisely what was wrong with Roemer for one of the new power bases in the state Republican Party, the new Christian Right. Evangelicals in the state, where Jimmy Swaggart was based, and where the Roman Catholic bishops were strong, pushed for the toughest anti-abortion law in the country. The legislature received telegrams from Mother Theresa and phone calls from the Vatican. Mother Theresa turned out to be a priest in Lafayette; the Vatican appeared to have a 504 area code number. Roemer vetoed the bill but for the first time in the twentieth century a governor's veto was overridden.[43]

The vigorously mobilized new Christian Right was not the only feature of the new Republican strength in Louisiana. From 1968 to 1992, with the exception of 1976, the national Republican strategy depended on courting southern white votes. As the biographer of George Wallace, Dan Carter, has shown, middle-income, and lower-middle-income voters enjoyed an unbroken rise in real income from the 1940s to the mid-1960s. But from the mid-1970s to the mid-1990s, the purchasing power of the median wage earner had declined in real terms. Government was no longer the beneficent friend of these taxpayers as Edwin Edwards believed; instead, government, and the welfare state in particular, was the enemy. Explanations of these taxpayers' plight in terms of international competitiveness and technological change carried little weight. Americans who felt betrayed by this turn of events found it easier in Carter's phrase to be "demonizing and scapegoating the powerless." In a time of economic hardship it was easy to return to a competitive and harsh form of race relations. Two targets, both racially nuanced, were affirmative action and welfare. Affirmative action and minority set-asides deprived well-qualified whites of jobs, many believed, and gave them instead to less well-qualified members of the new black middle class. Welfare created an underclass of dependants, mainly blacks. Hard-earned taxpayers' dollars, so the argument went, were supporting idle and irresponsible welfare mothers. One white hospital technician at LSU said, "we work so that they can have baby after baby."[44]

No one had a surer feel for those frustrations than former Nazi and Klansman David Duke, a man who admired George Wallace: "Both of us were talking about a lot of issues that the establishment politicians weren't talking about."[45]

The son of a Goldwater Republican and an alcoholic mother, Duke's first racial enthusiasms were for Citizens' Council literature. But he soon moved on to be obsessed by Jews. As a history major at LSU he proclaimed himself a National Socialist. In 1973 Duke joined the Ku Klux Klan. He wrote *African Atto,* a seventy-page manual purporting to teach streetfighting techniques to blacks in preparation for the coming race war with whites, and *Finders Keepers,* a sex guide which celebrated the joys of oral sex "quite a bed-time snack...low on calories." In 1980 Duke left the Klan, unable to shake its old-fashioned violent image, and formed the National Association for the Advancement of White People. But, as he said in 1985, "My basic ideology, as far as what I believe about race, about the Jewish question, is the same." What Evelyn Rich, a graduate student investigating nazi groups, Beth Rickey, a Louisiana Republican, and the Louisiana Coalition Against Racism showed was that these Nazi and anti-semitic views were not some youthful aberration by Duke but were views that he sustained right through the 1980s. He still holds those views. This year he announced the formation of the National Organization for European American Rights.[46]

In 1989 Duke was elected to the state legislature from District 81, next to New Orleans. In 1990 he ran for the Senate against veteran incumbent, conservative Democrat Bennett Johnston and polled 43 percent of the vote, including 59 percent of the white vote, smashing Johnston in white working-class and rural neighborhoods, the old bastions of the Long forces. The next year he pushed Governor Roemer into third place in the first gubernatorial primary. Edwin Edwards and Duke were the two leading candidates in the first primary with only two percentage points between them. If the voters who voted for other Republican candidates voted for Duke in the second primary, the former Klansman and Nazi would be easily elected governor of Louisiana.[47]

So began what one journalist described as "the gubernatorial run-off from hell." The choice was an unenviable one—between the lizard and the wizard, between the bigot and the crook. It was also not widely realized that it was a campaign between two compulsive womanizers and gamblers. Edwards's personal habits were well known. It was not known that Duke slept with different women most nights of the campaign or that he enjoyed gambling at Las Vegas, and later Monte Carlo, as much as Edwards. Aides to Duke, worried about the number of women he slept with, told him that a labor union was planning to set up a prostitute with drugs to trap him. Duke worried about the story for an afternoon but then reverted to his normal practice.[48]

Edwards found that much of his traditional appeal to a beneficent government that provided for the common welfare cut no ice, even with many white voters who had benefited from his largesse. But he was saved by two factors.

First, African Americans, scared by the prospect of a Duke victory, registered and then voted in record numbers for Edwards.[49]

Second, enough white Louisianans were fearful that Duke's victory would damage the state's economy by deterring tourists, convention business, and outside investment. Focus groups had shown Buddy Roemer's aides that voters were prepared to excuse Duke almost anything that would normally disqualify a candidate—his draft evasion, his failure to pay taxes, the fact that he had never had a job, his plastic surgery. Many viewed his Nazi and Klan background with sympathy—Hitler had some good ideas. What they were worried about was a pocketbook issue—a Duke victory would cost the state jobs. Roemer had failed to exploit this issue. Edwards did not make the same mistake. Business leaders immediately offered money to the Edwards campaign —and Edwards raised massive sums outside the state from Hollywood and New York. The main newspapers abandoned any pretense of impartiality and targeted Duke. Republican leaders, however reluctantly, disowned Duke and endorsed Edwards. These developments made possible a massive media and TV blitz against Duke and an equally massive effort to get out the black vote. Duke was damaged by his failure on television to identify the three main employers in Louisiana and the exposure of his alleged Christian credentials— the church he claimed to belong to did not exist. Edwards won three out of four of Roemer's supporters, and defeated Duke by 61 percent to 39 percent, despite the fact that 60 percent of voters still thought Edwards was a crook.[50]

But what did Edwards have to offer Louisiana from the governor's mansion? He once said that the best thing would be for him to be elected and then die. His style of pork and welfare liberalism was bankrupt, especially as it would be suicidal to raise taxes. His only answer was to legalize gaming. In Louisiana, the legislature feared to put the issue to the people, many legislators feared to take a public stand in favor of gambling. But the combined impact of gambling money and some sleight of hand by legislative leaders with the voting machines—trapping some opponents with green yes lights on by closing the machines early—led to the passage of a gambling law which vested vast power in the governor who controlled the state gambling board. Edwards's children quickly moved to work for companies seeking gambling licenses and the results we see today. As one Republican opponent noted, "It's a huge amount of money interacting with old-fashioned Louisiana politics. That's a very deadly combination." As another said, "Edwards promised us Caesar's wife, and he gave us Caesar's Palace."[51]

After 1991, Duke may have been unable to sustain a viable future in the Republican Party. But voters did not repudiate his views. The single most important fact about Duke's race for governor was that, despite all the Klan and Nazi baggage, he still had secured 56 percent of the white vote. Most of his support could be accounted for by the "Normal Republican Vote." What he failed to do was to win urban and Acadian votes that usually go Republican. In 1991 in neighboring Mississippi Kirk Fordice had got elected on almost exactly the same platform as Duke, targeting welfare mothers and affirmative action, tough on law and order, and advocating low taxation. The difference was that he was endorsed by the national party and did not have Duke's disreputable past. In 1995 Fordice was reelected. As veteran Mississippi white liberal Frank Smith told me, he may have been polished up a bit, but "he's still the same racist reactionary bastard he always was." In Louisiana Mike Foster was elected at the same time in 1995 as a Republican, referring to New Orleans as "the jungle," with a platform almost identical to Duke's four years earlier and endorsed by Duke. He defeated black congressman Cleo Fields overwhelmingly. He did not repudiate the endorsement he received from Duke. Only when Duke was called before a grand jury in 1999 did it emerge that Foster had also bought Duke's mailing list for $152,000 during the 1995 campaign.[52]

In 1999 Foster was reelected. He was the first candidate this century in the conservative reform tradition ever to win a second election. Why?

First, he ran against a black candidate again, this time congressman William Jefferson. Second, unlike other reform/good government candidates, for all his rhetoric, he did not practice retrenchment. It was discovered after the election that the number of people on the state payroll had actually increased in Foster's first term. In January after his election, it became clear that the state faced a budget deficit next year of anywhere between $500 million and $1 billion, a deficit his opponent had predicted but which Foster and his supporters had dismissed as ridiculous.[53]

Finally, Foster promised increased government spending. He promised to call a special session to raise teachers' pay to the regional average. When he called this special session in 2000, he blithely announced that he was not going to ask for teachers' pay rise after all.

V

How is it that when other southern states are awash with tax revenues, Louisiana faces yet another budget crisis? The fiscal crisis facing the state is directly related to the particular legacy of race, corruption, and democracy that I have tried to outline here: on the one hand, the consequences for public governance of the legacy of corruption and, on the other, the results of the racial myopia of the good government reformers.

The commissioner of administration said the budget deficit is the result of a tax system based "on an economy that came out of the dark ages," a system that relied on oil and gas taxes and sales, gambling, tobacco, and gasoline taxes that have scarcely grown in recent years. It continues to privilege property owners and income tax payers. Louisiana's tax system according to the most recent survey underperformed by 1.8 percent of state Gross Domestic Product when compared to Florida, Texas, and Georgia. This annual shortfall of $1.2 billion would solve the budget crisis and fund the teachers' raise. The single most important factor in this shortfall is the relative low property tax collections. The homestead exemption was originally designed to prevent poor families from losing their homes for taxes. Thanks to the democratic and corrupt system of assessment it has turned effectively into a subsidy for middle-class homeowners. The governor, responding to his party base, wants to raise, not to lower, the exemption.[54]

Gambling might have been the answer but Louisiana has been incapable of the professional and expert governance that would make gambling work for the state. Gambling has been unable to provide the benefits to education that the state lottery in Georgia or the casinos in Mississippi have brought. As James Gill wryly observed,

> When the gamblers came to town, we were promised a new prosperity without the pain of taxes. Yet now in the palmiest days of the Republic, Harrah's struggles, the state is spectacularly broke and teachers are still waiting for their raise.

Meanwhile, Mississippi raised its teachers' salaries 8 percent in 1999, and 3 percent in each of the previous two years. The Magnolia state voted a further 30 percent increase for the next six years.[55]

One reason for the lack of growth in tax revenues is that what economic growth there is in Louisiana comes almost entirely from the lowest of the low-paid sector service jobs. As a result, income tax revenues in Louisiana are rising far more slowly than the national average. When oil and gas were booming, Louisiana simply failed to invest in the infrastructure, notably in education, that might have attracted the high-tech research-based industries that have been the lifeline of, for example, North Carolina. Virginia can advertise to attract industry on television and boast of 15,000 Ph.D.s in science and engineering. Louisiana cannot make any such claim. When other states have seen the crucial linkage between economic development and higher education research and development, the governor of this state has called for a financial boycott of one of the state's leading universities. In a global economy where capital can move anywhere why should firms invest in a state that cannot provide honest and efficient government.[56]

Other states respond immediately to queries from potential outside investors. The Louisiana Department of Economic Development has been so slow that the recent special session voted to establish a privatized Louisiana, Inc. to replace it. But there is one thing Louisiana is quick at. MS Carbonate are planning to build a $4 billion urea fertilizer plant just over the border in Mississippi. The company is reconsidering because it may take a year to get the necessary environmental clearances from the Mississippi government. A spokesperson said they were considering moving the plant to Louisiana because, he said, they know they can get those permits quickly in Louisiana. No wonder that Louisiana is second only to Texas in the nation as the state with the worst water pollution record. Almost half's the state's industrial facilities have expired clean water permits.[57]

Over fifty years ago, the distinguished political scientist V. O. Key foresaw the ending of the old structures of southern politics. The collapse of segregation, the enfranchisement of African Americans, the reapportionment of state legislatures, and the arrival of a two-party system would benefit the previously excluded have-nots in the South and greatly strengthen the forces of liberalism. He envisaged a biracial coalition of lower-income whites and blacks united in common economic interests. The class-based politics of Louisiana appeared to offer promising ground for Key's optimism.[58]

Instead, in the South, and in Louisiana in particular, we have a racially polarized politics in which the Republicans secure only white support and the Democrats receive over 90 percent of the African American vote. It has been difficult for most Democrats in statewide and presidential elections in the South to purse the task of biracial politics. The task of maximizing the black turnout and at the same time securing 35–40 percent of the white vote necessary to win has been beyond the political skills of many southern politicians. In Louisiana the Democrats have occasionally been helped by the propensity of the Republicans to shoot themselves in the foot and nominate extremist candidates like Duke, or Woody Jenkins in 1996, "that unspeakable hypocrite," as one Republican described him to me. The open primary system, complained one Republican leader, means that "good solid candidates from the mainstream . . . get shunted out." But even Jenkins came within 5,000 votes of victory and the 1995 and 1999 gubernatorial elections demonstrate the stark racial polarization of the state.[59]

In the first of the Mellon lectures in 2000, Zell Miller painted a rosier picture. Drawing on the results in Alabama, Georgia, and South Carolina, he pointed to the potential cross-racial alliance between urban blacks and suburban whites united in a common interest in economic growth and quality education.[60]

That progressive biracial coalition seems a long way off in Louisiana.

First, suburban whites in Louisiana seem disposed to stick with the economic conservatism and white exclusivity of the Republican Party. Perhaps because they have yet to see the dynamic growth that has shaped other parts of the South, perhaps because so few of them are in-migrants, they seem more interested in low taxes and cultural conservatism than in issues of growth and quality education. There is no sign that the Republican Party itself is going to follow the advice of its chief Baton Rouge pollster and "develop programs and messages that attract significant support from black voters."[61]

Given the attitude of the majority of white voters, black leaders have faced an unenviable choice between a moderate policy aimed at coalition-building with moderate white Democrats and a racially exclusionary policy concentrating on black power. All too often it seems to black leaders, white politicians who court the black vote ignore their concerns, once elected, and pursue policies designed not to upset white sensibilities. However, an emphasis on black racial solidarity can bring local power but at the cost of wider influence. There are more black elected officials in Louisiana than any state in the nation other than Mississippi. African Americans have attained power in cities like New Orleans or in rural districts but they do not have the revenue base to solve the problems of their impoverished black constituents. Dutch Morial had to confront the chronic problems of the Crescent City when both the federal government and the state governments were slashing their aid—which had provided over half the city's revenue. African American male political leaders in Louisiana first gained significant political opportunities in the poverty programs in New Orleans controlled by Moon Landrieu or in the 1970s Edwards administrations. Like their white counterparts they appear to have opted for personal profit, patronage, and access to the white power structure for personal and group recognition, rather than for policy input designed to restructure Louisiana government in favor of the have-nots in the state. These are not policies designed to foster the coalition-building Miller was talking about.[62]

The future both for the have-nots in Louisiana and for the state's economy look bleak. The legacy of corrupt welfare liberalism and racial moderation has produced a system of public governance that has proved incapable of delivering a modernized economy. The legacy of good government and racial and economic conservatism has equally failed to produce a vision that can see beyond the next tax cut or the next toxic waste dump. Politics as TV wrestling is a great spectator sport and it has been for me a subject of endless fascination over the past forty years, but I have to confess, as I head to the airport, that the quality of governance it provides is more easily coped with at a distance of three thousand miles.[63]

10

The Dilemma of Biracial Politics in the South since 1965

1. Predictions

I want to start with three predictions.

In 1949 the Texas-born political scientist V. O. Key Jr. identified four devices that perpetuated conservative hegemony in the South: one-party rule, a restricted electorate, notably the disfranchisement of blacks, the malapportionment of state legislatures, notably the vast overrepresentation of the black belt, and racial segregation. If these devices were eliminated, Key believed that the "underlying southern liberalism will be mightily strengthened." He envisaged a vigorous democracy in which party competition for popular support would bring long overdue benefits to the have-nots in the South, who had lost out, he argued, over the long run in factionalized, disorganized politics. He looked forward to class replacing race as the dominant force of southern politics, in which biracial coalitions of lower-income blacks and whites would seek to complement political democracy with economic democracy. He already saw the template of these coalitions in the elections in the late 1940s of some young, liberal white politicians, a "new generation" of southerners whose arrival Franklin Roosevelt had predicted a decade earlier.[1]

In 1957 Martin Luther King Jr. powerfully laid out the benefits that would accrue if African Americans were given the ballot. "Give us the ballot," he demanded at the Prayer Pilgrimage, and they would end lynching, elect judges who will "do justly and love mercy," implement the *Brown* school desegregation decision, and "fill the legislature with men of goodwill."[2]

Characteristically in 1965 Lyndon Johnson made two contradictory predictions about the Voting Rights Act. At times he fatalistically assumed that he was handing over the South to the Republican Party for the next thirty years, driving whites into the GOP camp. At other times, notably when Larry O'Brien briefed him on the 1964 elections, he excitedly saw the black vote in the South as the "key" to a future liberal Democratic Party in the South.[3]

Key was simply wrong. Class did not replace race as the major determinant of southern politics. As one Washington political consultant observed during a campaign in Mississippi, "Race here is like sex at a horny prep school. You can't have a conversation without discussing it." Only a handful of Key's New Deal–style, biracial coalitions emerged at the state level in the South— arguably, Edwin Edwards in Louisiana in the 1970s, Cliff Finch in Mississippi in 1975, a feeble rhetorical gesture from George Wallace in 1982. The frustration of lower-income whites with a government that imposed racial change but failed to halt cultural change, spilled over into a hostility to government intervention in the economic sphere that made Key's liberal hopes chimerical.[4]

Johnson had both parts of his contradictory prediction right. Fatalism was his path largely. As Lewis Gould has pointed out, for a consummate party politician Johnson was actually not very interested in local party building while he was president. Whites did flock to the Republican Party: after 1964 a majority of southern whites never again voted for a Democratic presidential candidate. As for African Americans, they overwhelmingly supported the Democrats and the Democratic Party changed. For example, Congress became more liberal between 1970 and 1990 and southern Democratic congressmen became ideologically much closer to their northern colleagues.[5]

But the dilemmas of biracial politics suggest that the more common pattern, particularly in statewide politics, is that Democrats who need to supplement an African American base with possibly 35 to 40 percent of white votes in order to win, increasingly espouse conservative social and economic policies to secure that biracial politics.

The way Johnson's and Key's predictions have worked out have in good measure shaped the extent to which Martin Luther King Jr.'s optimism was justified. One look at the current Louisiana state legislature is probably enough itself to cast doubt on his hope to "fill the legislature with men of good will." In fact, the shape of biracial politics has left African American politicians with uncomfortable decisions to make. The results, the extent to which King's faith in the ballot was justified, are, at best, ambiguous.

2. Initial Counter-revolution

There were some immediate dramatic gains for African Americans as a result of the passage of the Voting Rights Act in 1965. Newly registered black voters in Dallas County, Alabama, flocked to the polls to help defeat their nemesis, Sheriff Jim Clark. But the more notable immediate impact of the Act was often to strengthen the hand of conservatives determined to resist racial change—Lurleen Wallace as a surrogate for her husband in Alabama, Claude Kirk in Florida, John Bell Williams in Mississippi, Lester Maddox in Georgia, and William Brock in Tennessee. In part this conservative surge reflected the counter-mobilization of white voters in response to black registration: in Alabama white registration figures went up from 69.2 percent to 89.6 percent in the two years after the 1965 Act. In part, it reflected the fact that rural and small-town whites had to confront the reality of desegregation and the civil rights movement for the first time and to confront African American leaders who talked in a language not of supplication but of non-negotiable demands.[6]

Until 1964, whites in rural eastern North Carolina, as I argued in chapter 7, could believe that they would largely escape the token racial change that business leaders had accepted for the urban areas of the state. After 1964, their racial supremacy was challenged by civil rights demonstrations in small towns, newly emboldened African American political leadership, and real school desegregation. At the same time, white economic security was imperiled by the mechanization of tobacco harvesting. The scapegoats for the plight of whites could be found in protesting, flag-burning students in Chapel Hill, an unelected Supreme Court that subverted both law and order and religion, and a profligate federal government that spent the hard-earned dollars of white taxpayers on welfare recipients and rioters. At first the Klan and George Wallace tapped into their fears. But eventually whites in the East found a savior in Jesse Helms. His appeal to their cultural and religious conservatism as well as their economic insecurity was but a forerunner of what would happen in the South as a whole with the rise of the Christian Right and the economic tribulations of a generation of white southerners whose median wage earner would see his purchasing power decline in real terms from the 1970s onward. A similar process, described in chapter 13, occurred in Tennessee, another token compliance state, where the Republicans secured their only Senate and gubernatorial gains in the South in 1970.[7]

3. The New South Politicians

But change was coming. The first manifestation was the development of biracial coalitions that cut across class lines of blacks and affluent whites. Affluent whites might be economically conservative but they had a shared interest with blacks in peaceful racial change. One such coalition behind the candidacy of Albert Brewer almost defeated George Wallace in 1970. The second was the failure of some of the good ole boy segregationists, like Lester Maddox and Orval Faubus, to win comeback elections with the old messages. The third testimony to the new importance of the black vote was the transmogrification of some of the old segregationists as they sought at least to make peace with their old black enemies and to recognize patronage and pork-barrel needs of their black constituents. Thus, George Wallace would eventually be rewarded by an honorary degree from Tuskegee, and Strom Thurmond would receive the Distinguished Service Medal from the South Carolina Conference of Black Mayors.[8]

Most important was the rise of New South politicians: young, attractive candidates who were conservative enough on social and economic issues to appeal to white voters and moderate enough on racial issues to satisfy their black constituents. Across the South there were new faces adept at this coalition building: Reubin Askew in Florida, Jimmy Carter in Georgia, Edwin Edwards in Louisiana, Dale Bumpers in Arkansas, James Hunt in North Carolina, and Bill Waller and William Winter in Mississippi. In the 1971 gubernatorial election in Mississippi there were still old fire-eating segregationists, for example, the radio evangelist Jimmy Swan and the author of *Black Monday*. Bill Waller, the prosecutor of Byron Delay Beckwith was appalled that a photograph might appear of him talking to a black television reporter. But in the run-off that year between Waller and Lieutenant Governor Charles Sullivan, racial issues were absent for the first time ever in Mississippi elections. Four years later, Cliff Finch and most other candidates in the state would want black faces on their campaign literature.[9]

The policy outputs of this biracial politics should not be underestimated. There was a dramatic increase in black officeholding in the South. Mississippi became the state with the most elected black officials in the country. African American mayors took control of cities like Atlanta, Richmond, Birmingham, and Charlotte. *Overt* racism was largely eliminated from the South's politics. The desegregation of the public sphere was a routine part of civic life. Day-to-day race relations were significantly less tense as whites accepted "visible blacks" in positions of authority. There were significant black employment gains in the public sector. The desegregation of higher education and Title VII of the Civil Rights Act opened up jobs in the private sector for middle-class black professionals. Basic public services for black communities were transformed. Voting, John Dollard pointed out seventy years ago, is not merely an honorific function. Perhaps the most dramatic consequence of biracial politics was the improvement in law enforcement that resulted from the responsiveness of elected sheriffs and appointed police chiefs to the new political realities and to their newly empowered black constituents.[10]

Yet the policy gains of this biracial politics were precisely circumscribed. New South governors were very much in the "business progressive" tradition: they concentrated on efficient and honest government and measures designed to attract outside investment and the in-migration of skilled, managerial, and professional workers. Roads, airports, education, and racial harmony were the targets. Spending on welfare or measures designed to reduce still-persistent economic and racial inequality or to protect workers were not part of their agenda.[11]

But if there were limitations to this New South politics, the 1970s would in the future appear to be a sort of golden age of biracial politics in the region. Exemplars of the new politics like William Winter and James Hunt would be defeated when they sought election to the U.S. Senate in 1982 and 1984. Locally successful black coalition builders like Harvey Gantt and Andrew Young were defeated in bids for statewide office. Others like Richard Arrington and John Lewis were deterred from even running statewide. What replaced the New South governors in the 1980s and 1990s were politicians who were even more fervently committed to low taxation and limited government and even more hostile to any redistributionist element in government policy.

4. Lily-White Republicans

The Republican Party of the 1970s was schizophrenic. Alongside traditional moderate Republicans, either from the mountain areas or from the white suburbs, like James Holshouser, Winthrop Rockefeller, and Linwood Holton, were the candidates, like Jesse Helms and Strom Thurmond, who had followed Barry Goldwater's dictum and gone "hunting where the ducks were" appealing to southern white conservatives. Republican gains had been stalled by Watergate, by Jimmy Carter, and by the difficulty of competing with Democrats at the local level. They were excessively reliant on presidential coattails and on the voter-recognition of high-profile figures like Helms and Thurmond, well known before they became Republicans.

What changed were the rise of the Christian Right and the anti-tax, anti-government climate of the Reagan years.

The Christian Right, taking as its model the mobilization of the churches by the civil rights movement in favor of the 1964 Civil Rights Act, energized evangelical voters on the lifestyle issues of the 1960s and 1970s, on abortion, on gays and on women, on sex education, the family, but perhaps in the South, most importantly, on the issue of school prayer. On all these issues the Religious Right tapped into frustration that unelected, unaccountable judges, bureaucrats, and public-interest lawyers were driving through a Rights Revolution that ran contrary to both traditional cultural values and to majority white sentiment. There was little doubting their partisan attachment. As Wayne Flynt noted, evangelical Christians "virtually turned their churches into Republican precinct headquarters." As late as 1980 only 29 percent of Southern Baptist ministers considered themselves Republican, by 1985, 66 percent did. The Southern Baptist Convention gave a platform to Ford, Reagan, and Bush; it denied the podium to the two presidents who were actually Southern Baptists, Carter and Clinton. Religious Right themes were an automatic response for many Republican candidates: the accusation that opponents like James Hunt and Harvey Gantt had received funds from gay rights groups or that Paul Hubberd was a member of the National Education Association which wanted to let homosexuals teach in schools, the need to support prayer in school, or the slogan against Jewish Democrat congressman Elliott Levitas that it was time to elect a Christian to Congress. Mike Huckabee's signature line was "When I was in school they passed out Gideon bibles. Today they pass out condoms." When half the voters in South Carolina identify themselves as evangelicals, the Christian Coalition—with over 125,000 members in the state and its capacity to deliver one million information packs at churches on election eve—clearly is in a position to wield a powerful influence in Palmetto state elections. Over thirty years after a Democratic governor of Alabama stood in the schoolhouse door with the National Guard to try and prevent desegregation, a Republican governor of Alabama promised to stand in the courthouse door with the National Guard to prevent the removal of the Ten Commandments from the courtroom.[12]

The overwhelming popularity of Ronald Reagan and George Bush among white southerners tapped into a conservatism that not only reflected lifestyle concerns but also historical white southern suspicion of the efficacy of government intervention and collective action. Faith in the ability of the federal government to do the right thing declined dramatically nationally from the high point of the early 1960s. White southerners who faced not only declining real incomes but also collapsing oil and gas revenues were committed even more to limits on government spending and to tax cuts, especially if taxes were spent on programs primarily designed to benefit the black poor. National liberals and Democrats were now convenient whipping boys. When Congressman Tommy Robinson from Arkansas switched to the Republicans in 1989 he stated, "I could no longer stomach staying in a party run by the likes of Teddy Kennedy and Jesse Jackson . . . The Arkansas Democrat is nothing like the national Democrat. They're hard-working people, they believe in God, and motherhood and chivalry and apple pie, and the eastern liberals have pointy heads, and they carry big briefcases around with nothing inside but ham sandwiches." Teddy Kennedy is to southern Republicans what Vito Marcantonio was to their McCarthyite predecessors: a candidate can be tarred as a liberal by the accusation that they voted 86 percent with Teddy Kennedy.[13]

Even in this favorable ideological and economic climate, Republican success was still a top-down phenomenon. Presidential success had yet to be translated into the long-predicted full-scale realignment. It was difficult to unseat long-serving incumbents—disproportionately Democrats—who could, in particular, deliver federal projects and defense spending to their regions and who were often finely attuned to local issues. The Republicans were not helped by the reluctance of very conservative Democrats to leave the party: veteran Mississippi congressmen Sonny Montgomery and Jamie Whitten or, even more important, George Wallace. It was harder outside presidential election years to tar local Democrats with the national liberal brush. There was a self-perpetuating shortage of experienced Republican candidates since there was little incentive for aspiring politicians at the local level to throw their lot in with the thin ranks of Republican activists.[14]

But the 1990s changed all that. Continued success at the Senate level and in the state houses was followed by additional success in the House, the capture of state offices below the governor, the capture of state supreme courts, even the control of some branches of state legislatures. The 1994 congressional earthquake was particularly important in the South: not only did the anti-incumbent tide run strong but it was easy to tap into anti-Clinton, anti-liberal sentiment. On all indicators—party identification, the size of the vote in party primaries, the number of local contested elections—the Republican Party was genuinely competitive. Testimony to the self-perpetuating nature of this growth was the quickened pace of party-switching by elected Democrats; U.S. senator Richard Shelby was merely the most prominent of fifty-eight Democratic state officials who switched to the Republicans between the 1994 elections and March 1998. There were confident predictions that the South was about to become a one-party Republican region—and as the electorate became more suburban, white, and middle-class such predictions were plausible.[15]

How important was race to Republican success? You do not have to argue that all Republicans are racist to argue that racial exclusivity is at the heart of Republican Party, much as Barry Goldwater had originally hoped, and Lyndon Johnson had feared.

Dan Carter has effectively argued that the Republican Party nationally and regionally went after the Wallace vote, successfully tapping the rage of ordinary white voters. The party specialized in "demonising and scapegoating the powerless," according to Carter. Racially nuanced targets, affirmative action and welfare, became central to the Republican appeal. Jesse Helms ran a memorable ad in 1990 of a voter tearing up a job rejection slip, with the voice-over saying that the voter was qualified but the job had been given to a minority. Welfare mothers, usually black, were supported, so the argument went, by hard-earned white taxpayers' dollars. Advertisements, as in Kirk Fordice's campaign in Mississippi, always portray welfare recipients as black. It is argued that this is racial conservatism, a product of conservative individualism, not racism, but the effect is the same. Equally it is difficult to forget the segregationist origins of most of the leading television evangelists of the Religious Right.[16]

Southern Republicans do not seek out black voters.

In Virginia they have. George Allen and Jim Gilmore both obtained 20 percent of the black vote and in a close election that can be decisive. It also leaves Virginia with a Republican-controlled legislature in the year 2001. But elsewhere in the South Republicans do not follow that strategy. In Alabama the state party chairman mused that they should—he was warned off by county chairmen who said they would lose white votes. In Louisiana the party's chief pollster in Baton Rouge argued the party should "develop programs and messages that attract significant support from black voters." There is no evidence the state GOP is moving in that direction.[17]

On the contrary, Republicans launch their own voter registration drives in white areas only and they aim to depress the black vote by a variety of ballot security measures of which we became only too familiar in the 2000 presidential election in Florida but were used by Helms in 1990, warning voters in black areas of potential five-year prison sentences for voting irregularities. Republicans supported African American majority districts in a successful effort to create whiter, potentially Republican districts. They use hot-button racial issues—opposition to extension of the Voting Rights Act, support for the Confederate flag. They use campaign ads that clearly exploit racial identity—"The Choice is Yours" over a picture of the white Republican and his black opponent or an ad consisting of a picture of the Democratic candidate sitting next to Joe Reed, black leader of the Alabama Democratic Council.[18]

Louisiana makes the point starkly as I suggest in chapter 10. Former Klansman David Duke may have been disowned by the national Republican Party when he ran as the Republican candidate for governor in 1991, but it is crucial to recognize, as a GOP activist reminded me in 2000, that state party officials did not repudiate Duke. There were a handful of leading Republicans who did, but they were the exceptions. He still won a majority of white votes, most of whom were regular Republican voters. His stance on welfare, affirmative action, law and order, and low taxation was a mainstream Republican position identical to that of Kirk Fordice, who was elected in

1991 in neighboring Mississippi, but who was not disowned by the national party. It was also identical to that of the Republicans' successful candidate for the Louisiana governorship in 1995 and 1999. Mike Foster twice defeated African American opponents, did not repudiate Duke's endorsement, and paid $152,000 for Duke's mailing list to use in the 1995 campaign.[19]

Republicans often lament the fact that they cannot secure the African American vote. A Virginia congressional candidate complained that she walked in the parade on Martin Luther King Day and did not pick up enough black votes to fill five phone booths. They loftily say that genuine competition for black votes would be the best for blacks: they would gain if Democrats could not take their vote for granted. Said one Republican political consultant, "It would be good for blacks, for the country, and the Republicans if the black vote became competitive. The Democrats could nominate David Duke and get all the black vote."[20]

But is difficult to see why African Americans should vote at the moment for southern Republicans. As black Mississippi congressman Benny Thompson puts it, for blacks to vote for Republicans, "it's like the chicken voting for Colonel Sanders."[21]

5. Democratic Coalition-Builders

Faced with the successful Republican appeal to white voters, modern-day Democrats in the South have faced the same dilemma radical Republicans faced under Reconstruction. How do you maximize the African American vote yet pick up the 35–40 percent of the white vote needed to win statewide elections? This squaring of the electoral circle requires political skills that, as under Reconstruction, have at times looked impossible.

In fact during the 1980s, Democrats did manage to pull off this feat. For example in 1986 they won back the six Senate seats that had been lost on Reagan's coattails in 1980. In part they were able to do this because they had not yet completely lost the support of rural conservatives, and in part because of their success in mobilizing African American voters. One reason they could attract white votes at the same time as securing black support was the degree of tolerance shown to centrist white candidates by African American leaders. The other was that white Democratic candidates could approach the black vote surgically. As one white Mississippi candidate noted, "I have found that in the black community they truly have opinion leaders. There was a time when it was more prevalent in the white community too. But that's not the case anymore and it sure makes a difference in how you reach for black votes." Black leaders could be approached and either act as surrogates for the candidate or act as escorts into the black community, particularly the churches, especially as in the 1980s black churchgoers were three times more likely to vote than non-churchgoers. Black voters could also be targeted by tailor-made advertisements on black radio. For a candidate trying to attract white support the beauty of this approach was that it was largely invisible from the white electorate, at least in local elections. Black leaders were pragmatic and did not expect too much. Said one in Virginia about the Democratic candidate they were backing, "[He] didn't make promises we all knew he couldn't keep. We said to him, listen we know you can't change the world, but at least you know we're here."[22]

The irony was that this strategy of mobilizing the black vote at one remove was very reminiscent of the strategy white moderates used in the 1950s when they secured black support at arm's length—relying on intermediaries to the black community who would deal with black leaders who could deliver the black vote. In 1960 Terry Sanford actually arranged to lose the black vote in Durham, North Carolina, in the first primary of the gubernatorial election that year, to avoid being targeted as the candidate of the black bloc vote in the run-off. The obvious downside of this strategy is a watering down of white politicians' perceptions of the immediacy of black demands.[23]

Could this strategy survive the revived Republican onslaught of the 1990s?

In 1991 Zell Miller, then governor of Georgia, mapped out his model for the successful biracial Democratic electoral coalition. He told the Southern Democratic Caucus in Raleigh that the problem for southern Democrats was simple: "for too many presidential elections we have had things backwards. We have chosen to fight on social issues rather than to run on the economic issues that shape the daily lives of American families." He made no apology for standing for sex education, the ERA, and a woman's right to choose and in opposition to the state anti-sodomy law. But his overriding concern was to win over white voters on the economy issue. "We must ask why CEOs make 90 times what shopworkers can earn; why big executives have golden parachutes while working people have no health insurance... these issues are the bottom line for the pocket book of working Americans." This speech, along with Miller's political consultants James Carville and Paul Begala, became the path to the White House for Bill Clinton.[24]

The Republican breakthrough of the 1990s plus Bill Clinton's travails suggested that the final triumph of the Republicans was close. But in 1998 Democrats won the governorships of Alabama, South Carolina, and Georgia and won Senate races in North and South Carolina that looked problematic. In March 2000 in a lecture in Tulane, Miller drew lessons from these campaigns and indicated how Democrats could build biracial coalitions in the future.

First, Democrats had to be conservative enough on social issues. "Unlike their GOP counterparts, every southern Democrat who runs for governor must still prove that he is not a wild liberal. That means he won't let all the crooks out of jail, raise taxes, pour the public's money down a variety of ratholes, double everybody's welfare check, allow the burning of the American flag, let serial ax murderers escape the electric chair, or take down the Christmas tree at the Governor's mansion. If they don't prove it, they lose it. It's that simple."

But the positive message was that Democrats had identified a crucial cross-racial interest for two key voting groups: urban blacks and suburban whites. Both had a common interest in economic growth and quality education. Neither had an interest in Religious Right social conservatism. African Americans traditionally did not in any case. But suburban whites who migrated in from the North were also socially liberal and not evangelically fundamentalist. They were the sort of voters who had voted for Miller's HOPE scholarships funded by ring-fenced lottery money which had been the model for Democratic successes in South Carolina and Georgia.[25]

6. Unpalatable Choices for African American Voters

This dynamics of biracial politics are unpromising for African Americans in the South and leave them with uncomfortable choices. The incentives for coalition building for southern blacks are limited. On the one hand, the Republicans are a racially exclusive party. On the other, the Democratic Party in its efforts to build a biracial coalition seeks black support, but appears to take that support for granted and instead pursues policies designed primarily not to upset white sensibilities.

Yet independent black politics as practiced by Charles Evers in Mississippi or by the black militants portrayed by Nahfiza Ahmed in Mobile simply paves the way for right-wing white success.[26]

Within the Democratic Party, the prospects for African Americans seeking statewide office are not promising. Doug Wilder's victory in 1989 in Virginia did not preview future success in gubernatorial or senatorial races as Harvey Gantt, Cleo Fields, and William Jefferson have found out. And Wilder only just won in 1989, saved by the last-minute support of pro-choice suburban white women, and he ran well behind the rest of the Democratic ticket.[27]

At the local level the difficulty of getting white support led to the drive to eliminate at-large and multi-member districts after the *Gingles* case. It is not surprising that African Americans opted for the creation of black majority districts that dramatically increased the number of black congressmen but which made other districts more white and more susceptible to Republican control. It is true that when Court decisions overturned some of those districts, black representatives like Cynthia McKinney in Georgia or Mel Watt in North Carolina won in their new white majority districts, but they won because as incumbents they had been able to build up a visible constituency record of service for both races. It was by no means clear that new black candidates could win such a seat in an open race. Many whites used to praise Mike Espy's overtures to whites in his Mississippi Second District and were prepared to vote for him in subsequent elections, but he won the seat in the first place without that white support.[28]

In opting for maximizing the number of black lawmakers at the expense of the slippery goal of dispersing black voters and exercising a liberalizing effect in a greater number of white districts, African American leaders made an understandable decision in the light of the existing state of biracial politics. Not surprisingly, they have opted for local power—for the chance of getting jobs for black constituents, for getting contracts for black businessmen, and for getting black access to local power and influence. Gavin Wright illustrated the success of increasing numbers of black officials in the South, increasing far faster than in the rest of the nation. But there is a cost. In Louisiana, which has more elected black officials than in any state other than Mississippi, African Americans have obtained power in cities like New Orleans or in rural districts but they do not have the revenue base to solve the problems of their impoverished black constituents. Dutch Morial had to confront the chronic problems of the Crescent City when both the federal government and the state governments were slashing their aid—which had provided over half the city's revenue. African American male political leaders in Louisiana first gained significant political opportunities in the poverty programs in New Orleans controlled by Moon Landrieu and then in the state programs controlled by Edwin Edwards. Like their white counterparts they appear to have opted for personal profit, patronage, and access to the white power structure for personal and group recognition rather than for policy input designed to restructure Louisiana government in favor of the have-nots in the state.[29]

Of course, the vote has transformed the African American experience as Adam Fairclough highlighted: the elimination of apartheid, the opening up of employment, and the administration of justice are vital gains. Gavin Wright emphasized the positive statistics of black-owned businesses, the rise in black median income, and the sustained black in-migration since 1970. But how are African American politicians to tackle the problems of the Arkansas Delta outlined by Nan Woodruff or of the inner cities spotlighted by Tim Tyson? How are they to tackle the desperate problems of, for example, New Orleans schools, or, what seems astounding to European eyes, the problems of inadequate accesss to healthcare, soaring infant mortality rates, and low birth weights in the richest country in the world.[30]

At the moment, African American politicians can secure symbolic victories —they can desegregate the Shoals Creek golf course, they will eliminate the Confederate flag as a state symbol. These are important issues. But, as Nancy McLean pointed out, retaining affirmative action, for example, has been decoupled from redistributive social policies. At a time when no politician in the Western world seems to dare to talk intelligently about progressive taxation, when the southern Republican vision seems to look no further than the next tax cut or the next toxic waste dump, and when Democrats can see only some form of gambling as a revenue source for government programs to support reform of the infrastruture, it is unclear that biracial politics is going to deliver the benefits for which Dr. King once hoped.[31]

11

~

Southern New Dealers Confront the World: Lyndon Johnson, Albert Gore, and Vietnam

1. Two Southern New Dealers

Jack Robinson, the young man from Carthage who ran Albert Gore's Senate office from 1956 to 1964, remembered:

> [A]fter Johnson was sworn in, just a few days later, he [Gore] comes to the office and says, "Jack R. I've got the call from the President and he wants to see me." Which means why don't you drive with me over to the White House. He says, "I won't be long, just wait here," at the south end you know. And again, you know, it's not Lyndon, it's the president. So he comes out, it didn't take long. And I said, "Well, what happened?" He said, "Well, the president said, 'Albert, you know we're both old school teachers, and what I would like to do is to take the eraser and wipe the slate clean.'" And I said, "Well what did you say?" He said, "Mr. President, I agree." He was so serious, you know. Well it wasn't two weeks that each was smacking against the other again.[1]

Gore and Johnson were very similar. They were born within a year of each other in the hill country of Tennessee and Texas. Both struggled to go to college: Gore would raise enough of a crop to pay for tuition for a semester or two at Middle Tennessee State Teachers College, then go back to the farm, raise another crop and return to college. Johnson scrounged a bewildering variety of jobs at South West Texas State and taught Mexican Americans for a year at Cotulla to enable him to complete his degree at San Marcos. Both taught—Gore in one-room schools in Smith County, Johnson in Houston—

181

but not for long. Both were natural politicians—Gore's classmates recall that he would stay in his room on a Saturday night at college to write postcards to people back in Smith County because he knew he would be running for office one day; Johnson was a political whirlwind even at San Marcos. Gore was elected superintendent of education for Smith County, then served as campaign manager for a rising Tennessee politician, Gordon Browning, and became Browning's commissioner of labor. Johnson went to Washington as Congressman Richard Kleberg's secretary and then became state NYA administrator for Texas.[2]

They were elected to Congress within a year of each other in 1937–38. They were elected in the old style of patronage-oriented southern Democratic Party politics in which a plethora of candidates with few issues to divide them contested primary elections. Both circumvented the local county seat elites who usually delivered their counties' votes by taking their case directly to the people, mounting vigorous campaigns to establish their name recognition. Johnson reached out to the tiniest and most isolated communities in his district and completely overturned the "leisurely pace normal in Texas elections." Gore played the fiddle with a small band to attract a crowd on Saturday afternoons in courthouse squares across his district.[3]

But if Gore and Johnson were elected in the old-style of local, patronage-oriented politics, they came to represent a new style of issue-oriented politics in the South. They were typical of "a new generation of leaders" whom Roosevelt identified in the region and were elected to state legislatures, statehouses, and Congress in the late 1930s and 1940s. Johnson and Gore would be elected to the Senate in 1948 and 1952: Johnson would defeat the rigidly conservative, popular governor, Coke Stevenson; Gore would defeat the veteran chair of the Senate Appropriations Committee and ally of Boss Crump of Memphis, Kenneth McKellar. Both would do so by dauntingly vigorous personal campaigns. While Johnson used a helicopter to follow a punishing schedule across the state, the stately Stevenson deigned to give one address in each county seat. While Gore crisscrossed Tennessee in a relentless daily schedule of stump speeches and television broadcasts, the enfeebled McKellar largely remained in his hotel while supporters hit the campaign trail as surrogates.[4]

Johnson and Gore both saw the economic development of the South as the key to the elimination of the grinding poverty of which they had firsthand knowledge. They championed cheap public power and water resource development to modernize agriculture and stimulate industrial development: they had seen what the great projects on the Lower Colorado River and on the Tennessee Valley could achieve; they could see the benefits of rural electrification. Whereas for southern conservatives, the federal government was the problem, for southern New Dealers like Johnson and Gore the federal government was the solution. Federal aid, they believed, was essential to solve the region's health care and educational problems. Cheap credit from the Reconstruction Finance Corporation would liberate the region's entrepreneurs. In the battle to develop the region's infrastructure, Johnson and Gore would be allies from the late 1930s to the Great Society: most notably, on interstate highways, federal aid to education, and Medicare.[5]

Johnson and Gore had particular enthusiasms for special aspects of federal investment in the South. For LBJ it was the space program that brought such spectacular benefits to Alabama and Florida but above all to Houston. For Gore it was atomic power. He had been made privy by FDR to the developments at Oak Ridge. He was as enthusiastic about the peaceful use of atomic power as he was for the Tennessee Valley Authority. In his senate campaign in 1952 he vowed to make Tennessee the "atomic capital" of the nation. Despairing of the slowness of private industry to develop nuclear reactors on the scale of the British, in 1956 he secured passage with Johnson's help of a Senate bill for government financing of reactor construction. The bill floundered in the House.[6]

They were both racial moderates. Like most southern liberals in the postwar South they tried to concentrate on economic issues—to avoid upsetting lower-income white voters and in the genuine belief that economic progress would gradually induce racial change. Neither prepared their constituents for the prospect of desegregation. But when the South started to resist the *Brown* decision, both demurred. Neither signed the Southern Manifesto. Gore supported Johnson when LBJ masterminded passage of the 1957 Voting Rights Act. Like other southern moderates—Jack Brooks, Jim Wright, and Dante Fascell—Gore did not support Johnson's 1964 Civil Rights Act but he was not part of the southern team that filibustered against it. He did, however, support the 1965 Voting Rights Act and the 1968 Open Housing Act. Just as Johnson cemented the loyalty of southern blacks to the Democratic Party, so African Americans overwhelmingly supported Gore in 1970, even if he made no special effort to reach out to African Americans as a group.[7]

Gore may have been more of a Populist on economic issues than LBJ: he distrusted tax cuts, pushed for tax reform, and constantly lamented policies of high interest rates. But both men admired and cultivated rich and successful businessmen: for Johnson, George Brown of Brown and Root and some of the independent oilmen; for Gore, Bernard Baruch and Armand Hammer. Raised in economic insecurity, both strove to achieve financial success. Johnson made his money while in office through his radio and TV empire in Austin. Gore had more modest goals while in office—he set up a local food and feed mill with Grady Nixon, which gave him enough financial security to contemplate the Senate race in 1952. He also set up a cattle breeding business with Armand Hammer. They consoled each other over the loss of their prize Angus bull, the 382, and Hammer suggested they place an obituary of the 382 in the *American Angus Journal.* But Gore made serious money after he left office. Setting up as a lawyer in Washington with Hammer's Occidental as one of his clients, Gore became chair of the Island Creek Coal Company, one of Hammer's subsidiaries, and he traveled the world negotiating one to one with foreign heads of state like Ceausescu of Rumania and with the Chinese government.[8]

Johnson and Gore, therefore, had much the same political agenda. They were natural allies and worked hard to like each other. Gore rejoiced in Johnson's Senate victory in 1948. They flattered each other and joked about their respective herds of cattle. They visited each other's ranches and their wives got on well. Gore gave Johnson a much-appreciated pig for his ranch, and they spoke in each other's states. In particular, Johnson called Gore over to Texas to speak in the last week of the 1956 campaign as he and Rayburn tried to keep the state in Democrat hands. Johnson cast Texas votes for Gore's vice presidential bid in 1956. Gore had the greatest admiration for Johnson's legislative expertise: he supported the Great Society legislation enthusiastically.[9]

Yet in many ways they were too similar. Both saw themselves as potential southern presidents, Gore was never a member of the southern caucus, and he was never part of Johnson's inner circle. He was too uncompromising for the majority leader who was always anxious to compromise. As Harry McPherson recalled:

> He [Johnson] had a terrible time with Gore. They had a lot in common politically, but Gore had the damnedest ability to offend through a kind of righteous pomposity that would drive Johnson right up the wall and me too. I used to just despise it. He always looked like a Baptist bishop standing back there speaking of the outrageous thing that had just been perpetrated on the people by the Establishment. Then Gore was also terribly ambitious.

As Gore's admirer, Adrian Fisher recalled, Gore was "a hard man to put pressure on," and Johnson wanted to be able to pressure everybody. Where Johnson was a friend of J. Edgar Hoover, Hoover targeted Gore from 1953 onward. Gore was far friendlier with Johnson's Texas nemesis Ralph Yarborough than with Johnson. He was also close to other senators whom Johnson often humiliated—like Paul Douglas of Illinois and Herbert Lehman of New York—or tough men Johnson could not control—like Gore's closest ally, Mike Monroney of Oklahoma.[10]

Johnson kept Gore off the Finance Committee for a long time. He undercut Gore's efforts to investigate campaign finances in 1956. From 1958 onward, the conservative Buford Ellington, whom Gore regarded as a "dolt," was Johnson's point man in Tennessee. Much as Gore needed Johnson's support, he chafed at the deference required to the majority leader. In 1960 he led an effort to undermine Johnson's absolute control of the Democratic Policy Committee. Gore invited all the likely Democratic presidential candidates to Tennessee in 1960. He saw no reason to feel inferior to any of them, and he supported Kennedy rather than Johnson for the presidency in 1960. He thought that Johnson was too subservient to the big money interests. He also thought that Johnson was the meanest man in Washington, and he meant "mean" as in cruel. When Kennedy was elected and Johnson became vice president, Gore must have thought that his days of having to defer to Johnson were finally over. By the time Kennedy's second term would be completed in 1968, Gore might have a realistic chance of being the first southern president. When Johnson attempted to continue as vice president to control the Democratic caucus and keep his majority leader's office, Gore was the leader of the powerful minority that effectively drove Johnson off. Gore spoke with the unguarded vehemence of someone who would not have to worry about Johnson again. They maintained some of the niceties while LBJ was vice president. Gore inserted LBJ's speeches in Berlin in the *Congressional Record* and praised their wisdom. In turn, Johnson consulted Gore on a speech he was to make in Nashville. He made elaborate protestations that he had not encouraged Buford Ellington to run against Gore in 1964. But Johnson also coldly ensured that Gore, who knew more about the control of nuclear weapons than any man in the Senate, was excluded from the congressional delegation that helped negotiate the test ban treaty in Washington. When Kennedy was assassinated, Gore must surely have realized that he would never again have the chance to be president.[11]

Despite Gore's support of Great Society legislation, he infuriated LBJ by his opposition to the tax cut, his opposition to the nomination of Henry Fowler as secretary of the treasury, and his repeated criticism of the high interest rates and tight money in the later Johnson years.[12] But it was foreign policy that was to see a lasting and bitter breach between the two southern New Dealers.

2. Southern Internationalists

World affairs played no part in Johnson and Gore's election to Congress in the late 1930s. But the two rural, small-town congressmen found themselves in Washington when issues of preparedness and war were all-consuming. Following the lead of Cordell Hull, who had once represented Gore's district, Gore was a strong supporter of preparedness and intervention. Johnson, following the lead of his New Deal circle of friends, was equally supportive of Roosevelt's foreign policy. Both Johnson and Gore served in the war for strictly limited periods—Johnson at the start in the Far East, Gore near the end in Europe. Bryce Harlow, future Republican top-ranking official in the Eisenhower and Nixon administrations, worked in General Marshall's office and remembered that he had been given the task of getting service experience for New Deal congressmen who were up for reelection and had voted for the draft but not served themselves, though of draft age:

> So I had the task of giving a hand-conducted tour through the armed forces in time of war … to get them in for a special basic training, and in for a little advanced training, and then for a special shipment to a combat area, and a special escort through a combat area, special return to the United States and special discharge. So then they would be veterans who had served in combat, so they could approach the voters unassailably the following year.

Harlow certainly exaggerated: Gore, for example, only enlisted after he was reelected in 1944 and he had to resign his congressional seat, unlike Johnson. But although both Johnson and Gore would appeal to fellow veterans after the war, neither had the sort of tough wartime experience that profoundly shaped so many southerners, white and black. As supporters of preparedness, intervention, and the Roosevelt-Hull wartime foreign policy, Johnson and Gore, however, were like most southern politicians who were internationalist irrespective of whether they were conservative or liberal on domestic policy. One exception was the right-wing of the Democratic Party in Texas: Johnson would effectively portray Coke Stevenson as an isolationist in 1948.[13]

It was natural for Gore and Johnson to be strong defenders of containment, the Marshall Plan, and the creation of NATO. The United States, Gore announced, "will oppose totalitarian aggression under whatever name and by whatever means it seeks to subjugate and oppress." Unlike southern conservatives and more so than Johnson, Gore was a supporter of foreign economic aid, but skeptical of military aid.[14]

Gore had an independent streak. He advocated a dehumanized atomic belt across the Korean peninsular through radiological contamination in order to end the Korean War. Although he backed Truman's dismissal of McArthur, despite a firestorm of constituency protest, he wanted Truman to sack Acheson and replace him with someone who would contribute to the "unity and solidarity of the country." Johnson helped Richard Russell defuse the controversy over the sacking of McArthur and helped the Eisenhower administration defeat the Bricker amendment. He generally supported Eisenhower against the isolationists in the president's own party. But he was profoundly influenced by the loss of China—which he blamed for McCarthyism and for Truman's loss of influence with Congress.[15]

Gore and Johnson were therefore conventional cold war liberal Democrats committed to global containment who chided the Eisenhower administration for its inflexible yet lethargic response to the Soviet threat. The all-encompassing nature of the anti-communist mentality was summed up by the rebuttal point that Gore prepared for Kennedy in 1960 to scotch Nixon's claims about success in the struggle against Communism:

> Within the lifetime of Mr. Nixon Communism was confined to a rented room in Zurich, Switzerland. Today it dominates 40 per cent of the world's people, one-third of its geography and one-third of its industrial power.
>
> Eight years ago Communism was being contained in Eastern Europe and Southeast Asia. Today its influence has penetrated the Middle East, notably the UAR and Iraq, Laos and Cambodia in Asia, Guinea and Ghana in Africa; and Latin America, particularly Cuba.[16]

There were important differences: Gore traveled widely, Johnson did not. Gore inspected nuclear facilities in Britain and Japan and highways in Latin America; he was an active member of the Interparliamentary union, visited Europe frequently, and inspected foreign aid administration in the Middle East and Southeast Asia. Johnson inspected U.S. military facilities in Europe in 1945, attended a NATO leaders' conference in Paris in 1956, and went to Mexico in 1958 to meet President Mateos (though you will find no mention of these last two trips in Robert Caro's 1,170 pages on LBJ's time in the Senate). According to George Reedy, Johnson feared that he would be accused of taking foreign junkets. Gore had a deep, personal interest in foreign policy and studied the issues for himself. He was very much involved in Geneva discussions of nuclear disarmament and tariff reduction. He cherished his eventual seat on the Foreign Relations Committee. Johnson was serious about foreign policy, made a decisive intervention in the decision not to commit troops to Vietnam in 1954, and received presidential briefings as Majority Leader, but foreign policy did not absorb his interest. Johnson had neither the time nor the inclination to get heavily involved in foreign policy. When Albert Gore arranged an informal Roundtable discussion group of senators to hear speakers like Dean Acheson and George Kennan, Johnson was always invited but he never attended.[17]

How would these southern liberal internationalists confront Vietnam?

3. Two Southerners Confront Vietnam

John Culver, then a representative from Iowa, remembered being summoned to the White House with other members of the House Foreign Affairs Committee and the Senate Foreign Relations Committee, and the two Appropriations committees:

> It was during the build up, the request for more funding to carry this out and there was this very elaborate full briefing and all the foreign policy members of this group participated and were asked back and even Mac Bundy, and the budget director and so forth. Everyone was served a couple of strong scotches and quite relaxed and by the time everyone sat down for the briefing and Johnson sat in the front of course, and the members would go up in turn and get their particular briefing, their presentation of the briefing and I had this feeling that he was sitting in a director's chair, because he sat up there with his drink and would not hesitate to interrupt the briefer and say to Bob, "Bob, tell me about this" and to Dean " be sure to mention this." And of course it was awkward because he kept interrupting but every time, in fairness, every time that he asked them to make a point or to comment in one way or another, it strengthened the political presentation and clearly he was making points that he thought would appeal and resonate well with the congressmen and senators there. When the briefings were formally finished, he stood up in front of the group and said he would take any questions that anybody asked. He was pretty relaxed at that time and I remember a number of questions. But the question I remember was that posed by Al Cederberg, who was the ranking Republican on the House Appropriations Committee, a longtime house member from Michigan. And he raised his hand and he said, "Mr. President," he said, "I agree with you about this war thing!" And that was exactly what he said, "I agree about this war thing, but what I don't understand is how we give them all this money and they don't do what we want them to." Johnson said... "Cederberg, let me tell you something," he said, "my home county in Texas is Blanco County in Texas, and a number of years ago the boys came into my office and said, Lyndon, we gotta get ourselves a sheriff, who should we get? And I said, boys you should go out and get yourself a good-looking man and make sure he doesn't drink or smoke or think the girls are pretty and he's honest and bring him in here to me. And after a few months they came in and sure enough they had a boy that checked out with every particular. Good, big, strong, handsome man, so I reached in my drawer and there's a big shiny badge and it said "Sheriff, Blanco County, Texas." I took it and put it right on his chest and he was the proudest man in Blanco County. And in the first six months, Cederberg, he was the best sheriff Blanco County in Texas probably ever had but the seventh month

he started to smoke and the eighth month he started to drink too much, the ninth month he thought everybody's wife was his girl friend and about the tenth month every time you paid a fine in Blanco County, Texas, he thought it was supposed to go in his bank account. So about the eleventh or twelfth month we had to fire him and get ourselves a new sheriff. Now I ask you, Cederberg, if Lyndon Johnson can't even keep a sheriff in Blanco County, Texas, how do you think I can keep a government in Vietnam?" So everybody had a great laugh at that and of course upon reflection, the tragedy was, he didn't follow the moral and the wisdom of his own story.[18]

In order to keep a government in Vietnam, Johnson, fully aware of the deficiencies of successive Saigon regimes, had first eschewed direct military action—he would not commit troops until there was a stable government in the South. Until there was a stable government, the United States could not afford to negotiate. As one after another South Vietnamese governments failed and defeat became imminent in 1964 and 1965, the rationale reversed. Military action was needed in order to create a stable government that could then negotiate. The bombing started in February 1965 to give time for a strong enough government to emerge and to convince the North of U.S. resolve so that the North would call off its surrogate forces in the South. As that bombing failed, so troops were sent in the spring of 1965 in what increasingly looks like the point of no return. In July 1965 the major escalation occurred when 175,000 troops were sent and authorized to fight an offensive war. Over the next two years, more and more troops were committed and the bombing changed from a calibrated exercise designed to demonstrate American resolve to an all-out campaign to destroy Hanoi's capacity to wage war. The Tet Offensive in 1968 demonstrated that the massive commitment of American forces had at best produced stalemate, with the prospects of more and more and more troops, more and more casualties, and no end in sight. Only then did Johnson stop the escalation and seek a negotiated settlement.

Joseph Fox, the wealthy Yale alumnus who established the Fox International Fellowship program, once told me that the purpose of this graduate exchange program with universities around the globe was to ensure that there would never again be an American president who was as ignorant of the rest of the world as Lyndon Johnson. (Fox made this comment before the election of George W. Bush.) But Johnson was no ignorant Texas rube in foreign affairs. It is true that, of course, he could be boorish and blustering with foreign leaders, notably Harold Wilson and Lester Pearson. He disliked having to meet many of them. He had little interest in seeing ambassadors about to go overseas.[19]

His style of operation could certainly be distinctive. He appeared to extrapolate from Texas to the wider world. John Kenneth Galbraith reported wryly on an LBJ visit to India in 1961 that Johnson "carries all precincts visited and would run well nationwide." Jack Hood Vaughn was a Foreign Service officer in Africa deputed to look after the vice president on a trip there. One morning he drove Johnson into the countryside, which Johnson ignored and, instead, harangued Vaughn with a three-hour monologue about how much money he had made and how many women he had slept with. After lunch he suddenly noticed Vaughn and asked him who he was. Vaughn explained that he was in Africa because that was where the State Department believed the important events were taking place, but that his real interest was in Latin America. Johnson suddenly sat up alert. "I'm very interested in Latin America," he said, "tell me where we are going wrong there." Vaughn thought nothing more about it and was not in communication with Johnson again. Three years later he was working in the fields in Bolivia when a message came that the White House wanted to talk to him. He assumed the messenger meant the house belonging to the local landowner, and ambled back to find the president on the phone. "Jack," the voice boomed, "remember what you told me about Latin America? We've got a problem in the Canal Zone and I've just made you ambassador to Panama."[20]

Recent work on the foreign policy of the Johnson administration seems to me to show that, first, in the rest of the world Johnson understood the limitations of American power and he and his advisers acted with skill and sensitivity in areas like Cyprus, the Middle East, and the Indian subcontinent where their options were limited and their efforts to restrain warring powers were modestly successful. The record was mixed, notably in Latin America where the shadow of Castro tended to distort policy. But successes outweighed failures. Second, as Thomas Schwartz has brilliantly demonstrated, the administration handled a succession of problems in Europe from the issue of a multilateral nuclear force, the withdrawal of the French from NATO, to the balance of payments deficit and the tensions in the international trade and monetary order, with considerable skill. Notably, Johnson understood and handled De Gaulle better than many of his career diplomats. Third, Vietnam did not preclude progress being made in foreign policy in other areas of the world. It did not halt efforts to improve relations with the Soviets and to carry forward Strategic Arms Limitation talks. It was the Soviet invasion of Czechoslovakia that halted that progress. As John Dumbrell has recently concluded, "it is churlish to deny that, in very broad terms, LBJ's Soviet policy was part of 'what went right' with his Presidency." Nor did it prevent exploration of an opening to China; indeed administration officials thought that Vietnam might facilitate that opening. The fact that it did not was due to China's internal politics, not American policy.[21]

Nor was Johnson a mindless warmonger who thought that victory for the world's strongest power could come easily in Vietnam. He was acutely aware that the war might destroy the Great Society programs, which he so cherished. He was under no illusions about the difficulties of a ground war in Asia: southern conservatives and old-time Senate colleagues like Richard Russell and Allen Ellender were among those who most strongly believed that such a war could not be won and told him so. No one can read the telephone transcripts of 1963–64 without having a profound sense of his agonizing over the Vietnam situation. Johnson knew from the CIA and from McNamara how limited the impact of the bombing was. Both war game simulations and the CIA told him that bombing the North would not weaken North Vietnam's resolve or affect the capacity of the indigenous Viet Cong to fight in the South. Far from glib optimism, what Fredrik Logevall has convincingly demonstrated is that "A startling aspect of the war is the pronounced pessimism at the center of American strategy in Vietnam." Johnson complained bitterly that the only advice he received from the generals was to bomb and bomb again. He gave the opportunity to dissenters like George Ball to make their case. He did not browbeat his advisers into only giving him advice he wanted to hear. He was a force for restraint—he sanctioned neither the invasion of the North nor the unlimited bombing of the North for fear of unleashing a world war with the Soviets and China: options which are newly fashionable among conservative revisionist historians. According to these recent arguments, Johnson should have invaded the North in the summer and fall of 1964 and reacted with massive bombing retaliation to the November 1 and December 24, 1964, attacks at Ben Hoa and the Brink Hotel. Johnson did not listen to intelligence estimates that the Chinese would not have responded and the intelligence agencies failed to pick up how many North Vietnamese had already been infiltrated into the South. Misled by this American restraint the North Vietnamese felt free to commit ground troops to the South. This argument rests on an extraordinarily glib assessment of the feasibility of an invasion of the North and, even if that were successful, the possibility of creating a successful, popular, and anti-communist South Vietnamese government.[22]

Given Johnson's overriding concern for the Great Society, given his caution, given his realistic awareness in other areas of the world of the limitations on American power, why did Johnson take the United States into a war about whose outcome he was so pessimistic? The question is particularly acute since so many of his political allies, his majority leader, Mike Mansfield, his long-time friend and chair of the Senate Foreign Relations Committee, William Fulbright, and his father-like mentor Richard Russell, all cautioned against American involvement. At least twenty Democratic senators shared this view, as did prominent columnists like Walter Lippmann and papers like the *New*

York Times. The question is also acute since there was an option for negotiation, rather than escalation, available throughout Fredrik Logevall's "the long 1964," an option championed not merely by De Gaulle, but by Washington's allies overseas, all convinced of the hopelessness of the Saigon regime and the war-weariness of the South Vietnamese people. Negotiation with a view to a neutralized South Vietnam also fitted the agenda of the Soviet Union, North Vietnam, and China. The Soviets did not want to be drawn into a competition with China as to who would most generously aid the North Vietnamese. The North Vietnamese themselves did not wish to see the conflict Americanized since they believed that the South was theirs for the taking in due course. The Chinese wanted to eliminate any possible threat to their southern border.

Why did that political master manipulator, Lyndon Johnson, not seek to build a coalition for that option of negotiation and withdrawal after his 1964 landslide victory, particularly in 1965 which Hubert Humphrey called "the year of minimum political risk for the Johnson administration"?

For some historians, Johnson's commitment to the war in 1965 was all but inevitable: it was the logic of global containment, the logic of Kennedy's extravagant rhetoric to defend freedom wherever it was threatened, a continuation of the Kennedy policy put forward to Johnson irresistibly by Kennedy's key advisers, Dean Rusk, McGeorge Bundy, and Robert McNamara that the United States had to demonstrate its staying power in the cold war. The fundamental and largely unchallenged assumptions of a whole generation of foreign policy decision-makers led to, first the bombing, and then the commitment of ground troops in 1965. For others it was Johnson's war. While a Kennedy, skeptical of military solutions and more sensitive to international opinion, might have finessed an exit strategy after the 1964 elections, Johnson, an instinctive hawk, dominated the decision-making on Vietnam, keeping Vietnam on the back burner in 1964, but all the time waiting for the opportunity for a stronger military response and rejecting any option for negotiation and withdrawal.[23]

It is true that a picture of Lyndon Johnson as the prisoner of any advisers is implausible. It is also true that Johnson kept decision-making much more narrowly based than Kennedy. His dislike of public dissent and disagreement that might force his hand led him to keep decision-making in the hands of himself and his key advisers, Rusk, McNamara, and Bundy. He liked the assurance that all options had been explored but did not like the reflective personal consideration of those options or the intellectual give and take that Kennedy enjoyed. But equally, the notion that Rusk, McNamara, and Bundy, because of personal ambition and misplaced loyalty to the president, simply told a hawkish Johnson what he wanted to believe is also implausible. There is a difference between advisers telling a president what he wants to hear, irrespective of their own views, and advocating their own preferred course of action to a president in terms that they knew he was likely to respond to. To my mind, the evidence is heavily in favor of the latter interpretation. Andrew Preston's new study of McGeorge Bundy seems to me admirably to capture the force and consistency of Bundy's role as a presidential adviser. Bundy's worldview encompassed the necessity of using military force, a contempt for appeasement and a consistent anti-communism. His toughness was limited only by his genuine abhorrence of nuclear weapons. Thus, Bundy supported détente with the Soviet Union but détente in Europe was predicated on strength in Southeast Asia. If Vietnam collapsed, America could not sustain détente in the rest of the world. As Johnson took over from Kennedy and the situation in South Vietnam worsened, Bundy and his NSC Vietnam specialist, Michael Forrestal, worked to discourage any talk of negotiation and neutralization: the American position had to be strengthened, otherwise negotiation simply meant a Communist takeover. Increasingly, he came to believe that a military response was needed to stave off defeat. He and his brother advocated the detailed military planning and the drafting of a congressional resolution that were called into play in the Tonkin Gulf crisis. Preston argues that from September 1964 Bundy was less an adviser carrying out the president's wishes and more an advocate preparing the way for the introduction of ground troops. The campaign intensified once the November election was out of the way. Bundy and McNamara presented Johnson with a stark choice. No longer could he afford to wait for a stable South Vietnamese government. To avoid defeat in Vietnam American involvement had to escalate. Bundy worked with McNamara in 1965 to assuage the president's doubts about committing ground troops.[24]

Consistently Bundy and McNamara presented their arguments in terms that Johnson would find difficult to resist: the need for continuity with the Kennedy administration, the dangers of appeasement, the need to honor commitments, that negotiation could only lead to a Communist takeover, that takeover would have a domino effect in Southeast Asia, that the loss of Vietnam would have the same domestic negative political consequences for Johnson as the loss of China did for Truman.[25]

These arguments certainly resonated with Johnson. Anxious to follow his predecessor's foreign policy line, he understandably saw Bundy and McNamara as the main sources of knowledge of what that policy would be. Johnson constantly feared that any weakening in his stance on South Vietnam would be denounced by the surviving Kennedys and their coterie. Lest this view seem unduly paranoid, it is important to remember how late in the day both Robert and Edward Kennedy became dissenters on Vietnam.[26]

Johnson found it easy to believe that to negotiate a withdrawal would be to cut and run, to appease aggression. The domino effect on the rest of Southeast Asia loomed large for Johnson as it did, indeed, for the Australian and New Zealand governments. He explained the need for containment graphically to the London journalist Louis Heren. He compared the Vietcong to a young man trying to seduce a girl. Johnson was the girl but he reversed the role to demonstrate what he meant. "You can remember," he said, "putting your hand on a girl's knee and sliding it up her thigh until she told you to stop." The thought, recalled Heren, "of him protecting his virginity was ridiculously funny, until his powerful fingers first clenched my knee and then my thigh. I cannot recall the thoughts that passed through my mind but was immensely relieved when his fist relaxed."[27]

When Johnson's foreign policy advisers developed second thoughts on the war and abandoned the government, they left a president who had bought their arguments only too well, who had expressed his goals in rhetoric that made disengagement difficult, and who now had true-believer advisers like Walt Rostow who did not share the new-found skepticism of Bundy and McNamara. The world was full of elite advisers who were prescient doves in retrospect, but when a historian looks at Bundy, Michael Forrestal, John McNaughton, Averill Harriman, Maxwell Taylor, and Roger Hilsman he finds that at the time they were the staunchest advocates of an interventionist Vietnam policy.

But Johnson, as Lloyd Gardner has compellingly argued, also saw Vietnam through the eyes of a New Dealer. Like Texas in the 1930s, it was ripe for infrastructure development. His billion-dollar development plan, laid out in his Johns Hopkins speech of 1965 would enable the region to be transformed in the same way as the New Deal had changed the South. For the Tennessee Valley, read the Mekong Delta. Johnson liked to believe that other Asian leaders shared his vision, and for a time he believed that Ho Chi Minh would find the bait of that development plan irresistible. LBJ never quite understood why Ho did not react like Lister Hill or John Sparkman or himself to the promise of cheap electrical power. Johnson had faith that Americans, self-evidently imbued with the public-spirited zeal and the faith in economic growth of the New Deal, could go into South Vietnam and pacify it by winning over the hearts and minds and building a new nation. And, according to Gardner, defeat in Vietnam would not only unleash a right-wing backlash that would destroy the Great Society but would also call into question America's ability to sustain the ambitious projects of the War on Poverty.[28]

But the grubby reality was different. Johnson's instinctive search for the middle way, which served him brilliantly in Congress, led him to be mired in an unsatisfactory policy that produced stalemate. He avoided bombing that would lead to direct confrontation with the Soviets and Chinese but nevertheless steadily increased the bombing targets until there was virtually nothing else to bomb. He rejected the more extreme demands for troop increases but did agree to a succession of relatively modest troop increases that produced the dreadful casualties he so feared. He launched countless peace offensive and bombing halts but undercut those efforts by his refusal to allow the NLF or the Vietcong at the conference table. All the time he hoped against hope that he would get the quick victory that would mean that he would not have to confront the next demand for escalation. Yet he instinctively knew that the war could only be won on the ground over a long period. He believed that incremental steps and the choice of the middle way preserved his room for maneuver and kept his options open. In fact, each small step foreclosed options and made disengagement more difficult. It took the public relations crisis of the Tet offensive and looming electoral humiliation in the primaries to provoke a major reassessment and to launch negotiations on terms less favorable than would have been available three years earlier.[29]

How did Albert Gore, fellow southern liberal internationalist and committed cold warrior, react to the same Vietnamese crisis?

Gordon Petty, Gore's doctor, recalled the spring of 1965:

> I remember one time when he was in the Senate and I was practicing medicine here and some bill was up before Congress that affected medicine quite a bit and I went to talk to him about it. And he was always very personable with me and kindly. He gave me whatever time I wanted. And we talked quite a little while about this medical bill that was coming up and discussed it at length and he was very open minded about it. He could see both sides to it and when we got through I said, "Albert, what are you doing and when are you coming back to Carthage?" He says, "About twenty minutes." "That's a coincidence," I said, "What are you doing tonight?" He said, "Nothing." I said, "Well, I happen to have tickets to the Vanderbilt basketball game. Would you be interested in going to a basketball game." "Oh, I'd love to," he said. And he said, "Pick me up." We arranged a time and I drove by and picked him up. When Albert got in the car he said, "Now, Gordon, I've had my mind so torn up by problems of state lately and probably you're having the same problem with problems of medicine. Let's forget it all tonight and just let it all hang out and just relax and let our hair down and have a good time." I said, "That sure suits me." We started out and drove down the road about twenty miles and I was chatting along and he'd just sort of grunt and answer yes or no. It was obvious that his mind was on something else. And finally I just turned to him and said, "Albert, you said we were

going to whoop it up tonight and have a good time, relax. And you haven't opened your mouth hardly the whole time. What's wrong?" He said, "Well, something has developed that I just can't get out of my mind. The President is about to commit the fighting troops in Vietnam." He says, "It is one of the worst mistakes that the United States has ever been involved in. We have no business there. The French fought in Vietnam for twenty years and finally they gave up and went home and now we are getting sucked into the same problem." And he said, "We have no business there, heretofore we've had manufacturers selling equipment, military equipment over there and just advisors over there to advise them how to use it." But he said, "Now the President is about to commit fighting troops." He said, "It will go down in history as one of the worst mistakes our country has ever made." He said, "I called the President this morning from my office in Washington and discussed it with him quite a while and he's committed to do it." He said, "Before I left up there to come here I called him and talked to him again and went over to the White House and talked to him and tried to talk him out of it." He says, "Then after I got home to Carthage I called him again and talked to him again about it. There's no changing him. He's going to commit fighting troops. It's a mistake." Says, "We'll lose a lot of good American boys. It'll cost a whole lot. We will fight a war that can't be won." And he said, "It will just drag on, and on, and on and just be a mess." How true it was. Just think of the foresight that Albert had there.[30]

In 1954 Gore got his staff to provide background material on Indochina, and their findings led him to take a lead with Lyndon Johnson in opposing the commitment of U.S. ground troops to rescue the French. In 1959 Gore and Gale McGhee from Wyoming were sent to Southeast Asia to examine allegations of corruption in the aid program. In Vietnam, McGhee saw "one of the most hopeful, exciting areas around the globe... one of the most imaginative and exciting land development programs anywhere in the world." He was so heartened that he believed "the United States might well consider sending thousands of foreigners, particularly other Asians and Africans... to see what American aid has been able to achieve in the interests of an undeveloped state." Gore, by contrast, found Diem to be a leader "whose authoritarian policies seem to be growing instead of diminishing." He found the aid policies extravagant "and, at least questionable, if not entirely mistaken." It was these findings that led him to question U.S. policy in executive sessions of the Foreign Relations Committee during the Kennedy administration and to plead with Kennedy at a personal meeting with the president in August 1963 to plan for a quick withdrawal from the country.[31]

Gore was influenced by the people round him. He and Pauline kept a keen eye on the young reporter David Halberstam, who served on the *Tennessean* in the fifties. They took great pride in his achievements when he went to the *New York Times*. As a result, when Halberstam sent back from South Vietnam his skeptical reports on the progress of the American effort, Gore, in contrast to Kennedy and McNamara, accepted Halberstam's viewpoint. Pauline Gore thought Halberstam had done a "terrific reporting job" and had played a great part in bolstering Buddhist morale in 1963. Two of Gore's oldest political friends were Chester Bowles and J. K. Galbraith with whom he had worked closely over price control at the Office of Price Administration during and after World War II. Both Bowles and Galbraith, especially from their vantage point as ambassadors to India, warned that military success in Vietnam was unlikely and that nationalist sentiment should not be confused with communism. These skeptical voices also made Gore unconvinced by Johnson's grandiose plans to provide a New Deal–style makeover of Vietnam. Johnson's social reform rhetoric did, however, influence one of Gore's oldest political mentors, David Lilienthal. Lilienthal, who had so influenced Gore as chair both of the TVA and the Atomic Energy Commission, became an active supporter of, and participant in, Johnson's development activities in Vietnam. But the New Deal rhetoric of both LBJ and Lilienthal was offset for Gore by his own observations in 1959 and by the skepticism of his friends.[32]

Yet Gore, like Fulbright and McCarthy, voted for the Tonkin Gulf resolution. He claimed he was misled by Johnson and bitterly regretted his vote. He complained that every time he and other Vietnam dissenters went round to see the president, Johnson would pull the resolution out of his pocket and remind them that they had voted for it. In the summer of 1964 Gore believed that Johnson was a force for restraint against the military. Gore may have been misled by Johnson and his advisers but, facing the possibility of Goldwater nationally and a surprisingly strong right-wing Republican challenge to his own reelection in Tennessee, Gore was only too keen to be over-persuaded.[33]

In late 1964 and 1965, however, he made it clear that he thought a military victory in Vietnam was impossible: in January 1966 he was one of the first leading politicians to call for a negotiated settlement. Through August 1965 he gave President Johnson the benefit of the doubt. But as the reality of the American troop buildup became clear, Gore regretted his earlier reticence and made his opposition to the war clear: he was convinced that it would prove to be "an historical, tragic mistake." No military victory was possible "unless one imagines that he can throw gravel into the Mississippi until it is successfully damned" and no political victory was likely given the nature of the war they were fighting and its inevitable effect on the civilian Vietnamese population. "Perhaps even more importantly in this regard, it has been, and is now becoming even more so, white man against yellow man. Racism is big in this equation, so is religion, so is anti-colonialism." No matter, he later said, "how pure our motives, the United States cannot master the revolutionary, nationalistic tide that is sweeping the world." He played a prominent role in the Foreign Relations Committee exposure of the American dilemmas in Vietnam. Two mistakes had been made, he believed. It had become an American war; bombing was ineffective because "the strength and manpower of the Vietcong is still predominantly indigenous to South Vietnam." Military victory could only be achieved "at tremendous cost which is out of proportion to the vital interests of this country" and at the risk of a war with China which might well lead to nuclear war. Like Johnson, Gore feared war with China. His fear of the dangers of escalation in Vietnam went back to his 1951 fears in Korea about endlessly swapping lives with the Chinese, and the possibility of a nuclear holocaust. As someone who had taken a keen interest in Europe and in Soviet relations, perhaps influenced by his friendship with Armand Hammer, Gore saw Vietnam threatening the improvement of relations with the Soviets, which he took to be crucial to future world security and far more important to America's national interest than Vietnam.[34]

Gore took some heart from early moves of the Nixon administration, which appeared to rule out total military victory, and boasted of troop withdrawals. But, initial hopes of Nixon soon gave way to the conviction that the president was following the same old policy. Gore believed that a "phased withdrawal of increments of U.S. troops" was simply a device to buy time for the administration at the negotiating table. There was no prospect of a negotiated settlement as long as retaining the oppressive Thieu-Ky regime was nonnegotiable. As long as the goal was a "South Korea-type client state," or as Fulbright put it "the puppet government in South Vietnam," there could be no settlement. Meanwhile, casualties since Nixon took office rose remorselessly: 46,000 killed by November 1969. Each week Gore inserted the casualty figures in the *Congressional Record*. "'Vietnamization,' whatever that means and on whatever secret timetable it has been laid out, is another blind alley." He noted indeed that in 1969 at one point U.S. troop figures increased, not decreased. At the same time, his belief in meaningful negotiations meant that he did not support Senate moves to lay down a deadline for unilateral withdrawal of American troops. Such a condition would tie the hands of negotiators just as much as the commitment to the Thieu regime.[35]

Gore did not like campus disturbances and the radical side of the antiwar movement. He always supported appropriations for the war effort on the grounds that he did not want to harm the servicemen who had been sent overseas. His record on the war demonstrated a certain consistency. Unlike many opponents of the war, he was an opponent of the war long before Nixon's election freed many Democrats to be part of the mainstream anti-war movement. Although he was not as public and strident an opponent as Wayne Morse or Ernest Gruening, or indeed Frank Church, he had pressed his skepticism about the war hard both in 1963 and early 1965 and made every effort to get both Kennedy and Johnson to see his way. Like other critics, he did not spell out how negotiations would secure American aims, but he did not perpetuate the comfortable myth that somehow the Americans could have negotiations and a noncommunist Vietnam. The breakdown of his relations with Johnson meant that he did not, like other dissenters—George Aiken, Mike Mansfield, Stuart Symington, even Wayne Morse—attempt to curry favor with the president and keep the president informed about the inner workings of the Senate Foreign Relations Committee. Nevertheless, Gore, like the other doves, showed why they failed to be effective during the Johnson administration. The motives of some of them could too easily be dismissed as the result of thwarted ambition and personal resentment. They rarely organized: they found it hard enough to maintain a common front, even on the Senate Foreign Relations Committee. Too often, notably before the major escalation in July 1965, but particularly in 1964, they were reluctant publicly to challenge a Democratic president.[36]

4. Denouement

Johnson puzzled over the war to his dying day. As the Johnson Library was being completed, Harry Middleton noted that "Particularly with Vietnam did he want the record complete, every meeting and memorandum, the documentation for every action included." In reflecting on the war, he expressed three contradictory stances, Middleton recalled, "To some...he expressed the wish that he had taken stronger action and gone for military victory." To Leonard Marks, he seemed to regret that "he had not simply declared his objectives achieved in Vietnam and brought the troops home." To others, "he endlessly probed the alternatives, exploring the what ifs, always coming back to the conviction that he could have taken no other course."[37]

Gore never wavered in his belief that his course of action on Vietnam was right. "If I have ever," he told Gene Sloan in November 1969, "been right about anything in my entire life then I was right in opposing our involvement in the Vietnam War. I cannot claim a perfect record because I permitted myself to be misled into voting for the Tonkin Gulf resolution. I am confident that I was right in opposing escalation of the war. Indeed, except for the role that I and others played in this regard, we may well have been in war with Red China today."[38]

But Gore's stance on the war left him isolated in the Tennessee Democratic Party. Gore recalled that the war issue was so bitter that, for the first time in his life, people would walk across the street rather than shake his hand. He was at odds with the governor of the state, Buford Ellington. As a result, at the Democratic National Convention at Chicago in 1968 he received no support in the Tennessee delegation controlled by Ellington at the 1968 Convention, either for the peace plank he supported or for the nomination of George McGovern. Tennessee delegates studiously and conspicuously ignored his speech for the peace plank. In 1970 Hudley Crockett, Ellington's press secretary and former Nashville TV anchor, suddenly resigned from the Ellington administration and challenged Gore in the Democratic primary. As Crockett recalled, "It was a matter of are you going to support your troops. You gonna support your people. And you don't undermine and he just got out of touch. . . . but it was a major issue." Crockett rehearsed all the arguments that the Republicans would make in the general election and Gore only just defeated him. Crockett won over 45 percent of the vote and kept Gore's margin of victory to under 32,000. As the *Tennessean* noted, Crockett's votes "picked up steadily as he moved westward across the state into the counties that supported George Wallace in 1968."[39]

The appeal to the Wallace voters was what animated both Richard Nixon's southern strategy and Republican William Brock's campaign against Gore in the 1970 general election. The southern strategy was based on an appeal to racial conservatism—a go-slow on school desegregation and opposition to busing—together with an appeal to regional pride—the appointment of southerners to the Supreme Court—and an appeal to law and order —against both urban crime and campus protest—and an appeal to traditional values—patriotism and conservative morality. The Brock campaign followed this strategy to the letter. Brock's carefully crafted TV ads focused on busing, on supporting the president on the war, on controlling government spending to curb inflation, on combating crime by appointing judges who would put criminals in jail and a Supreme Court that would not tie the hands of the police, on opposition to gun control, on stronger drug laws and enforcement, and the expulsion of violent student protesters. The slots were thirty or sixty seconds and showed Brock talking to ordinary Tennesseans: a parent, a veteran, a pensioner, a farmer, hunters, constituents who had been helped, disaffected Democrats, the wife of a POW, a textile worker, a young man. The message was that Brock listened and took local issues seriously, unlike Gore. The repeated mantra was—"Bill Brock believes in the things we believe in."[40]

Gore's position on the war fitted in to what his opponents in Tennessee considered part of a general "radical liberal" worldview.

A Knoxville evangelist explained why he could not vote for a senator who "seems to think that Tennessee is located somewhere between Connecticut and Massachusetts." Or in Spiro Agnew's formulation, Gore believed "that Tennessee is located somewhere between the *New York Times* and the *Greenwich Village Voice*." Gore's votes against the nominations to the Supreme Court of Haynesworth and Carswell confirmed such views. They were strengthened in the last stages of the campaign when the Brock team focused, to Gore's disgust, on Gore's votes against school prayer.[41]

Gore was defeated in 1970—the only success claimed by Nixon's southern strategy that year. In one sense, the 1970 Tennessee elections simply confirmed the rising Republicanism in the state, highlighted by Howard Baker's victory in the Senate race four years earlier. William Brock, however, identified Gore's "position on the Supreme Court nominees and RN's VN policies as major factors" in his victory. Jimmy Stahlman, editor of the *Nashville Banner,* sent two exultant telegrams after the election. Referring to the defeat of both Gore and the Democratic gubernatorial candidate, John Jay Hooker, whom Stahlman hated even more than he hated Gore, Stahlman telegrammed Richard Nixon at San Clemente the day after the election, WE GOT 'EM BOTH, ONE WITH EACH BARREL. GLADYS JOINS IN BEST TO YOU AND PAT. The next day he sent a telegram to Lyndon Johnson: THANK GOD, WE HELPED GET RID OF ONE OF YOUR ARCH ENEMIES. NO ACKNOWLEDGEMENT NECESSARY.[42]

12

The Anti-Gore Campaign of 1970

With Michael S. Martin

I

At the end of 1968 Albert Gore knew he was in trouble. His opposition to the Vietnam War, his moderation on civil rights, his support of Great Society liberalism, and his advocacy of tax reform had alienated many in Tennessee. The Democratic National Convention in Chicago in August had starkly illustrated his estrangement from major elements of the state Democratic Party. The Tennessee delegation was handpicked by Governor Buford Ellington. When Gore made an impassioned speech for a peace plank in the party platform, he received rousing cheers from other delegations. Tennessee delegates responded with studied indifference, sitting on their hands, ostentatiously reading their newspapers or talking and walking around. Gore cast a lonely vote for George McGovern. The rest of the delegation followed Ellington's lead. The governor had been a favorite-son candidate in part in anticipation of a draft LBJ move, in part in the hope of wringing concessions from Hubert Humphrey. In the end, Ellington and the delegation voted for Humphrey.[1]

There was no love lost between Ellington and Gore. Gore had campaigned strongly for Ellington in the general election in 1958 after the segregationist won a hotly contested and divided Democratic primary. But, according to John Seigenthaler, Gore regarded the governor as a "dolt." While Ellington was Lyndon Johnson's point man in Tennessee, Gore and LBJ were too similar and too ambitious to get along. Gore mistrusted Johnson's ties to moneyed interests, Johnson was exasperated by what he and his friends regarded as the insufferably self-righteous Gore. As Adrian Fisher, who worked for LBJ and was an admirer of Gore, recalled, Gore was a "hard man to put pressure on" and Johnson wanted to put pressure on everybody. The result was that even before the split over Vietnam, "each was smacking against the other again," no matter how often they tried to mend their fences. Ellington, who left the White House with Johnson's blessing to run for governor in 1966, simply believed that Gore was jealous of Johnson, "Gore for some reason felt he had been the bridesmaid too long, not the bride. He had seen himself pushed aside by Johnson, which can build up in any man." The consequence of the Gore-Ellington split, the bitterness between the Ellington camp and supporters of his 1966 opponent John J. Hooker, and the disinterest in Democratic Party organization by President Johnson meant that the state party organization was in a shambles. That absence of an effective state party would be particularly important for Gore, who had never built up a political organization of his own, but had relied on goodwill, on the Kefauver organization or on the state party.[2]

Gore also knew that the Republican party in Tennessee had been transformed. When he was first elected to the Senate in 1952 he garnered 74 percent of the general election vote. In 1958 he pushed that up to 79 percent. But in 1964 Goldwater supporter and Memphis public relations man Dan Kuykendall had polled 46.4 percent against him. Two years later Howard Baker Jr. had won the other Senate seat against Frank Clement comfortably and was on his way to building up the strongest political base of any of the first generation of southern Republican senators. In 1968 the Democratic presidential candidate Humphrey only polled 28 percent of the vote. Middle and western Tennessee white Democrats had switched to George Wallace. His 34 percent enabled Nixon to carry the state. Gore knew that the Republicans would mount a strong challenge in 1970. If Gore was in any doubts about the extent of anti-Democratic backlash, he had only to look at the defeat of his closest Washington friend, Oklahoma senator Mike Monroney in October 1968.[3]

Gore also knew that he was perceived as having lost touch with the state. One pollster reported that "he is frequently criticized on the basis of being out of touch with the state, a "politician" who appears on the scene a few months before election time to take popular stands on controversial issues— and once elected is seldom seen or heard from by his constituents." Said one voter, "He's a politician. Until six months before the election we never hear from him, then you start getting mail, films, and so on." Gore might vigorously refute the charge—he was in Tennessee at some point in forty-three weeks in both 1967 and 1968—but his allies did not deny the substance of the complaints.[4]

Gore held a family council of war over Christmas 1968 and considered whether he should run again. He decided to and immediately reorganized his calendar to be as visible in Tennessee as possible. For the next two years his weekly schedule was usually to be in Nashville Friday afternoon to catch the chance to be on the local newscast that night, Knoxville and Chattanooga on Saturday to get TV exposure there, Memphis on Sunday for similar television coverage, and his Memphis office Monday morning for constituency work.[5]

II

Gore's intensive preparations were clearly with a Republican challenge in mind. It is unlikely that he anticipated serious opposition in the Democratic primary. For a long time, it appeared that this calculation was correct. Major Democrats in the state were reported to be considering a Gore challenge— Buford Ellington, Ray Blanton—but none materialized. As late as March there was no opposition at all. Then two political unknowns, Stanford Andress and retired admiral Herman Frey, announced. Between them they would receive less than 4 percent of the Democratic primary vote. Andress was a travel agency executive and former detective from Madison who identified himself very clearly with George Wallace. Frey campaigned on a platform of "Go in to win or get out" in Vietnam and promised to protect the interests of the state's many military facilities.[6]

But at the last minute, Ellington's press aide and former TV news executive Hudley Crockett announced. It was difficult to see this as anything other than an Ellington-inspired move. Crockett left Ellington's service for the duration of the primary, then returned to the administration when the primary was over. Crockett's was a political neophyte: his name had never surfaced in any press speculation about possible opponents for Gore. But, if his organization was hastily put together, he was a confident, articulate public performer. His campaign previewed almost all the main themes that Brock would pursue against Gore in the general election. Republicans in Chattanooga complained that he "out-brocked Brock." He argued that Gore was out of touch with Tennessee voters, that he failed to represent Tennessee's interests in Washington. He found confirmation in this charge in the decision by Gore to hire Charles Guggenheim to come to Tennessee to prepare his TV commercials and in fund-raising dinners organized by liberals in Washington for Gore. Guggenheim was, according to Crockett, a "high-powered out-of-state image maker obviously paid by powerful out-of-state friends to try to build a new image for an out-of-touch candidate." He criticized Gore and the Foreign Relations Committee for opposing Nixon's Vietnam policy and lambasted the senator for his votes against the nomination of Supreme Court justices south-erners Haynsworth and Carswell. Crockett supported Nixon's and Brock's plans for revenue sharing and fervently opposed gun control. These were all issues that would loom large in Brock's campaign against Gore.[7]

As an indication of the potential anti-Gore vote that Brock could expect to pick up in the general election, Crockett made an impressive showing. He won over 45 percent of the vote and kept Gore's margin of victory to under 32,000. As the *Tennessean* noted, his votes "picked up steadily as he moved Westward across the state into the counties that supported George Wallace in 1968." Crockett carried Shelby County and the four western congressional districts. He was endorsed not only by the conservative *Nashville Banner* but the *Memphis Commercial Appeal,* which had in the past backed Gore. Crockett's vote certainly boded well for a strong Republican race against Gore in the November election.[8]

III

William E. Brock, wealthy son of the Chattanooga candy manufacturer, had been a key figure in expanding the Tennessee Republican Party out of its his-toric, rural, mountain base in the East. Coming out of the U.S. Navy, enthused by the Eisenhower candidacy, Brock and other likeminded Jaycees had for the first time attempted to organize the party across the state and to bring middle- and upper-class whites from the suburbs into the party. Brock himself had been the first congressman to break out of the mountain redoubt by winning the Third District seat in Chattanooga and Hamilton County. He and his fellow ideologues chafed at what they took to be the top-down approach of the traditional eastern leadership of the party, first under B. Carroll Reece, then under Howard Baker. East Tennessee Republicans, they argued, had been too ready to accede to Democratic dominance in the rest of the state in return for local control of patronage. Brock and his allies wanted to make the Republican Party an identifiably conservative and statewide party. Where Baker cringed at the Goldwater candidacy, Brock gloried in it. He sought to prevent the party swinging to the left in the aftermath of the Arizonan's defeat. He supported his young protégé Jack McDonald's efforts to wrest control of the Young Republicans National Federation away from former Republican National Committee chairman Hugh Scott. But, like other southern Republicans, he latched on to Richard Nixon's candidacy in 1968 and was one of ten "surrogate" speakers for Nixon in the campaign.[9]

When Brock's pollsters in 1969 surveyed his prospects for state-wide election in Tennessee in 1970 they identified only one possible Republican rival for the senatorial nomination, Memphis congressman Dan Kuykendall. They argued that Brock's ability to raise funds was more important than Kuykendall's name recognition across the state and they believed, accurately, that an early indication by Brock that he would seek the Senate seat would pre-empt the Kuykendall candidacy. What they did not predict was that there would be a Republican opponent for Brock and that that Republican candidate would be the country singer and veteran of eighty cowboy movies Tex Ritter. Journalists believed, and Ritter later confirmed, that he had been put up to run by members of Howard Baker's staff, although Baker himself announced a policy of strict neutrality in both senatorial and gubernatorial primaries.[10]

Just as Crockett's campaign against Gore previewed Brock's campaign against the senator, so Ritter's campaign against Brock previewed Gore's campaign against his challenger. Ritter argued that Brock was too conservative to defeat Gore, that a candidate from the mainstream was needed to pick up dissident Democrat voters. Ritter vowed that, unlike Brock, he would not "have my picture made with prominent members of the John Birch society." He castigated Brock as the "against" man, the negative congressman who was lukewarm on TVA and had voted against Hill-Burton hospital funds and against funds for the Appalachian Regional Commission. Ritter criticized Brock's votes for the ABM system and the supersonic jet project. He dismissed Brock's advocacy of a constitutional amendment against busing as impractical. He pointedly refused to attend a Billy Graham Crusade in Knoxville. He maintained he did not want to "use the crusade for political gain." Both Brock and Nixon attended. In highlighting Brock's negative votes on issues affecting Tennessee and distancing himself from too blatant a religious and cultural conservatism, Ritter's campaign closely resembled Gore's later attacks on Brock.[11]

Ritter was no mere singer. He was a political science major from the University of Texas and studied law at Northwestern. But it was the country stars who appeared on the campaign trail with Ritter who attracted the crowds. His bandwagon round Tennessee brought a galaxy of stars to warm up the audience—including Roy Acuff, Ernest Tubb, Loretta Lynn, Dolly Parton, and Porter Waggoner. And after his speech, Ritter himself would usually sing the "Boll Weevil Song" and "High Noon." However, just like Roy Acuff in 1948, Ritter attracted the audiences but not their votes. He won only 23 percent of the Republican primary votes, polling just over 50,000.[12]

IV

Ritter's campaign therefore did not interrupt Brock's well-planned campaign or encourage him to soften his approach. Brock's pollsters indicated that the war was the issue most troubling Tennesseans but that, in addition, there were three major areas that provoked "active response or extreme vulnerability."

A. The continuing deterioration of public regard for the law, as symbolized by the violent campus incidents and the weakness of school administrations in coping with them.
B. The national trend toward increased welfare support and priority for Negroes, many of whom appear unwilling to help themselves.
C. The expanding influence of the federal government in general and the Supreme Court in particular, in the day-to-day affairs and activities of the state and local community.

The tactics for Brock in exploiting this vulnerability were clear, his strategists argued,

In the general election campaign a contrast must first be drawn between political philosophies, as shown in the voting records. Brock is a Nixon conservative. Gore is a Kennedy liberal. There is little doubt that the deciding political force in Tennessee is the Wallace voter. Indications are that the Wallace people would support Brock and actively vote for him against Gore. They should not be courted but great pains should be taken to see that they are not offended.

The drive to capture the lower- and middle-income white voters who had voted for Wallace in 1968 was not only Brock's strategy, it was the key element of Richard Nixon's southern strategy. Gore rather promoted himself as Nixon's Number One Target in 1970, but there is little doubt that the White House was very keen to defeat him. Not only did the Gore race offer an excellent chance to pick up Wallace voters, but Gore himself exasperated Nixon and his allies almost as much he had irritated Lyndon Johnson. Gore's relentless and increasingly scornful attacks on Nixon's Vietnam policy, so Nixon believed, hurt the chances of Nixon securing an honorable settlement in Vietnam by encouraging the North Vietnamese to stand firm. The White House was intimately involved in the Brock campaign from the start. Brock's administrative assistant, William Timmons, had gone on to be a deputy assistant to the president. He believed that the Brock-Gore race should "become a testing ground of Nixon-Kennedy strength as well as Brock-Gore." Brock's political consultants were Treleavan Associates, who had run Nixon's media campaign in 1968. His campaign manager was Kenneth Rietz from Treleavan. As early as October 1969 the White House and Rietz agreed that grant announcements, patronage appointments, and presidential visits would be carefully coordinated to aid the Brock campaign.[13]

Brock's strategists laid out a timetable in May 1969 that they followed with great precision. It set out target dates for fund-raising, appointment of county chairmen, door-to-door canvassing, all culminating in a Phase III media blitz in October 1970. The campaign itself ran with military precision with carefully staged events and a meticulous timetable which made sure that the candidate had time between 4 and 6 P.M. to freshen up and to be always in bed by 11, so as always to look his best on television. Larry Daughtrey described this new brand of campaigning in April 1970:

> Brock's first day left no doubts that the message will be delivered by a tautly managed and efficient organization. His itinerary was charted out, in writing, to the minute, and there was a time-table for applause by the mini-skirted girls at each rally... All the little touches of polish were there: a short, patriotic speech, a little (but not too much) time for hand-shaking, different colored buttons to distinguish between party, press, and security, a device heretofore limited to presidential campaigns. "Broadcast media" representatives were given a Nashville telephone number they can call to get a tape-recorded comment from the candidate daily.

The contrast with Gore's campaign could not have been more stark. As always, his vigorous campaigning was highly personal, chaotic, with a volunteer staff, no transport for the press, no advance men, and little money.[14]

Nixon's southern strategy to capture Wallace Democrats for the Republicans would be successful. In 1972 an estimated three-quarters of Wallace voters in the South voted Republican. The strategy was based on an appeal to racial conservatism—a go-slow on school desegregation and opposition to busing—together with an appeal to regional pride—the appointment of southerners to the Supreme Court—and an appeal to law and order—against both urban crime and campus protest—and an appeal to traditional values—patriotism and conservative morality. The Brock campaign followed this strategy to the letter. Brock's carefully crafted TV ads focused on busing, on supporting the president on the war, on controlling government spending to curb inflation, on combating crime by appointing judges who would put criminals in jail and a Supreme Court that would not tie the hands of the police, on opposition to gun control, on stronger drug laws and enforcement, and the expulsion of violent student protesters. The slots were thirty or sixty seconds and showed Brock talking to ordinary Tennesseans: a parent, a veteran, a pensioner, a farmer, hunters, constituents who had been helped, disaffected Democrats, the wife of a POW, a textile worker, a young man. The message was that Brock listened and took local issues seriously unlike Gore. The repeated mantra was—"Bill Brock believes in the things we believe in."[15]

The implication was, of course, that Albert Gore did not believe in what Tennesseans believed in. He was an "ultra liberal" in Brock's words or in Spiro

Agnew's formulation when he spoke in Memphis in September a "radical liberal." Agnew charged that Gore was to "all intents and purposes Southern regional chairman of the eastern liberal establishment." As a Knoxville evangelist supporting Brock said, he could not vote for someone "who seems to think Tennessee is located somewhere between Connecticut and Massachusetts." Agnew claimed that Gore believed "that Tennessee is located somewhere between the *New York Times* and the *Greenwich Village Voice*."[16]

On *Face the Nation* in October, Brock asserted that Gore "has refused to stand up for the South and for Tennessee." The appeal to regional interest and racial conservatism was highlighted by Gore's vote against the nomination of Nixon's two southern Supreme Court nominees, Clement Haynsworth and Harold Carswell. One of Gore's constituents left him in no doubt that Brock would be the beneficiary of his stance:

> Your vote against Judge Haynsworth marks you as a gutless coward who has sold his soul to the corrupt union bosses and the black militants. It is little comfort to know that you'll get your "reward" some day.
> I just want you to know that I'm going to do everything in my power to see you're rewarded NEXT YEAR. I'm going to work tirelessly for Bill Brock... We want to rid this nation's government and the Union-owned Senate of our long-haired, vacuous, arrogant, anti-American disgraceful Senator.
> You make me sick.
> PS And don't waste my hard-earned tax dollars, which you so love to redistribute to the lazy, by having your staff send me one of your innocuous form letters.[17]

Brock appealed to Tennesseans to support their president, not to "handcuff" him in foreign policy. He defended the Cambodia invasion. He accused Gore and the other senators of undercutting the president's peace efforts by trying to set a timetable for withdrawal. Gore was betraying American soldiers who were sacrificing their lives for their country. His antiwar statements were being used to brainwash American POWs in Vietnam. In return, Nixon came to east Tennessee to speak to huge crowds in Johnson City and to appeal for Brock's election to support him in his efforts to secure a peace that would discourage, not encourage, aggressors.[18]

To Brock supporters, Gore's stance on Vietnam encapsulated a worldview that was alien to Tennessee. Henry Loeb, the mayor of Memphis and a bitter opponent of Gore, summed up this view:

> The basic immorality is not backing our fighting men in Vietnam, and in not winning the war, and I mean it. From that immorality, we go to rationalization on smut and pornography, turning away from prayer etc.

As the *Tennessean* reporters described Brock's early campaign, he "hits the 'new left' in the Senate and terrifies people with threats of pornography and dope in high schools in Tennessee." Brock kept hammering away. The robbing and the riots and the vandalism and the muggings go on," he said. "This tidal wave of crime and violence" had to be stopped.[19]

Brock summed up simply this appeal to traditional racial and social values. The election gave Tennesseans "opportunity to vote against violence and permissiveness, for a balanced Supreme Court, against forced busing and for the President's policy for a lasting peace in Vietnam."[20]

Just as Brock believed the Wallace voters were the key, so did Gore. He hoped to appeal to them by stressing economic issues, not racial or social ones. In a vigorous campaign Gore took the attack to factory gates, stockyards, and courthouse squares. He called the roll on all Brock's votes against programs that benefited Tennessee and stressed, in contrast, what he had done throughout his career for lower-income voters. By mid-October polls for both Brock and Hooker suggested that this bid by Gore to reclaim the Wallace voters was succeeding.[21]

Brock, however, was able to unleash both a new issue and also the media blitz for the end of the campaign that had been planned for since May 1969. The opportunity to develop a new issue came when Howard Baker tacked on a rider to the Equal Rights Amendment in the Senate on October 13 that allowed voluntary prayer in public buildings. The rider was one that Baker and his father-in-law Everett Dirksen had routinely tried to pass ever since Baker had been in the Senate. It passed after a perfunctory debate; Gore voted against it without any impact; and the sponsors of the ERA withdrew the amendment, knowing the Senate would not pass it in that form. Brock latched on to this vote with alacrity. He announced that "I have and will continue to support school prayer. In contrast Albert Gore has gone on record against school prayer on three separate occasions." Three days later a full-page ad appeared in the *Banner,* announcing, "ALBERT GORE HAS TAKEN POSITION AGAINST SCHOOL PRAYER THREE TIMES." Many ministers asserted the importance of the division of church and state. Vanderbilt divinity students deplored Brock's "syrupy pietism." Baptist Gore was shocked at the injection of the religious issue into the campaign. But for Brock the issue, a complex one to rebut so late in the campaign, was a perfect fit for the campaign to appeal to traditional cultural values.[22]

Brock had no TV ads prepared on prayer in school, but he compensated with newspaper advertisements and leaflets. It was part of the media blitz in the final ten days of the campaign that Brock's campaign had planned for. As Kenneth Rietz told David Broder of the *Washington Post:*

We had 18 per cent undecided in our polls—mostly Wallaceites who were anti-Gore but not pro-Brock or pro-Republican...Now we're really going after the undecided with the four big issues we've saved for the last ten days—prayer, busing, gun control, and the judges.

On each issue the TV and press ads relentlessly put over the message that Gore was at odds with the people of Tennessee. As Gene Graham, Gore's press secretary, bitterly observed, "Make it read from right to left—John T. Scopes, race, race and race."[23]

<h1 style="text-align:center">V</h1>

Brock's strategy worked. In the battle for Wallace votes, Gore's economic appeal made headway in Middle Tennessee but not sufficient to offset the wholesale defection of Wallace voters in the West. Whereas in Nashville Gore retained the support of nearly 60 percent of the lower-income white voters, in Memphis he only won 27.3 percent. In the state as a whole, Brock won by 52.1 percent to 47.9 percent.[24]

Yet Gore was the only major prize for the Republican southern strategy in 1970. Why did Brock succeed while Republicans in other southern states did not?

Elsewhere in 1970 New South Democratic politicians put together a biracial, cross-class alliance of affluent whites committed to economic growth and racial moderation and blacks. As Randy Sanders has shown, successful Democrats in 1970 campaigned for the governorships as new faces who, in a rather fuzzy and indeterminate way, were racial moderates. Gore was neither a new face nor fuzzy. He was unlikely to appeal to affluent whites because of business opposition to his economic policies. In addition, gubernatorial candidates were not encumbered by clear policy stances on either the war or on the Supreme Court candidates. Gore, by contrast, as an anti-war senator had established a clear record as a target on these two key issues. William Brock himself identified Gore's "position on the Supreme Court nominees and RN's VN policies as major factors" in his victory.[25]

Local factors clearly played a part. The unexpected strength of Republican gubernatorial candidate Winfield Dunn from Memphis clearly helped Brock in western Tennessee in a way that a Nashville candidate like Maxey Jarman could not have done. Equally, the imploding candidacy of Democrat John J. Hooker harmed Gore. The Hooker camp refused to pool forces with Gore despite the best efforts of Gore's protégé Gilbert Merritt, who was Hooker's brother-in-law and finance director. Hooker's backers refused to countenance such a move. Later it became clear they needed Gore more than he needed them as Hooker's campaign was beset by the fall-out from the collapsed Minnie Pearl chicken franchise. The failure to merge campaigns hurt Gore because he needed the organization of the Hooker team to compensate for his own lack of organization. The failure to merge also significantly reduced the amount of financial backing from the national AFL-CIO, who would have provided far greater financial support if the campaigns had been unified.[26]

The particular circumstances of Howard Baker's rider that made the school prayer issue a salient one was also important. It was an early foretaste of what the Religious Right could do for the southern Republicans. As Gore's Davidson County campaign director Jim Sasser recalled, "That amendment put Brock over the top."[27]

But, in the final analysis, the politics of race, as Gene Graham observed, were crucial. Brock did not run a crude race-baiting campaign. When Republican candidate Albert Watson in South Carolina ran just such a campaign in 1970 he lost. Brock himself had supported desegregation in Chattanooga. But he was appealing to a white backlash against the federal government in which race was intimately involved as part of the defense of traditional local values whether on prayer, guns, or busing. The trajectory of white backlash had a different path in Tennessee than it did in the Deep South. In the Deep South, states which had been at the center of the defiance of racial change in the 1950s were the sites of New South successes in 1970. On the one hand, there had been a dramatic increase in black voting. On the other, economic leaders had mobilized to mediate what they now recognized as inevitable desegregation. New South racial moderates could triumph there. In states like Tennessee and North Carolina, which had practiced token compliance in the 1950s, the post-1965 rise in black voting was less dramatic and less important. Equally, the timing of white backlash was different. Token compliance in the late 1950s and early 1960s had implicitly promised white voters in the black belts of west Tennessee and eastern North Carolina that they would be spared desegregation. By the late 1960s it was clear that they would not be spared. Voters in west Tennessee responded by defeating Albert Gore; two years later in eastern North Carolina whites would elect Jesse Helms.

Acknowledgments

My deep gratitude to Jim Patterson and Larry Malley, who conceived of the notion of this book. Ann Holton and Sophie King prepared the manuscript in Cambridge with exemplary care. Julie Watkins, Sarah White, Debbie Self, Tom Lavoie, and Larry himself drove through the project in Fayetteville. I am much in the debt of all of them.

Bill Leuchtenburg and Jim Patterson were my inspiration when I started as a New Deal historian and have helped my in countless ways since the early 1970s. My many scholarly debts to southern historians will be evident in the text. Those debts are also obligations of friendship, since I have been fortunate to work in a field where collegiality, mutual support, and friendship are the norm. It would be impossible to acknowledge everybody who has helped me in the United States over the past twenty-five years, but I would be remiss if I did not thank, in particular, Dan and Jane Carter, David and Jean Chalmers, David Chappell, Jim and Lyra Cobb, Charles and Brenda Eagles, Walter Edgar, Wayne Flynt, Steve Gillon, Charles Joyner, Richard Lowitt, Jeff and Kelly Norrell, and Pat Sullivan for their southern hospitality.

Southern archivists from Beaumont to Charlottesville and Clemson to Thibodeaux have been amazingly cooperative and helpful. They have gone out of their way to secure permissions to work on collections, to open up their holdings on Sundays, public holidays, and other days when they would normally have been closed, to let me roam around in as-yet unprocessed collections, and to provide donuts in Fayetteville on a Saturday morning. They have made traversing the South a delight.

The essays in this book necessitate some very specific thanks.

An invitation from John Boles led to the introductory essay on "Southern History from the Outside." Valeria Gennaro Lerda, Lothar Honnighausen, and Jan Nordby Gretlund introduced me to the world of continental scholars of the American South in the European Southern Studies Forum in 1988. Chapters 2 and 3 were first delivered as papers at the forum's meetings in Berlin and Bonn, and an earlier version of chapter 10 at the gathering in Aero. A colloquium, organized by the late Stuart Kidd and Bob Garson, was the occasion for chapter 4, an opportunity to honor David K. Adams for the leadership he provided for New Deal scholarship and American Studies in Britain.

My work on the Southern Manifesto, chapters 5 and 6, has been supported by grants from the American Council of Learned Societies, the University of

Newcastle Research Fund, the North Carolina Fund, the British Academy, and the fund attached to my Cambridge chair. Chapter 6 was also the result of an invitation to a memorable conference organized by Betsy Jacoway and Fred Williams on the fortieth anniversary of the Little Rock Crisis.

Ted Ownby's invitation to the 1999 Porter L. Fortune symposium in southern history at the University of Mississippi was responsible for chapter 7. Vernon Burton and Bo Moore gave me the chance to participate in the pioneering Citadel conference on the civil rights movement in South Carolina in 2003 and the privilege of sharing a platform with Fritz Hollings and the late John C. West. Those two veteran politicians could not have been more gracious and patient.

Thanks to Sylvia Frey, Emily Clark, and Betty Wood, Cambridge and Tulane linked up for a series of Atlantic World conferences, starting in 1996. Sylvia also arranged for me to be the Andrew W. Mellon visiting professor at Tulane in 2000. Chapter 9 was my farewell lecture there. Chapter 10 was delivered at the 2001 Tulane-Cambridge conference. I am also grateful to Zell Miller, who came to New Orleans to give a characteristically incisive lecture while I was visiting Tulane.

British historians of modern America owe a great deal to the encouragement and support of the late Hugh Davis Graham. Thanks to Hugh and to Lisa Pruitt, director of the Albert Gore Research Center at Middle Tennessee State University, I was invited in 2001 to write the biography of Albert Gore Sr. Fleming Wilt for the Samuel Fleming Foundation and Jack Robinson Sr. have been indispensable to that project. Lisa and Betty Rowland at the Gore Center have made me welcome in Murfreesboro and provided everything that a researcher could ask for. Michael Martin and Sean Smith have been exemplary research assistants. Michael and I wrote chapter 12, which was originally given as a paper at the 2003 Tennessee Conference of Historians. Chapter 11 is the other initial product of the biography project. It was given as the Charles Griffin Memorial Lecture at Vassar in 2004. Bob Brigham, who had earlier been an outstanding Visiting Senior Mellon Scholar in Cambridge, was the generous organizer and host.

Since returning to Cambridge in 1992 I have been privileged to work with an outstanding community of Americanists as we have attempted to make Cambridge the leading center for the study of the United States outside North America. Bill Dusinberre, the late Mark Kaplanoff, Michael O'Brien, the late Peter Parish, Andrew Preston, Colin Shindler, Mike Sewell, David Reynolds, John Thompson, Betty Wood, and Josh Zeitz have provided a most supportive and intellectually stimulating environment. In the manner in which the British Ph.D system operates I have supervised Ph.Ds on subjects from the Apalachicola slave maroon to Native Americans under the

New Deal to Walt Rostow to Jimmy Carter's post-presidency. I have learned from all my students, but in particular from those working on modern southern history: Jen Black, David Perkins, Simon Hall, Catherine Maddison, Tim Minchin, Steve Tuck, and Clive Webb. Visiting Pitt Professors in American History who have worked on the South have been an added bonus for someone living in small market town in the Fens: Gavin Wright, Dan Carter, Sylvia Frey, John Shelton Reed, Stanley Engerman, and Jim Roark.

I have been fortunate to work on the modern South and on the civil rights movement at a time when the subject has attracted a large number of talented British scholars. Like the rest of us, I owe a huge debt to Adam Fairclough, whose work showed the way and set the standard. Brian Ward has been a constant friend and collaborator since he succeeded me at Newcastle in 1991.

Ruth has had to put up with more than should be asked of any partner over the past thirty years. What I owe Ruth is incalculable and cannot adequately be expressed here. Her love and support have made this work possible, as has her admonition, "Have you ever thought of just getting on with it?" Nick and Chris need to know that my pride in their achievements far exceeds any satisfaction I may take in my own career. This book is dedicated to them.

Tony Badger
Cambridge 2007

Notes

Introduction

1. Herbert Nicholas, "The Education of an Americanist," *Journal of American Studies* 14 (April 1980): 15–16.

2. I did manage to get to the papers of Albert Gore Sr. at Murfreesboro, Tennessee first. It seems likely that I may also have been first to use the papers of Jack Brooks in Beaumont, Texas, since the boxes were still in the cellophane wrappers that they had been in when they arrived from Washington. But otherwise, Bill has beaten me every time.

3. Sir Anthony Jenkinson, *America Came My Way* (London: A Barker, 1936), 143; Nick Clarke, *Alistair Cooke: The Biography* (London: Weidenfeld and Nicholson, 1999), 115.

4. Anthony J. Badger, "Huey Long and the New Deal," in *Nothing Else to Fear: New Perspectives on America in the Thirties,* ed. Stephen W. Baskerville and Ralph Willett (Manchester: Manchester University Press, 1985), 65–103. Tony Badger, "'When I Took the Oath of Office, I Took No Vow of Poverty': Race, Corruption, and Democracy, 1928–2000" (Mellon Lecture Series, 2000), copy in the author's possession.

5. Anthony J. Badger, *Prosperity Road: The New Deal, Tobacco, and North Carolina* (Chapel Hill: University of North Carolina Press, 1980); Michael Sewell, "British Responses to Martin Luther King, Jr., and the Civil Rights Movement, 1954–68," in *The Making of Martin Luther King and the Civil Rights Movement,* ed. Brian Ward and Tony Badger (London: Macmillan, 1996), 206; Charles Martin, "The Rise and Fall of Jim Crow in College Sports: The Case of the Atlantic Coast Conference," *North Carolina Historical Review* 76 (July 1999): 253–84; and Timothy B. Tyson, *Blood Done Sign My Name* (New York: Crown, 2003).

6. Michael O'Brien, "C. Vann Woodward and the Burden of Southern Liberalism," *American Historical Review* 78 (June 1973): 589–604. Michael has explored his own intellectual history with characteristically stylish irony and self-deprecation in the introduction to the paperback edition of *The Idea of the American South, 1920–1941* (Baltimore and London: Johns Hopkins University Press, 1990), ix–xv, and "The Apprehension of the South in Modern Culture," *Southern Cultures* 4, 4 (1998): 3–18.

7. Tony Badger, "Southerners Who Refused to Sign the Southern Manifesto," *Historical Journal* 42 (June 1999): 517–34; "Whatever Happened to Roosevelt's New Generation of Southerners?" in *The Roosevelt Years: New Perspectives on American History, 1933–1945,* ed. Robert A. Garson and Stuart S. Kidd (Edinburgh: Edinburgh University Press, 1999), 122–38; "'Closet Moderates':

Why White Liberals Failed, 1940–1970," in Ted Ownby, ed., *The Role of Ideas in the Civil Rights South* (Jackson: University Press of Mississippi, 2002), 83–112. Harold Cooley, future chair of the House Agriculture Committee, had been elected as a pro-New Dealer in 1934, Charles Deane, elected in 1946, had first run in 1938. Thurmond Chatham was a prominent Liberty League member and supporter of Wendell Wilkie in the 1930s.

8. Tony Badger, "Confessions of a British Americanist," *Journal of American History* 79 (September 1992): 515–23.

9. Sir David Williams to Tony Badger, May 29, 1991 (copy in the author's possession).

10. James Cobb, "European Scholars Can't Get Enough of the South," *University of Georgia Alumni Magazine* 82 (June 2003): 4. Willie Morris, *North toward Home* (Boston: Dell, 1967), 399. Alger Hiss, who drafted the first AAA contract for flue-cured tobacco in 1933, understood the South perfectly well. He liked to be read to, as he had read aloud to Oliver Wendell Holmes. I read to him that summer of 1984 chapters of Patricia Sullivan's Emory Ph.D. dissertation that became her path-finding book, *Days of Hope: Race and Democracy in the New Deal Era* (Chapel Hill: University of North Carolina Press, 1996). Some southern New Dealers who loomed so large in that book, like Clark Foreman and Virginia Durr, had been old friends of his.

11. Timothy J. Minchin, *What Do We Need a Union For?: The TWUA in the South, 1945–1955* (Chapel Hill: University of North Carolina Press, 1997); Clive Webb, *Fight against Fear: Southern Jews and Black Civil Rights* (Athens and London: University of Georgia Press, 2001); Stephen G. N. Tuck, *Beyond Atlanta: The Struggle for Racial Equality in Georgia, 1940–1980* (Athens and London: University of Georgia Press, 2001).

12. Henry H. Lesesne, *A History of the University of South Carolina, 1940–2000* (Columbia: University of South Carolina Press, 2001).

13. Tony Badger, "From Defiance to Moderation: South Carolina Governors and Racial Change" (Paper given at The Citadel Conference on the Civil Rights Movement in South Carolina, March 7, 2003, copy in the author's possession). *The* [Columbia, S.C.] *State,* March 8, 2003.

14. Jack E. Davis, Review of Stephen G. N. Tuck, *Beyond Atlanta: The Struggle for Racial Equality in Georgia, 1940–1980,* in *American Historical Review* 107 (December 2002): 1595–96.

15. Davis, review of *Beyond Atlanta,* 1595.

Chapter One

1. V. O. Key Jr., *Southern Politics in State and Nation* (New York: Knopf, 1949), 298–311. Dan T. Carter has vividly described the persistence of the colorful, personal campaigns in the face of forces of modernization in the South in "Southern Political Style," in *The Age of Segregation: Race Relations in the South, 1890–1954* ed. Robert Haws (Jackson: University Press of Mississippi, 1978).

2. Although published later, Seymour Martin Lipset and Earl Raab, *The Politics of Unreason* (London: Heinneman, 1970), 167–203, encapsulated that tradition.

3. Allan P. Sindler, *Huey Long's Louisiana State Politics, 1920–1952* (Baltimore, Md.: Johns Hopkins University Press, 1956), 45–116; Arthur M. Schlesinger Jr., *The Politics of Upheaval* (Boston: Houghton Mifflin, 1960), 42–69.

4. T. Harry Williams, *Huey Long* (New York: Knopf, 1969), 1–9, 409–19, 636–40, 748–62, 835–37.

5. Barton J. Bernstein, "The New Deal: The Conservative Achievements of Liberal Reform," in *Towards a New Past: Dissenting Essays in American History,* ed. Barton J. Bernstein (New York: Pantheon Books, 1967), 263–68; Robert S. McElvaine, "Thunder without Lightning: Working-Class Discontent in the United States, 1929–1937" (unpublished Ph.D. dissertation, State University of New York, Binghamton, 1974), 217–46.

6. Glen Jeansonne, "Challenge to the New Deal: Huey P. Long and the Redistribution of National Wealth," *Louisiana History* 21 (1980): 331–39; Alan Brinkley, "Huey Long, the Share Our Wealth Movement and the Limits of Depression Dissidence," *Louisiana History* 22 (1981): 17–34; Alan Brinkley, *Voices of Protest: Huey Long, Father Coughlin and the Great Depression* (New York: Knopf, 1982).

7. Sindler, *Huey Long's Louisiana,* 1–39; Key, *Southern Politics,* 156–81; Williams, *Huey Long,* 82–91.

8. Williams, *Huey Long,* 119–25, 191–213, 264–65, 273–75.

9. Williams, *Huey Long,* 280–311, 492–525, 546–52.

10. George B. Tindall, *The Emergence of the New South* (Baton Rouge: Louisiana State University Press, 1967), 219–52; Brinkley, *Voices of Protest,* 31.

11. Henry C. Dethloff, "The Longs: Revolution or Populist Retrenchment," *Louisiana History* 19 (1978): 407.

12. Williams, *Huey Long,* 423–25, 546.

13. Williams, *Huey Long,* 521–23.

14. Brinkley, *Voices of Protest,* 31.

15. James C. Cobb, *The Selling of the South: The Southern Crusade for Industrial Development, 1936–1980* (Baton Rouge: Lousiana State University Press, 1982) 157.

16. Brinkley, *Voices of Protest,* 31; Jeansonne, "Challenge to the New Deal," 336–37; John Robert Moore, "The New Deal in Louisiana," in *The New Deal, the State and Local Levels,* ed. John Braeman et al. (Columbus: Ohio State University Press, 1975), 142–43.

17. Thomas A. Krueger, *And Promises to Keep: The Southern Conference for Human Welfare* (Nashville: Vanderbilt University Press, 1967).

18. Williams, *Huey Long,* 547–49; Mark T. Carleton, *Politics and Punishment: The History of the Louisiana State Penal System* (Baton Rouge: Louisiana State University Press, 1971), 111–26.

19. Williams, *Huey Long,* 701–6.

20. Michael J. Cassity, "Huey Long: Barometer of Reform in the New Deal," *South Atlantic Quarterly* 72 (1973): 261–66.

21. Dethloff, "The Longs," 411.

22. Floyd Martin Clay, *Coozan Dudley LeBlanc: From Huey Long to Hadacol* (Gretna, La.: Pelican Publishing, 1973), 85–86.

23. Jeansonne, "Challenge to the New Deal," 337.

24. Williams, *Huey Long,* 743.

25. Williams, *Huey Long,* 290–95, 421, 732–45.

26. Williams, *Huey Long,* 755.

27. Brinkley, *Voices of Protest,* 26.

28. Jack Bass, *Unlikely Heroes* (New York: Touchstone, 1981), 26–27.

29. Clay, *Coozan Dudley LeBlanc,* 100–114.

30. Williams, *Huey Long,* 737.

31. Williams, *Huey Long,* 253–54, 368, 391–93, 406, 756–57, 819, 828, 862, 876.

32. Sindler, *Huey Long's Louisiana,* 104.

33. Williams, *Huey Long,* 487–88, 757, 820–21.

34. Williams, *Huey Long,* 354, 387–90.

35. Glen Jeansonne, *Leander Perez Boss of the Delta* (Baton Rouge: Louisiana State University Press, 1977), 70–73.

36. Hodding Carter, "Huey Long, American dictator," in *The Aspirin Age,* ed. Isabel Leighton (New York: Simon and Schuster, 1949), 343.

37. Williams, *Huey Long,* 365–67, 394–96.

38. Williams, *Huey Long,* 486.

39. James T. Patterson, *The New Deal and the States Federalism in Transition* (Princeton, N.J.: Princeton University Press, 1969), 26–49.

40. Anthony J. Badger, "The New Deal and the Localities," in *The Growth of Federal Power in America,* ed. R. Jeffreys Jones and B. Collins (Edinburgh: Edinburgh University Press, 1984), 108–9.

41. Richard Lowitt, *George W. Norris: The Triumph of a Progressive, 1933–1944* (Urbana: University of Illinois Press, 1978), 135–36; Burton K. Wheeler, with Paul F Healey, *Yankee from the West* (New York: Doubleday, 1962), 280–86.

42. Williams, *Huey Long,* 581, 602–4; Martha Swain, *Pat Harrison: The New Deal Years* (Jackson: University Press of Mississippi, 1978), 28.

43. Brinkley, *Voices of Protest,* 56–61.

44. Ronald L. Feinman, *Twilight of Progressivism: Western Republican Senators and the New Deal* (Baltimore, Md.: Johns Hopkins University Press, 1981), 48–116.

45. Williams, *Huey Long,* 636–40, 689–92, 793–99, 812–13.

46. Wheeler, *Yankee from the West,* 282.

47. Betty Marie Field, "The Politics of the New Deal in Louisiana, 1933–1939" (Unpublished Ph.D. dissertation, Tulane, 1973), 33–46. This excellent dissertation has unaccountably been ignored in the recent literature.

48. Donald Holley, *Uncle Sam's Farmers: The New Deal Communities in the*

Lower Mississippi Valley (Urbana: University of Illinois Press, 1975), 75–76; Field, "The Politics of the New Deal," 39.

49. Brinkley, *Voices of Protest,* 63–64.

50. Williams, *Huey Long,* 640.

51. Field, "The Politics of the New Deal," 57–61.

52. Tindall, *Emergence of the New South,* 475.

53. Field, "The Politics of the New Deal," 7–13.

54. Field, "The Politics of the New Deal," 14–31, 90–109; Moore, "The New Deal in Louisiana," 147.

55. Field, "The Politics of the New Deal," 9.

56. Field, "The Politics of the New Deal," 97.

57. Carter, "Huey Long," 357.

58. The best account of the scandals remains Harnett T. Kane, *Louisiana Hayride: The American Rehearsal for Dictatorship, 1928–1940* (New York: Wm. Morrow, 1941). For Earl Long's postwar liberalism, see Numan V. Bartley and Hugh D. Graham, *Southern Politics and the Second Reconstruction* (Baltimore, Md.: Johns Hopkins University Press, 1975), 24–25.

59. Lyle Dorsett, *Franklin D. Roosevelt and the City Bosses* (Port Washington, N.Y.: Kennikat Press, 1977), 88; Bruce Stave, *The New Deal and the Last Hurrah: Pittsburgh Machine Politics* (Pittsburgh: University of Pittsburgh Press, 1970), 142–47.

60. For the obstacles to political realignment in the 1930s, see Patterson, *The New Deal and the States,* 168–93, and Badger, "The New Deal and the Localities," 112–16.

61. Moore, "The New Deal in Louisiana," 146.

62. Moore, "The New Deal in Louisiana," 150, 158.

63. Moore, "The New Deal in Louisiana," 161

64. Moore, "The New Deal in Louisiana," 152–56.

65. Moore, "The New Deal in Louisiana," 154, 161.

66. Cassity, "Huey Long," 256–57, 261, 264–66; Paul Mertz, *New Deal Policy and Southern Rural Poverty* (Baton Rouge: Louisiana State University Press, 1978), 132–38.

67. Williams, *Huey Long,* 837.

68. Williams, *Huey Long,* 708.

69. Brinkley, *Voices of Protest,* 143–68.

70. Donald W. Whisehunt, "Huey Long and the Texas Cotton Acreage Control Law of 1931," *Louisiana Studies* 13 (1974): 142–53; Robert Snyder, "Huey Long and the Cotton Holiday of 1931," *Louisiana History* 18 (1977): 135–60.

71. Williams, *Huey Long,* 530–33.

72. H. L. Mitchell, *Mean Things Happening in This Land* (Montclair, N. J.: Allanhead, Osmun, 1979), 30.

73. Cassity, "Huey Long," 261.

74. John L. Shover, *Cornbelt Rebellion: The Farmer's Holiday Association* (Urbana, 1965), 187–216.

75. Williams, *Huey Long,* 707.

76. Brinkley, *Voices of Protest,* 71–75; Jeansonne, "Challenge to the New Deal," 336.

77. Brinkley, *Voices of Protest,* 194–203, for an analysis of the social background of Long's followers. For an analysis that stresses the working-class nature of Long's support, see McElvaine, "Thunder without Lightning," 244–46. Williams, *Huey Long,* 8.

78. Brinkley, *Voices of Protest,* 144–48, 156–59.

79. Williams, *Huey Long,* 825–27.

80. Jeansonne, "Challenge to the New Deal," 337.

81. Glen Jeansonne, "Partisan Person: An Oral History Account of the Louisiana Years of Gerald L. K. Smith," *Louisiana History* 23 (1982): 154.

82. Williams, *Huey Long,* 202–3, 816–17.

83. Williams, *Huey Long,* 583–93.

84. Williams, *Huey Long,* 815–16; Jack Irby Hayes Jr., "South Carolina and the New Deal, 1932–1938" (Unpublished Ph.D. dissertation, University of South Carolina, 1972), 474–75.

85. Brinkley, *Voices of Protest,* 218–20; Williams, *Huey Long,* 533–34; Martha Swain, *Pat Harrison,* 127–29, points out that both Bilbo and Pat Harrison were scared of Long, despite Long's failure to back the winning candidate in the 1935 Mississippi gubernatorial primary.

86. Brinkley, *Voices of Protest,* 169–86.

87. Brinkley, *Voices of Protest,* 207–9; Robert E. Snyder, "Huey Long and the Presidential Election of 1936," *Louisiana History* 16 (1975): 117–44.

88. Millard L. Gieske, *Minnesota Farmer Labourism: The Third Party Alternative* (Minneapolis: University of Minnesota Press, 1979), 220–22; John E. Miller, *Governor Philip LaFollette: The Wisconsin Progressives and the New Deal* (Columbia: University of Missouri Press, 1982), 81–83, 90.

89. Williams, *Huey Long,* 801–2; David H. Bennett, *Demagogues in the Depression: American Radicals and the Union Party, 1932–1936* (New Brunswick, N.J.: Rutgers University Press, 1969), 1–180.

90. Jeansonne, "Partisan Person," 154.

91. Bennett, *Demagogues in the Depression,* 222–57.

92. Brinkley, *Voices of Protest,* 216.

Chapter Two

1. The book which pointed the way forward for local studies of the New Deal was James T. Patterson, *The New Deal and the States: Federalism in Transition* (Princeton, N.J.: Princeton University Press, 1969). An attempt to summarize those studies was Anthony J. Badger, "The New Deal and the Localities," in *The Growth of Federal Power in American History,* ed. Rhodri Jefreys-Jones and Bruce Collins (Edinburgh: Scottish Academic Press, 1983),

102–15. The essays in James C. Cobb and Michael V. Namaroto, eds., *The New Deal and the South* (Jackson: University Press of Mississippi, 1984), very usefully summarize existing work on the South in the 1930s.

2. Roger Biles, *Memphis in the Great Depression* (Knoxville: University of Tennessee Press, 1986), 74–79.

3. V. O. Key Jr., *Southern Politics in State and Nation* (New York: Knopf, 1949), 306, 310.

4. Anthony J. Badger, *Prosperity Road: The New Deal, Tobacco and North Carolina* (Chapel Hill: University of North Carolina Press, 1980), 65; Roger D. Tate Jr., "Easing the Burden: The Era of Depression and New Deal in Mississippi," Ph.D. dissertation (University of Tennessee, 1978), 87; Gilbert C. Fite, *Cotton Fields No More: Southern Agriculture, 1865–1980* (Lexington: University Press of Kentucky, 1984), 126, 62; Pete Daniel, "The New Deal, Southern Agriculture and Economic Change,'" in Cobb and Namaroto eds., *The New Deal and the South,* 37–61.

5. Richard S. Kirkendall, *Social Scientists and Farm Politics in the Age of Roosevelt* (Columbia: University of Missouri Press, 1967), 227–32, 240–42, 244–47; Paul Mertz, *New Deal Policy and Southern Rural Poverty* (Baton Rouge: Louisiana State University Press, 1978), 179–220; Donald S. Holley, *Uncle Sam's Farmers: The New Deal Communities in the Lower Mississippi Valley* (Urbana: University of Illinois Press, 1975).

6. David E. Conrad, *The Forgotten Farmers: The Story of Sharecroppers in the New Deal* (Urbana: University of Illinois Press, 1965); Donald H. Grubbs, *Cry from the Cotton: The Southern Tenant Farmers Union and the New Deal* (Chapel Hill: University of North Carolina Press, 1971); Mertz, *New Deal Policy,* 20–178; Peter H. Irons, *The New Deal Lawyers* (Princeton, N.J.: Princeton University Press, 1982), 156–80; Pete Daniel, *Breaking the Land: The Transformation of Cotton, Tobacco, and Rice Cultures since 1880* (Urbana: University of Illinois Press, 1985), 90–109, 155–83; Sidney Baldwin, *Poverty and Politics: The Rise and Decline of the Farm Security Administration* (Chapel Hill: University of North Carolina Press, 1968).

7. Walter J Stein, *California and the Dust Bowl Migration* (Westport, Conn.: Greenwood, 1973), 1–26; Badger, *Prosperity Road,* 200–204; Harvard Sitkoff, *A New Deal for Blacks: The Emergence of Civil Rights as a National Issue, vol. 1, The Depression Decade* (New York: Oxford University Press, 1978), 53.

8. Gavin Wright, *Old South, New South: Revolutions in the Southern Economy since the Civil War* (New York: Basic Books, 1986), 226–35; Warren C. Whatley, "Labor for the Picking: The New Deal in the South," *Journal of Economic History* 43 (1983): 905–29.

9. Pete Daniel, "The Transformation of the Rural South: 1930 to the Present," *Agricultural History* 55 (1981): 231–48.

10. George B. Tindall, *The Emergence of the New South, 1913–1945* (Baton Rouge: Louisiana State University Press, 1967), 505–39; J. Wayne Flynt, "The New Deal and Southern Labor," in Cobb and Namaroto, eds., *The New Deal*

and the South, 63–95; John W. Hevener, *Which Side Are You On? The Harlan County Coal Miners, 1931–1939* (Urbana: University of Illinois Press, 1979); James A. Hodges, *New Deal Labor Policy and the Southern Cotton Textile Industry, 1933–41* (Knoxville: University of Tennessee Press, 1986); Philip Taft, *Organizing Dixie: Alabama Workers in the Industrial Era* (Westport, Conn.: Greenwood, 1981), 76–120.

11. Taft, *Organizing Dixie,* 96–110; Hodges, *New Deal Labor Policy,* 86–118, 141–79.

12. Taft, *Organizing Dixie,* 116–19; Daniel Nelson, "'The Rubber Workers' Southern Strategy: Labor Organizing in the New Deal South, 1933–1943," *The Historian* 46 (1984): 319–38; Jack Irby Hayes, "South Carolina and the New Deal, 1932–1938" (Ph.D. Dissertation, University of South Carolina, 1972), 311–405.

13. R. Jefferson Norrell, "Labor at the Ballot Box: Birmingham's Big Mules Fight Back, 1938–1948" (unpublished ms. in the author's possession).

14. Tindall, *The Emergence of the New South,* 473–504; Douglas L. Smith, "The New Deal and the Urban South: The Advancement of a Southern Urban Consciousness during the Depression Decade" (Ph.D. dissertation, University of Southern Mississippi, 1978), 62–89, 136–271; Michael S. Holmes, *The New Deal in Georgia: An Administrative History* (Westport, Conn.: Greenwood, 1975), 34–38.

15. Hayes, "South Carolina and the New Deal," 199–203; Holmes, *The New Deal in Georgia,* 28.

16. Tindall, *The Emergence of the New South,* 487–91; Tate, "Easing the Burden," 55; Thomas E. Williams, "Children and Welfare in a Segregated Society; Mississippi, 1900–1970" (unpublished ms. in the author's possession); Lee J. Alston and Joseph P. Ferrie, "Labor Costs, Paternalism, and Loyalty in Southern Agriculture: A Constraint on the Growth of the Welfare State," *Journal of Economic History* 45 (1985), 95–117.

17. Sitkoff, *A New Deal for Blacks* 34–57.

18. Sitkoff, *A New Deal for Blacks,* 58–83; Smith, "The New Deal and the Urban South," 39–40.

19. Morton Sosna, *In Search of the Silent South: Southern Liberals and the Race Issue* (New York: Columbia University Press, 1977), 60–87; John A. Salmond, *A Southern Rebel: The Life and Times of Aubrey Willis Williams, 1890–1965* (Chapel Hill: University of North Carolina Press, 1983), 43–218; John T. Kneebone, *Southern Liberal Journalists and the Issue of Race, 1920–1944* (Chapel Hill: University of North Carolina Press, 1985), 115–74; Charles W. Eagles, *Jonathan Daniels and Race Relations: The Evolution of a Southern Liberal* (Knoxville: University of Tennessee Press, 1982), 23–120.

20. Anthony Dunbar, *Against the Grain: Southern Radicals and Prophets* (Charlottesville: University of Virginia Press, 1981).

21. Sosna, *In Search of the Silent South,* 88–104, 140–46; Mertz, *New Deal Policy and Southern Rural Poverty,* 223–52; James C. Cobb, *The Selling of the*

South: The Southern Crusade for Industrial Development, 1936–1980 (Baton Rouge: Louisiana State University Press, 1982), 1–34.

22. Tindall, *The Emergence of the New South,* 625, 633; Virginia Van der Veer Hamilton, *Lister Hill: Statesman from the South* (Chapel Hill: University of North Carolina Press, 1987), 70–86.

23. Tindall, *The Emergence of the New South,* 607–11; James T. Patterson, *Congressional Conservatism and the New Deal: The Growth of the Conservative Coalition in Congress, 1933–1939* (Lexington: University Press of Kentucky, 1967), 1–13, 64–67.

24. Sitkoff, *A New Deal for Blacks,* 102–38; Robert A. Garson, *The Democratic Party and the Politics of Sectionalism, 1941–48* (Baton Rouge: Louisiana State University Press, 1974).

25. Lionel Patenaude, *Texans, Politics and the New Deal* (New York: Garland, 1983), 75; Tindall, *The Emergence of the New South,* 642–49; William Anderson, *The Wild Man from Sugar Creek: The Political Career of Eugene Talmadge* (Baton Rouge: Louisiana State University Press, 1975), 168.

26. Patterson, *Congressional Conservatism,* 140–45.

27. Richard B. Henderson, *Maury Maverick: A Political Biography* (Austin: University of Texas Press, 1970), 133–86; Chester Morgan, *Redneck Liberal: Theodore Bilbo and the New Deal* (Baton Rouge: Louisiana State University Press, 1985).

28. Hollinger F. Barnard, ed., *Outside the Magic Circle: The Autobiography of Virginia Foster Durr* (University: University of Alabama Press, 1985), 162; Hamilton, *Lister Hill,* 83, 211–82.

29. Wright, *Old South, New South,* 236; Numan V. Bartley, "The Era of the New Deal as a Turning Point in Southern History," in Cobb and Namaroto, eds., *The New Deal and the South,* 143; Smith, "The New Deal and the Urban South," 537.

30. Sitkoff, *A New Deal for Blacks,* 58–101, 139–335.

31. Badger, *Prosperity Road,* 225–27; Harvard Sitkoff, "The Impact of the New Deal on Black Southerners," in Cobb and Namaroto, eds., *The New Deal and the South,* 117–34; Patricia Sullivan, "Southern Reformers, the New Deal and the Formation of the Civil Rights Movement" (unpublished ms. in the author's possession).

32. Numan V. Bartley and Hugh D. Graham, *Southern Politics and the Second Reconstruction* (Baltimore, Md.: Johns Hopkins University Press, 1975), 24–50; Sullivan, "Southern Reformers," Patricia Sullivan, "Gideon's Southern Soldiers: New Deal Politics and Civil Rights Reform, 1933–1948" (Ph.D. dissertation: Emory University, 1983), 100–92; Tate, "Easing the Burden," 191, 198; Williams, "Children and Welfare in a Segregated Society."

33. Fite, *Cotton Fields No More,* 163–206.

34. Harvard Sitkoff, *The Struggle for Black Equality, 1954–1980* (New York: Hill and Wang, 1981), 15–16; Wright, *Old South, New South,* 264–69.

35. James C. Cobb, *Industrialization and Southern Society, 1877–1984* (Lexington: University Press of Kentucky, 1984), ch. 3.

Chapter Three

1. Gilbert C. Fite, *Cotton Fields No More: Southern Agriculture, 1865–1980* (Lexington: University Press of Kentucky, 1984); Pete Daniel, *Breaking the Land: The Transformation of Cotton, Tobacco and Rice Cultures since 1880* (Urbana: University of Illinois Press, 1985); Jack Temple Kirby, *Rural Worlds Lost: The American South, 1920–1960* (Baton Rouge: Louisiana State University Press, 1982).

2. Gavin Wright, *Old South, New South: Revolution in the Southern Economy since the Civil War* (New York: Basic Books, 1986); James C. Cobb, *The Selling of the South: The Southern Crusade for Industrial Development, 1936–1980* (Baton Rouge: Louisiana State University Press, 1982); James C. Cobb, *Industrialization and Southern Society, 1877–1984* (Lexington: University Press of Kentucky, 1984).

3. Tony Badger, "How Did the New Deal Change the South?" *Looking Inward, Looking Outward: From the 1930s through the 1940s,* ed. Steve Ickingrill (Amsterdam: VU University Press, 1990), 166–83; Kirby, *Rural Worlds Lost,* 64–69; Wright, *Old South, New South,* 226–35.

4. Kirby, *Rural Worlds Lost,* 22, 54–55.

5. James C. Cobb, "'Somebody Done Nailed Us on the Cross': Federal Farm Policies and Welfare Policy and the Civil Rights Movement in the Mississippi Delta," *Journal of American History* 77 (1990): 912–36; see also Neil McMillen, *Dark Journey: Mississippi in the Jim Crow Era* (Urbana: University of Illinois Press, 1989), 151.

6. Badger, "How Did the New Deal Change the South?" 167; Cobb, "'Somebody Done Nailed Us on the Cross,'" 912.

7. Kirby, *Rural Worlds Lost,* xvi.

8. John L. Thomas, "'The Road Not Taken': Perspectives on Post-Frontier America," Commonwealth Fund Lecture 1986 (copy in the author's possession), 16.

9. Pete Daniel, "The New Deal, Southern Agriculture and Economic Change," *The New Deal and the South,* ed. James C. Cobb and Michael V. Namaroto (Jackson: University Press of Mississippi, 1984), 42.

10. Pete Daniel, "The Transformation of the Rural South: 1930 to the Present," *Agricultural History* 55 (1981): 233, 247–48.

11. Ferrol Sams, *Run with the Horsemen* (Atlanta: Peachtree Publishers, 1982), 1–16.

12. Ernest J. Gaines, *A Gathering of Old Men* (London: Heinemann, 1984), 96–97.

13. Harry Crews, *Childhood: A Biography of a Place* (London: Secker and Warburg, 1979).

14. Maya Angelou, *I Know Why the Caged Bird Sings* (London: Virago, 1984); Pauli Murray, *Pauli Murray: The Autobiography of a Black Activist, Feminist, Lawyer, Priest and Poet* (Knoxville: University of Tennessee Press, 1989); Anne

Moody, *Coming of Age in Mississippi* (New York: Dial Press, 1968); Charles Evers, with Grace Halsall, *Evers* (New York: World Publishers, 1971); McMillen, *Dark Journey*, 124, 194.

15. Gaines, *A Gathering of Old Men*, 99.

16. Theodore Rosengarten, *All God's Dangers* (London: Cape, 1975).

17. Nell Irvin Painter, *The Narrative of Hosea Hudson: His Life as a Negro Communist in the South* (Cambridge: Harvard University Press, 1979).

18. Kirby, *Rural Worlds Lost*, 154.

19. Ferrol Sams, *The Whisper of the River* (New York: Penguin, 1986) 3, 467.

20. Fred Powledge, *Journeys through the South* (New York: Vanguard Press, 1979).

21. John Egerton, *The Americanization of Dixie: The Southernization of America* (New York: Harper's Magazine Press, 1974), 25, 210–11.

22. Carl Degler, *Place over Time. The Continuity of Southern Distinctiveness* (Baton Rouge: Louisiana State University Press, 1977).

23. George Brown Tindall, "Beyond the Mainstream: The Ethnic Southerners," *Journal of Southern History* 40 (1974): 3–18.

24. John Shelton Reed, *The Enduring South: Subcultural Persistence in Mass Society* (Chapel Hill: University of North Carolina Press, 1974); John Shelton Reed, *One South* (Baton Rouge: Louisiana State University Press, 1982); John Shelton Reed, *Southern Folk, Plain and Fancy: Native White Social Types* (Athens: University of Georgia Press, 1986).

25. See Ruth A. Banes, "Southerners Up North: Autobiographical Indicators of Southern Ethnicity," *Perspectives on the American South: An Annual Review of Society, Politics and Culture,* ed. James C. Cobb and Charles R. Wilson, vol. 3 (New York: Gordon and Beech, 1985), 1–16.

26. Willie Morris, *North Toward Home* (London: Macmillan, 1968), 398–99.

27. John Shelton Reed, "Up from Segregation," *Virginia Quarterly Review* 40 (1984): 373–93.

28. Albert Murray, *South to a Very Old Place* (New York: McGraw-Hill, 1971), 79–80.

29. Kirby, *Rural Worlds Lost*, 302.

30. Sams, *The Whisper of the River,* 33, 213.

31. *USA Today,* August 14, 1991.

Chapter Four

1. Carl Elliott Sr. and Michael D'Orso, *The Cost of Courage: The Journey of an American Congressman* (New York: Doubleday, 1992), 43–44, 54, 72–73.

2. See Frank Freidel, *FDR and the South* (Baton Rouge: Louisiana State University Press, 1965).

3. Anthony Badger, "Local Politics and Party Re-Alignment in the Late Thirties: The Failure of the New Deal", *Storia Nord Americana* 6 (1989): 77.

4. Badger, "How Did the New Deal Change the South?" in *Looking Inward, Looking Outward: From the 1930s through the 1940s,* ed. Steve Ickringill (Amsterdam: VU University Press, 1990), 174.

5. Badger, "Local Politics," 77–86; Badger, "How Did the New Deal Change the South?" 174; Roger Biles, *The South and the New Deal* (Lexington: University Press of Kentucky, 1994), 149; Lionel Patenaude, *Texans, Politics and the New Deal* (New York: Garland, 1983), 75; Alan Brinkley, *The End of Reform: New Deal Liberalism in Recession and War* (New York: Knopf, 1995).

6. Patricia Sullivan, *Days of Hope: Race and Democracy in the New Deal Era* (Chapel Hill: University of North Carolina Press, 1996), 69, 84–92, 141–49, 273, 275.

7. Sullivan, *Days of Hope,* 169–247; Patricia Sullivan, "Southern Reformers: The New Deal and the Movement's Foundation," in *New Directions in Civil Rights Studies,* ed. Armstead Robinson and Patricia Sullivan (Charlottesville: University of Virginia Press, 1991), 81–104; Robert Korstad and Nelson Lichtenstein, "Opportunities Found and Lost: Labor, Radicals and the Early Civil Rights Movement," *Journal of American History* 75 (1988): 786–811; Adam Fairclough, *Race and Democracy: The Civil Rights Struggle in Louisiana, 1915–1972* (Athens: University of Georgia Press, 1995), xii, xiv.

8. John Egerton, *Speak Now against the Day: The Generation before the Civil Rights Movement in the South* (New York: Knopf, 1995), 10–11, 71, 113, 148, 220.

9. Ira Katznelson, Kim Geiger, and Daniel Kryder, "Limiting Liberalism: The Southern Vote in Congress," *Political Science Quarterly* 108 (1993): 283–306.

10. Katznelson et al., "Limiting Liberalism," 296; Numan V. Bartley and Hugh Davis Graham, *Southern Politics and the Second Reconstruction* (Baltimore, Md.: Johns Hopkins University Press, 1975), 24–50.

11. Bruce Schulman, *From Cotton Belt to Sunbelt: Federal Policy, Economic Development, and the Transformation of the South, 1938–1980* (New York: Oxford University Press, 1991), 63–111; Gavin Wright, *Old South, New South: Revolutions in the Southern Economy since the Civil War* (New York: Basic Books, 1986), 239–74; Numan V. Bartley, *The New South, 1945–1980: The Story of the South's Modernization* (Baton Rouge: Louisiana State University Press, 1995), 1–16.

12. Virginia Van der Veer Hamilton, *Lister Hill: Statesman from the South* (Chapel Hill: University of North Carolina Press, 1987), 70–86.

13. Jordan A Schwarz, *The New Dealers: Politics in the Age of Roosevelt* (New York: Knopf, 1993), 59–96, 194–245, 249–94; Robert A. Caro, *The Years of Lyndon Johnson: The Path to Power* (New York: Knopf, 1982), 472.

14. Schulman, *From Cotton Belt to Sunbelt,* 127–34; Tony Badger, "Fatalism not Gradualism: The Crisis of Southern Liberalism, 1945–1965," in *The Making of Martin Luther King and the Civil Rights Movement,* ed. Brian Ward and Tony Badger (London: Macmillan, 1996), 77–78.

15. Caro, *The Path to Power,* 389–436; Billie Burdick Kemper, "Lindley

Beckworth: Grassroots Congressman" (M.A. thesis, Stephen F. Austin State University, 1980), 33–38, in Lindley Garrison Beckworth Papers, Barker Center for American History, University of Texas, Austin; Randall Bennett Woods, *Fulbright: A Biography* (Cambridge: Cambridge University Press, 1995), 65–69; George E. Sims, *The Little Man's Big Friend: James E. Folsom in Alabama Politics, 1946–1958* (Tuscaloosa: University of Alabama Press, 1985), 21–39.

16. Roger D. Tate Jr., "Easing the Burden: The Era of Depression and New Deal in Mississippi" (Ph.D. dissertation, University of Tennessee, 1978), 191, 198.

17. Timothy J. Minchin, *What Do We Need a Union For? The TWUA in the South, 1945–1955* (Chapel Hill: University of North Carolina Press:, 1997), 15–19; Michelle Brittain, "Making Friends and Enemies: Textile Workers and Political Action in Post–World War II Georgia," *Journal of Southern History* 63 (1997): 97–98, 104.

18. Judy Barrett Litoff and David C Smith (eds.), *Dear Boys: World War II Letters from a Woman Back Home* (Jackson: University Press of Mississippi, 1991), 90.

19. C. C. Hodge to George Andrews, March 5, 1945, Papers of George Andrews, Auburn University.

20. David Reynolds, *Rich Relations: The American Occupation of Britain, 1942–45* (New York: Harper Collins, 1995), 54, 71–88, 148–54, 302–24, 439–45; Donald Cunnigen, "Men and Women of Goodwill: Mississippi's White Liberals" (Ph.D. dissertation, Harvard University, 1988), 560; Rowan T. Thomas, *Born in Battle: Round the World Adventures of the 513th Bombardment Squadron* (Philadelphia, 1944), 78, 192–93, 318–20.

21. Frank E. Smith, *Congressmen from Mississippi: An Autobiography* (New York: Pantheon, 1964), 64–92; Dennis Mitchell, "Frank E. Smith: Mississippi Liberal," *Journal of Mississippi History* 48 (1986): 89–93.

22. Jim Wright, *Balance of Power: Presidents and Congress from the Era of McCarthy to the Age of Gingrich* (Atlanta: Turner Pub, 1996), 18–30, 40; Interview with Jim Wright, November 18, 1996. Stuart Long Interview, Texas Oral History Collection, Woodson Research Center, Rice University, Houston.

23. Jim Lester, *A Man for Arkansas: Sid McMath and the Southern Reform Tradition* (Little Rock, Ark.: James W. Bell, 1976), 8–31, 52; Sidney S. McMath interview with John Egerton, September 8, 1990, Southern Historical Collection, Chapel Hill.

24. Interview with Dante Fascell, February 27, 1997; Claudia Townsend, *Dante Fascell: Democratic Representative from Florida* (Ralph Nader Congress Papers: Citizens Look at Congress, 1972), 1.

25. Schulman, *From Cotton Belt to Sunbelt,* 112–34, 321.

26. Minchin, *What Do We Need a Union For?* 48–68, 199–209.

27. James A Burran, "Racial Violence in the South during World War II" (unpublished Ph.D. dissertation, University of Tennessee, 1977).

28. Jennifer Brooks, "From Fighting Nazism to Fighting Bossism: Southern

World War Two Veterans and the Assault on Southern Political Tradition" (paper delivered to the Southern Historical Association, New Orleans, November 1995. I am very grateful to Dr Brooks for permission to quote from this paper).

29. Fairclough, *Race and Democracy,* 141; Michael Heale, *McCarthy's Americans: Red Scare Politics in State and Nation, 1935–1965* (London: Macmillan, 1998), 273–76.

30. Badger, "Fatalism, not Gradualism," 67–95; Tony Badger, "The Constraints of Southern Liberalism" (paper delivered at the Southern Intellectual History Circle, Birmingham, 1997; copy in author's possession); Tony Badger, "Southerners Who Did not Sign the Southern Manifesto" (paper delivered at the Organization of American Historians, San Francisco, April 1997).

31. Caro, *The Path to Power,* 449.

Chapter Five

1. I developed these arguments in "The Southern Manifesto" a paper given at the Southern Historical Association meeting in Orlando, November 1993 (copy in the author's possession).

2. Fulbright referred to "one of the most-respected and liberal-minded Southerners in the Senate" who signed the Manifesto without reading it in an interview with Stewart Alsop, clipping *Washington Post* April 8, 1956, Box 71, J. William Fulbright Papers, University of Arkansas, Fayetteville. Carl Eliott Sr. and Michael D'Orso, *The Cost of Courage: The Journey of an American Congressman* (New York: Doubleday, 1992), 178–82.

3. Draft Statement, n.d. Box 48, Fulbright Papers. Transcript, Columbia University Oral History Program Interview, 1970, pp. 28–29, copy in Brooks Hays Papers, University of Arkansas, Fayetteville.

4. John Stennis, Oral History Interview, June 17, 1972, Lyndon Baines Johnson Library, Austin. Sanford P. Dyer, "Lyndon Johnson and the Politics of Civil Rights, 1935–60: The Art of Moderate Leadership" (Ph.D.: Texas A and M, 1978), 102–7. Robert Dallek, *Lone Star Rising: Lyndon Johnson and His Times, 1908–1960* (New York: Oxford University Press, 1991), 138–43, 496–97. Robert Mann, *The Walls of Jericho: Lyndon Johnson, Hubert Humphrey and Richard Russell* (New York: Harcourt Brace, 1996), 159–66.

5. Memo, George Reedy to Lyndon Johnson, July 12, 1956, Box 423, Office Files of George Reedy, 1956–57, Lyndon Baines Johnson Library, Austin. There is no evidence that Russell was anxious to protect Walter George, even though politicians like Ross Bass, Albert Gore, and Paul Douglas appeared to accept that argument. The success of the campaign to paint the Manifesto as designed purely for home consumption and therefore to restrain Northern criticism was noted by columnist Peter Edson, *Birmingham Post-Herald,* March 26, 1956. For Johnson's distaste at the divisive oratory, *Dallas Morning News*, March 13, 1956. For Russell's reaction, Charles J. Bloch to Richard B. Russell, March 21, 1956;

Russell to Arch Rowan, March 27, 1956; Richard B. Russell Papers, University of Georgia, Athens. Harry Byrd to E. H. Ramsey, May 1, 1956, Harry F. Byrd Papers, University of Virginia, Charlottesville.

6. *Beaumont Enterprise*, July 30, 1956

7. *Austin-American,* March, 1, 6, 13, August 1, 3, 1956.

8. Franklin Jones to Wright Patman, February 2, 1956, Box 80A; Wright Patman to newspaper editors n.d., Speech Notes, TV Speech, Box 79C; *Wright Patman's Congressional Record* Box 73A, Kenneth Simmons tv speech n.d, *Simmons for Congress News,* Box 73C; Simmons speeches, June 29, 1956, July 19, 1956, Box 80B; Wright Patman to R. B. Morrison, February 23, 1956, Morrison to Patman, March 7, 1956, Box 80A; Patman Press release, March 23, 1956, Box 79C, Wright Patman Papers, Lyndon Baines Johnson Library, Austin. Two of the other Texas signers had views more like Martin Dies's. Right-wing views on states rights, the economy and subversion went alongside traditional views on race for John Dowdy and Clark Fisher. Even someone as conservative as W. R. "Bob" Poage viewed Dowdy as a "perfectly honest and sincere reactionary" and Fisher as an "extreme reactionary." W. R. Poage Oral History Interview, vol. 5, 20–21, 23, W. R. Poage Papers, Baylor Collection of Political Materials, Waco.

9. Jim Wright, *Balance of Power: Presidents and Congress from the Era of McCarthy to the Age of Gingrich* (Atlanta: Turner Publishing, 1996), 19–30, 48. Interview with Jim Wright, November 18, 1996. James Wright to Jim Wright, February 26, 1956, Jim Wright to ——— letter and statement March 14, 1956, Statement, March 22, 1956, Wright to ——— April 20, 1956, Wright to ——— April 20, 1956, Jim Wright Collection, Texas Christian University, Fort Worth. (The anonymity of Wright's correspondents is a condition of citing material from these papers.) Stuart Long Interview, Texas Oral History Collection, Woodson Research Center, Rice University, Houston. The voluminous papers of Jack Brooks have been deposited at Lamar University, Beaumont, where they lie uncataloged in their original boxes. I was kindly allowed to examine these but could turn up no material for 1956. Brooks was four days older than Wright, entered Law School at the same time, and was elected to Congress in 1954, backed by organized labor and the oil workers.

10. Albert Thomas to M. E. Walter, August 12, 1937, Box 15, Thomas Biography, Box 18, Albert Thomas Papers, Woodson Research Center, Rice University. Joe Kilgore Interview, Sam Rayburn Papers, Barker Center for American History, University of Texas, Austin. Interview with Jim Wright, November 18, 1996. Bruce Alger Speech, September 24, 1956, Bruce Alger Papers, Dallas Public Library. Bruce Alger Oral History Interview, East Texas State University and Dallas Public Library.

11. Interview with Jim Wright, November 18, 1996. Oral History Interviews: O. C. Fisher, Frank Ikard, Joe Kilgore, George Mahon, J. R. Parten, Homer Thornberry, Rayburn Papers.

12. Sam Rayburn to Miss M. R. Bruton, July 3, 1954, Rayburn Papers. Wright, *Balance of Power,* 54.

13. J. T. Rutherford, Allan Shivers Oral History Interviews, Rayburn Papers. Jim Wright, *You and Your Congressman* (New York: Putnam's, 1976), 107–9. *Austin-American*, March 8, 1956. Memorandum on campaign for control of Texas delegation, Box 419.2, Reedy Office Files.

14. ——— to Jim Wright, March 20, 1956, ——— to Wright n.d., Larry King to Craig Raupe, August 6, 1956, Wright Papers. Jack Brooks to Charles B. Deane, August 7, 1956, Charles B. Deane Papers, Southern Baptist Historical Collection, Wake Forest University, Winston-Salem. Henry Wade vs. Bruce Alger debate, Wade speech, September 17, 1956, Alger Papers.

15. Interview with Jim Wright, November 18, 1996. *Beaumont Enterprise,* July 29, 1956. Poage Oral History Interview, vol. 3, p. 815, Poage Papers.

16. *New York Times,* March 12, April 3, 1956. Speech draft 1956, Estes Kefauver to P. L. Prattis, May 19, 1956, Kefauver to B. L. Fonville, May 10, 1956, Estes Kefauver Papers, University of Tennessee, Knoxville.

17. Albert Gore to Mrs. Talley, October 12, 1954, Albert Gore Papers, Middle Tennessee State University, Murfreesboro. James B. Gardner, "Political Leadership in a Period of Transition: Frank G. Clement, Albert Gore, Estes Kefauver and Tennessee Politics, 1948–1956" (Ph.D. Vanderbilt University, 1978), 500–670. Interview with Albert Gore Sr., December 1, 1990.

18. Albert Gore Interview, March 13, 1978, Southern Oral History Program, Southern Historical Collection, Chapel Hill. Interview with Albert Gore Sr., December 1, 1990. Donald Davidson to Albert Gore, March 12, 1956, Fred Childress to Gore, March 12, 1956, Sims Crownover to Gore, April 19, 1956, Gore Papers.

19. Interview with Albert Gore, December 1, 1990. Albert Gore to Pat Hughes, April 12, 1956, Gore Papers. *Nashville Tennessean* March 13, March 18, 1956.

20. Hugh Davis Graham, *Crisis in Print: Desegregation and the Press in Tennessee* (Nashville, Tenn.: Vanderbilt University Press, 1967), 29–90. Miss Jean Scraggs to Albert Gore, January 18, 1956, Gore Papers.

21. Spessard L. Holland to Mrs. A. L. Anderson, March 27, 1956, Spessard Holland Papers, University of Florida, Gainesville. *Miami Herald*, March 8, 11, 1956. Interview with Dante Fascell, February 27, 1997.

22. Interview with Dante Fascell, February 27, 1997. *Miami Herald*, March 11, 12, 1956. Taylor, *Fascell,* 9.

23. *Raleigh News and Observer,* March 13, 1956. Howard W. Smith was the congressional leader responsible for securing signatures from the North Carolina delegation. The successive lists in his papers show the order in which the North Carolina delegation signed up, Howard W. Smith Papers, University of Virginia, Charlottesville.

24. Clipping, *Henderson Times-News,* March 14, 1956; Harold D. Cooley to H. Q. Dorsett, March 13, 1956, Harold Dunbar Cooley Papers, Southern Historical Collection, Chapel Hill.

25. Ralph J. Christian, "The Folger-Chatham Congressional Primary of 1946," *North Carolina Historical Review* 53 (1976): 25–53. *Raleigh News and Observer,* May 18, 1954. *Winston-Salem Journal,* May 18, 1954.

26. *Greensboro Daily News,* September 2, 1955. *Winston-Salem Journal,* September 12, 1955. Comment, James L. Sundquist, April 8, 1987. John A. Lang to Charles B. Deane, April 23, 1956, John A. Lang Papers, East Carolina Manuscript Collection, East Carolina University, Greenville.

27. Charles B. Deane to Walter Lambeth, October 22, 1952, Deane Papers. Interview with Charles B. Deane Jr., September 12, 1989.

28. Charles B. Deane to Fay Allen, November 21, 1951, Deane Papers.

29. Notes for schools and colleges [n.d.], Notes, November 22, 1956, Deane Papers.

30. Charles B. Deane to Herman Hardison, March 27, 1956, Deane Papers.

31. Interview with Charles B. Deane Jr., September 12, 1989. Charles B. Deane to Mrs. P. A. Wood, July 28, 1956, Lang Papers. Lewis Cannon to Charles B. Deane, March 15, 1956; Leaflet [n.d.], Deane to James E. Griffin, May 7, 1956, J. B. Hood to Deane, April 24, 1956, Nina Duke Wood to Deane, July 26, 1956, Deane Papers.

32. Anon to Thurmond Chatham [n.d], Dallas Gwynn to Chatham, March 24, 1956; I. F. Young to Chatham, May 13, 1956, Thurmond Chatham Papers, North Carolina Division of Archives and History, Raleigh.

33. Debnam Adverts, Cooley Papers. *Raleigh News and Observer,* March 17, 1956. Memorandum, March 19, 1956, Waldemar Eros Debnam Papers, East Carolina Manuscript Collection, East Carolina University, Greenville.

34. L. Van Noppen to Thurmond Chatham, March 8, 1956, Ralph Scott adverts, Chatham Papers. *Greensboro Daily News,* April 10, 13, 1956. *Winston-Salem Journal,* April 19, 1956.

35. Ermine B. Hampton to Barbara Dearing [n.d.], Debnam Adverts, Cooley Papers. *Raleigh News and Observer,* March 14, April 6, 1956. Anthony J. Badger, *North Carolina and the New Deal* (Raleigh: North Carolina Division of Archives and History, 1981), 89.

36. Harold Cooley to E. L. Cannon, April 3, 1956, Nashville (NC) speech, April 7, 1956, Henderson speech, May 17, 1956; WTVD speech, Cooley Papers. Thurmond Chatham to Hiden Ramsay, May 31, 1956, Chatham to Ralph Howland, June 5, 1956, Chatham Papers.

37. Interview with Frank Smith, November 1995.

38. Walter Jackson, "White Liberal Intellectuals, Civil Rights, and Gradualism, 1954–60," in *The Making of Martin Luther King and the Civil Rights Movement,* ed. Brian Ward and Tony Badger (London: Macmillan, 1996), 96–114.

39. Numan Bartley, *The New South, 1945–1980* (Baton Rouge: Louisiana State University Press, 1995), 175–76.

Chapter Six

1. In working on this chapter, the author has been very fortunate to receive advice and assistance from Carolyn Abel, Brent Aucoin, Betty Austin, Andrea Cantrell, David Chappell, Robert Frizzell, Willard Gatewood, Elizabeth Jacoway, John Kirk, William E. Leuchtenburg, Elaine McNeil, and Randall Woods. The author also wishes to thank the editors of the *Arkansas Historical Quarterly* for granting permission to use a portion of the article they published entitled "'The Forerunner of Our Opposition': Arkansas and the Southern Manifesto of 1956." Richard Kluger, *Simple Justice* (New York: Random House, 1975), 593–94.

2. Kluger, *Simple Justice,* 716–47.

3. Jim Lester, *A Man for Arkansas: Sid McMath and the Southern Reform Tradition* (Little Rock, Ark.: Rose Publishing Co., 1976), 82, 157–59, 162–66; Roy Reed, *Faubus: The Life and Times of an American Prodigal* (Fayetteville: University of Arkansas Press, 1997), 85–127, 168–69; Sidney McMath Interview, by John Egerton, September 8, 1990, Southern Oral History Program, University of North Carolina, Chapel Hill.

4. Brooks Hays Interview, Columbia University Oral History Program, Lawrence Brooks Hays Papers, Special Collections Division, University of Arkansas Libraries, Fayetteville, Arkansas.

5. Virgil T. Blossom, *It Has Happened Here* (New York: Harper and Brothers, 1959).

6. McMath Interview, University of North Carolina.

7. *Arkansas Gazette,* March 4, 1956.

8. Julianne Lewis Adams and Thomas DeBlack, *Civil Disobedience: An Oral History of School Desegregation in Fayetteville, Arkansas, 1954–1965* (Fayetteville: University of Arkansas Press, 1994), 1–11.

9. Neil McMillen, *The Citizens' Council: Organized Resistance to the Second Reconstruction, 1954–64* (Urbana: University of Illinois Press, 1971), 94–95.

10. *Arkansas Gazette,* March 16, 1956.

11. Ibid.

12. Ibid.

13. *Arkansas Democrat,* January 8, February 25, 1956; *Arkansas Gazette,* February 26, 1956.

14. *Arkansas Democrat,* January 29, 1956; *Arkansas Gazette,* February 25, 26, 1956.

15. Reed, *Faubus,* 176–78; *Arkansas Gazette,* February 25, 26, 1956.

16. *Arkansas Democrat,* January 23, February 8, 1956.

17. Anthony J. Badger, "The Southern Manifesto of 1956," paper delivered at the annual meeting of the Southern Historical Association in Orlando, Florida, 1993.

18. *Arkansas Gazette,* February 7, 18, 24, 1956.

19. *Arkansas Gazette,* July 22, 1956. Typed sheet in 1956 scrapbook, Papers of William F. Norrell, Special Collections Division, University of Arkansas,

Fayetteville. Oren Harris to Gus Jones, May 22, 1944; Harris to Rev. H. Nabors, June 25, 1942; Campaign File Loc. 1370, 13–4-12, Paul Geren; Oral History transcript, University of Texas, Oral History Project, Papers of Oren Harris, Special Collections Division, University of Arkansas, Fayetteville.

20. Wilbur Mills Interview, Papers of Sam Rayburn, Barker Center for American History, University of Texas. Brooks Hays Interview (1975) with Walter Brown and Bruce Parham, Brooks Hays Papers; Wilbur Mills Interview, Former Members of Congress Oral History Project, Library of Congress, Washington, D.C. I am greatly indebted to William E. Leuchtenburg for this reference. The Wilbur Mills Papers at Hendrix College, Conway, Arkansas, contain clippings suggesting that Mills's signing of the manifesto (and his later efforts to seat Dale Alford when Alford's defeat of Brooks Hays was challenged) harmed his long-term efforts to become Speaker of the House of Representatives.

21. Miss Alice Santamaria to J. William Fulbright, March 12, 1956; Miss Anne Ferrante to Fulbright, March 15, 1956; Mrs. E. T. Meijer, March 21, 1956; Fulbright to Dr. J. Kenneth Shamblin, March 14, 1956; Papers of J. William Fulbright, Special Collections Division, University of Arkansas, Fayetteville, Arkansas.

22. *Washington Post,* April 9, 1956; typed statement [n.d.], Fulbright Papers; Anthony J. Badger, "Southerners Who Did Not Sign the Southern Manifesto," paper delivered at the annual meeting of the Organization of American Historians in San Francisco, Calif., 1997.

23. Typed statement [n.d.] Fulbright Papers.

24. Randall B. Woods, *Fulbright: A Biography* (Cambridge, Eng.: Cambridge University Press, 1995), 207–11. The original Thurmond draft is in the Papers of J. Strom Thurmond, Clemson University. Fulbright's and Thurmond's papers contain both the Russell draft and the revisions by Fulbright, Holland, Sparkman, and Daniel. I am very grateful to William E. Leuchtenburg for providing me with the reference to the Price Daniel Oral History Interview, University of North Texas, Denton. John Sparkman to John Nolen, June 23, 1956, Papers of John Sparkman, W. S. Hoole Library, University of Alabama, Tuscaloosa. Typed commentary on the manifesto drafts, box 17, Thurmond Papers.

25. Final draft, Thurmond Papers.

26. Randall B. Woods, "Dixie's Dove: J. William Fulbright, the Vietnam War, and the American South," *Journal of Southern History* 9 (1994): 541; Fulbright to Mrs. Walter Bell, August 31, 1948; Clipping *Washington Post,* April 8, 1956, Fulbright Papers.

27. Jim Hale to Fulbright, March 14, 1956; Memo from John Erickson to Fulbright [n.d.], Fulbright Papers.

28. Woods, *Fulbright,* 202–4.

29. Gordon McNeil to Fulbright, March 19, 1956, Fulbright Papers. Gordon McNeil is the husband of the sociologist Elaine McNeil, who was very active in desegregation in Fayetteville; Adams and DeBlack, *Civil Disobedience,* 149–57.

Elaine McNeil, "Policy-Maker and the Public," *Southwestern Social Science Quarterly* 39 (1958): 95–99. Jeff Packham to Fulbright, March 13, 1956; Mrs. J. O. Powell to Fulbright, March 15, 1956, Fulbright Papers.

30. W. Johnson to Fulbright, March 13, 1956, Fulbright Papers.

31. J. William Fulbright and Seth Tilman, *The Price of Empire* (New York: Pantheon Books, 1989), 94; Donald K. Campbell to Fulbright, March 12, 1956, Fulbright Papers.

32. Woods, "Dixie's Dove," 538, 541.

33. Woods, "Dixie's Dove," 540–41; Numan Bartley, *The New South, 1945–1980* (Baton Rouge: Louisiana State University Press, 1995), 175–76; Woods, *Fulbright,* 211.

34. Brooks Hays Interview, 1970, 26–28, Columbia University Oral History Program, Brooks Hays Papers.

35. Brooks Hays Interview, 1970, 26–28, Columbia University Oral History Program, Brooks Hays Papers; Brooks Hays Interview, 1971, 26, Lyndon Baines Johnson Library, Brooks Hays Papers.

36. John Ward Interview with Orval Faubus and Brooks Hays, June 4, 1976, in the Brooks Hays Papers. Faubus was referring to the two (not one) North Carolina congressmen who were defeated in primaries less than two months after refusing to sign the manifesto; Harold Cooley was the Tar Heel congressman who race-baited the race-baiter to keep his seat. In addition to the three North Carolina representatives, three senators and nineteen (seventeen from Texas) congressmen from the southern states also refused to sign; none of these others was defeated.

37. Orval Faubus Interview, by John Kirk, December 3, 1992, Newcastle University Oral History Program.

38. My analysis differs slightly from Roy Reed's in his indispensable biography of Faubus. Reed sees Faubus, like the moderates, responding to mass segregationist sentiment. I argue that Faubus helped create the sentiment to which he and the moderates claimed to be prisoners. Reed, *Faubus,* 356–57.

39. *Arkansas Gazette,* March 4, 1956.

Chapter Seven

1. Terry Sanford interview with Jack Bass and Walter DeVries, Southern Oral History Program. Southern Historical Collection, Chapel Hill. Margaret Birdsong Price interview with the author, May 20, 1970. *Raleigh News and Observer,* January 23, 2000

2. John William Coon, "Kerr Scott, the 'Go Forward' Governor: His Origins, His Program and the North Carolina General Assembly" (M.A., University of North Carolina, 1968), 32–65. For the Trigg appointment, see Box 10, especially J. S. Davis to W. Kerr Scott, April 28, 1949, Scott to Davis, May 19, 1949, Papers of Governor W. Kerr Scott, North Carolina Division of Archives and History, Raleigh.

3. Coon, "Kerr Scott," 33–39. Timothy J Minchin, *What Do We Need a Union For? The TWUA in the South, 1945–1955?* (Chapel Hill: University of North Carolina Press, 1997), 81–82, 91.

4. Campaign Speech, 1936, Papers of W. Kerr Scott, North Carolina Division of Archives and History, Raleigh. Rob Christiansen, "The Scotts of Haw River," *Raleigh News and Observer,* January 17, 1999.

5. Julian M. Pleasants and Augustus M. Burns III, *Frank Porter Graham and the 1950 Senate Race in North Carolina* (Chapel Hill: University of North Carolina Press, 1990), 5–17, 156–59.

6. Jesse Helms to W. Kerr Scott, September 16, 1949, Governor W. Kerr Scott Papers.

7. Steve Niven, "The Slow Burn Rebellion of Forgotten Americans: White Backlash in North Carolina, 1964–68." I am extremely grateful to Steve Niven for a copy of this paper. David Cecelski, *Along Freedom Road: Hyde County, North Carolina, and the Fate of Black Schools in the South* (Chapel Hill: University of North Carolina Press, 1994), 155–58. Robert W Scott, Oral History Interview, 1986, Southern Oral History Program, Southern Historical Collection, Chapel Hill.

8. Tony Badger to Iris and Kenneth Badger, February 23, 1970 (in the author's possession). Thad Stem to Jonathan Daniels, October 5, 1970, Papers of Jonathan Daniels, Southern Historical Collection, Chapel Hill.

9. John Egerton, *Speak Now against the Day: The Generation before the Civil Rights Movement in the South* (New York: Knopf, 1995), 10–11. Patricia Sullivan, *Days of Hope: Race and Democracy in the New Deal Era* (Chapel Hill: University of North Carolina Press, 1996), 69, 84–92, 141–49, 169–247, 273, 275. Patricia Sullivan, "Southern Reformers, the New Deal and the Movement's Foundation," in *New Directions in Civil Rights Studies,* ed. Armstead Robinson and Patricia Sullivan (Charlottesville: University of Virginia Press, 1991), 81–104. Adam Fairclough, *Race and Democracy: The Civil Rights Struggle in Louisiana, 1915–1972* (Athens: University of Georgia Press, 1995), xii, xiv. Robert Korstad and Nelson Lichtenstein, "Opportunities Found and Lost: Labor, Radicals and the Early Civil Rights Movement," *Journal of American History* 75 (1988): 786–811. Minchin, *What Do We Need a Union For?* 26–118. Jennifer Brooks, "From Fighting Nazism to Fighting Bossism: Southern World War II Veterans and the Assault on Southern Political Tradition" (unpublished paper in the author's possession). Pamela Tyler, *Silk Stockings and Ballot Boxes: Women and Politics in New Orleans, 1920–1963* (Athens: University of Georgia Press, 1996), 78–168. Leslie Gale Parr, *A Will of Her Own: Sarah Towles Reed and the Pursuit of Democracy in Southern Public Education* (Athens: University of Georgia Press, 1998), 144–85.

10. Tony Badger, "Whatever Happened to Roosevelt's New Generation of Southerners?" in *The Roosevelt Years: New Essays on the United States, 1933–1945,* ed. Robert A. Garson and Stuart Kidd (Edinburgh: Edinburgh University Press, 1999), 122–38. Ira Katznelson, Kim Geiger, and Daniel Kryder, "Limiting

Liberalism: The Southern Vote in Congress," *Political Science Quarterly* 108 (1993): 283–306. Tony Badger, "Fatalism, Not Gradualism: Race and the Crisis of Southern Liberalism, 1945–1965," in *The Making of Martin Luther King and the Civil Rights Movement,* ed. Brian Ward and Tony Badger (London: Macmillan, 1996). Frank Smith, *Congressman from Mississippi* (New York: Pantheon Books, 1964), 69–74. Tony Badger, "Southerners Who Refused to Sign the Southern Manifesto," *Historical Journal* 42, 2 (1999): 517–34. John Drescher, *Triumph of Goodwill: How Terry Sanford Beat a Champion of Segregation and Reshaped the South* (Jackson: University Press of Mississippi, 2000), 10–14. Nahfiza Ahmed, "Race, Class, and Citizenship: The Civil Rights Struggle in Mobile, Alabama, 1925–1985" (Ph.D., Leicester University, 1999), 108–22.

11. Elaine M. Paull to Terry Sanford, May 31, 1954, W. Kerr Scott Papers. Badger, "Fatalism Not Gradualism," 87–88.

12. Minchin, *What Do We Need a Union For?* 48–68, 199–209. Bryant Simon, *A Fabric of Defeat: The Politics of South Carolina Millhands, 1910–1948* (Chapel Hill: University of North Carolina Press, 1998), 221.

13. James C. Cobb, "World War II and the Mind of the Modern South," in *Remaking Dixie: The Impact of World War II on the American South,* ed. Neil R. McMillen (Jackson: University Press of Mississippi, 1997), 6–9. Brooks, "Fighting Nazism." Brian Lewis Crispell, *Testing the Limits: George Armistead Smathers and Cold War America* (Athens: University of Georgia Press, 1999), 8–74. Thad Stem to Jonathan Daniels, September 24, 1967, Jonathan Daniels Papers.

14. Bruce J. Schulman, *From Cotton Belt to Sunbelt: Federal Policy, Economic Development, and the Transformation of the South, 1938–1980* (New York: Oxford University Press, 1991), 321. Carl Grafton and Anne Permaloff, *Big Mules and Branchheads: James E. Folsom and Political Power in Alabama* (Athens: University of Georgia Press, 1985), 62. Badger, "Southerners Who Refused to Sign the Southern Manifesto," 517–34.

15. Kari Frederickson, *The Dixiecrat Revolt and the End of the Solid South* (Chapel Hill: University of North Carolina Press, 2001), 101–73. Pete Daniel, *Lost Revolutions: The South in the 1950s* (Chapel Hill: University of North Carolina Press, 2000), 257, 281–82. Pleasants and Burns, *Frank Porter Graham,* 121.

16. Carl Elliott and Michael D'Orso, *The Cost of Courage: The Journey of an American Congressman* (New York: Doubleday, 1992), 181. Sullivan, *Days of Hope,* 221–75. Morton Sosna, *In Search of the Silent South* (New York: Columbia University Press, 1977), 165. Michael Klarman, "How *Brown* Changed Race Relations: The Backlash Thesis," *Journal of American History* 81 (1994): 81–118.

17. Sullivan, *Days of Hope,* 221–75. Korstad and Lichtenstein, "Opportunities Found and Lost," 786–811. Fairclough, *Race and Democracy,* xiii. Numan Bartley, *The New South, 1945–1980* (Baton Rouge: Louisiana State University Press, 1995), 70, 73.

18. Numan Bartley, comment, Fortieth Anniversary of Little Rock Conference, University of Arkansas at Little Rock, September 27, 1997. Klarman, "How *Brown* Changed Race Relations," 81–118. Korstad and Lichtenstein, "Opportunities Found and Lost," 786–811. Jim Sleeper, "Color Blind," *New Republic,* March 2, 1998.

19. Gary Huey, *Rebel with a Cause: P. D. East, Southern Liberalism and the Civil Rights Movement, 1953–71* (Wilmington, Del.: Scholarly Resources Inc., 1985), 106–8. Alan Brinkley, *The End of Reform: New Deal Liberalism in Recession and War* (New York: Knopf, 1995), 265–71.

20. Frank Smith, interview with the author, November 7, 1995. Maury Maverick Jr. Interview, Texas Oral History Interview, Woodson Research Center, Rice University, Houston. Michael Heale, *McCarthy's Americans: Red Scare Politics in State and Nation, 1935–1965* (Athens: University of Georgia Press, 1998), 214–17. William J. Billingsley, *Communists on Campus: Race, Politics, and the Public University in Sixties North Carolina* (Chapel Hill: University of North Carolina Press, 1999), 1–87.

21. Calvin Trillin, "Reflections: Remembrance of Moderates Past," *New Yorker,* March 21, 1977.

22. David Chappell, *Inside Agitators: White Southerners in the Civil Rights Movement* (Baltimore, Md.: Johns Hopkins University Press, 1994), 1–49. David Chappell, "The Divided Mind of Southern Segregationists," *Georgia Historical Quarterly* 82, 1 (1998): 45–72. David Chappell, "Religious Ideas of Segregationists," *Journal of American Studies* 32, 2 (1998): 237–62. J. Mills Thornton III, "Miunicipal Politics and the Course of the Movement," in *New Directions in Civil Rights Studies,* ed. Armistead Robinson and Patricia A Sullivan (Charlottesville: University of Virginia Press, 1991), 41–44. Badger, "Fatalism Not Gradualism," 77–78, 85–86. Fairclough, *Race and Democracy,* 35.

23. Badger, "Fatalism Not Gradualism," 85. Badger, "Southerners Who Did Not Sign the Southern Manifesto," 534.

24. Smith, *Congressman from Mississippi,* 77–92. Dennis J. Mitchell, "Frank E. Smith: Mississippi Liberal," *Journal of Mississippi History* 48 (1986): 91–93. Frank Smith to Hodding Carter, August 26, 1949, quoted in Dennis J. Mitchell, "Frank Ellis Smith: Mississippi Liberal" (unpublished manuscript), 86. Badger, "Fatalism Not Gradualism," 77–78.

25. Robert J. Norrell, *Reaping the Whirlwind: The Civil Rights Movement in Tuskegee* (New York: Knopf, 1985), 85.

26. Brooks Hays, Interview, Columbia Oral History Program, Lawrence Brooks Papers, Special Collections Division, University of Arkansas Libraries, Fayetteville, Arkansas; J. William Fulbright to Mrs. Walter Bell, August 31, 1948, Papers of J. William Fulbright, Special Collections Division, University of Arkansas, Fayetteville. Randall B. Woods, *Fulbright: A Biography* (Cambridge: Cambridge University Press, 1995), 114–19, 52.

27. Sidney McMath Interview, by John Egerton, September 8, 1990, Southern Oral History Program, Southern Historical Collection, University of North

Carolina, Chapel Hill. Bartley and Graham, *Southern Politics and the Second Reconstruction,* 38–40, 76–78. Earl Black, *Southern Governors and Civil Rights* (Cambridge, Mass.: Harvard University Press, 1976), 45.

28. Terry Sanford Interview, May 14, 1976, Southern Oral History Program, Southern Historical Collection, Chapel Hill. Drescher, *Triumph of Goodwill,* 16–19.

29. May 17, 1954, Statement, Sanford statement [n.d], W. Kerr Scott Papers. Albert Gore to Mrs. Talley, October 12, 1954, Papers of Albert Gore, Gore Research Center, Middle Tennessee State University. Estes Kefauver to P. L. Prattis, May 19, 1956, Kefauver to B. L. Fonville, May 10, 1956, Papers of Estes Kefauver, University of Tennessee, Knoxville. Robert Dallek, *Lone Star Rising: Lyndon Johnson and His Times, 1908–1960* (New York: Oxford University Press, 1991), 445.

30. Albert Gore Interview, March 13, 1976, Southern Oral History program, Southern Historical Collection, Chapel Hill. Richard Russell to Walter R. McDonald, February 15, 1956, Papers of Richard Russell, Richard B. Russell Library, University of Georgia, Athens.

31. Fulbright interview with Stewart Alsop, *Washington Post,* April 8, 1956, Box 71, J. William Fulbright Papers, Special Collections Division, University of Arkansas Libraries, Fayetteville. Sam Englehardt to John Sparkman, March 15, 1956, Papers of John Sparkman, W. S. Hoole Library, University of Alabama, Tuscaloosa. Typed statement [n.d.], Fulbright Papers. Randall B. Woods, "Dixie's Dove: J. William Fulbright, the Vietnam War, and the American South," *Journal of Southern History* 9 (1994): 541. Memorandum, John Lang, February 3, 1956, Papers of Charles B. Deane, Southern Baptist Historical Collection, Wake Forest University, Winston-Salem. William Cochrane interview with the author, September 1988. Brooks Hays Interview, 1970, 26–28, Columbia University Oral History Program, Hays Interview, 1971, 26, Lyndon Baines Johnson Library, Brooks Hays Papers.

32. Jack Bass, *Unlikely Heroes: The Dramatic Story of the Southern Judges of the Fifth Circuit Who Translated the Supreme Court's* Brown *Decision into a Revolution for Equality* (New York: Simon and Schuster, c. 1981), 68–74, 78–80. Virginia Van der Veer Hamilton, *Lister Hill: Statesman from the South* (Chapel Hill: University of North Carolina Press, 1987), 212–55. Virginia Durr to Hugo Black, November 1962, Virginia Foster Durr Papers, Arthur and Elizabeth Schlesinger Library, Cambridge, Mass. (I am very grateful to Pat Sullivan for this reference).

33. Tony Badger, *Race and War: Lyndon Johnson and William Fulbright* (Reading: University of Reading, 2000), 11–12.

34. William Cochrane interview. "North Carolina's Man on the Hill," *Carolina Alumni Review* (Spring 1984): 13–14. Jonathan Houghton, "The Politics of Sly Resistance: North Carolina's Response to *Brown*" (Paper given at the Organization of American Historians' meeting, April 11, 1991). Sylvia Ellis, "The Road to Massive Resistance: North Carolina and the Brown Decision"

(Graduate paper in the author's possession). Drescher, *Triumph of Goodwill,* 51–52.

35. Sidney McMath interview, by John Egerton, September 8, 1990. Jim Lester, *A Man for Arkansas: Sid McMath and the Southern Reform Tradition* (Little Rock, Ark.: Rose Publishing Co., 1976), 233–35.

36. Sims, *The Little Man's Big Friend,* 175–88.

37. Badger, "Southerners Who Did Not Sign the Southern Manifesto," 532–34. James C. Cobb, *The Selling of the South: The Southern Crusade for Industrial Development, 1936–1980* (Baton Rouge: Louisiana State University Press, c. 1982), 122–50.

38. Badger, "Southerners Who Did Not Sign the Southern Manifesto," 525–32. Tony Badger, "Albert Gore Sr. and Civil Rights," paper given at the Gore Research Center, Middle Tennessee State University, Murfreesboro, November 8, 1997 (copy in the author's possession). Charles L. Fontenoy, *Estes Kefauver: A Biography* (Knoxville: University of Tennessee Press, 1980), 236–43, 285–301.

39. Badger, *Race and War,* 7, 10–11.

40. Virginia Van der Veer Hamilton, *Lister Hill: Statesman from the South* (Chapel Hill: University of North Carolina Press, 1987), 170. John Horne to Lister Hill, October 20, 1955, Ed Dunnelly to Lister Hill, January 25, 1956, Tully A. Goodwin to Lister Hill, February 22, 1956, Bart P Chamberlain to Lister Hill, February 22, 1956. Papers of Lister Hill, W. S. Hoole Library, University of Alabama, Tuscaloosa. John Sparkman Interview, January 31, 1974, Southern Oral History Program, Southern Historical Collection, Chapel Hill, N.C.

41. Elliott, *The Cost of Courage,* 212–58.

42. Chappell, "The Divided Mind of Southern Segregationists," 45–72.

43. J. D. Messick to Terry Sanford, April 16, 1954; Sanford to Messick, April 24, 1954; W. Kerr Scott to Clark Brown, June 15, 1954; W. Kerr Scott Papers. Sims, *The Little Man's Big Friend,* 167–68. Sidney McMath Interview, by John Egerton, September 8, 1990. Terry Sanford interview, May 14, 1976, Drescher, *Triumph of Goodwill,* 162–63. Dante Fascell interview with the author, February 27, 1997.

44. Bass and Thompson, *Ol' Strom: An Unauthorized Biography of Strom Thurmond,* 123, 131. Edwin E. Dunaway interview with John A. Kirk, September 26, 1992. (I am very grateful to John Kirk for permission to quote from this interview.)

45. Bartley, *The New South,* 174; Woods, *Fulbright,* 211.

46. J. Mills Thornton, "Challenge and Response in the Montgomery Bus Boycott," *Alabama Review* 33 (1980): 163–235. Nahfiza Ahmed, "Race, Class and Citizenship," chapters 4, 5.

47. Hollinger F. Barnard, ed., *Outside the Magic Circle: The Autobiography of Virginia Foster Durr* (University: University of Alabama Press, 1985), 32. John A. Salmond, *The Conscience of a Lawyer: Clifford J. Durr and American Civil*

Liberties, 1899–1975 (Tuscaloosa: University of Alabama Press, 1990), 208. John A. Salmond, *A Southern Rebel: The Life and Times of Aubrey Willis Williams, 1890–1965* (Chapel Hill: University of North Carolina Press, 1983). Drescher, *Triumph of Goodwill,* xv.

48. Bartley and Graham, *Southern Politics and the Second Reconstruction,* 71.

49. Bartley and Graham, *Southern Politics and the Second Reconstruction,* 56–57, 67–68, 111–34.

50. Cobb, *The Selling of the South,* 149. Davison M. Douglas, *Reading, Writing and Race: The Desegregation of the Charlotte Schools* (Chapel Hill: University of North Carolina Press, 1995), 88, 103. Glenn T. Eskew, *But for Birmingham: The Local and National Movements in the Civil Rights Struggle* (Chapel Hill: University of North Carolina Press, c. 1997), 111–12, 189–90, 235–36, 269–97. Grafton and Permaloff, *Big Mules and Branchheads,* 165–66, 189–90. Robert Gaines Corley, "The Quest for Racial Harmony: Race Relations in Birmingham, Alabama, 1947–63' (Ph.D., University of Virginia, 1979), 180–86.

51. Bartley and Graham, *Southern Politics and the Second Reconstruction,* 138–41, 162–63. Woods, *Fulbright,* 663.

52. Linda Flowers, *Throwed Away: Failures of Progress in Eastern North Carolina* (Knoxville: University of Tennessee Press, 1990), 52.

53. Cecelski, *Along Freedom Road,* 39. Frank A. Rouse, interview, Southern Oral History Program, Southern Historical Collection, Chapel Hill.

54. Tony Badger, "The Rise and Fall of Bi-Racial Politics in the South," in *The Souths of the 1990s,* ed. Jan Nordby Gretlund (Columbia: University of South Carolina Press, 1999), 30–45.

55. Bartley, *The New South,* 466.

Chapter Eight

1. Marcia G. Synott, Desegregation in South Carolina, "Sometime between 'Now' and 'Never,'" in *Looking South: Chapters in the Story of an American Region,* ed. Winfred B. Moore and Joseph F. Tripp (Westport, Conn.: Greenwood, 1989), 51–64. Marcia G. Synott, "Federalism Vindicated: University Desegregation in South Carolina and Alabama, 1962–63," *Journal of Policy History* 1, 3 (1989): 292–318, John G. Sproat, "'Firm Flexibility': Perspectives on Desegregation in South Carolina," in *New Perspectives on Race and Slavery in America: Essays in Honor of Kenneth M. Stampp,* ed. Robert H. Abzug and Stephen E. Maizlish (Lexington: University Press of Kentucky, 1986), 164–84; John G. Sproat, "'Pragmatic Conservatism' and Desegregation in South Carolina" (unpublished paper kindly provided to me by Professor Sproat); Maxie Myron Cox Jr., "1963—The Year of Decision: Desegregation in South Carolina" (Ph.D. University of South Carolina, 1996); Walter B. Edgar, *South Carolina: A History* (Columbia: University of South Carolina Press, 1998), ch. 22; Gordon E.

Harvey, *A Question of Justice: New South Governors and Education, 1968–1976* (Tuscaloosa: University of Alabama Press, 2002).

2. *The Economist*, November 30, 2002.

3. Charles Joyner communication to the author, February 20, 2003. Dan T. Carter communication to the author, June 17, 1985, Strom Thurmond, interview with James Banks, July 1978, Southern Historical Collection, Chapel Hill. Sproat, "Firm Flexibility," 182; Harriet Keyserling, *Against the Tide: One Woman's Political Struggle* (Columbia: University of South Carolina Press, 1998), 111; Rembert Dennis, interview with Jack Bass, March 4, 1975, Southern Historical Collection, Chapel Hill and South Caroliniana Library.

4. Michael Klarman, "How *Brown* Changed Race Relations: The Backlash Thesis," *Journal of American History* 81 (1994): 81–118. Numan Bartley, *The New South, 1945–1980* (Baton Rouge: Louisiana State University Press, 1995), 70, 73. Numan Bartley, comment, Fortieth Anniversary of Little Rock Conference, September 27, 1997.

5. Harvey, *A Question of Justice*, 8; Edgar, *South Carolina*, 552.

6. John Carl West, Interview with Herbert J. Hartsook, 1997, Modern Political Collections: Oral History Project, South Caroliniana Library. I am extremely grateful to Governor West for allowing me to consult this interview.

7. Tony Badger, "Whatever Happened to Roosevelt's New Generation of Southerners?" in *The Roosevelt Years: New Essays on the United States, 1933–45*, ed. Robert A. Garson and Stuart Kidd (Edinburgh: Edinburgh University Press, 1999), 122–38. Jennifer Brooks, "From Fighting Nazism to Bossism: Southern World War II Veterans and the Assault on Southern Political Tradition" (unpublished paper in the author's possession).

8. Nadine Cahodas, *Strom Thurmond and the Politics of Southern Change* (New York: Simon and Schuster, 1993), 89, 96, 132.

9. Cahodas, *Strom Thurmond*, 177.

10. Kari Frederickson, *The Dixiecrat Revolt and the End of the Solid South, 1932–1968* (Chapel Hill: University of North Carolina Press, 2001), 180. David W. Robertson, *Sly and Able: A Political Biography of James F. Byrnes* (New York: Norton, 1994), 496, 501–2, 511–12.

11. Sproat, "Firm Flexibility," 166.

12. Robertson, *Sly and Able*, 507–10. Synott, "Federalism Vindicated," 299; Tony Badger, "Closet Moderates: Why White Liberals Failed, 1940–1970," in *The Role of Ideas in the Civil Rights South*, ed. Ted Ownby (Jackson: University Press of Mississippi, 2002), 97–98.

13. Robertson, *Sly and Able*, 513–20. Raymond Wolters, *The Burden of Brown: Thirty Years of School Desegregation* (Knoxville: University of Tennessee Press, 1984).

14. Robertson, *Sly and Able*, 520–21.

15. Walter Jackson, "Northern White Liberals and Civil Rights, 1955–1965," in *The Making of Martin Luther King and the Civil Rights Movement*, ed. Brian Ward and Tony Badger (London: Macmillan, 1996).

16. Howard H. Quint, *Profile in Black and White* (Washington, D.C.: Public Affairs Press, 1958), 101–4.

17. Quint, *Profile in Black and White*, 35, 101, 117–28. Edgar, *South Carolina*, 524–30.

18. Timothy Tyson, "Dynamite and 'The Silent South': A Story from the Second Reconstruction in South Carolina," in *Jumpin' Jim Crow: Southern Politics from Civil War to Civil Rights*, ed. Jane Dailey, Glenda Elizabeth Gilmore, and Bryant Simon (Princeton, N.J.: Princeton University Press, 2000), 275–97.

19. Calvin Trillin, "Reflections: Remembrances of Moderates Past," *New Yorker*, March 21, 1977. Quint, *Profile in Black and White*, 35, 46. Marcia G. Synott, "Alice Norwood Spearman: Civil Rights Apostle to South Carolina," in *Beyond Image and Convention: Explorations in Southern Women's History*, ed. Janet L. Coryell, Martha H. Swain, Sandra Gioia Treadway, and Elizabeth Hayes Turner (Columbia: University of Missouri Press, 1998), 184. Tony Badger, "The Southern Manifesto of 1956" (Paper delivered at the Southern Historical Association meeting, 1993, copy in the author's possession).

20. Orville Vernon Burton, Terence R. Finnegan, Peyton McCrary, and James W. Lowen, "South Carolina," in *Quiet Revolution in the South: The Impact of the Voting Rights Act, 1965–1990*, ed. Chandler Davidson and Bernard Grofman (Princeton, N.J.: Princeton University Press, 1984), 195.

21. Quint, *Profile in Black and White*, 86, 163; Earl Black, *Southern Governors and Civil Rights: Race, Segregation and Campaign Issues in the Second Reconstruction* (Cambridge, Mass.: Harvard University Press, 1976), 82–83. West Interview, 1997.

22. West Interview, 1997. Quint, *Profile in Black and White*, 97. Cahodas, *Strom Thurmond*, 231–32.

23. Hollings interview with Marcia Synott, 1980, Modern Political Collections, South Caroliniana Library. Synott, "Desegregation in South Carolina," 59–60; "Federalism Vindicated," 302.

24. Synott, "Federalism Vindicated," 302.

25. Sproat, "Firm Flexibility," 170.

26. Elizabeth Jacoway and David R. Colburn, eds., *Southern Businessmen and Desegregation* (Baton Rouge: Louisiana State University Press, 1982). James C. Cobb, *The Selling of the South: The Southern Crusade for Industrial Development, 1936–1980* (Baton Rouge: Louisiana State University Press, 1982).

27. Donald Russell, Interview, July 6, 1992, Oral History Project, Modern Political Collections, South Caroliniana Library. George McMillan, "Integration with Dignity: The Inside Story of How South Carolina Kept the Peace," *Saturday Evening Post*, March 16, 1963. Joseph C. Ellers, *Getting to Know Clemson University Is Quite an Education: Determination Makes Dreams Come True* (Blueridge Publications, 1987), 48–58. West interview, 1997.

28. Synott, "Federalism Vindicated," 293. Hollings interview, 1980.

29. Synott, "Federalism Vindicated," 311. John Seigenthaler, interview with the author, February 27, 2003.

30. Cox, "1963—The Year of Decision," 84–85, 171. Henry H. Lesesne, *A History of the University of South Carolina, 1940–2000* (Columbia: University of South Carolina Press, 2002), 137–50.

31. Cox, "1963—The Year of Decision," 345–469. Paul Lofton, "Calm and Exemplary: Desegregation in Columbia, South Carolina," in Elizabeth Jacoway and David R. Colburn, eds., *Southern Businessmen and Desegregation* (Baton Rouge: Louisiana State University Press, 1982), 70–81.

32. Edgar, *South Carolina*, 543–45. Sproat, "Pragmatic Conservatism," 21–22, 24–27. Harvey, A *Question of Justice*, 118–19.

33. West interview, 1997. West interview with Jack Bass and Walter DeVries, 1974, Southern Historical Collection.

34. West interview, 1997. West interview, 1974. Harvey, A *Question of Justice*, 123–40.

35. Timothy J. Minchin, *Hiring the Black Worker: The Racial Integration of the Southern Textile Industry, 1960–1980* (Chapel Hill: University of North Carolina Press, 1999), 3. West interview, 1997. West interview, 1974.

36. Cox, "1963—Year of Decision," 219–58. Orville Vernon Burton, Terence R. Finnegan, Peyton McCrary, and James W. Lowen, "South Carolina," in *Quiet Revolution in the South: The Impact of the Voting Rights Act, 1965–1990*, ed. Chandler Davidson and Bernard Grofman (Princeton, N.J.: Princeton University Press, 1984), 200–203. Minchin, *Hiring the Black Worker*, ch. 1, 2.

37. Vernon Burton in "A Monumental Labor': Four Scholars Assess Walter Edgar's *South Carolina: A History*," *South Carolina Historical Magazine* 100 (1999): 264.

Chapter Nine

1. James Lee Burke's novel, *A Stained White Radiance* (London: Arrow, 1993), 181–82. Edward F. Haas, "Black Cat, Uncle Earl, Edwin and the Kingfish: The Wit of Modern Louisiana Politics," *Louisiana History* 29 (1988): 213; Tony Badger, "Confessions of a British Americanist," *Journal of American History* 79 (1992): 515–23.

2. Burke, *A Stained White Radiance*, 32.

3. *New Orleans Times-Picayune*, August 13, 1995.

4. *New Orleans Times-Picayune*, July 8, November 5, 1995.

5. *New Orleans Times-Picayune*, November 7, 1995.

6. *New Orleans Times-Picayune*, January 9, 21, 23, 30, February 1, 8, 15, March 1, April 1, 2000. Tyler Bridges, *Bad Bet on the Bayou: The Rise of Gambling in Louisiana and the Fall of Edwin Edwards* (New York: Farrar, Straus and Giroux, 2001), 313–51.

7. Allan P. Sindler, *Huey Long's Louisiana: State Politics, 1920–1952* (Baltimore, Md.: John Hopkins University Press, 1956), 1–52. V. O. Key Jr., *Southern Politics in State and Nation* (New York: Knopf, 1949), 157–64.

8. T. Harry Williams, *Huey Long* (New York: Knopf, 1969), 4–6, 702–6.

9. Williams, *Huey Long,* 119–25, 191–213, 264–65, 273–75.

10. Stan Opotowsky, *The Longs of Louisiana* (New York: E. P. Dutton, 1960), 134–38. Michael L. Kurtz and Morgan D. Peoples, *Earl K. Long: The Saga of Uncle Earl and Louisiana Politics* (Baton Rouge: Louisiana State University Press, 1990), 263–64.

11. Kurtz and Peoples, *Earl K. Long,* 29, 57, 266.

12. William J. "Bill" Dodd, *Peapatch Politics: The Earl Long Era in Louisiana Politics* (Baton Rouge: Claitor's Publishing Division, 1991), 150–52.

13. Tyler Bridges, *The Rise of David Duke* (Jackson: University Press of Mississippi, 1994), 198–200. John McGinnis, *The Last Hayride* (Baton Rouge: Darkhorse Press, 1984), 10–32.

14. Williams, *Huey Long,* 467. Haas, "Black Cat," 229. Kurtz and Peoples, *Earl K. Long,* 107–8. McGinnis, *The Last Hayride,* 202. Bridges, *The Rise of David Duke,* 200.

15. Williams, *Huey Long,* 280–311, 492–525, 546–52; Kurtz and Peoples, *Earl K. Long,* 129–32.

16. McGinnis, *The Last Hayride,* 19–32; Bridges, *The Rise of David Duke,* 199.

17. See above chapter 1.

18. William Ivy Hair, *The Kingfish and His Realm: The Life and Times of Huey P. Long* (Baton Rouge: Louisiana State University Press, 1991), 293. Thomas A. Becnel, *Senator Allen Ellender of Louisiana: A Biography* (Baton Rouge: Louisiana State University Press, 1995), 248–50. Robert Mann, *Legacy of Power: Senator Russell Long of Louisiana* (New York: Paragon House, 1992), 318, 361.

19. Williams, *Huey Long,* 365–67, 394–96.

20. Williams, *Huey Long,* 290–95, 421, 732–45, 873–75.

21. Williams, *Huey Long,* 825. Hair, *The Kingfish and His Realm,* 293, 380 fn. 52. Michael L. Kurtz, "Organized Crime in Louisiana History: Myth and Reality," *Louisiana History* 24 (1983): 355–76.

22. Harnett T. Kane, *Louisiana Hayride: The American Rehearsal for Dictatorship, 1928–1940* (New York: Wm. Morrow, 1941), 163–455. Mark T. Carleton, *Politics and Punishment: The History of the Louisiana State Penal System* (Baton Rouge: Louisiana State University Press, 1971), 135, 148–49.

23. Michael L. Kurtz, "Political Corruption and Organized Crime in Louisiana: The FBI files on Earl Long," *Louisiana History* 29 (1988): 229–52. Kurtz and Peoples, *Earl K. Long,* xiii, 86–89, 137–38, 190–93.

24. Kurtz and Peoples, *Earl K. Long,* 125.

25. McGinnis, *The Last Hayride,* 18. John Maginnis, *Cross to Bear: America's Most Dangerous Politics* (Baton Rouge: Darkhorse Press, 1992), 36–38. *New York Times,* May 10, 31, 1970, May 6, 1971, 1973, October 6, 26, December 3, 1976, January 14, 1978.

26. McGinnis, *The Last Hayride,* 23–30. Haas, "Black Cat," 222.

27. Bridges, *Bad Bet on the Bayou,* 34–37.

28. Edward F. Haas, "Political Continuity in the Crescent City: Toward and in Interpretation of New Orleans Politics, 1874–1986," *Louisiana History* 39 (1998): 17.

29. William, *Huey Long,* 3. Maginnis, *Cross to Bear,* 229–31.

30. Williams, *Huey Long,* 702–6. Alan Brinkley, *Voices of Protest: Huey Long, Father Coughlin and the Great Depression* (New York: Knopf, 1983), 31–34. Hair, *The Kingfish and His Realm,* 170–71, 202, 223, 274–75, 303–4. Glen Jeansonne, "Huey Long and Racism," *Louisiana History* 23, (1992): 265–82. Adam Fairclough, *Race and Democracy: The Civil Rights Struggle in Louisiana* (Athens: University of Georgia Press, 1995), 21–23, 29, 44.

31. Fairclough, *Race and Democracy,* 35, 179–86, 228–29. Kurtz and Peoples, *Earl K. Long,* 194–210. Harris Wofford, *Of Kennedy and Kings* (New York: Farrar, Straus, Giroux, 1980), 162.

32. Kurtz and Peoples, *Earl K. Long,* 211–29.

33. Fairclough, *Race and Democracy,* 369–70, 378–80, 408–15, 444.

34. Fairclough, *Race and Democracy,* 464. Arnold R. Hirsch, "Simply a Matter of Black and White: The Transformation of Race and Politics in Twentieth-Century New Orleans," in *Creole New Orleans: Race and Americanization,* ed. Arnold R. Hirsch and Joseph Logsdon (Baton Rouge: Louisiana State University Press, 1992), 288–319.

35. See above chapter 1. *New Orleans Time Picayune,* March 3, 2000.

36. Williams, *Huey Long,* 441, 688, 784. Pam Tyler, *Silk Stockings and Ballot Boxes: Women and Politics in New Orleans, 1920–1963* (Athens: University of Georgia Press, 1996), 32–77.

37. Jerry Purvis Sansom, *Louisiana during World War II: Politics and Society, 1939–1945* (Baton Rouge: Louisiana State University Press, 1999), 55–137. Michael L. Kurtz, "Government by the Civics Book: The Administration of Robert F. Kennon, 1952–56," *North Louisiana Historical Association* (1981): 22, 53–61. John Wilds, *Thirty Years and Five Governors: That's Public Affairs Research* (Baton Rouge: Public Affairs Research Council, 1980). Gus Weill, *You Are My Sunshine: The Jimmie Davis Story* (Gretna: Pelican Publishing Company, 1995), 75–77.

38. Kurtz, "Government by the Civics Book," 57. Fairclough, *Race and Democracy,* 222–24, 322–23. Weill, *You Are My Sunshine: The Jimmie Davis Story,* 67.

39. Edward F. Haas, *De Lesseps S. Morrison and the Image of Reform: New Orleans Politics, 1946–1961* (Baton Rouge: Louisiana State University Press, 1986), 67–81, 256–82.

40. Liva Baker, *The Second Battle of New Orleans: The Hundred-Year Struggle to Integrate the Schools* (New York: Harper Collins, 1996), 367–409. Clarence Mohr and Joseph Gordon, *Tulane: The Emergence of a Modern University, 1945–1980* (Baton Rouge: Louisiana State University Press, 2001), 130–60, 191–242. James Gill, *Lords of Misrule: Mardi Gras and the Politics of Race in New Orleans* (Jackson: University Press of Mississippi, 1997), 221–45.

41. *New York Times,* June 8, 1994.

42. Maginnis, *Cross to Bear,* 43–53, 109–16. Tyler Bridges, *The Rise of David Duke* (Jackson: University Press of Mississippi, 1994), 197, 203.

43. Maginnis, *Cross to Bear,* 134–52.

44. Dan T. Carter, "Legacy of Rage," *Journal of Southern History* 62 (1996): 3–26. Bridges, *The Rise of David Duke,* 208.

45. Bridges, *The Rise of David Duke,* 240.

46. Bridges, *The Rise of David Duke,* 1–84, 113–18, 159–60.

47. Bridges, *The Rise of David Duke,* 139–93, 206–16.

48. Maginnis, *Cross to Bear,* 76–78.

49. Charles S. Bullock III, Ronald Keith Gaddie, and John C. Kuzenski, "The Candidacy of David Duke as a Stimulus to Minority Voting," in *David Duke and the Politics of Race in the South,* ed. John C. Kuzenski, Charles S. Bullock III, and Ronal Keith Gaddie (Nashville: Vanderbilt University Press, 1996), 99–114.

50. Bridges, *The Rise of David Duke,* 211–12, 227–37. Douglas D. Rose with Gary Esolen, "DuKKKe for Governor," in *The Emergence of David Duke and the Politics of Race,* ed. Douglas Rose (Chapel Hill: University of North Carolina Press, 1992), 196–241.

51. Bridges, *Bad Bet on the Bayou,* 50–269. *New York Times,* June 8, 1994.

52. John Heppehn, Wayne Parent, Gregory Veek, and Carville Earle, "David Duke and the Normal Republican Vote: The Two Faces of Louisiana in the 1991 Gubernatorial Election," *Southern Studies* (1995): 53–74. Frank Smith, interview with the author, November 1995. *New Orleans Times-Picayune,* November 1995, January 12, 2000, February 11, 2000. Edward F. Renwick, Wayne Parent, and Jack Wardlaw, "Louisiana," in *Southern Politics in the 1990s,* ed. Alexander Lami (Baton Rouge: Louisiana State University Press, 1999), 294–96.

53. *New Orleans Times-Picayune,* January 22, 2000.

54. *New Orleans Times-Picayune,* February 15, April 9, 2000.

55. *New Orleans Times-Picayune,* April 21, 2000.

56. *New Orleans Times-Picayune,* February 20, 2000, March 31, 2000.

57. *New Orleans Times-Picayune,* March 14, 19, 21, 31, 2000.

58. Key, *Southern Politics,* 670.

59. James Farwell, interview with author, November 1996. Renwick, Parent, and Wardlaw, "Louisiana," 283, 296–300.

60. Zell Miller, "The Dilemmas of Modern Southern Politics: The Opportunities for Democratic Governors," March 20, 2000 (copy in the author's possession).

61. Renwick, Parent, and Wardlaw, "Louisiana," 304.

62. Hirsch, "Simply a Matter of Black and White," 304–19.

63. On May 25–26, 2006, Cambridge University hosted the fourth Tulane-Cambridge conference. In "Hurricane Katrina: Historians the First Responders," scholars from Tulane powerfully and movingly examined Katrina and its impact in its historical context. The conference amply demonstrated the tragic consequences of the quality of governance that I described in 2000.

Chapter Ten

1. V. O. Key Jr., *Southern Politics in State and Nation* (New York: Knopf, 1949), 670.

2. Quoted in Robert P. Steed, Laurence W. Moreland, and Tod A. Baker, *Southern Parties and Elections: Studies in Regional Political Change* (Tuscaloosa: University of Alabama Press, 1997), 9.

3. Mark Stern, *Calculating Visions: Kennedy, Johnson, and Civil Rights* (New Brunswick, N.J.: Rutgers University Press, 1992), 212–14.

4. James M. Glaser, *Race, Campaign Politics and the Realignment in the South* (New Haven, Conn.: Yale University Press, 1996), 167.

5. Lewis Gould, "Never a Deep Partisan: Lyndon Johnson and the Democratic Party, 1963–1969," in *The Johnson Years, Vol. 3: LBJ at Home and Abroad,* ed. Robert A. Divine (Lawrence: University of Kansas Press, 1994), 21–52. Layne Hoppe, "Increasing Liberalism among Southern Members of Congress, 1970–1990, with an Analysis of the 1994 Congressional Elections," in Steed, Moreland, and Baker, *Southern Parties and Elections,* 109–30.

6. Numan V. Bartley and Hugh Davis Graham, *Southern Politics and the Second Reconstruction* (Baltimore, Md.: Johns Hopkins University Press, 1975), 51–135.

7. See above chapter 7 and below chapter 12.

8. Bartley and Graham, *Southern Politics,* 136–83.

9. Randy Sanders, *Mighty Peculiar Elections: The New South Gubernatorial Campaigns of 1970 and the Changing Politics of Race* (Gainesville: University of Florida Press, 2002). Adam Nossiter, *Of Long Memory: Mississippi and the Murder of Medgar Evers* (Reading, Mass.: Addison Wesley, 1994), 156–63, 170–71.

10. John Shelton Reed, "Up from Segregation," *Virginia Quarterly Review* 60 (1984): 373–99. Margaret Edds, *Free at Last: What Happened When Civil Rights Came to Southern Politics* (Bethesda, Md.: Adler and Adler, 1987), 51–76, 95–123, 193–238. John Dollard, *Caste and Class in a Southern Town* (New Haven, Conn.: Yale University Press, 1937), 211. Frank Parker, *Black Votes Count: Political Empowerment in Mississippi after 1965* (Chapel Hill: University of North Carolina Press, 1997), 197–209.

11. Numan V. Bartley, *The New South, 1945–1980: The Story of the South's Modernization* (Baton Rouge: Louisiana State University Press, 1995), 398–416. James C. Cobb, *The Selling of the South: The Southern Crusade for Industrial Development* (Baton Rouge: Louisiana State University Press, 1982), 179–268. Earl Black and Merle Black, *Politics and Society in the South* (Cambridge, Mass.: Harvard University Press, 1987), 125–51, 197–209.

12. Peter Applebome, *Dixie Rising: How the South Is Shaping America's Values, Politics and Culture* (New York: Times Books, 1996), 7, 52–55. Tod A. Baker, "The Emergence of the Religious Right and the Development of the Two-Party System in the South," in *Political Parties in the Southern States: Party Activists in Partisan Coalitions,* ed. Tod A. Baker et al. (New York: Praeger, 1980), 135–47.

Wayne Flynt, "The Transformation of Southern Politics, 1954 to the Present," in *A Companion to the American South,* ed. John Boles (Oxford: Oxford University Press, 2002), 500. *The State,* November 1, 1993. Alexander P. Lamis, ed., *Southern Politics in the 1990s* (Baton Rouge: Louisiana State University Press, 1999), 84, 173, 229.

13. Lamis, *Southern Politics,* 167.

14. Glaser, *Race, Campaign Politics and Realignment,* 15.

15. Lamis, *Southern Politics,* 44–45.

16. Dan T. Carter, *The Politics of Rage: George Wallace, the Origins of the New Conservatism, and the Transformation of American Politics* (New York: Simon and Schuster, 1995), 451–68. Dan T. Carter, *From George Wallace to Newt Gingrich: Race and the Conservative Counterrevolution, 1963–1994* (Baton Rouge: Louisiana State University Press, 1996), xi–xiii. Dan T. Carter, "Legacy of Rage: George Wallace and the Transformation of American Politics," *Journal of Southern History* 62 (1997): 13–17. Lamis, *Southern Politics,* 81, 255.

17. Zell Miller, "The Dilemmas of Modern Southern Politics: Challenges and Opportunities for Southern Democratic Governors," March 20, 2000 (copy in the author's possession). Lamis, *Southern Politics,* 245, 304.

18. Lamis, *Southern Politics,* 84, 228–29.

19. See above chapter 9.

20. Glaser, *Race, Campaign Politics and the Realignment,* 192, 194.

21. Glaser, *Race, Campaign Politics and the Realignment,* 163.

22. Glaser, *Race, Campaign Politics and the Realignment,* 75–79, 104, 120.

23. See above chapter 7.

24. Richard Hyatt, *Zell: The Governor Who Georgia HOPE* (Macon, Ga.: Mercer University Press, 1987), 350–53.

25. Miller, "The Dilemmas of Modern Southern Politics: Challenges and Opportunities for Southern Democratic Governors." Miller's optimism looked more problematic with the defeat in 2002 of Democratic governors in the states where they had been successful in 1998.

26. Nossiter, *Of Long Memory,* 173–94. Nahfiza Ahmed, "Race, Class and Citizenship: The Civil Rights Struggle in Mobile, 1925–1985" (Ph.D. dissertation, University of Leicester, 1999).

27. Lamis, *Southern Politics,* 140–42.

28. Richard K. Scher, Jon L. Mills, and John J. Hotaling, "Voting Rights in the South after *Shaw* and *Miller:* The End of Racial Fairness," in Steed, Moreland, and Baker, *Southern Parties and Elections,* 9–36. Steven A. Holmes, "For Very Strange Bedfellows, Try Redistricting," *New York Times* 23 July 1995. Glaser, *Race, Campaign Politics and the Realignment,* 143–47. Kevin A. Hill, "Does the Creation of Majority Black Districts Aid Republicans? An Analysis of the 1992 Congressional Elections in Eight Southern States," *Journal of Politics* 57 (1995): 384–401. John R. Petrocik and Scott Desposato, "The Partisan Consequences of Majority-Minority Redistricting in the South, 1992 and 1994," *Journal of Politics* 60 (1998): 613–33.

29. Richard K. Scher, *Politics in the New South: Republicanism, Race and Leadership in the Twentieth Century* (Armonk, N.Y.: M. E. Sharpe, 1997), 255–58. Alvin J. Schneider, "Political Mobilization in the South: The Failure of a Black Mayor in New Orleans," in *The New Black Politics: The Search for Political Power*, ed. Michael B. Preston, Lenneal J. Henderson Jr., and Paul Puryear (London: Longman, 1982), 221–37. Arnold R. Hirsch, "Simply a Matter of Black and White: The Transformation of Race and Politics in Twentieth-Century New Orleans," in *Creole New Orleans: Race and Americanization*, ed. Arnold R. Hirsch and Joseph Logsdon (Baton Rouge: Louisiana State University Press, 1992), 283–319.

30. Adam Fairclough reflected on the conclusions of his *Race and Democracy: The Civil Rights Struggle in Louisiana* (Athens: University of Georgia Press, 1995), and anticipated *Better Day Coming: Blacks and Equality, 1890–2000* (New York: Penguin, 2002). Gavin Wright drew on his "The Civil Rights Revolution as Economic History," *Journal of Economic History* (June 1999). Tim Tyson's paper drew on material for his latest project, *Deep River: African American Freedom Movements in the Twentieth-Century South*. Nan Woodruff's paper discussed themes highlighted in her book *American Congo: The African American Freedom Struggle in the Delta* (Cambridge, Mass.: Harvard University Press, 2003).

31. Glenn T. Eskew, *But for Birmingham: The Local and National Movements in the Civil Rights Struggle* (Chapel Hill: University of North Carolina Press, 1997), 338–40. Nancy Maclean's paper foreshadowed her book, *Freedom Is Not Enough: The Opening of the American Workplace* (Cambridge, Mass.: Russell Sage Foundation Books, Harvard University Press, 2006).

Chapter Eleven

1. Jack Robinson Sr., interview with the author.

2. Albert Gore Sr., *Let the Glory Out: My South and Its Politics* (New York: Viking, 1972), 38–42. Albert Gore Sr., Interview, Southern Historical Collection, Chapel Hill. Gore, MTSU interview. Robert Dallek, *Lone Star Rising: Lyndon Johnson and His Times, 1908–1960* (New York: Oxford University Press, 1991), 62–92. Robert Caro, *The Years of Lyndon Johnson: The Path to Power* (New York: Knopf, 1982).

3. Dallek, *Lone Star Rising*, 125–56. Caro, *The Path to Power*, 389–444. *Carthage Courier*, May 5, 1938.

4. Tony Badger, "Whatever Happened to Roosevelt's 'New Generation of Southerners?'" in *The Roosevelt Years: New Perspectives on the United States, 1933–1945*, ed. Robert A. Garson and Stuart Kidd (Edinburgh: Edinburgh University Press, 1999), 122–38. Tony Badger, "'Closet Moderates': Why White Liberals Failed, 1945–1972," in *The Role of Ideas in the Civil Rights South*, ed. Ted Ownby (Jackson: University Press of Mississippi, 2002), 86–88. Dallek,

Lone Star Rising, 298–348. Robert Caro, *The Years of Lyndon Johnson: The Means of Ascent* (New York: Knopf, 1988). David Lilienthal, *The Journal of David Lilienthal,* vol. III, *The Venturesome Years, 1950–55* (New York: Harper and Row, 1964), 256, 333. James B. Gardner, "Political Leadership in a Period of Transition: Frank G. Clement, Albert Gore and Estes Kefauver in Tennessee Politics, 1948–1956" (Ph.D. Vanderbilt University, 1978), 158–75, 239–76, 302–26. Nashville, *The Tennessean,* July 1– July 31, 1952.

5. Jordan A. Schwarz, *The New Dealers: Power Politics in the Age of Roosevelt* (New York: Knopf, 1993), xi–xvii, 195–294. Lawrence O'Brien, Memo to President, September 24, 1964, White House Central File Name File, LBJ Library. Albert Gore to Mrs. Alex Shell, September 11, 1964, C15, Capitol Commentary, July 12, 1965, C44 Gore Papers. Gore, *Let the Glory Out,* 177–82.

6. Dallek, *Lone Star Rising,* 529–34. Campaign Speech, June 7, 1952, Box 12, Gore to *Memphis Commercial Appeal,* October 31, 1951, Gore House Papers. *New York Times,* April 17, 18, 1951. Albert Gore to Clinton Anderson, December 14, 1956, copy in Box 44, LBJ Congressional File, Lyndon Baines Johnson Library. Albert Gore to Ben West, mayor of Nashville, March 8, 1957. B53, Legis. Gore Senate Papers. Gore statement, provided to Mrs. T. Roy Reid for Democratic Women's Club Newsletter, February 4, 1957, B11, Dept., "AEC—General," 1957, Gore Senate Papers. Gore to *St. Louis Post Dispatch,* June 29, 1956. B51, Legis., "AEC—S2725," 1956, Gore Senate Papers.

7. Tony Badger, "Southerners Who Refused to Sign the Southern Manifesto," *The Historical Journal* 42, 2 (1999): 517–19, 525–27. Tony Badger, "Albert Gore Sr. and Civil Rights," Paper at the Gore Research Center, November 8, 1997.

8. Dallek, *Lone Star Rising,* 189–92, 247–52, 409–16. Albert Gore Sr. and Mrs. Pauline Gore, interview with the author, December 1, 1990. Albert Gore interview with Jack Bass, Southern Historical Collection, Chapel Hill, 1974, Albert Gore Oral History Interview, JFK Library. Gore, *Let the Glory Out,* 143–47, 187–91.

9. Albert and Pauline Gore to Lyndon Johnson, October 6, 1948, Gore to Johnson, December 10, 1957, Johnson to Gore, December 19, 1957, Johnson to Gore, November 6, 1956, Box 44, Johnson to Gore, August 30, 1956, Johnson to Gore, June 16, 1959, Box 71, U.S. Senate Master File, Johnson Library.

10. Harry McPherson, Oral History, 1, 28; Adrian Fisher, Oral History, 1, 18, Johnson Library.

11. Robert Caro, *Master of the Senate: The Years of Lyndon Johnson* (New York: Knopf, 2002), 670, 674–75, 680, 858–59, 1035–39. Gore to Lyndon Johnson, January 12, 1960, Box 44, LBJ Congressional File, LBJ Library.

12. Jack Valenti to Johnson March 5, 1966, Mike Manatos to Johnson, April 5, 1967, Box 207, White House Central File, Johnson Library.

13. Gore Newspaper Articles, May 6, 1939, June 24, 1939, May 18, 1940, August 31, 1940, September 7, 1940, March 16, July 14, 1941, November 17, 1941, Gore House Papers, Papers of Albert Gore, Gore Research Center, Middle Tennessee State University. Bryce Harlow, Oral History Interview, February 28,

1979, Michael Gillette, Johnson Library. Joseph A. Fry, *Dixie Looks Abroad: The South and U.S. Foreign Relations, 1789–1973* (Baton Rouge: Louisiana State University Press, 2002), 201–9. The Hull papers at the Library of Congress reveal a mutual admiration society with Gore—Gore was point man for Hull at the 1940 convention. Gore, *Let the Glory Out,* 63. Dallek, *Lone Star Rising,* 197–98, 225–30, 316.

14. Dallek, *Lone Star Rising,* 290–95. WSM Transcripts, March 14, 1947, Gore House Papers. Fry, *Dixie Looks Abroad,* 222–31.

15. *New York Times,* April 17, 18, 1951. Albert Gore to Ashford, April 28, 1951, Box 13, Gore House Papers. Dallek, *Lone Star Rising,* 433–37. Caro, *Master of the Senate,* 372–82, 522–41.

16. Ken O'Donnell to Bob Kennedy, October 26, 1960, Box 1066, Campaign File, Folder One, Pre-presidential papers, John F. Kennedy Library.

17. Dallek, *Lone Star Rising,* 507, 542. George Reedy, Oral History Interview with Michael Gillete, August 17, 1983, 43–50, Johnson Library. Robinson interview. William Conrad Gibbons, *The U.S. Government and the Vietnam War: Executive and Legislative Roles and Relationships, Part One: 1945–60* (Princeton, N.J.: Princeton University Press, 1986), 191–96. Albert Gore to Lyndon Johnson, May 13, 1959, Box 366, Papers of the Democratic Leader, 1951–1961, Johnson Library.

18. John Culver, interview with the author, December 8, 2003.

19. Joseph Fox, comment to the author, Feburary 1997.

20. Robert Dallek, *Flawed Giant: Lyndon Johnson and His Times, 1961–73* (New York: Oxford University Press, 1998), 15, 84–85. Bill Stott, interview with the author, September 22, 1998.

21. Warren Cohen and Nancy Bernkopf Tucker, eds., *Lyndon Johnson Confronts the World: American Policy, 1962–1968* (New York: Cambridge University Press, 1994), and H. W. Brands, *Beyond Vietnam: The Foreign Policies of Lyndon Johnson* (College Station: Texas A and M University Press, 1999), provide contrasting views of both Johnson's foreign policy skill and of the impact of Vietnam on other foreign policy issues. Thomas Alan Schwartz, *Lyndon Johnson and Europe: In the Shadow of Vietnam* (Cambridge, Mass.: Harvard University Press, 2003), makes a powerful case for Johnson's skill in dealing with Europe. For relations with the Soviets, John Dumbrell, *President Johnson and Soviet Communism* (Manchester: Manchester University Press, 2004), 185. For the attempts to open up relations with China, see Andrew Dodds, "The China Opening in Perspective, c. 1961–1976" (Ph.D. dissertation, Cambridge University, 2002).

22. David M. Barrett, *Uncertain Warriors: Lyndon Johnson and his Vietnam Advisers* (Lawrence: University Press of Kansas, 1993), 60–61, 190–94. Dallek, *Flawed Giant,* 242, 254–55, 261, 275, 386, 458, 462, 479. Fredrik Logevall, *Choosing War: The Lost Chance for Peace and the Escalation of the War in Vietnam* (Berkeley and Los Angeles: University of California Press, 1999), xvi. Mark Moyar, "American Entry into the Vietnam War, 1964–65" (Ph.D. dissertation, Cambridge University, 2003).

23. Logevall, *Choosing War,* xiii.

24. Andrew Preston, "The Little State Department: McGeorge Bundy, the NSC Staff and the Vietnam War, 1961–65" (Ph.D. dissertation, Cambridge University, 2001).

25. Preston, "The Little State Department"; Logevall, *Choosing War,* 90–94, 228–35, 315–19.

26. Edward Kennedy, interview with the author, December 10, 2003.

27. Louis Heren, *No Hail, No Farewell* (London: Weiderfeld ad Nicolson, 1970).

28. Lloyd Gardner, *Pay Any Price: Lyndon Johnson and the War for Vietnam* (Chicago: I. R. Dee, 1995). For an excellent analysis of the Johnson search for the middle ground and its consequences in foreign policy, see Dumbrell, *Johnson and Soviet Communism,* 180–81.

30. Gordon Petty, interview with the author, April 2004.

31. Harry McPherson, *A Political Education: A Washington Memoir* (Austin: University of Texas Press, 1995), 103. Background Material on Indochina for possible use in speech by Senator Gore, Research-Foreign Policy-Indochina, 1954, Gore Senate Papers. Gale McGhee's Senate Summary, Gore letter to the editor, January 10, 1960, B 64 Gore Senate Papers, Hodges, "Gore," ch 1. Appointment Index-Albert Gore, August 1, 1963, off record, Kennedy Library

32. Albert Gore to David Halberstam, May 6, 1964, Pauline Gore to Halberstam, November 22, 1963, Gore Senate Papers, John Kenneth Galbraith, *A Life in Our Times: Memoirs* (London: Deutsch, 1981), 144. John Kenneth Galbraith, *Name-dropping* (London: Aurum, 1999), 193–94. Tony Badger, *Race and War: Lyndon Johnson and William Fulbright* (Reading University, 2000), 24–27. Steve M. Neuse, *David Lilienthal: The Journey of an American Liberal* (Knoxville: University of Tennessee Press, 1996), 275–81.

33. Albert Gore, interview with the author, December 1, 1991.

34. Capitol Commentary. April 19, August 2, 1965, Gore to Edward J. Meeman, November 26, 1965, *Congressional Record,* May 8, 1969. Gore to Jonathan Bingham, January 3, 1968, Senate Remarks February 16, 1966, Gore to Jeffery B. Hamilton, November 8, 1966, Hubert Humphrey to Gore, November 16, 1967, Gore to Humphrey (not sent), Gore to Humphrey, December 1, 1967, Gore Senate Papers. Robert Clyde Hodges, "Senator Albert Gore Sr. and the Vietnam War" (Master's thesis, University of Kentucky), ch. 2. Edward Jay Epstein, *Dossier: The Secret History of Armand Hammer* (New York: Carroll and Graf, 1996), 166, 173, 189, 199, 202, 208, 211. Gore Statement, February 16, 1966, p. 13, Gore to Jeffery B. Hamilton, November 8, 1966, Gore Senate Papers. *New York Times,* November 20, 1968.

35. *Congressional Record,* May 8, 1969, 4828–30, September 9, 1969, 10339–42, November 4, 1969, 13658–63; Gore to J. W. McGinley, December 2, 1969, Gore Senate Papers. *Congressional Record,* August 25, 1970, 14155–56. Robert Clyde Hodges, "Senator Albert Gore Sr. and the Vietnam War" (Master's thesis, University of Kentucky), ch. 2.

36. For the best analysis of the congressional opponents of the war, see Randall Woods, ed., *Vietnam and the American Political Tradition* (Cambridge: Cambridge University Press, 2003).

37. Harry Middleton, *LBJ: The White House Years* (New York: H. N. Abrams, 1990), 258–60.

38. Gore to Gene H. Sloan, November 20, 1969, Gore Papers.

39. Albert Gore Sr., *Let the Glory Out*, 211. *Memphis Press-Scimitar,* August 20, 1968; *The Tennessean,* August 29, September 1, 1968. Tony Badger and Mike Martin, "The Anti-Gore Campaign of 1970" (paper given at the Tennessee Conference of Historians, 2003, copy in the author's possession). Hudley Crockett, interview with the author, July 2004. *The Tennessean,* August 9, 1970.

40. A complete set of Brock TV Commercials is held at the Julian P. Kanter Political Commercial Archive, University of Oklahoma.

41. *Nashville Banner,* August 23, September 23, 1970. J. Lee Annis Jr., *Howard Baker: Conciliator in an Age of Crisis* (New York: Madison Books, 1995), 55–56. *Nashville Banner,* October 19, 22. Gore Final TV broadcast, Julian P. Kanter Political Commercial Archive, University of Oklahoma.

42. White House Special Files: Staff Member and Office Files: John D. Erlichman, Alphabetical Subject Files, 1963–73, Box 23. 1970, Postelection analysis, Nixon Presidential Materials Project, James Stahlman tel to Richard Nixon, November 3, 1970, Stahlman tel to Lyndon B. Johnson, November 4, 1970, Papers of James G. Stahlman, Special Collections, Alexander Heard Library, Vanderbilt University.

Chapter Twelve

1. Albert Gore Sr., *Let the Glory Out: My South and Its Politics* (New York: Viking, 1972), 211. *Memphis Press-Scimitar,* August 20, 1968. *The Tennessean,* August 29, September 1, 1968. Nashville delegate Kenneth Schoen cast his half vote for Eugene McCarthy.

2. John Seigenthaler, interview with the author, February 27, 2003. Adrian Fisher, Oral History Interview, LBJ Library. Buford Ellington, Oral History Interview, LBJ Library. Jack Robinson Sr., interview with the author, January 23, 2003.

3. Numan V. Bartley, *Southern Politics and the Second Reconstruction* (Baltimore, Md.: Johns Hopkins University Press, 1975), 104–6, 123, 153. Earl and Merle Black, *The Rise of Southern Republicans* (Cambridge, Mass.: Belknap Press, 2002), 94–96. Jack Robinson Sr. interview.

4. Gore, *Let the Glory Out,* 213–14. Washington Report, June 1968, December 1969, C44 Albert Gore Senate Papers, Gore Research Collection, Middle Tennessee State University, Murfreesboro. Jack Robinson Sr. interview.

5. Gore, *Let the Glory Out,* 214.

6. *Chattanooga Free-Press,* January 11, 1970. *Memphis Press-Scimitar,* February 26, 1970. *The Tennessean,* May 7, 9, 16, June 6, July 9, 10.

7. *Chattanooga Free-Press,* June 21, 1970. *The Tennessean,* July 11, 1970. *Nashville Banner,* May 27, June 11, 24, 1970.

8. *The Tennessean,* August 9, 1970. *Memphis Commercial Appeal,* July 12, 1970.

9. Interviews with William E. Brock, William C. Cater, and William L. Carter, Southern Oral History Project, Southern Historical Collection, Chapel Hill. Jack Bass and William DeVries, *The Transformation of Southern Politics: Social Change and Political Consequence since 1945* (New York: Basic Books, 1976), 292–95. Press Releases and clippings, Box 12, Papers of William E. Brock, Special Collections, University of Tennessee, Knoxville.

10. Poll and Strategy, Box 14, Brock Papers. *The Tennessean,* April 12, May 5, June 28, July 23, 1970

11. *The Tennessean,* January 6, February 26, April 12, May 3, 26, June 30, July 7, 9, 31, August 1, 1970.

12. *The Tennessean,* April 12, June 2, June 7, July 26, 1970

13. William E. Timmons to President, August 8, 1970, President's Office Files, Richard M. Nixon Presidential Materials, National Archives. Jim Allison to Harry Dent, October 9, 1969, John Stuckey to Bill Brock, n.d., Box 31, Brock Papers.

14. Polls and Strategy, Box 14, Brock Papers. Kenneth Rietz to staff, November 24, 1969, Box 31, Brock Papers. Richard Harris, "How the People Feel," *New Yorker,* 1972. *The Tennessean,* April 5, 1970.

15. A complete set of Brock TV Commercials is held at the Julian P. Kanter Political Commercial Archive, University of Oklahoma.

16. *Nashville Banner,* August 23, September 23, 1970.

17. *Nashville Banner,* October 5, 1970. Mrs. Glenda G. Grigsby to Albert Gore, n.d., A46 Issue Mail, 1969, Supreme Court, 9 of 10, Gore Papers.

18. *Nashville Banner,* May 22, 1970. *The Tennessean,* June 13, September 27, 1970.

19. Henry Loeb to William O'Hara, copy to Gore, June 5, 1970, B44, Gore Papers. *The Tennessean,* July 26, 1970. *Nashville Banner,* October 6, 10, 1970.

20. *Nashville Banner,* October 31, 1970.

21. Richard Harris, "How the People Feel," *New Yorker,* 1972. Gore, *Let the Glory Out,* 266.

22. J. Lee Annis Jr., *Howard Baker: Conciliator in an Age of Crisis* (New York: Madison Books, 1995), 55–56. *Nashville Banner,* October 19, 22. Gore Final TV broadcast, Julian P. Kanter Political Commercial Archive, University of Oklahoma.

23. Harris, "How the People Feel"; Gene Graham, "Gore's Lost Cause," *New South* (1971): 26–34.

24. Bartley and Graham, *Southern Politics,* 150.

25. Randy Sanders, *Mighty Peculiar Elections: The New South Gubernatorial Campaigns of 1970 and the Changing Politics of Race* (Gainesville: University of Florida Press, 2002), 1–10. White House Special Files: Staff Member and Office Files: John D. Erlichman, Alphabetical Subject Files, 1963–73, Box 23, 1970, Postelection analysis, Nixon Presidential Materials Project

26. Seigenthaler interview. Gilbert Merritt, interview with the author, February 24, 2003.

27. Annis, *Howard Baker,* 56.

Index

259

TONY BADGER, a specialist in post–World War II Southern political history, is Paul Mellon Professor of American History at Cambridge University and Master of Clare College. He is the author of a number of books, including *Prosperity Road: The New Deal, Tobacco, and North Carolina*; *North Carolina and the New Deal*; *The New Deal: The Depression Years, 1933-1940*; *The Making of Martin Luther King and the Civil Rights Movement* (with Brian Ward); and *Contesting Democracy: The Substance and Structure of American Political History* (with Byron Shafer). He was selected by the Gore Biography Project at the Albert Gore Research Center, Middle Tennessee State University, to write a biography of the late senator.